The Book of God

The Book of God

Secularization and Design in the Romantic Era

COLIN JAGER

PENN

University of Pennsylvania Press

Philadelphia

10 9 8 7 6 5 4 3 2 1

Published by
University of Pennsylvania Press
Philadelphia, Pennsylvania 19104-4112

Library of Congress Cataloging-in-Publication Data

Jager, Colin.
  The book of God : secularization and design in the romantic era / Colin Jager.
    p. cm.
  Includes bibliographical references and index.
  ISBN-13: 978-0-8122-3979-9 (acid-free paper)
  ISBN-10: 0-8122-3979-2 (acid-free paper)
    1. Theology in literature.   2. English literature—18th century—History and criticism.
3. English literature—19th century—History and criticism.   4. Romanticism—Great
Britain.   5. Natural theology—History.   6. Secularization (Theology)—History.
7. Intelligent design (Teleology).   8. God—Proof, Teleological.   9. Religion and
literature—England—History.   I. Title.

PR448.T45J34   2007
820.9'382—dc22   2006042190

For Wendy

This, no tomorrow hath, nor yesterday;
Running it never runs from us away,
But truly keeps his first, last, everlasting day.

Contents

Preface   ix

Introduction: Nature Is the Book of God   1

1. The Argument Against Design from Deism to Blake   41

2. Arbitrary Acts of Mind: Natural Theology in Hume's *Dialogues Concerning Natural Religion*   58

3. Theory, Practice, and Anna Barbauld   73

4. Natural Designs: William Paley, Immanuel Kant, and the Power of Analogy   102

5. *Mansfield Park* and the End of Natural Theology   124

6. Wordsworth: The Shape of Analogy   158

7. Reading with a Worthy Eye: Secularization and Evil   188

8. Religion Three Ways   201

   Afterword: Intelligent Design and Religious Ignoramuses; or, the Difference Between Theory and Literature   216

Notes   229

Selected Bibliography   259

Index   265

Acknowledgments   273

Preface

The intimation that the starry heavens and the fertile earth are the very Book of God, "wherein to read his wond'rous Works," as Milton put, is an old, old idea; old as the Protestant Reformation, old as medieval cosmology, old as the Christian Scriptures and the Classical orators, old as the ancient Psalmist avowing that "the heavens declare the glory of God." The bookish metaphor may indeed be inescapable for any vaguely religious sensibility, though it describes most acutely a world of proliferating Protestant textuality, wherein the world is a book to be read both intensively and rationally.

What to make of this Book of God? How to read it, interpret it, or translate it? It is both legible and inscrutable. Saints and sages and scholars have pondered it, artists and poets have meditated on its mysteries; but none has resolved it or wholly evaded it or given the book its definitive reading.

Secularization is a process that blurs the very words of the Book of God. It muddies syntax, creates ambiguity, makes vague or uncertain declarations formerly clear and distinct. Secularization makes reading itself a problem—which is why, though it manifests itself in a thousand ways, its relationship to literary culture is especially rich.

* * *

This book is about secularization—as a general concept and in relation to certain literary texts from the late eighteenth and early nineteenth centuries. Secularization has often been coordinated with the social and cultural movements of this period; for some readers, romantic literature has seemed a secular scripture, preserving or humanizing a spiritual sensibility while abandoning religious belief and institutional affiliation; for others, romanticism has seemed to offer a prescient critique of that same spiritualizing tendency. The truth is more complicated than either of these.

Secularization itself remains, within literary study, an analytically fuzzy category that usually tells us as much about the self-understanding of modern-day interpreters as it does about the historical period under consideration. I deal with this phenomenon throughout the book and address it directly in the introduction and in the final chapters. Another part of my argument, and the chief subject of Chapters 1 through 6, focuses the question of secularization in England during the period from David Hume to Jane Austen by examining what is often termed "the argument from design." According to that argument, the miraculous adjustment of means to ends evident in the natural world must be intentional, not random. Any designer capable of imagining and constructing such a world must be divine, and so only God is the sort of being who could make a world so marvelously fitted together. Nature, according to one common metaphor, is "the Book of God"—a series of revelations that parallel and complement the revelations of scripture. Implicitly or explicitly, this sensibility dominated mainstream theology in England from 1675 to 1850. As recent debates about "intelligent design" indicate, it has never really gone away.

To argue for the importance of design during the romantic period seems, on the face of it, to suggest two possibilities. The first would argue that design's persistence means that secularization did not happen—or did not happen, at any rate, during the romantic era. Alternatively, one could argue that because design depends upon a scientific worldview, its persistence during the romantic period is in fact further demonstration that secularization *did* happen. It would be well, however, to insist that before we decide whether secularization happened, we understand the term, how and by whom and under what conditions it is invoked, and what it purports to explain. The way to do this is to proceed both conceptually and historically—that is, to consider secularization as an analytic concept *and* to consider how that concept is cashed out at a specific historical moment. In bringing the historical discourse of design together with certain texts of the romantic period, then, my goal is not to offer a study of influence but rather a study of secularization's explanatory power.

The texts I consider here include representatives of the old canon (William Wordsworth), the newer canon (Jane Austen), and the not-quite-yet canon (Anna Barbauld). I grant equal time to the philosophical and theological arguments of David Hume and William Paley. Though the book is positioned with one eye on romantic studies, I cannot claim to have offered a comprehensive account (were such possible) of the relationship between romanticism and religion. That relationship would have to take in more than the argument from design, which is why Wordsworth, much of whose poetry can be read very well through the lens of design, gets more attention here than either Coleridge or Percy Shelley, whose more capacious religious interests render design a less pressing matter.

My interest is in isolating aspects of the design argument that cut across canons as well as genres, and I have no particular stake in defining certain texts as "romantic." It might nonetheless be observed that despite the various revisions of romanticism accomplished over the past decades, the narrative of secularization has provided substantial continuity in scholarly thinking about the period. Romantic exceptionalism has been under revision for some time, but we are only now beginning to challenge an interpretation of the period in which religion gives way to a secularized modernity posited as inevitable. This book contributes to that project.

To ask or search I blame thee not, for Heav'n
Is as the Book of God before thee set,
Wherein to read his wond'rous Works.

—*Milton*, Paradise Lost, *1674*

The great book of the universe lies open to all mankind; and he who
cannot read in it the name and titles of its Author, will probably de-
rive but little benefit from the labours of any commentator.

—Edinburgh Review, *1803*

Introduction
Nature Is the Book of God

This book argues that a religious form—design—is complexly entwined with romantic-era writing. If true, this claim complicates the long-standing association of romanticism with the narrative of secularization. According to that narrative, religion may have "influenced" the era's literature, but rather in the way that theories of Christian eschatology "influenced" the idea of historical progress. In each case religious content is transformed into something else (that is, secularized) by the forward march of history. M. H. Abrams's book *Natural Supernaturalism* (1971), which describes romanticism as "the secularization of inherited theological ideas and ways of thinking," is the most distinguished and important contribution to this understanding of the period. "The process," Abrams writes, "has not been the deletion and replacement of religious ideas but rather the assimilation and reinterpretation of religious ideas, as constitutive elements in a world view founded on secular premises."[1] Yet the account of secularization upon which Abrams relies is open to a series of objections. Empirically it is not the case that modernity equals secularization in any straightforward way. In addition, the historical change that the word "secularization" tries to capture does not reside solely or even primarily at the level of ideas and beliefs (where Abrams places it), but incorporates habits, dispositions, and postures that are themselves carried out and performed within changing institutional contexts. Thus if secularization is understood not as a loss of belief but rather as an example of the differentiation that characterizes modernity—a differentiation that necessarily entails neither religious decline nor the privatization of religion as a form of feeling or emotion—then we can start to analyze our own investment in secularization as that which underwrites and legitimates romanticism.

This book, then, has two aims, analytically distinct but necessarily related. The specific aim is to offer a detailed reading of the presence and power of design arguments during the late eighteenth and early nineteenth centuries, focusing particularly on design's relation to texts that anticipate and constitute early British romanticism. The larger aim is to argue from the fact of design's cultural importance toward a revised understanding of secularization and the ideas of religion that secularization entails. Both of these aims require that the terms "design," "romanticism," and "secularization" acquire some analytic clarity. To that I turn first.

Design

Though various in application and detail, all design arguments during the seventeenth and eighteenth centuries are inductive arguments for the existence of God. They begin empirically, with what can be seen or discovered in the natural world, and work their way upward to the creator of that world. They are literally arguments *from* design *to* God, and thus presuppose an individual's ability to perceive marks of design in the natural world.[2] Technically speaking, design arguments are both teleological and analogical. They are *teleological* because they are interested in the seemingly purposive features of the natural world, in things—such as bird's wings or eyelids—that appear to have been designed with a specific function in mind. In the eighteenth century, therefore, design arguments depend upon practices of close observation and tend to describe the world in mechanistic or functionalist terms. In these ways design arguments mesh nicely with a basically "enlightenment" temperament. Design arguments are *analogical*, meanwhile, because they reason from known instances of design to unknown ones; indeed they often depend at least implicitly upon a ratio of the type *a:b::c:d*. Sometimes, in addition, we find a deductive tendency within design arguments, for the theologian may be inclined to deduce attributes of the deity from what he observes of the world. So beneficence follows from the smooth functioning of the creation, whereas eternal and self-sufficient existence follows from the fact that the designer must exist prior to the design, and so on. Cutting design into inductive and deductive halves, however, is a bit too neat for a theological tradition that tends to move back and forth between them as a matter of habit, and that frequently invokes the conclusions of the argument without bothering to delineate each of the steps. This, indeed, is the twofold difficulty of writing about design: first, that its intellectual ambition leads away from careful philosophical delineation and toward a certain capaciousness; and second, that many writers, most of them nontheologians, tended to invoke it outside the context of systematic exposition, as a kind of sensibility. These factors make design an elusive quarry.

Most eighteenth-century clergymen, as enlightened as they may have been, were not agnostic about God's existence. Indeed, the argument from design operates best in an atmosphere that assumes from the beginning that the firmament declares God's handiwork. The chief end of nature, in other words, is to showcase its creator's glory; the miraculous discoveries that science is making about the world are but further examples of its design. This is the teleological presupposition that underpins an apparently inductive procedure, and while such a union may be philosophically problematic, the intellectual labor that issues from it actually draws strength from this dual heritage.[3] With one foot solidly in the older camp of Aristotelian teleology and the other firmly planted in the newer camp of inductive reasoning, design draws justification both from the ever-expanding ambitions of natural philosophy and from the venerable conventions of traditional theology. This means, in turn, that the impulse behind the avid collecting of empirical data is underwritten by both scientific progress and traditional Christian apologetics. Design's teleological framework offers a formal means of acknowledging diversity in both culture and nature, and a method for gathering that diversity into a whole posited as the natural and inevitable culmination of its various parts. Within this overarching frame, specific natural objects are both susceptible to analysis and part of a larger system that is itself available to analysis. Meanwhile individuals are placed within a rational institutional framework that both grants and regulates freedom: final causes belong to God, while immediate and efficient causes, both social and scientific, become the legitimate objects of human investigation and agency.[4]

Natural theology is the set of ideas, practices, and intellectual habits that surround this argument from design. The phrase "natural theology" sometimes refers to the more general idea that humans can have direct knowledge of God apart from revelation, but in this book I use the term to refer to the teleological orientation exemplified by the argument from design. In this respect, the natural theology that characterizes the design argument should be distinguished from the neo-Platonism that so influenced English theology and philosophy in the seventeenth century. Although neo-Platonism also posited an orderly cosmos and linked such heavenly order to social hierarchies, it tended to emphasize the inherent form or structure of which such hierarchies were a part. The tradition of the Great Chain of Being is one manifestation of this Platonic tradition. Though the Great Chain may be "temporalized"— that is, seen to produce higher forms over time—it posits static relationships between the members of the Chain, and the Chain itself is conceived in an intrinsically hierarchical fashion. In contrast, eighteenth-century natural theology tends to justify hierarchy instrumentally, and indeed some versions abandoned the notion of hierarchy altogether. Order is not an end in itself; rather, the particular and unique purpose of every creature works together complementarily, each enabling the other to achieve the end that is already built into it. In this respect design is integral to what Charles Taylor calls a "modern social imaginary."[5]

The point is worth emphasizing. Far from being old-fashioned or retrograde, natural theology is a characteristically *modern* phenomenon. It both shapes and reflects the slow transformation into a world organized around the flourishing of autonomous individuals, what Taylor calls a "new . . . moral order of society" which eventually gave rise to new social forms: the market economy, the public sphere, and the idea of a self-governing people.[6] This does not mean, of course, that natural theologians saw themselves as participating in an intellectual or social vanguard; indeed, precisely because it was such an influential set of ideas among England's formally educated, natural theology during the eighteenth and early nineteenth centuries accommodated a range of political and social opinions along a broad spectrum of intellectual elites.[7] The premise that the intricate works of nature point to a divine and benevolent final cause helped to formalize and publicize a felt convergence of religious belief and scientific investigation that already existed in the minds of the educated classes. And it allowed orthodox clergy to pursue scientific interests that reaffirmed a stable and ordered universe, not a chaotic and implicitly revolutionary one. For the great majority of British intellectuals, science and theology were mutually informing means of investigating God's world; design was not, consequently, invoked to suture a widening gap between "science" and "religion," as some accounts suggest, because its practitioners did not in general recognize that gap to begin with. On the contrary, natural theology expresses what has been rightly termed an "intellectual consensus."[8] It simply confirmed at the level of reason what everybody already supposed to be true: that the natural world contained abundant evidence of its magnificent creator. If natural theology is "conservative," then, such conservatism is to be found not in its religious content but in its characteristic intellectual posture, which is dedicated not to novelty but to multiple examples, to repetition and reiteration. It is science, but with an accent—for it is also a habit of mind, a way of intellectually addressing the materials of the world.

It may help at this juncture to consider an example. John Tillotson, Archbishop of Canterbury from 1691 to 1694, was famous throughout his career for sermons that combined piety with rational presentation. Here is Tillotson's refutation of the claim that the world came about by chance, from "The Wisdom of Being Religious," the first sermon in a volume of selected sermons published two years after his death:

For I appeal to any man of reason whether any thing can be more unreasonable, than obstinately to impute an effect to chance which carries in the very face of it all the arguments and characters of a wise design, and contrivance? Was ever any considerable work, in which there was required a great variety of parts and a regular and orderly disposition of those parts, done by chance? Will chance fit means to ends, and that in ten thousand instances, and not fail in any one? How often might a man after he had jumbled a set of letters in a bag, fling them out upon the ground before they would fall into an exact Poem, yea or so much as make a good discourse in Prose? And may not a little *Book* be as easily made by chance, as this great *Volume* of the world? How long might a man be in sprinkling colours upon Canvas with a careless hand, before they would happen to make the exact Picture of a man? And is a man easier made by chance than his Picture? How long might twenty thousand *blind men*, which should be sent out from the several remote parts of *England*, wander up and down before they would all meet upon *Salisbury-plains* and fall into rank and file in the exact order of an Army? And yet this is much more easy to be imagined, than how the innumerable blind parts of matter should rendezvous themselves into a world. A man that sees *Henry* the *Seventh's* Chappel at *Westminster* might with as good reason maintain (yea with much better, considering the vast difference betwixt that little structure and the huge fabrick of the world) that it was never contrived and built by any man, but that the stones did by chance grow into those curious figures into which they seem to have been cut and graven; and that *upon a time* (as tales usually begin) the materials of that building, the stone, morter, timber, iron, lead, and glass, happily met together and very fortunately rang'd themselves into that delicate order in which we see them now so close compacted that it must be a very great chance that parts them again. What would the world think of a man that should advance such an opinion as this, and a Book for it? If they would do him right, they ought to look upon him as mad.[9]

Several things stand out in this argument. Most notable, perhaps, is its prolixity. Tillotson's elegant Latinate phrasing allows him to spin out his analogies at great length yet with absolute clarity: the sentences uncurl themselves in a manner almost erotic, but their structure is rigorously focused. Equally important is the sense that Tillotson has stopped almost arbitrarily; once the form of the argument is in place, he might have gone on listing analogies forever. Finally, the power of the argument depends upon the way that it accumulates its examples, rather than upon the precise operations of logic. We could say that Tillotson in effect asks his hearers to do some of the work along with him: he provides the clever analogies, and the listener makes the application. Less sympathetically, we could say that this argument is a rhetorical one, depending for its effect upon the persuasiveness of its manner. Prolixity, multiple examples with an arbitrary stopping point, and the related sense that the argument is carried more by the force of language than the power of logic: these three qualities make Tillotson's sermon a paradigmatic instance of a design argument.

Of course design arguments have been around for a long time: they turn up in Cicero, in the Psalms, in the New Testament, in Aquinas. Though it functions in historically particular ways, the idea that nature is another "Book of God," to be set beside the scriptural Book of God, is evidently a compelling one.[10] The most important sacred text for articulating the relationship between these two books is Psalm 19:

> The heavens declare the glory of God; and the firmament sheweth his handywork.
> Day unto day uttereth speech, and night unto night sheweth knowledge.
> *There is* no speech nor language, *where* their voice is not heard.
> Their line is gone out through all the earth, and their words to the end of the world.[11]

Importantly, the remainder of the Psalm turns from this celebration of nature to contemplate a more directly interventionist God:

> The law of the LORD *is* perfect, converting the soul: the testimony of the LORD *is* sure, making wise the simple.
> The statutes of the LORD *are* right, rejoicing the heart: the commandment of the LORD *is* pure, enlightening the eyes. (Psalm 19:7–8)

Natural theology is a place to begin, apparently, but not a place to end. Saint Paul sounds a similar note in the New Testament book of Romans:

> For the wrath of God is revealed from heaven against all ungodliness and unrighteousness of men, who hold the truth in unrighteousness;
> Because that which may be known of God is manifest in them; for God hath shewed *it* unto them.
> For the invisible things of him from the creation of the world are clearly seen, being understood by the things that are made, *even* his eternal power and Godhead; so that they are without excuse. (Romans 1:18–20)

Like the psalmist, Paul assumes that evidence of a designer is obvious— obvious enough, even, to condemn those who ignore it by rendering them "without excuse." But his intellectual interest clearly lies elsewhere, for this passage initiates the set of arguments that culminates in the famous conclusion in Romans 8:1: "*There is* therefore now no condemnation to them which are in Christ Jesus, who walk not after the flesh, but after the Spirit."

Despite these contextualizations of natural theology, the initial verses of Psalm 19 could be easily extracted and made to stand alone as an argument for God's existence instead of simply an expression of a religious orientation. This process of disembedding is on display when Joseph Addison writes in *The Spectator* of means for strengthening religious faith:

> The last Method which I shall mention . . . is frequent Retirement from the World, accompanied with religious Meditation. . . . In Courts and Cities we are entertained with the Works of Men, in the Country with those of God. One is the Province of Art, the other of Nature. Faith and Devotion naturally grow in

the Mind of every reasonable Man, who sees the Impressions of Divine Power
and Wisdom in every Object on which he casts his Eye. The Supream Being has
made the best Arguments for his own Existence, in the Formation of the Heavens and the Earth, and these are Arguments which a Man of Sense cannot for-
bear attending to, who is out of the Noise and Hurry of Human Affairs.

After quoting the first three verses of Psalm 19, Addison then concludes:

As such a bold and sublime manner of Thinking furnishes very noble Matter for
an Ode, the Reader may see it wrought into the following one.

I.

The Spacious Firmament on high,
With all the blue Etherial Sky,
And spangled Heav'ns, a Shining Frame,
Their great Original proclaim:
Th' unwearied Sun, from day to day,
Does his Creator's Pow'r display,
And publishes to every Land
The Work of an Almighty Hand.

II.

Soon as the Evening Shades prevail,
The Moon takes up the wondrous Tale,
And nightly to the listning Earth
Repeats the Story of her Birth:
Whilst all the Stars that round her burn,
And all the Planets, in their turn,
Confirm the Tidings as they rowl,
And spread the Truth from Pole to Pole.

III.

What though, in solemn Silence, all
Move round the dark terrestrial Ball?
What tho' nor real Voice nor Sound
Amid their radiant Orbs be found?
In Reason's Ear they all rejoice,
And utter forth a glorious Voice,
For ever singing, as they shine,
"The Hand that made us is Divine."[12]

Addison's loose paraphrase of the first three verses of Psalm 19 turns an
expression of religious devotion into an argument about the origin of
that devotion's object: where in the original psalm the heavens had declared God's *glory*, they now point to "their great Original." Even more
strikingly, Addison takes the psalmist's image of nature's voice tran-
scending the limitations of local languages and turns it into a brief for
Reason's universality. In both cases he shifts the emphasis toward the
capacities of human knowledge, a shift undertaken because he alters

the psalmist's basic question. The question hovering in the background of the psalm itself could be rendered as "How are we to understand all of nature, even when silent, as declaring God's glory?" Addison's background question, by contrast, is more straightforwardly rational: "How can we know that God made the nature that we see?" *The Spectator* thus reflects the bivalent nature of design arguments. On the one hand, Addison implies that orthodoxy is vulnerable to skeptical attack, and so he wheels out the design argument for defensive purposes. On the other hand, that rational defense is embedded within a culture of habitual devotion, what Addison calls the "proper Means of strengthning and confirming [Faith] in the Mind of Man" (141), that seeks to transcend merely reasonable arguments and address itself to postures and disciplines of religious living organized teleologically, not inductively.

A revealing contrast to Addison's rendering is Isaac Watts's 1719 hymn "The Heavens Declare Thy Glory, Lord," also inspired by Psalm 19. In Watts's version, each verse turns on a firm distinction between Nature and Scripture:

> The Heavens declare thy Glory, Lord,
> In every Star thy Wisdom shines:
> But when our Eyes behold thy Word
> We read thy Name in fairer Lines.

> Nor shall thy spreading Gospel rest
> Till thro' the World thy Truth has run;
> Till *Christ* has all the Nations blest
> That see the Light, or feel the Sun.[13]

For the nonconformist Watts, nature is decidedly *not* equal to scripture as a locus of God's revelation; indeed, nature here does not even have the preparatory, subservient status that it does for the psalmist and for Saint Paul. Apparently Watts is not very interested in Addison's implicit questions and the empirical philosophical background from which they derive. For Watts, knowledge comes through revelation, not through "Reason's Ear," a position that effectively short-circuits the epistemological question of *how* one comes to know something. Nature for Watts is a pleasant but largely irrelevant form of revelation, a potential distraction from a focus on the gospels, which replace the sun as the true source of light. Yet Watts, despite his influence—he wrote almost 600 hymns—was in this respect less a man of his times than was Addison. "The Spacious Firmament on High" expressed a sensibility that permeated the culture of eighteenth-century elites, a sensibility suspicious of arguments from revelation, and one that appealed simultaneously to a thin conception of rationality ("Reason's Ear") and to a thicker, more embedded culture of faith's inculcation.

Certainly design is less vulnerable to skepticism when it is embedded in a larger apparatus of belief and practice. If one already thinks that God made the world, then the world will offer up evidence in support of that thought. In *Paradise Lost*, for instance, Raphael scolds Adam for wondering if the excess of stars suggests divine inefficiency, but his speech is a contextualization of natural theology, not a rejection of it:

> This to attain, whether Heav'n move or Earth,
> Imports not, if thou reck'n right; the rest
> From Man or Angel the great Architect
> Did wisely to conceal, and not divulge
> His secrets to be scann'd by them who ought
> Rather admire.[14]

Admiration of the stars, not learning how they move, is the real meaning of reckoning right. But within the context of admiration, the search for answers is blameless, because it will be undertaken in the proper direction, namely from principle to observation and not the other way around.[15] Thus before chastising Adam, Raphael reassures him:

> To ask or search I blame thee not, for Heav'n
> Is as the Book of God before thee set,
> Wherein to read his wond'rous Works. (8.66–68)

Here Milton offers his readers a compact lesson in design arguments. Human curiosity, combined with limited knowledge, encourages us to reason in the wrong manner: we try to figure out something about God based on what we can see around us. This is natural. But it still needs to be corrected: we need to be reminded, as Raphael reminds Adam, to begin not with what we can observe but with what we know about God. If we're "reck'n[ing] right," questions about the behavior of the stars assume their proper place as signifiers of God's creative power. Raphael's reminder has the effect of recalling Adam to a better sense of himself, which for Milton is the same thing as reminding Adam that God made him—that God, not human power to reason and observe, is the condition of human autonomy. So Raphael's reminder re-embeds Adam in a different (and for Milton, deeper) sort of natural state, one that paradoxically requires the artifice of a pedagogical situation. Design's brief quest for autonomy, and its resubmergence into a larger apparatus of belief, thus stands for Milton as an allegory of human nature in general.

In the many natural theologies published in the latter half of the seventeenth century, design is likewise part of a larger texture of argument. In the neo-Platonic works of Edward Stillingfleet and Ralph Cudworth, the power of the argument is assumed but not dwelt upon. In John Wilkins's *Of the Principles and Duties of Natural Religion* (1675), possibly the

most influential example of natural theology for the first part of the
eighteenth century, design is one of four arguments for the existence
of God.[16] But something happened to design arguments between 1700
and 1850—between, to speak schematically, the moment when Newton
made uniformity the guarantor of modern science, and the moment
when Darwin offered a naturalistic explanation for what had until then
looked like divinely instituted order. In brief, Raphael's dictum was reversed, and design began to stand more or less on its own.

Initially, the design argument gained in prominence and prestige as
freethinking and deism began to play a larger role in the worries of the
orthodox in the 1690s. John Ray's *The Wisdom of God Manifested in the
Works of Creation* (1691) is centrally devoted to it. The year 1691 also
marks the first Boyle lecture, a series funded by Robert Boyle's estate,
whose declared aim was to defend orthodoxy against "notorious Infidels,
viz. Atheists, Deists, Pagans, Jews and *Mahometans*," in the service of which
the design argument was crucial ammunition.[17] The first of the Boyle lec-
turers, Richard Bentley, had been a tutor to Stillingfleet's son; his final
three lectures in the series deployed an argument from design that
leaned heavily on Newton's *Principia*. Where Bentley had ended with natural theology, Samuel Clarke's 1704 and 1705 Boyle lectures began
there, building a system of ethics and a theory of revelation upon a cosmological foundation.[18] Clarke's strategy would become paradigmatic
for natural theologians. At the far end of the century, William Paley did
in fact write his books on ethics (*Principles of Moral and Political Philosophy*,
1785) and on revelation (*Evidences of Christianity*, 1794) before turning to
the argument from design (*Natural Theology*, 1802). But he wrote in the
Preface to this last book that his works had "been written in an order the
very reverse of that in which they ought to be read."[19] This is a dramatic
shift from the order commended in *Paradise Lost*. Raphael would have
told Paley that his recommendation was exactly wrong.

This visibility of the design argument, while manifestly a sign of its cultural importance, is also a mark of its weakness. I noted previously that
design arguments work best if one is already committed to their worldview: one is more likely to feel persuaded by Tillotson's analogies, for instance, if one is already sympathetic to his general approach. It follows
that the increasing autonomy of reason over the course of the eighteenth
century represents a major liability for design. In directing their readers
to begin with the argument from design, writers from Clarke to Addison
to Paley count heavily upon a rhetoric of reasonableness; by prioritizing
epistemology, they seem to ignore the predispositions, habits, and various visceral intensities their readers bring with them. In this, of course,
they are typical of their age. And, for just that reason, they open themselves to critique. David Hume, in particular, was able to exploit design's

reliance upon reason and argument. Hume's *Dialogues Concerning Natural Religion* argued that, far from being an authentic inductive procedure, design arguments reasoned circularly, presupposing the very creator whose existence they claimed to demonstrate. Yet Hume also understood, as I argue in detail in the second chapter of this book, that the social field in which design operated, not the intellectual persuasiveness of the argument itself, accounted for its staying power. Demonstrating that natural theology depends upon something like circular reasoning does little to dislodge its hold, because that hold depends less on firm arguments than on a set of intellectual and emotional habits of which design is only a part. Intellectual historians have tended to emphasize Hume's critique of design *arguments* while playing down his rueful acknowledgment that the customs and habits inculcated by a wider culture of design were largely impervious to purely intellectual demolition. Yet the importance of this second aspect can hardly be overemphasized. It is one of the things that accounts for the persistence, and even the growth, of design.

A second liability for design flows from this same source. Scholars have noted that the growing autonomy of reason during the eighteenth century also means that *feeling*, in its turn, becomes a more vexed phenomenon.[20] While Hume thinks of the passions as social, Fanny Price, the heroine of Jane Austen's *Mansfield Park*, is a character whose depth of feeling arises from her *a*sociality: she is silent and retiring, and she refuses to participate in the forms of sociability available to her. Design has a difficult time dealing with a discourse, like the one to which Fanny subscribes, that understands religion as a set of authentic feelings. Here we verge upon a more general eighteenth-century trend in which increased importance attached to proper feelings accompanies a lack of confidence in the most effective means of inculcating them and a vagueness in the language used to describe them. Edmund Burke's entire career, from his early writings on aesthetics through his counterrevolutionary broadsides to his impeachment of Warren Hastings, could be regarded as an attempt to fix this problem and place proper feeling once again on a firm foundation.

Between "feeling" and "reason," however, subsists another set of nonrational elements such as habit and custom. Burke's defense of what he calls "prejudice" depends upon these elements, and design, too, operates most powerfully when it works upon this ground. As a largely repetitive and tradition-laden discourse, design aims not to produce new feelings but to produce old ones again, so that they become embedded more firmly within the mental and bodily lives of persons. Although natural theology presents itself as a strictly reasonable series of inferences, then, its strength resides in the largely unarticulated predispositions, habits, and attitudes that live below the threshold of reason. In one sense, of course, these tacit assumptions cannot be articulated, for to do so would disembed them and dissipate their force. On the other hand, reiteration and repetition can serve as powerful methods of enculturation and personal discipline. As we shall see, design is best understood as a series of practices or habits that register the nascent anxieties of a developing modernity in which, paradoxically, tacit assumptions need to be stated so that they can become tacit again.

Design sits squarely in the middle of what would become familiar modern divisions between science and religion, reason and feeling. In this respect it expressed a tension for which there was not yet a name. In his 1667 *History of the Royal Society*, Thomas Sprat gives voice to that tension when he declares that the Society's Fellows, in revealing the orderliness of the world, will also be revealing the goodness of the creator: "[I]t lies in the *Natural Philosopher's* hands," writes Sprat, "best to advance that part of *Divinity*: which, though it fills not the mind, with such *tender,* and *powerful contemplations,* as that which shews us Man's *Redemption* by a *Mediator,* yet it is by no means to be pass'd by unregarded: but is an excellent ground to establish the other."[21] Sprat's language is an example of what sociologists call differentiation: we can see how theology in its modern disciplinary sense is separating out from what Sprat calls "natural philosophy." Science, indeed, will establish the "ground" for the theological concept of redemption. Along the way theology acquires an affective language (*"tender* and *powerful contemplations"*) foreign to the more dispassionate investigations of the Royal Society. In time, Sprat's distinction would become a genuine opposition: between faith and reason, between religion and science.[22] The increasing autonomy of these domains would eventually prove too much for design to handle.

Lest this sound too dramatic, however, let us remind ourselves that the differentiation that would eventually render science an autonomous domain happened gradually and over many years. Writing two hundred years after Sprat, having absorbed not only Newton but also Darwin, John Stuart Mill is still willing to allow design a seat at the scientific table—albeit a rather humble one. Design arguments, he notes, have a "really scientific character;" but he goes on to note that design's analogical character makes it "impossible to estimate precisely": "It may be very strong, when the known points of agreement . . . are numerous and the known points of difference few; or very weak, when the reverse is the case: but it can never be equal in validity to real induction."[23] Analogy is not science ("real induction") but it is not simply rhetoric either; and Mill's ambivalence at this late date makes it less surprising that during the romantic period design's powerful analogical language is still able to express a basically unified sensibility even amid the gradual differentiation of science and religion.

The "Theology" section of the liberal *Analytical Review* for November 1790 provides a revealing snapshot of the way design continued to be taken for granted around the turn of the century. That section opens with an enthusiastic review of the third volume of Hugh Blair's *Sermons* and includes a lengthy excerpt from a sermon entitled "The Creation of the World considered, as displaying in the Great Creator, Supreme Power, Wisdom, and Goodness." The world, writes Blair,

presents such an astonishing conjunction of power, wisdom, and goodness, as cannot be beheld without religious veneration. Accordingly, among all nations of the earth, it has given rise to religious belief and worship. The most ignorant and savage tribes, when they looked round on the earth and the heavens, could not avoid ascribing their origin to some invisible designing cause, and feeling a propensity to adore. . . .[24]

After this classic instance of the design argument, the *Review* offers a short and critical account of a sermon by Thomas Twining entitled "On the Abuse of Reason": "though the general principles of this discourse be admitted in their full extent," says the reviewer, "it will still remain a question with many, whether Christianity does in fact teach any truths, which can properly be called mysteries, or require men to assent to any propositions, which reason cannot fully comprehend" (327). Having dispensed with Twining's emphasis on mystery and revelation in a manner that seems deliberately to recall the language of the deist debates in the early part of the century, the *Review* offers, on the following page, a positive analysis of a sermon by Samuel Neely entitled "The Ocean; Displays of the Divine Perfections in it; and the Moral Instructions to be derived from it": "The history of nature is so obviously connected with theology, and so easily applied to illustrate and confirm its principles," declares the *Review*, "that it is astonishing it is so seldom resorted to as a fund of interesting topics of discourse for the pulpit. . . . The writer has enumerated many particulars respecting the ocean, which serve to illustrate the wisdom and goodness of God" (329). Taken together, these three reviews offer a picture of natural theology as both embedded and precarious. They tell us simultaneously that natural theology is barely alive and that it is prospering; that it figures importantly in the sermons of one of the eighteenth century's most popular preachers and that it rarely appears in "discourse for the pulpit."

The historical evidence does not really bear out the *Review*'s assertion that theology rarely resorts to nature, but this is less interesting than the fact that the journal distinguishes nature *from* theology even as it declares the two discourses "obviously connected." This is similar to the distinction that Sprat had made back in 1667, and it is born out by the way in which the *Review* divides the relevant intellectual terrain. For despite the *Review*'s endorsement of the sentiments of Blair and Neely, it nevertheless sequesters them to the "Theology" section; a lengthy section on "Natural Philosophy" in the September issue, meanwhile, never mentions the possible theological implications of science's discoveries. That section opens with an account of the transactions of the Royal Society: William Herschel on the discovery of two new moons orbiting Saturn, some papers on luminous arches and "heavy inflammable Air," and on volcanoes, each one summarized in great detail. Strikingly, the *Review* is clearly unsatisfied with the Society's current transactions: "Can it be supposed that these great men have bid adieu to philosophical pursuits? can it be supposed that their researches are not worth communicating? or can they be imagined to be so little awake to the true interests of the society as to withhold them?" (44). Here the *Review* advocates for the process of intellectual differentiation that Sprat had identified many years earlier: it calls upon scientists to imagine for themselves a more public role. The implication is that science is, or could be, interesting for its own sake and not necessarily for what it can tell its audience about the divine creator.

Dominating the *Review*'s November issue, finally, are the events in France and the publication that very month of Edmund Burke's *Reflections on the Revolution in France*. From this perspective, the *Review*'s endorsement of Blair and Neely, and its concomitant rejection of Twining on the grounds of unnecessary mysteriousness, resonates powerfully with the radical and liberal complaint that Burke fetishized monarchical power and mystery—a critique shortly to be made (in)famous by Mary Wollstonecraft, herself a frequent contributor to the *Review*. Here natural theology, particularly in the differentiated state in which the *Review* understands it (that is, as obviously connected to, but not the same as, natural philosophy), emerges as coordinate with a basically enlightenment *political* project of transparency and reason, to be set against all those who would cloak power, either divine or temporal, in mystery. In these guises and permutations, then, the *Review* gives us a snapshot of design toward the end of the eighteenth century as a full participant in the various intellectual currents that occupied the minds of England's intellectual elites.

Romanticism

After a century and more of frequent iteration, design had achieved such cultural saturation by the late eighteenth century that it is little wonder romantic poetry was sometimes read according to its dictates. The *British Critic*'s lengthy review of Wordsworth's *Excursion*, for instance, placed the poem in a tradition of spiritual meditation beginning with Joseph Hall and Robert Boyle. Where Hall and Boyle had devised a technique for transmuting everyday objects into occasions for praising God, the *Critic* pushes this technique in a teleological direction: "Moreover, by considering all things sensible with respect to some higher power, we are more likely to get an insight into final causes, and all the wonderful ways of Providence."[25] The inculcation of this sensibility is the chief end of all worthy poetry, the writer claims: "It would be a very engaging task to trace the progress of descriptive poetry with a view to this principle, to mark how the great hierophants of nature have instinctively used it as the true key to her high mysteries" (453). All poetry, in other words, offers a version of the design argument. The *Critic* then deploys this revised literary history in order to position Wordsworth as the inheritor of a tradition stretching back to ancient Greece, taking in "our own best and oldest bards" (454) and Milton, skipping over the "artificial manners" of the neoclassical period, and landing firmly in what used to be called preromanticism:

the shackles however were burst by Thomson and Collins and Akenside, and, since their day, the works of nature have not wanted observers able and willing to deduce from them lessons, which Providence, if we may speak it without presumption, intended them to convey. But none have ever entered so profoundly into this theory of their art as those commonly known by the name of the Lake Poets, particularly Mr. Wordsworth. (455)

This is a familiar romantic genealogy. Yet it aims to install *The Excursion*, not the as-yet unpublished *Prelude*, as the culmination of poetic history; those readers disappointed by the direction that Wordsworth's politics and poetry had taken could therefore find in such teleological spiritualizing plenty of material for suspicion.

Most obviously, that suspicion can originate in a skeptical or secular sensibility: this is the position of Percy Shelley, William Hazlitt, and the critical tradition that contrasts Wordsworth's so-called "Great Decade" with the long slow twilight of his career. But suspicion of romanticism's teleological impulse can also come from those more, not less, devout than Wordsworth. Thus Coleridge's *Aids to Reflection* (1825), for example, contains a running attack on William Paley, and we find Coleridge worrying in his marginalia over the typical Cambridge undergraduate reared on the "Grotio-Paleyian Scheme of Christian Evidence."[26] Coleridge's increasing orthodoxy makes him suspicious of the way that Wordsworth's verse lends itself to the very same natural pieties that the *Critic* celebrates. And it is here that the devout Coleridge finds common ground with the skeptical Percy Shelley, who declared in the Preface to *Prometheus Unbound* (1819) that "[f]or my part I had rather be damned with Plato and Lord Bacon, than go to Heaven with Paley and Malthus."[27] It was reading *The Excursion*, we might recall, that finally convinced Shelley of Wordsworth's apostasy. As Mary Shelley records in her journal, Percy "brings home Wordsworths Excursion of which we read a part—much disapointed [*sic*]—He is a slave—."[28] The figure of slavery here contrasts intriguingly with the analogous figure in the *British Critic*, where Wordsworth appears as the inheritor of those poets who have "burst the shackles" of convention and liberated poetry to become a vehicle for design arguments.

The literary genealogy proposed by the *British Critic* identifies a persistent strain within Wordsworthian romanticism that can be easily joined to a sensibility attracted to design—and it thus defines the terms of a debate about the religious affinities of romanticism that still continues. In the specific case of Percy Shelley, on whom we may dwell for a moment longer, the conceptual orientation of the design argument, with an intellectual heritage that is Aristotelian, naturalist, and empirical, will seem like an anathema, for Shelley's intellectual heritage is Platonic, mystical, and idealist. Shelley's hostility toward Paley springs from his belief that Paley was an apologist for the status quo who offered spiritual justification for things as they are. As such, he represented direct competition for the reformist Shelley, who wished to imagine the world differently. Still, the broadside directed at Paley in the "Preface" to *Prometheus Unbound* is a bit surprising, even if we adjust for irony. Grouping Paley with Thomas Malthus may be a familiar romantic reaction against enlightened reason and utilitarian calculus, but in framing his criticism in the theological terms of heaven and hell, Shelley's rhetoric exposes a certain tension between the language of religion and that of reason. If Paley is an example of what Shelley does not want to be, is this because, as the rhetoric of heaven and hell suggests, he advocates a religious worldview that seems anachronistic and retrograde? Or is it because, as the link to Malthus suggests, he represents enlightenment's endgame, the kindly face of a world-destroying Reason in which freedom is really submission? Is Paley, that is to say, too unmodern, or is he too much the representative of a kind of modernity that Shelley abhors? The answer matters in part because many of us have learned to view religion as the residue of a prior age, a doomed holdout against the process of modernization. If Paley is in fact real competition for Shelley's kind of romanticism—if Shelley's argument, that is to say, recognizes Paley's religious and moral vision as a possible way of imagining what it means to be modern—then he cannot simultaneously be dismissed as retrograde. Thus Shelley's ambivalence: he wants to relegate religion to the past *and* to articulate a different future from the one that religion lays out.

Scholars have long recognized design as an informing, if vague, background presence in the romantic era. Asserted relationships between the harmony and unity of a natural scene and the moral or devotional disposition of its human observers draw upon the tradition of design— but also, potentially, upon neo-Platonism and Spinozism.[29] Most writers did not respect the neat divisions of intellectual history, but rather used whatever arguments and insights served their purposes. In "A Refutation of Deism," Percy Shelley attacks a version of the design argument derived from Paley, but this is far from his only target.[30] Book Five of Wordsworth's *Prelude*, meanwhile, turns on the notion that nature is God's Book:

> Hitherto
> In progress through this verse my mind hath looked
> Upon the speaking face of earth and heaven
> As her prime teacher, intercourse with man
> Established by the Sovereign Intellect. (5.10–14)[31]

The speaker goes on to propose an analogy between God's Book and human books: "Thou also, man, hast wrought," he says (5.17), though he must immediately face the fact that human books decay.[32] The "Dream of the Arab" passage that shortly follows is a complicated rewriting of Rene Descartes's dream of the "two books" of science and poetry, itself a revision of the two books of Nature and Scripture.[33] If the *British Critic* thought that design was the key to literary history, the truth is that, precisely because of its ubiquity, design is hard to isolate from the general stew of late eighteenth-century political, philosophical, and religious thinking and writing.

Rather than provide an exhaustive catalog of design references, then, I have focused in this book on places where discussions or acknowledgments of design verge upon the larger matter of secularization— secularization instantiated, registered, or resisted both at the level of the text itself and in later critical interpretations and appropriations. Thus romanticism is an important part of the story I wish to tell in part because of its reception in the twentieth century. Consequently, we must keep two sorts of romanticism in play: on the one hand, various texts that exemplify (without exhausting) what is now often termed "romantic-period writing"; on the other, a more abstract conception of romanticism, heavily influenced by the critical tradition, that through its powerful and frequently normative operations has influenced our understanding of secularization and religion.[34] At the most basic level, that normativity is captured in the vague sense that after the romantics it was possible to be "spiritual" without being "religious." Consider, then, how Shelley's dismissal of Paley functions to consolidate such a reading by embodying the dual conceptions of romanticism as period-specific writing and as normative worldview. Here we see the rejection, by a "romantic" writer, of a "romantic-period" writer, a rejection moreover that hinges on defining the latter as in thrall to orthodoxy while the former is free of it. This is sometimes called "romantic exceptionalism," and Shelley's example registers not only the link between romantic exceptionalism and secularization but also the manner in which that link constructs a persuasive intellectual genealogy for modern critics. M. H. Abrams, Harold Bloom, and Paul de Man, despite important methodological differences, share a reading of romanticism that turns upon extracting its exceptional figures from their cultural milieu by interpreting them as powerfully anticipating and addressing modern concerns—where modernity itself is understood as alienated (Abrams), iconoclastic (Bloom), or potentially demystified (de Man).

One powerful way in which romanticism has been tied to modernity through the auspices of secularization is the "two cultures" hypothesis, so-called after C. P. Snow's famous lecture of that name.[35] According to this hypothesis, the industrial revolution split intellectual culture in two, with the physical sciences on one side and the literary intellectuals on the other. Henceforth, science dedicated itself to progress and to the future, while literary culture became increasingly backward looking and conservative. Romantic-era writers of all political persuasions contributed to this sensibility, sometimes by conceiving of literary culture as distinct from that of science, more importantly by producing the sort of writing in which later generations could locate the idea of literary culture.[36] Although Snow does not speak much of religion, we need only turn to the work of Max Weber to find a powerful account of the way in which science gradually demystifies the universe. Against Weber's "iron cage," mystery and enchantment come increasingly to reside in versions of the literary, and so two faces of secularization emerge. The first is the rational scientific one, whose operations push a religious sensibility increasingly over to the literary side of the ledger. Yet writers, too, must live in the modern world, in which religious belief is increasingly pressured. So in accounts such as those of Matthew Arnold or John Ruskin, a religious sensibility, conceived now as the property of literature, of feeling, or of art, eventually becomes indistinguishable from that of spirit or culture more generally. This sensibility carries over into the twentieth century and the full institutionalization of literary study, when figures as various as T. S. Eliot, F. R. Leavis, and the American New Critics demote romanticism but retain the *idea* of a literary culture distinct from the workaday world.[37] This conception, in which literature enables human beings to hold on to a spiritual sensibility without having to commit themselves to a particular metaphysic, helps elucidate why, for a postwar generation of literary critics, romanticism appeared as an attempt to rescue "spirit"—that is, a secularized religion—from the anomie and fragmentation of a modern life increasingly dominated by science and instrumental rationality.

Progressive critics from Marx and Weber onward, meanwhile, depend upon the same basic opposition between humanistic and scientific cultures in order to launch their critiques of capital and rationalization—a tradition taken up most famously in the twentieth century by Adorno and the Frankfurt School.[38] By locating critical agency within the text itself, such progressive criticism installs cultural conflict within its own object of study. In effect, the literary object exposes its own impulses toward retrenchment, mystification, and religion. Thus particular critics might, like Abrams, celebrate a romanticism understood as the carrier of spiritual truths, or they might, like de Man, criticize those truths as mystifications and seek to uncover romanticism's counterspirit—but the difference in these critical approaches is itself enabled by the *shared* premise that literature had taken upon itself the role of cultural consolidation formerly reserved for religion. That shared premise itself is one reason that romanticism seems so inevitably entangled with the narrative of secularization.[39]

Let me here give two examples of that entanglement. The first is from a passage I noted previously: the discussion of books in Wordsworth's *Prelude*. When the speaker says that *hitherto* he has looked at nature as his "prime teacher" (5.13) he inaugurates the first in a series of attempts to create some distance between himself and nature—and in this instance the analogy between the Book of God and human books becomes the means for such separation. Yet there are two important respects in which the analogy of the Book of God to human books does not fully succeed. First, human books "must perish" (5.21), whereas Nature decays only to live again, a process famously described a bit later as "woods decaying, never to be decayed" (6.557). Second, while "the speaking face of earth and heaven" is designed as a way for God to communicate with humanity, books are a way for humanity to communicate with itself: "Thou also, man, hast wrought, / For commerce of thy nature with itself " (5.17–18). In other words, human productions are self-conscious in a way that divine productions are not. In his influential essay "Romanticism and 'Anti-Self-Consciousness,' " Geoffrey Hartman notes that the "disease" of self-analysis in *The Prelude* will lead eventually to the famous crisis of Books 9 and 10, but goes on to argue that it is Wordsworth's strength to overcome such paralyzing self-analysis by winning through to a mature theory of Imagination: "[a] way is to be found not to escape from or limit knowledge but to convert it into an energy finer than intellectual," he writes.[40] Hartman's dialectical apparatus comes from Hegel's interpretation of the Fall as a fall into self-consciousness. According to this strategy, the way back to a second innocence must come not through a reversion to an Edenic state, but rather, as Hartman quoting Hegel says: "the hand that inflicts the wound is also the hand that heals it."[41] In other words, the making of human artifacts, including books of poetry, both initiates a separation from a pre-lapsarian and apparently un-self-conscious world *and* heals the wound such separation entails by discovering the compensating power of the imagination. Hartman is consequently quite explicit about the secularization inherent in the romantic agon of self-consciousness: "There clearly comes a time when art frees itself from its subordination to religion or religiously inspired myth, and continues or even replaces these. This time seems to coincide with what is generally called the Romantic period."[42] If human books are to be understood analogously to the Book of God, then, it is an analogy pitched, we might say, toward an increasingly demystified (which is to say, for Hartman, self-conscious) future.

Interestingly, it is possible to contest Hartman's emphasis on consciousness but retain his constitutive link between romanticism and secularization. Andrzej Warminski does just this when he begins his reading of Book 5 by responding to Hartman: "what happens," he writes, "when . . . the second term of the triad Nature / Self-consciousness / Imagination is understood, is read, as a linguistic self-reflection . . . a linguistic turn of language upon language?"[43] This question disputes Hartman's basic presupposition that Wordsworthian romanticism is fundamentally about the relationship of nature and imagination. For Warminski (following de Man), the basic Wordsworthian problematic is rather the relationship of imagination and temporality. Thus, in his reading, the turn in Book 5 from God's Book to human books does not inaugurate secularization along the lines of a Hegelian fall into self-consciousness and consequent imaginative reparation, but emerges instead as an allegory for the barely glimpsed possibility that secularization need not be undertaken because it has always already happened in the anticipated death of the subject, a death that figures the death of divinity itself: "just as man's face may 'cover' or 'manifest' or figure no spirit or a dead spirit, so the 'speaking face' of Nature may 'cover' or 'manifest' or 'figure' nothing but a deathful spirit or a dead God," writes Warminski.[44] From this perspective, the hermeneutic tradition stretching from Hegel to Hartman stabilizes the very spiritual content whose sublation it takes itself to be narrating; Hartman's emphasis on self-consciousness keeps him nostalgically attached to the idea of Nature as

God's Book, and he thereby comes uncomfortably close to a mystified reading of Wordsworth and, by extension, romanticism itself.

The debate between Warminski and Hartman, which can stand in for a debate between phenomenological and deconstructive criticism, is more interesting now for its shared premises than for its methodological disagreements. Both critics read in such a way as to make it romanticism's distinct achievement to initiate a break with religion. Though they construe that break in different ways, they concur about what romanticism is breaking *from*: what eighteenth-century writers called "natural religion" or, somewhat more technically, "naturally theology," represented in *The Prelude* by the idea of Nature as the "speaking face" of the divine. Whether the romantic achievement takes the form of imaginative anti-self-consciousness or the tropological anticipation of death—whether, that is, it involves a redefined relationship to Nature or a definitive turn away from Nature—the object of critique is the same. For both critics, what is at stake is the legacy of romanticism itself, a legacy whose secularity must be established or preserved by rescuing it from the mistaken idea that Nature is the Book of God—an idea whose mistakenness both critics understand Wordsworth's poetry to implicitly register.

My second example of the way that romanticism has come to seem inevitably entangled with the narrative of secularization: Josef Haydn's oratorio *The Creation*, which premiered in 1798. Haydn was a quintessentially enlightened figure; his friends and acquaintances were largely well-educated and progressive elites, many of them Freemasons like himself. His optimistic and technically superb music is grounded by a dignified humanity; what one scholar calls his "sincere and cheerful piety" strikes a balance between God's majesty and human capacities.[45] The libretto for *The Creation* expresses a similar philosophy. It was probably written for Handel (who never set it) several decades earlier by someone variously referred to as Lidley or Liddel, about whom nothing else is known. As befits the time of its writing, it is optimistic, evincing a wonder in God's creation and confidence about humanity's place within it. Although it makes a few Platonic references to celestial harmony, its basic energies are decidedly those of natural theology: inductive, reasonable, and confident.[46] The libretto is an amalgam of *Paradise Lost* and the early chapters of Genesis, but it contains very little of Milton's actual theology; the Fall is alluded to only briefly, and persistent thematic concerns of *Paradise Lost* such as free will and God's foreknowledge are entirely absent. Theologically, then, the libretto could have been written by an Arminian Anglican, a deist, or a Freemason; "[t]he broader message," writes Nicholas Temperley, "seems distinctly 'ecumenical' in its appeal."[47] The libretto was in the possession of the London-based musical impresario Johann Peter Salomon, who was responsible for bringing Haydn to London in 1791 and again in 1794. It was adapted and translated into German by Haydn's friend Baron Gottfried van Swieten, and subsequently retranslated into English.

The German version of *The Creation* was premiered privately in Vienna in 1798, then publicly at the National Theatre in Vienna in March of 1799. The score was published in both English and German in February 1800 and the oratorio itself premiered at Covent Garden in March of 1800. *The Creation* rapidly entered the standard repertory of choral societies.[48] In the early years of the nineteenth century it became a European and eventually transatlantic phenomenon, with more than forty performances in Vienna before 1810; numerous performances throughout the German-speaking and Scandanavian countries; four performances in London in 1800; in Worcester, Hull, Hereford, Norwich, Stamford, and Gloucester during 1801–3; in Paris in 1800, Moscow in 1801, Spain in 1805, Italy in 1809, and Boston in 1819.[49] The publication of a piano-vocal score and the independent publication of extracts ensured further dissemination.

The Creation opens with a depiction of chaos in the key of C minor. These passages are unsettled and chromatic, with shifting harmonies and spare orchestral accompaniment, more the raw materials of music than music itself. "[A]nd the earth was without form, and void," reads the libretto, "and darkness was upon the face of the deep."[50] The subsequent depiction of God's creation of light is one of the most famous moments in all of Haydn's music. The libretto reads: "And God said; Let there be Light, and there was Light" (53). At this moment the orchestra bursts into a fortissimo C major chord, resolving the broken and unfinished character of the depiction of chaos. Haydn had apparently kept this moment a secret until the first performance in Vienna. As one contemporary observer wrote, "in that moment when light broke out for the first time, one would have said that rays darted from the composer's burning eyes. The enchantment of the electrified Viennese was so general that the orchestra could not proceed for several minutes."[51] This famous strike-of-light passage also establishes the fundamentally optimistic tone of the oratorio as a whole; in bringing order out of chaos and light out of darkness, it reveals Haydn's confidence in the natural world's accessibility to human understanding. Like God, the composer brings light to his creation—this time, appropriately enough, by electrifying it.

That confidence gets picked up at the end of day four, when Haydn returns to C major with the well-known choral passage "The heavens are telling the glory of God," a paraphrase of the opening verses of Psalm 19. With this chorus we can complete a story that began with our earlier discussion of this Psalm, for Haydn's setting of "The heavens are telling" became a familiar nineteenth-century hymn. There was one important change, however: the music was Haydn's, but the hymn's words are not those of Haydn's libretto but rather "The spacious firmament on high," Addison's well-known paraphrase of Psalm 19. Addison's confidence in "Reason's Ear," which can hear the hymn of praise that creation sings even when creation is literally silent, proves to be an apt revision of the libretto of *The Creation*, which at this juncture seems to carry a Christological implication: "In all the land resounds the word, / never unperceived, / Ever understood" (56). Especially within a Miltonic context, the resounding word could be taken to echo the "Word" (that is, Christ) from the gospel of John,[52] suggesting a complex relationship between the revelation available to all and the revelation contained specifically within Scripture. But Addison's paraphrase strips this ambiguity away, ironically bringing the passage closer to its original, non-Christological meaning, though with a decidedly enlightened spin:

What though, in solemn Silence, all
Move round the dark terrestrial Ball?
What tho' nor real Voice nor Sound
Amid their radiant Orbs be found?
In Reason's Ear they all rejoice,
And utter forth a glorious Voice,
For ever singing, as they shine,
"The Hand that made us is Divine."

Here creation's silence, which for Saint Paul and Isaac Watts, we recall, provides an opening for more direct kinds of divine revelation, is rendered completely accessible to Reason, delivering a clear message that rests content with an account of origins ("The Hand that made us is Divine") and thereby foreclosing upon any further doctrinal complications.

The ecumenical energy of the composite Addison / Haydn hymn suggests the manner in which a design sensibility permeated eighteenth-century intellectual culture. By contrast, when Haydn's oratorio appears in a pivotal passage in Mary Shelley's 1826 novel *The Last Man*, the effect is to darken, ironize, and secularize the optimistic and pious cultural milieu in which Addison and Haydn both participated. After a plague has wiped out most of the earth's inhabitants, the few straggling survivors make their way toward Switzerland, when they hear organ music coming from a rural church. The narrator, Lionel Verney, offers a rapturous and Platonizing apostrophe to music as the "language of the immortals." He then continues:

We all stood mute; many knelt. In a few minutes however, we were recalled to human wonder and sympathy by a familiar strain. The air was Haydn's "New-Created World," and, old and drooping as humanity had become, the world yet fresh as at creation's day, might still be worthily celebrated by such an hymn of praise. Adrian and I entered the church; the nave was empty, though the smoke of incense rose from the altar, bringing with it the recollection of vast congregations, in once thronged cathedrals; we went into the loft. A blind old man sat at the bellows; his whole soul was ear; and as he sat in the attitude of attentive listening, a bright glow of pleasure was diffused over his countenance; for, though his lack-lustre eye could not reflect the beam, yet his parted lips, and every line of his face and venerable brow spoke delight. A young woman sat at the keys, perhaps twenty years of age. Her auburn hair hung on her neck, and her fair brow shone in its own beauty; but her drooping eyes let fall fast-flowing tears, while the constraint she exercised to suppress her sobs, and still her trembling, flushed her else pale cheek; she was thin; languor, and alas! sickness, bent her form.[53]

Shelley's reference here is probably to Haydn's depiction of the close of the first day of creation, in which the libretto repeats the phrase "[a] new created world / springs up at God's command" (53). This section of the oratorio had been transcribed for piano and voice as a separate piece, which Shelley knew. Interestingly, this passage is one of the few places in *The Creation* that strikes a darker tone.[54] Coming immediately after the dramatic "and there was Light" passage, it pairs the fall of the rebel angels "with despairing cursing rage" (rendered in A minor) with the creation rising "at God's command" (rendered in A major).

Picking up on this darker tone, Shelley's account accomplishes a brilliant reversal of everything that *The Creation* had come to stand for. Depicting the oratorio as a carrier of enlightened values, she begins by contrasting the Aristotelian "human sympathy" of Haydn's "familiar strain" with the Platonizing, harmonious, and reverential attitude evoked by the (unnamed) musical selection that had preceded it. Though Lionel and Adrian continue to cling to the enlightened idea of human sympathy, the plague has revealed that idea as empty; any attempt to link sympathy and compassion to a religious vision by means of natural theology would ring hollowly in the contrast between the novel's "old and drooping . . . humanity" and what the music describes as the fresh creation springing up at God's command, for God is clearly nowhere to be found in the world of accelerating destruction that Lionel inhabits. In this respect we may say that Shelley is deliberately secularizing the familiar discourse of natural theology, not by contesting its inductive form of reasoning but by casting the entire tradition as an exercise in nostalgia: the world may have once sprung up at God's command, but that was a long time ago, and that story can now provide only the solace of a mystified backward glance for its few remaining inhabitants, who remember "vast congregations in once thronged cathedrals." Importantly, Shelley accomplishes this revision in part by restoring the Miltonic ethos that *The Creation* libretto had stripped away. The "blind old man" listening intently to the playing of his frail daughter recalls the blind Milton dictating *Paradise Lost* to his daughters. More dramatically yet, the reader of *The Last Man* knows, from the very outset of the novel, that Lionel, Adrian, and the few remaining inhabitants of the earth have embarked on a downward population spiral, one that in effect un-writes Milton's story by reducing the population all the way down to one, turning Lionel Verney into an Adam without an Eve.

Shelley's strategic use of *The Creation* thus stands for one possible fate of design within romanticism. The tradition of natural theology had dominated the 150 years between *Paradise Lost* and *The Last Man*, but Shelley's text works to revise Milton in such a way as to render natural theology an historical relic. If the Book of God had once been easy to read, it is now both obscure and obsolete. Human books, to pick up on the Wordsworthian thread that attracted both Hartman and Warminski, are all that remain legible in this world; as Lionel notes when he chooses a "few books" for his solitary journey around the globe, "the libraries of the world are thrown open to me" (367). In like manner, we recall, human books replaced the Book of God in *The Prelude*, becoming (for Hartman) a vehicle for consciousness as the carrier and redeemer of the Fall or (for Warminski) the experience of temporality and thus the tropological anticipation of death. Shelley's conclusion manages to combine these two differently secular readings of human books, for they become both a vehicle for Hartmanian anti-self-consciousness—a means by which Lionel tries to "conceal me from myself" (363)—and, with the book that Lionel himself writes, a nonredemptive anticipation of death. For unlike Wordsworth, Lionel has no audience for his autobiography: "I also will write a book, I cried—for whom to read?—to whom dedicated?" (364). To write, in this context, is to write for its own sake, to produce a literature not beholden to its audience. This undertaking is possible, Shelley suggests, only once the writer has gone beyond Wordsworth, with his penchant for teleological "slavery" as revealed in *The Excursion*, and achieved the difficult knowledge that his own death will bring an end to all meaning. To imagine a literature at the end of the world means giving up on the idea that books reference, however obliquely, the Book of God.

In this "death of the author" guise, romanticism spoke powerfully to critical movements such as deconstruction. I remark upon this affinity in order to draw out two distinct ways of understanding romanticism in the broader sense alluded to earlier—not, that is, merely a period-specific designation but as a concept that continues to variously inform our modernity. The first, linked most obviously to Abrams, is to plot romanticism as the secularization of inherited theological ideas, and then to read backward from a seemingly achieved modern secularity in order

to validate the romantic secularizing project. This method turns historical change over to the relatively impersonal forces of development, particularly the set of developments that sociologists call "modernization."
The second way of understanding romanticism's relation to modernity,
linked both to deconstructive and to historicist methodologies, relies on
a more explicitly interventionist model, wherein particular writers and
readers—Shelley, Warminski—help us recognize that the old certainties
no longer hold. This model sometimes positions these writers and readers in agonistic opposition to the tendencies of the literature they read.
For this group, romanticism finds its proper home in modernity not inevitably but contingently, because through the blindness and insight of
critical activity we have made a home for it here.

In turning now to address secularization directly, I wish to keep both
the modernizing and the interventionist versions of romantic modernity
in mind. I shall propose that the humanist technique of linking secularization to modernization, evident in the approaches of Abrams and
Hartman, wrongly supposes that modernity is a singular and historically
inevitable event rather than a multiple and contingent one. Meanwhile,
the posthumanist interventionist model characteristic of Warminski and
a variety of poststructuralist critics, while admirably alert to contingency,
tends to misread its own secularity as neutral and autonomous rather
than as determined by the intellectual stance itself. Both humanist and
posthumanist renderings of romanticism, that is to say, rely upon aspects of the secularization thesis that have been subjected to increasing
scrutiny by nonliterary scholars.

Secularization

What do we mean when we invoke "secularization"? In common use, the
term is often shorthand for a loss of belief or a decline in the authority of
religious institutions. Many secularization stories, moreover, assume a
causal relationship between these two, for it seems logical to assume that
people will abandon their personal religious commitments as religion
itself loses cultural power. Yet that assumption mixes individual and institutional foci, and it leads to some conceptual confusion. For one thing,
it supposes that religion is a set of beliefs that *can* be lost.[55] Abrams
makes this assumption in *Natural Supernaturalism*, for it is only in personal terms—that is, in the language of "belief" and "ideas" and their
"reinterpretation"—that he can claim romanticism as a revolution in
subjectivity.[56] In accounts such as this, institutional decline morphs into
the loss of religious content at the level of the individual. Empirically,
however, there is a problem with this account: in at least some parts of the
world, individual participation is *inversely* linked to religion's institutional

power. Indeed, institutional decline sometimes leads to the intensifica-
tion of religious content as it becomes more thoroughly internalized.

A second problem with the familiar account of secularization is that
the narrative of religious decline itself is empirically suspect. With the
important exception of Western Europe, the world is not more secular
than it was before modernization; it is, if anything, more *religious*.[57]
Some of its most rapidly modernizing societies are also its most intensely
religious. Even in the West, the relationship between modernization
and secularization is hard to pin down, for the process has played itself
out differently in northern Europe, in southern Europe, and in former
Eastern Bloc countries. The religious vibrancy of the United States,
meanwhile, further complicates the relation of secularization to modernization.[58] Current data suggest little change in religious participation
during the past fifty years in the United States, while evidence for earlier
eras indicates that modernization does not equal secularization in any
straightforward way. Meanwhile the most reliable data show that religious participation in England rose between 1800 and 1850 (the period
of most intense modernization and industrialization) and then held
steady or rose gradually until 1900; the period between 1890 and 1914
was probably the key turning point.[59]

The secularization thesis predicts that religion declines as societies
modernize, and yet the empirical data seem not to support the thesis or
to support it only partially. The secularization thesis itself has been so
persuasive, however, because of the way that it is embedded in modernization theory.[60] In this theory Western modernity provides a model for
all industrialized societies, which can be evaluated according to how far
they lag behind the Western template. The idea that industrialized societies develop according to a single, culture-neutral model in which complexity and reflexivity replace simplicity and tradition has exerted
considerable power within sociology through most of the twentieth century. Yet the supposedly inevitable convergence posited by modernization theory has not materialized, and as a variety of sociologists and
cultural theorists working under the rubric of "multiple modernities" or
"alternative modernities" have recognized, modernity is not a single entity but a multiply refracted one. These scholars argue that European
forms of modernity are not necessarily templates for other societies; although modernization may be largely inevitable, that process is dialectically shaped by the cultural traditions it encounters, so that modernity
itself must be understood, in the words of one scholar, as a "continual
constitution and reconstitution of a multiplicity of cultural programs."[61]
In a working paper originating in the Center for Transcultural Studies,
Charles Taylor and Benjamin Lee note that convergence theories of
modernity tend to conceive of "tradition" as a homogenous resistance to

modernization: "by holding people within a sacred horizon, a fixed community, and unchallengeable custom," they write, "[tradition] . . . hold[s] us back from 'development,' conceived as the unfolding of our potentiality to grasp our real predicament and apply instrumental reason to it."[62] Taylor and Lee argue that pitting tradition against modernity in this way distorts the actual historical changes that are underway, which are inevitably more complex and variable. If modernity is imagined as a variety of cultural programs, however, and not simply as whatever remains after tradition has been removed, then tradition and modernity can be understood as mutually informing entities.

If modernization is a myth, perhaps secularization is, too? To be sure, secularization as a theory of religious decline is deeply embedded in modernization theory. That is one reason for its uncontested status: secularization was taken for granted because it legitimated modernity. To the tension between tradition and modernity, between simple and complex societies, secularization offered both a persuasive theory of historical transformation and a legitimation of that transformation. There is of course a negative, Weberian, reading of this transformation, in which we are delivered from tradition only to find ourselves in the iron cage of instrumental rationality. But there is also the positive reading, in which the story of modernization is the story of the human capacity to shake itself free from the past, to maximize autonomy and grasp its freedom as an objective truth.[63]

It would be an overreaction, however, to dispense altogether with secularization, however tempting that may be.[64] In his book *Public Religions in the Modern World*, José Casanova very usefully distinguishes among the variety of meanings attached to secularization, notes their imbrication with a now-discredited modernization theory, and concludes that what must be salvaged from secularization theory is the concept of "differentiation"— that is, the emancipation of a variety of forms of cultural authority from religious control. One indisputable characteristic of modernity is that autonomous secular institutions now handle a huge variety of social tasks that were once the concern of religion; but though this change is massive and irreversible, Casanova insists that such differentiation does not necessarily entail either religious decline or religious privatization and marginalization. Only once we disarticulate differentiation from these other processes, he argues, can we understand why religion has returned so forcefully to the world stage in the past quarter century. Now, privatization and decline *may* follow in the wake of differentiation, and they sometimes have; but it is part of Casanova's nicely counterintuitive thesis that those religious cultures that embrace modern differentiation, such as the United States, actually resist or reverse religious privatization and decline. To be both modern and religious is not a contradiction in terms.

Etymologically, "secularization" in fact suggests differentiation: one of the word's original meanings was the movement of individuals and property from the realm of the church or monastery to the realm of the world. Most discussions of secularization, however, tend to refer not to a changed relationship within this world, but rather to a changed relationship between this world and the next, and thereby focus not on differentiated spheres but rather on such things as the privatization or loss of belief. Casanova argues that we must return to the earlier and more precise definition of secularization.[65] The consequences of this recommendation become immediately clear when we consider the very title of Abrams's book: *Natural Supernaturalism*. Abrams is interested in a changed relationship between "this world" and "the other world," a definition that entails a personalistic approach to religion and commits him to the hypothesis that modernization brings about a measurable loss in religious *belief*. By contrast, Casanova's version of secularization focuses on transformations *within* "this world," particularly what he calls "the differentiation and emancipation of the secular spheres from religious institutions and norms." "If before," he continues, "it was the religious realm which appeared to be the all-encompassing reality within which the secular realm found its proper place, now the secular sphere will be the all-encompassing reality, to which the religious sphere will have to adapt."[66] It is worth repeating that this reordering of the relations between religious and secular realms entails no necessary reordering of the relations either between the natural and supernatural worlds or between institutions and private beliefs.

In this book I will follow Casanova's definition of secularization as differentiation, and I will strive to distinguish it from theories of secularization that posit or predict religious decline. Theories of secularization embedded in modernization theory tend to take the industrial revolution as an implicit or even explicit touchstone; they thus foreshorten the historical time line and limit the range of meanings that "modernity" itself can have. Using differentiation rather than modernization as the key to secularization allows us to expand the time line and lift a teleological and normative burden from the concept of modernity. Differentiation is part of the experience of modernity, but its descriptive capacities allow for a sense of modernity itself as multiple, as an ongoing process of creating and reforming a plethora of cultural programs. Once modernization is rendered a more parochial and local affair, secularization can be freed from the linear and teleological assumptions that hover in the background whenever it is invoked.

Indeed, the argument from design registers and responds to a form of differentiation that precedes industrialization. We already saw this process at work in Sprat's *History of the Royal Society* in which he distinguishes between natural philosophy and the "tender and powerful contemplations" that characterize the Christian theology of redemption. In his *Novum Organum* (1620) Francis Bacon renders this situation in all its complexity. In a small section annexed to the text, Bacon writes: "For I want this primary history to be compiled with a most religious care, as if every particular were stated upon oath; seeing that it is the book of God's works, and (so far as the majesty of heavenly may be compared with the humbleness of earthly things) a kind of second Scripture."[67] Clearly Bacon is segregating empiricism from theology; but by means of analogy he is also comparing them. And Bacon is of course an extreme case; natural theology would by and large welcome the delicate dance between the separation and conjoining of these realms that analogy made possible.

Accordingly, Joseph Butler's 1736 book *The Analogy of Religion* deploys the figure of analogy even as it registers the power of Bacon's distinctions. Butler was rather skeptical of natural theology; his book tried to arrest its growing independence by contextualizing it within the confines of revealed religion. Moreover Butler does not want to treat reason and revelation as separate but equal the way that Bacon evidently does. Perhaps he guesses that revelation will be the loser if that happens. And yet he cannot help recapitulating the distinction because his apologetic purpose causes him to present revelation itself as extrasensory information.[68] Thus, although Butler writes that design arguments are useful, they offer neither absolute proof of God's existence nor direction for living a moral life. For those things, he says, we must turn to a "faculty within us"—an intuition of divine guidance.

Butler cannot put the cat back in the bag and fold reason into a comprehensive account of revelation as Aquinas can. This is not to say, however, that either Butler or Bacon is transforming religious content into "secular" content. Rather both men are engaged, from their different places, in reordering relations within this world. Both are skeptical of natural theology, though for different reasons, and yet both are attracted to analogies between reason and revelation precisely because analogy seems to figure the historical reordering of those domains that they are witnessing. The conflict that the analogy figures is not an abstract one between "religion" and "science," but rather a conflict between religious authority and a new method's quest for "differentiated autonomy."[69] Underwriting that conflict, the figure of analogy both distinguishes science from religion *and* holds these two in the same thought universe.

Neither Bacon nor Butler is offering design arguments for God's existence: they don't propose analogies between divine and human contrivance. For them, rather, the analogy of nature and scripture becomes a way to think of science and theology in roughly parallel ways. In this dispute over jurisdiction rather than over content we can see how analogy itself becomes a figure for secularization as differentiation rather than secularization as transformation. The design argument enters, meanwhile, when another analogy, between divine and human contrivance, supplements that initial differentiating analogy—something that happens within the context of the more comprehensive analogy by which nature becomes the Book of God. Thus, to anticipate a later stage of my argument: the romantic affection for metaphor and symbol inspires a progressive reading of romantic secularization as that which reorders the relationship of this world to the next world by transforming divine into human content. By contrast, if we restore the design argument to its place in the romantic era, then we can counterpose *analogy* to symbol and metaphor and thus understand romantic secularization as a form of differentiation, a reordering of categories *within* this world, just as Bacon understood analogy as a figure for the emancipation of science from theological control.

One social group whose differentiated autonomy is particularly apposite to this discussion is the group that Alvin W. Gouldner calls the "new class" of intellectuals.[70] In his introduction to *The Desecularization of the World*, Peter Berger notes the following exception to his "desecularization thesis":

There exists an international subculture composed of people with Western-type higher education, especially in the humanities and social sciences, that is indeed secularized. This subculture is the principle "carrier" of progressive, Enlightened beliefs and values. While its members are relatively thin on the ground, they are very influential, as they control the institutions that provide the "official" definitions of reality, notably the educational system, the media of mass communication, and the higher reaches of the legal system. They are remarkably similar all over the world today . . . . [R]egrettably, I cannot speculate here as to why people with this type of education should be so prone to secularization. I can only point out that what we have here is a globalized *elite* culture.[71]

Berger answers his own question, at least in part: the reason that these global elites are so prone to secularization is precisely that they *are* global elites. Tied together by a "Western-type" education grounded in "Enlightened beliefs and values," they understand their autonomy as inversely related to the power of religion. In other words, they adhere to modernization theory of the sort criticized by Taylor and Lee, for they imagine tradition as intrinsically opposed to such modern intellectual values as reflexivity. In fact, *The Desecularization of the World* describes an astonishingly multiple variety of modernities across the globe. In their inability to recognize this, the global elites remarked by Berger reveal the degree to which secularization as a theory of religious decline and marginalization operates as an ideology. It both offers a meaningful

explanation of a present reality and expresses the interests of a particular class of actors by universalizing a historically contingent state of
affairs.

In emphasizing the role of intellectual elites in the promulgation of
the secularization thesis as a theory of religious decline, I am following
Berger, Christian Smith, and others who have attended to the activities
of historically and culturally specific actors who deliberately set out to
achieve secularization. Objecting to the abstract nature of sociological
accounts of secularization, Smith argues that differentiation is often
brought about by the agency of particular elites. He demonstrates, for
example, how American intellectuals between 1870 and 1930, a set of
"professional definers, producers, legitimators, and distributors of social
knowledge," desired secularization because they believed that organized
religion threatened their own hard-won autonomy.[72] Intellectuals may
pursue secularization for personal or individual reasons, Smith concludes, but along the way they help to create and validate an intellectual
posture understood as intrinsically antagonistic to religion. Smith's
point is that the versions of critical thinking celebrated by intellectuals
are not expressions of true independence of mind so much as they are
expressions of class interest, carried out by historically specific actors
who, though small in number, are motivated to defend their privileged
location and are well situated "to construct reality through the production and control of knowledge."[73]

In his discussions of intellectuals Pierre Bourdieu has frequently
drawn our attention to "the social determinants of a posture which
tends to be experienced as a freely arrived-at, discretionary choice."[74]
Likewise, Smith argues that intellectual actors misrecognize the origins
of their own cultural authority when they mistake differentiation for
religious decline. Such actors interpret their own relative cultural autonomy not as the result of modern differentiation and consequent
fragmentation of cultural authority, but rather as the result of a religious
decline and consequent elevation of such intellectual values as criticism
and reflexivity. Paradoxically, differentiation is received as progress,
while intellectual actors themselves seem to exemplify progress in the
form of individual autonomy.

This relationship between differentiation and a progressive theory of
secularization is important to keep in mind when it comes to British romanticism and the history of its interpretation. Given that Western
Europe has experienced secularization as *both* differentiation *and* religious decline and transformation, the objections to secularization theory raised earlier may seem largely irrelevant to this study.[75] In other
words, why would it matter for interpreting *British* romanticism that secularization as commonly understood is not universally applicable, and

that the global South, for instance, is currently experiencing a massive surge in religious activity? That objection loses some of its force, however, when we recall that to take up a topic such as romanticism is also to take up its interpretation by later readers. Like the intellectual actors analyzed by Berger and Smith, the influential readers of romanticism have been elites who occupy relatively prominent positions within the cultural landscape. While secularization generally appears as merely a descriptive tool, then, among Western intellectuals it is also a normative theoretical construct, with its own values and assumptions. One cannot discuss secularization simply as an empirical matter, even within the context of Britain or Western Europe, for it is always also bound up in the values, desires, and self-understandings of those who wield it as a concept—and who wield it most powerfully when they assume a certain definition of secularization itself. To return to the two senses of romanticism I distinguished earlier, the question of secularization's relation to romanticism cannot be understood as delimited by the historical period 1780–1830; it must also be analyzed with regard to those modern interpreters of romanticism who seek, for a variety of institutional and personal reasons, to make it speak to their contemporary moment.

Here an illustration from Jane Austen's novel *Mansfield Park* (1814) is apposite. When Mary Crawford, upon hearing that prayers are no longer said in the family chapel at Sotherton, smilingly notes that "[e]very generation has its improvements," we should understand her words as an attempt to link the waning of religion to the inevitability of generational change.[76] In this way Mary tries to naturalize religious decline, but in fact her claim is invested in influencing a debate about whether religious decline *is* natural or whether the case at Sotherton is an aberration. And because Mary is talking to a prospective clergyman with whom she will, much to her surprise, fall in love, the narrator is having a little joke at her expense: Mary thinks she is stating the obvious, but the narrator unmasks the "obvious" as an interested position within an active debate, a position, moreover, that masks its partiality and claims objectivity by means of the aura of generational inevitability.

Mary Crawford, with her progressive transformation of religious into secular content, is an apt figure for those scholars who ushered romanticism into the academic mainstream between 1930 and 1960. These scholars were writing during the heyday of modernization theory, and linking romanticism to secularization supplemented this theory at the level of ideas, for it seemed axiomatic that newer secular ideas would defeat older religious ideas; if romanticism was a "revolution in ideas," then, it was a revolution that pointed directly to the sensibilities of the middle of the twentieth century. Spiritually speaking, it was an optimistic and ecumenical age. On the Protestant side, the World Council of Churches was founded in 1948, while the reforms of Vatican II (1962–65) promised a more generous and inclusive Catholicism. Meanwhile, under the influence especially of Mircea Eliade, the professional study of religion in midcentury was moving away from a Durkheimian emphasis on ritual and practice and toward a broadly syncretistic emphasis on myth, symbol, and idea, aspects of religion that were in principle sharable across cultural divides.[77] Finally, secularization theory was sweeping all before it. As a recent article on the history of secularization within sociology notes, "by the early 1970s, secularization was the reigning dogma in the field."[78] Abrams himself does not reference sociological material, but perhaps he could refer so casually in 1971 to the "historical commonplace" of "progressive secularization" because it seemed possible to find in romanticism (that is, at the level of subjectivity and "ideas") what his colleagues on the other side of campus were finding in the organization of cultural space.[79] Reading romanticism as a manifestation of secularization, then, meant that one avoided the Weberian nightmare of modernity as soulless rationalization and mechanization; romanticism could be a carrier of cultural modernity rather than societal modernization, a technique for preserving spiritual truths while overcoming both modern bourgeois anomie *and* the exclusive doctrinal content that had led historically to religious conflict.

So interpreted, romanticism seemed to fit into midcentury cultural movements like a hand in a glove. "In their various ways," writes Gene W. Ruoff, "many critics who flourished from the fifties through the seventies attempted to accommodate romantic texts to a sense of capacious spirituality, consistently undervaluing polemical dissonances in search of higher spiritual harmonies."[80] From this perspective, literature offers its readers a way to contextualize absolute religious claims within a more inclusive, if vaguer, spirituality. In Cleanth Brooks's famous formulation, for instance, literature is paradoxical, standing beside and gesturing toward the *doxa* that it does not name; such criticism demands of the reader only the willingness to check his or her preconceptions at the door.[81] Despite important methodological differences, romantic humanists such as Abrams and Earl Wasserman and mythological critics such as Northrop Frye subscribed to Brooks's belief that literature, properly understood, transcended doctrine. Accordingly, to elevate romanticism to a privileged status within the academy meant freeing it from doctrine; not coincidentally, this newly fashioned romanticism consolidated the position of the critic by establishing the importance of his or her profession and its ability to speak to the spiritual concerns of the age.

The cultural era to which these critical postures gave expression came to a startling end in 1979—the year of the Iranian Revolution and the year in which Jerry Falwell founded the Moral Majority in the United

States. In the 1980s, religion reassumed a public role on the world stage; as I write these words in 2005, religion's public reemergence seems, if anything, to be intensifying.[82] The part of the secularization thesis that links modernization to religious decline and privatization—that is, the aspect of the secularization thesis that the ecumenical intellectual culture of the 1950s, 1960s, and 1970s took for granted—has been empirically refuted by the events of the past quarter century. From this perspective, Jerome J. McGann's critique of romantic humanist idealism in *The Romantic Ideology* (1983) expressed at the critical level a cultural and historical trend just getting underway. In tune with this new era, McGann and the new historicists who followed in his immediate wake overturned a romanticism of spiritual harmonies, freeing romantic texts to become sites of contested value within arenas inflected by power. As Ruoff summed up the situation in 1990, "[t]he age of ecumenicism, which had followed a solid Wordsworthian program in accentuating . . . spiritual affinities while diminishing credal differences, is dead. Ecumenicism itself, which had seemed a turning point in the history of religions . . . now appears to have been a narrowly based cultural detour."[83] That a cultural detour might appear to a small group of Western intellectuals as a turning point in the history of religions is itself eloquent testimony to the manner in which a parochial set of analytic procedures can, under the right conditions, assume the mantle of universality.

And yet, if the historicist turn opened the way for a reconsideration of romanticism's relation to secularization, that path remained largely unexplored. The worldwide movements of desecularization and the reemergence of public religion seemed either irrelevant or aberrant to the materialist romantic historicism that followed McGann's intervention.[84] For that historicism, the urgent critical task was to strip romanticism of whatever vestiges of religion or spirit still remained (a task already being undertaken, from another direction, by de Manian deconstruction). McGann quite explicitly aimed to advance secularization by finding in romantic texts the very ideological conflicts structuring literary criticism in the last quarter of the twentieth century—and in this goal his project was ironically continuous with Abrams's: "From our present vantage," McGann wrote in a 1981 essay about Coleridge's *Ancient Mariner*, "what we must do is inaugurate our disbelief in Coleridge's 'poetic faith.' This Romantic ideology must be seen for what it is, a historical phenomenon of European culture, generated to save the 'traditional concepts, schemes, and values' of the Christian heritage."[85] The results of such critical disbelief have been consistently informative and sometimes stunning, not least in McGann's discussion of the *Ancient Mariner* in this same essay. A quarter century into a historicist *and* religious revival that have run roughly in tandem, however, we can measure what has been lost as well as gained by historicism's methodological commitment to a materialism that from the outset has regarded religion as its privileged, even exemplary, object of critique. Thus, to update Mc-Gann: from our present vantage, it does not really seem that the "traditional concepts, schemes, and values of the Christian heritage" need salvaging; from Seoul to Sao Paulo, those concepts, schemes, and values are doing pretty well on their own. What may need salvaging, rather, is a critical method that can account nonreductively for such persistence. That method would disarticulate secularization and religious decline and require a nuanced sense of religion's relationship to historical change.

Secularization, much like romanticism, is both an historical description and an object located within a contemporary interpretive environment. In the task of grasping this double valence, Casanova's discussion of differentiation and Smith's study of individual secularizing actors are both helpful. For Casanova, secularization means the process of differentiation attendant upon modernization—in short, a transformed relationship *within* this world. Smith reminds us, however, that the theory of secularization is deployed by agents with their own commitments and values. Like Mary Crawford and her happy thought that "every generation has its improvements," these agents may treat secularization not as a theory of differentiation but as a theory of religious decline, thereby positing their own intellectual values as the inevitable outcome of an objective historical process and installing those values in institutionally influential positions. Once again, this should not be interpreted to mean that critics who find secularization are wrong. My argument, rather, is that claims and assumptions about secularization must be subjected to the same sort of critical reflexivity that literary critics now habitually bring to discussions of race, class, and sexuality; we need to be alert, in other words, for the process by which norms get smuggled in as value-neutral descriptors. It turns out that those who believe in secularization's inevitability are a relatively small group of professional readers and interpreters. Because that belief contributes mightily to the cultural entitlement of this small group, it seems a worthwhile task to make it an object of analysis whenever we read the poetry and prose that gave birth both to it and to us.

Designs and Aims of This Book

Together with later chapters of the book, this Introduction addresses its largest claims: the definition of secularization as differentiation and the importance of reflexivity in treating the historical process that "secularization" names. Chapter 7 takes up these issues with reference to the transformation of evil from a metaphysical to a moral category, with Wordsworth's *Ruined Cottage* serving as the basis for the investigation; Chapter 8 considers the difficulties of bringing criticism together with the study of religion. The Afterword meditates upon the reemergence of design in the twenty-first century in the form of "intelligent design." I hope that these broader discussions will prove particularly interesting to those readers who are not professional literary critics, and to those literary critics who are not romanticists.

Chapters 1 through 6, meanwhile, contain the heart of the book's historical and literary argument. I begin with deism, one important interpretation of natural theology during the eighteenth century. Because deism, like natural theology, staked its claims on enlightened reason, it proved easy for romantic-era writers such as William Godwin and William Blake to fold their critiques of natural theology into a larger critique of the enlightenment project; at the same time, both writers register the power and appeal of the enlightenment critique of religion, thereby bequeathing to modern critics an either / or dynamic. Either natural theology is continuous with the enlightened project, in which case it is to be rejected on romantic grounds; or it is continuous with a religious project, in which case it is to be rejected on enlightened grounds. Chapter 2 then proposes a way out of this bind by focusing not on the epistemological truth of natural theology but rather on modes of practicing it. I argue that the primary contribution of David Hume's *Dialogues Concerning Natural Religion* is not its powerful critique of design's philosophical worthiness but rather its acknowledgment that the habits of mind and the structures of sociability associated with design can triumph *over* intellectual critique. By shifting analytic attention from argument to practice, Hume short-circuits the romantic / enlightenment opposition, and the models of critical reason that depend upon that opposition, thereby enabling a reading of the tradition of natural theology as substantially continuous over the eighteenth and early nineteenth centuries. Over the past decade a variety of critics have succeeded in troubling the perceived opposition between enlightened and romantic culture; these early chapters build upon that work by arguing that our standard definition of secularization as religious decline, premised as it is upon the enlightenment critique of religion, in fact works to secure that opposition.

The Humean emphasis on practice also accounts for my principle of selection throughout the book. This does not mean that all the writers studied here agree with one another, even implicitly; rather, I treat Hume's response to the design argument as a point of departure for a number of entwined but nevertheless analytically distinct responses to the issues that his skepticism raises. After a detailed discussion of Hume in Chapter 2, then, I proceed to considerations of Anna Barbauld (Chapter 3), William Paley (Chapter 4), Jane Austen (Chapter 5), and William Wordsworth (Chapter 6). Although these chapters can stand on their own, each brings design together with Casanova's definition of secularization as functional differentiation, for we witness such differentiation in each of these writers. Hume works to expose design as non-rational, thus widening the breach between faith and science. Barbauld, a participant in Britain's dissenting culture, accepts this breach in order to explore modes of *practicing* design linked decisively to the gendered body. Paley, though committed to scientific discourse, rewrites design as an "argument from perception" that attempts to short-circuit Hume's sundering of reason and religion. Meanwhile, Jane Austen's *Mansfield Park* demonstrates design's increasingly precarious hold on the differentiated realm of internal feeling, and Wordsworth's early career shows how the differentiated domain of literature takes over from design the task of consolidating a unified sensibility.

Insofar, then, as secularization is a form of functional differentiation, a transformed relationship *within* this world, each of these writers may be taken to exemplify it. Casanova's second claim is equally important, however: differentiation does not necessarily entail either religious decline or religious privatization. Accordingly, for some of the writers considered here differentiation leads to decline; for others it does not. We observe decline, for instance, in the set of linked concerns running from Hume through Paley to Austen. Beginning with Hume's sundering of feeling and reason, this trajectory interprets religious emotion as a private matter that does not lend itself to public ordering. *Mansfield Park* runs this increasingly privatized religion up against the demand that private feelings remain hooked up with establishment forms of Christianity. That demand can register only as coercion, for what has gone missing is a mechanism for mediating between official form and internal feeling; the result is the social chaos that Paley himself had intimated, and the consequent random assertions of authority practiced by Sir Thomas Bertram and by the narrator of *Mansfield Park* herself. In contrast to this trajectory, the set of concerns running from Hume (again) through Barbauld to Wordsworth exemplifies ways in which differentiation does *not* lead to religious decline. Transforming design into the experience of fancy (in the case of Barbauld) and analogy (in the case of Wordsworth), this trajectory takes the very fact of differentiation, in the form of the increasing autonomy of both literature and religious feeling, as an opportunity for celebrating varieties of expressive practice that supersede intellectual critiques of design's conceptual worthiness. Though I argue in the book's Afterword that it cannot finally be sustained, this distinction between practice and theory runs with varying degrees of explicitness throughout the book. Thus fancy and analogy appear as practices distinct from such "theoretical" categories as imagination and metaphor precisely because, while the latter try to take on and transform the traditional functions of religion, the former are distinguished by their noninstrumentality, the way in which they figure and embody a kind of formal contentment with the multiple opportunities opened up by differentiation.

Since these trajectories exist more or less side by side during the period, one logical conclusion is that despite its establishment credentials, it is easier for design to remain vibrant outside the boundaries of the official church. Thus the first trajectory, which links differentiation to religious decline, identifies what is conventional about Paley (his worry about social stability) and manifests that conventionality in the dying world of *Mansfield Park*. The second trajectory, in which differentiation does not lead to decline, finds poetic expression in the dissenting Barbauld and the religiously vague early Wordsworth. The conclusion that disestablishment actually fosters religious creativity may surprise those who wish to read religion in terms of ideology; in fact, however, it supports Casanova's thesis that cultures which embrace modernity remain religiously vibrant, and it accords with the empirical evidence throughout much of the world that modernization leads to increased religious diversity.

With Casanova's claim in mind, let me finally reemphasize that this book does *not* simply argue that romantic-era writers are more "religious" than we had thought, or that religion held out longer that we had thought against the tides of skepticism and materialism before eventually succumbing to them. That would be an oversimplification as bad as the oversimplification that sees in every romantic writer a precursor of the secular modern reader. Rather, I am seeking to use design and its cognates as a way to define secularization's analytic relationship to romanticism. That definition entails understanding secularization itself as differentiation rather than the transformation of religious content, so that we can see how religion finds ways to creatively appropriate the institutional transformations that characterize modernity. And it entails understanding at least some aspects of romanticism as complexly interwoven with the fabric of modernity. Romanticism has long been coordinated with modernity, of course, but if modernity is a multiple rather than single object in which secularization plays an imprecise and frequently vexed role, then deciding on the ways and means by which romanticism anticipates and legitimates modernity becomes a more complex and nuanced business.

Although those scholars working on "multiple modernities" are especially concerned with its relevance to analyzing non-Western societies, the concept is helpful for understanding historical change within the West as well. The experience of differentiation varies even within cultures bound together by nation, race, and religion; studying particular writers over a delimited historical range enables us to register how what Taylor and Lee call "modernity as lived from the inside" modulates all the way down to the level of the individual. Of course, at one level modernity is irresistible: the nation-state and the market economy have penetrated and transformed virtually all social institutions, and resistance to those changes has proved worse than useless. But those transformations can feel very different from the inside, as individual writers search, with varying kinds of success, for resources with which to speak to the ever-changing culture in which they live and move.

Chapter 1

The Argument Against Design
from Deism to Blake

Sometimes the apparent order of the universe seems like a "proof" of God's existence all by itself. Such apparent self-sufficiency is a temptation for the argument from design; it might tempt a writer to showcase natural order without giving sufficient attention to the way that order translates into an emotional and personal response. Eighteenth-century natural theologians themselves, writing within a framework that largely took Anglican Christianity for granted, often simply assumed the presence of the more personal, visceral, and habitual aspects of religious devotion, concentrating on apologetic and intellectual factors to the relative exclusion of all else.

The possibility that the Book of God may speak on its own, without intervention or interpretation from person or institution, was a bewitching idea even for the devout. In *Paradise Lost*, Raphael reminds Adam to place his rational questions within a proper devotional perspective, but many eighteenth-century thinkers seemed not to heed their own inner Raphael. Sir Richard Blackmore's 1712 epic poem *Creation* offers a case in point. Here is how his poem begins:

> No more of Courts, of Triumphs, or of Arms,
> No more of Valour's Force, or Beauty's Charms;
> The Themes of Vulgar Lays, with just Disdain,
> I leave unsung, the Flocks, the am'rous Swain,
> The Pleasures of the Land, and Terrors of the Main.
> How Abject, how Inglorious 'tis to lye
> Groveling in Dust and Darkness, when on high
> Empires immense and rolling Worlds of Light
> To range their Heav'nly Scenes the Muse invite?
> I meditate to Soar above the Skies,
> To Heights unknown, thro' Ways untry'd, to rise:
> I would th' Eternal from his Works assert,
> And sing the Wonders of Creating Art.[1]

This opening, though clearly indebted to the beginning of *Paradise Lost*, also departs sharply from Milton's program. Though Milton's invocation of the Holy Spirit is suitably audacious, its audacity is framed by the sacred story Milton retells and his own devotional relationship to his "heavenly Muse." Blackmore's more classical Muse inspires no such devotion, but simply invites the poet to pursue the project upon which he seems already to have decided. And that project is, of course, to "assert" God "from his works"—in other words, to offer, at great length and in extraordinary detail, an argument from design that, implicitly, bolsters Blackmore's own status as a "creator."

Blackmore's "Argument" for book I offers a glimpse of what is to come:

The Proposition. The Invocation. The Existence of a God demonstrated from the Marks of Wisdom, Choice and Art, which appear in the Visible World, and infer an Intelligent and Free Cause. This evinc'd from the contemplation, I. of the Earth. 1. Its Situation. 2. The Cohesion of its Parts, not to be solv'd by any Hypothesis yet produc'd. 3. Its Stability. 4. Its Structure, or the Order of its Parts. . . . II. The Existence of a God prov'd from the Marks and Impressions of Prudence and Design, which appear in the Sea. 1. In its Formation. 2. The Proportion of its Parts in respect of the Earthy. 3. Its Situation. 4. The Contexture of its Parts. 5. Its Brackish or Briny Quality. 6. Its Flux and Reflux. (57)

I spare the reader further detail. An "Argument" of this sort ensures that by the time any reader gets to the Miltonic opening lines, he or she already knows that the poem will devote its considerable energies to a detailed description of the organization and arrangement of the physical world, all the way down to the brackishness of the sea. Blackmore's sense of the world as a collection of parts organized into a harmonious whole evinces a substantial pleasure in the sheer amount of what can be said about the natural world; the detail and prolixity of the account even threaten to overwhelm its apologetic purpose. The capacious ambitions of the poem, too, tend ironically to focus the reader's attention not on the Creator but on the creation (and *Creation*) itself; the manifold splendors of the universe seem to exist for their own sake, while the claim to "assert" the existence of a Creator from an analysis of the Creation fades into the background.

Blackmore's *Creation* is a good example of the paradox built in to eighteenth-century natural theology. Publicly committed to reason and the inductive method, much of natural theology's energy came nevertheless from a prior assurance of God's existence, attributes, and requirements. Underneath Blackmore's endless descriptions lie deeply felt convictions, but those convictions shape themselves, and become visible, in accord with the demands and protocols of public reason. Looking back at such texts, we are likely to see a theology that has lost touch with feeling altogether. Despite the anachronism of such a view, it does accurately represent one historically important reading of natural theology. It is not hard to imagine a reading of Blackmore's poem in which its spiritual animation simply drops out altogether; on this reading, natural theology, coupled with the intellectual sensibilities of the age, generates a design argument whose unstated premise seems to be that understanding the world is the *only* prerequisite for understanding God. The name generally given to such a reading, of course, is deism.

Deism

The earliest formal statement of deism, thought to be authored by Charles Blount, appeared in a 1693 essay entitled "A Summary Account of the Deists [sic] Religion." This short document appears within a composite text called *The Oracles of Reason*, written by Blount, his disciple Charles Gildon, and others. According to the author, the deists' God is "Whatsover is Adorable, Amiable and Imitable by Mankind, . . . in one Supream infinite and perfect Being, *Satis est nobis Deus unus* [one God is enough for us]."[2] That God is to be worshipped neither by sacrifice nor through the offices of a mediator, but rather "by an imitation of God in all his imitable Perfections, especially his goodness and believing magnificiently [sic] of it" (89). If the language of "imitation" suggests that Blount is influenced here by neo-Platonism, the reduction of worship to virtuous acts receives a more Aristotelian inflection through reference to a natural law, ordained by God, which it is the duty of human beings to follow. Indeed, a later text in the *Oracles*, "Of Natural Religion," attributed to one "A. W.," reduces the matter to a tidy syllogism, suggesting how natural theology supports deism's universalist project: "That Rule which is necessary to our future Happiness, ought to be generally made known to all men. But no Rule of Revealed Religion was, or ever could be made known to all men. Therefore no Revealed Religion is necessary to future Happiness."[3] With such reasoning, we can observe how a general emphasis on reason, combined with the ever-growing prominence of natural theology, fosters a sensibility hostile to those who wish to add doctrines, rules, and temporal authorities to a natural religion that seems self-evident and self-sufficient.

Orthodox variants of natural theology operate with constant reference to unstated premises: they assume that the God whose existence they can produce through reason also exhibits qualities that cannot be reasonably demonstrated: compassion, mercy, grace, love, and so on. A. W.'s syllogism is more flat-footed. Like deism generally, it quite winsomely claims to be offering a consistent application of the principles of natural theology, challenging the likelihood of miracles and revelation on the grounds that a God capable of designing a well-functioning universe would surely have no need to interrupt the natural laws that God himself had created. This is an explicit denial of revelation—a denial, that is, that God speaks in ways other than through the publicly available language of nature. Revelations at the personal level, whether they claim special knowledge of God or whether they devote themselves to the cultivation of an inward piety, are at worst pernicious, at best purely supplementary.

Blount and the other authors of the *Oracles of Reason* operated somewhat precariously, but the aura of tolerance surrounding William and Mary's ascension to the throne in 1689, the revocation of the Licensing Act in 1693, and the general and increasing prominence of Lockean and Newtonian philosophy during the 1690s all helped to give deism a rather more solid, though still uncertain, footing. Uncertainty is the opening mood of John Toland's *Christianity Not Mysterious* (1696), which begins with the lament that "such is the deplorable Condition of our Age, that a Man dares not openly and directly own what he thinks of Divine Matters, tho it be never so true and beneficial, if it but very slightly differs from what is receiv'd by any Party, or that is establish'd by Law."[4] And yet Toland and the other deists who dominated the scene in the early eighteenth century were sufficiently sure of themselves to make clear the antiauthoritarian implications of their writing. "In natural religion the clergy are unnecessary," according to Lord Bolingbroke.[5] "The only way that Men can render immediate Honour to God," wrote Matthew Tindal, "is by worshipping him according to that Method they think most agreeable to his Will."[6] Here the right of individual self-determination, combined with a Newtonian faith in the uniformity of Nature, simultaneously undergirds an inductive argument for God's existence and prevents extending that argument to include a God who intervenes in creation. The hierarchies and authorities that claimed to interpret God's interventions or to represent him on earth are accordingly unnecessary. Because the God of the deists is himself thoroughly self-sufficient, writes Tindal, he "could have no Motive in requiring any thing from us, but as it naturally tends to promote our general Good," and each man knows his own "general Good" without help from authority.[7] This demand for consistency is aimed at the artifice of religious institutions, and so leads naturally to a critique of the social order and a presumed solidarity with those whom ecclesiastical and temporal authorities overlook. Deism's populist project comes through most clearly in this attention to audience. Toland writes in *Christianity Not Mysterious* that he has "endeavour'd to speak very intelligibly, and am not without hope that my Assertions do carry their own Light along with them. I have in many Places made explanatory Repetitions of difficult Words, by synonymous Terms of a more general and known Use. This Labour, I grant, is of no Benefit to Philosophers, but it is of considerable Advantage to the Vulgar" (xvii). Not only, then, is deism an enlightened event, but it claims to put its enlightenment in the service of the common folk.[8] "The Poor, who are not suppos'd to understand Philosophical Systems," Toland continues, "soon apprehended the Difference between the plain convincing Instructions of Christ, and the intricate ineffectual Declamations of the Scribes" (xix). He implies that the simplicity of the vulgar in effect makes them deists already; the task of the philosopher, accordingly, is simply to find his way back to the plain sense of things.

Christianity Not Mysterious does not treat the design argument directly, but Toland evidently shares an intellectual orientation with orthodox figures such as Blackmore and with the defenders of the design argument more generally. First, he proceeds on the assumption—again directly contrary to the procedure recommended by Milton's Raphael—that reason is religion's enabling condition. Toland describes his procedure as follows: "I prove first, that the true Religion must necessarily be reasonable and intelligible. Next I shew, that these requisite Conditions are found in Christianity. But seeing a Man of good Parts and Knowledg may easily frame a clear and coherent System, I demonstrate, Third, that the Christian Religion was not form'd after such a manner, but was divinely reveal'd from Heaven" (xxv–xxvi). Thus Toland will get, eventually, to a defense of divine revelation, but he will reason his way there. Second, when Toland defines reason itself he does so in language directly amenable to the analogical reasoning central to the design argument. Reason, he writes, is *"That Faculty of the Soul which discovers the Certainty of any thing dubious or obscure, by comparing it with something evidently known"* (14). By defining reason as the means by which we move from the known to the unknown, Toland implicitly defends analogy as the very essence of reason itself. Last, he makes a virtue of his inductive method: "That the mistaken Unbeliever may not say I serve a Hypothesis in the Defence of my Faith, like some who first imagine or receive an Opinion, and then study Proofs to establish it, I solemnly declare the thing is much otherwise; and that I hold nothing as an Article of my Religion, but what the highest Evidence forc'd me to embrace" (viii). This principle parallels that of orthodox natural theology, but Toland also goes orthodoxy one better by claiming to have drawn no conclusions whatsoever before he begins his reasoning. Like A. W.'s syllogism, but more subtly, Toland cancels the enabling paradox of natural theology—the already-in-place belief in the God about to be demonstrated.

The distinction between deism and orthodox design does not, then, reside at the level of ideas. Both, in effect, breathe the same air: they share a picture of an orderly universe, they concur that reason is a neutral arbiter of truth, and they believe in the capacity of human intellect to read the Book of God through a cognitive movement from the known to the unknown. The difference between deism and design, which emerges only when deism presses its inductive case to the point of denying any preconceptions whatsoever, resides ironically enough in something extrarational: in the deist's decision—personal, emotional, and historical—to leave the orbit of orthodoxy rather than remain within it. Notwithstanding Toland's claim to be moved only by the force of evidence, the very advent and influence of deism indicate that evidence is not really what matters. The *claim* that evidence is what matters, however, does suggest that reason is gradually carving out for itself a differentiated domain, one that under certain circumstances may come to stand in judgment over religion.

Blake and Analogy

The fact that orthodox theology and unorthodox deism both rely on the design argument tells us something about that argument's pervasiveness. It also means that rejecting one often means rejecting the other. When, near the end of century, William Blake lumps deism, design, and Lockean psychology into a single category called "Deism," he means therefore to indict not only a group of ideas but also an intellectual *posture*, an entire way of seeing the world. Northrop Frye's description of deism as Blake understood it is still the best: "In Deism," Frye writes, "there is not only the belief that the physical world is the only real one, but also a feeling of satisfaction at remaining within it."[9] Frye helps us to see that the object of Blake's critique is twofold: first, there is the mistake of thinking that the five senses can tell us everything there is to know about the world; but second, there is the emotional satisfaction and self-gratification that results from this mistake. This second aspect is the more pernicious simply because it is liable to spread to those who are not explicitly identified with deism's intellectual projects. It feels good to think that you can grasp the universe on your own strength—a good feeling that Blackmore as well as the deists understood. For Blake, then, Blackmore is as much a deist as is Toland, for each takes the world that comes to him through his senses and makes it the object of his faith. From this perspective, any distinction between deism and design is just so much hairsplitting.

Deism marks an intellectual posture that seeks to resolve oppositions— Blakean "contraries"—into a higher unity. In *The Marriage of Heaven and Hell*, this attitude is said to characterize all organized religion. Blake's point is that deism has changed the way people understand religion in general; under its influence, "religion" now means a shared impulse to discover the mysteries of the universe. Deism then poses this abstract conception of religion against its own contention that everything important about religion can be derived from accurate empirical observation. For Blake this is wrong on both counts: Christianity is a specific religious form, accessible only through a visionary and prophetic sensibility. He thinks that empiricism, by contrast, is intellectually exhausted.

Much of this argument is nascent already in one of the earliest texts in the Blake canon, *There Is No Natural Religion* (1788). Blake's first claim in this collection of aphorisms is that, because deism begins with sense perception, it cannot produce a new or original insight: "none can desire / what he has not perciev'd."[10] In beginning with objects of sense, deism limits its conclusions to objects of sense, for it excludes at the outset the faculty for new insights that Blake variously labels "poetry" or "prophesy": "If it were not for the Poetic or Prophetic character. / the Philosophic & Experimental would soon be at the ratio of all things / & stand still, unable to do other than repeat the same dull round over again" (b.vii). Blake also links the ratio to one of his most common and negative images, that of the "mill with complicated / wheels" (b.iv) that mechanically grinds everything down to the same level. The polemical contrast between poetic originality and the "same dull round over again" appears more famously in Blake's description of theology in *The Marriage of Heaven and Hell* (1790):

Any man of mechanical talents may from the writings of Paracelsus or Jacob Behmen, produce ten thousand volumes of equal value with Swedenborg's. and from those of Dante or Shakespear, an infinite number.[11]

All works of theology, according to this argument, are simply quotations of previous works; unlike the poetic faculty, they bring nothing new into the world.

In part, then, the term "deism" becomes for Blake a way to contrast the poetic faculty to what he sees as the deadening, reiterative, and spirit-destroying intellectual hubris of an entire century. That century's dominant narrative had relegated poetry to a marginal place while allowing Reason to conquer all areas of human endeavor. As Blake came to argue later in his career, the revolutionary energy of the American and French Revolutions was destined to burn out as well, because the prejudice against imagination in those enlightened revolutions guaranteed their eventual collapse into a new round of despotism: Napoleon replaces Louis, and the structure of similitude that characterizes deism carries on unscathed. Thus in *Jerusalem* (1804), "Voltaire Rousseau Gibbon Hume" are all accused of worshiping "the God of this World" by denying the need for prophesy and revelation, or what Blake often calls the "poetic faculty."[12] Blake accepts deism's reduction of the design argument into purely rational principles. When he rejects deism he thereby also rejects

the entire tradition of eighteenth-century natural theology by refusing to
see any difference that matters between the Blackmores and Tolands of
the world; like all Blakean "Deists," these men simply recirculate the
same tired, old ideas.

After Blake, it is easy to think of romanticism and design as intrinsically opposed. The Blakean rejection of similitude as a way of rejecting
enlightened values bears especially upon analogy, design's chief rhetorical figure. Almost always, though not always explicitly, design arguments
follow an analogical form when they reason from known instances of design in the material world to the hypothetical design of the universe itself. Perhaps William Paley made the most famous of these analogies
in 1802, when he compared the universe to a watch. Due to the obvious
designedness of the watch, Paley says, we know that a watchmaker made
it. The universe is like a watch in its contrivances and its complicated relation of means to ends; therefore, the universe, like the watch, must be
the product of design. This analogical form opens the argument from
design to the objection that it is biased in favor of similarities (between
watch and world) and ignores differences. As we shall observe at greater
length later in this book, David Hume and Immanuel Kant were particularly effective in bringing this kind of charge to bear against natural theology. Both philosophers realized that it was impossible not to think that
some things, such as watches, had been designed; what they objected to
was the habit of extrapolating analogically from watch to world. To
them, analogy was not only imprecise—it was positively promiscuous in
its ability to keep producing misleading similarities.

Negative readings of analogy have had a certain influence on literary
history as well.[13] Wallace Stevens, for instance, distinguishes between analogy as "imagination," which he says is the use of language authentic to
the poet, and analogy as "elaboration," which is derivative, inauthentic,
and "eighteenth century."[14] For Stevens, the bad form of analogy does not
develop internally but rather comes from outside both poem and poet,
and thus carries with it all sorts of extratextual traditional baggage. That
some of this baggage is religious baggage is not difficult to discern in a
poem such as "Sunday Morning" (1923), which pursues a deliberate strategy of disanalogy. No religious vision, the speaker tells us in this poem,

has endured

As April's green endures; or will endure
Like her remembrance of awakened birds,
Or her desire for June and evening, tipped
  By the consummation of the swallow's wings.[15]

We cannot, then, read divinity from our knowledge of the world. Quite
the contrary: the physical world is organized around death, whereas

heaven, though "so like our perishing earth," is static and changeless. Death, consequently, "is the mother of beauty," a thought that the speaker likes well enough to repeat twice. In contrast to this disarming honesty, poetry that insists on reaching toward heaven must commit itself to heaven's static and deathless world, surrendering the existential autonomy that the poem paints as the necessary and quiet heroism of modernity. In its continual reversion to natural images, then, "Sunday Morning" suggests that a proper reading of the physical world leads not to God but simply back to itself; the speaker rewrites natural theology through the auspices of a conception of poetry understood as beholden to nothing but its own process of earthly discovery. "Sunday Morning" thus offers a horizon against which we can view the critique of the analogical structure that Blake named the "ratio." In it, analogy becomes the enemy of true poetry.

Readers of metaphysical poetry know that analogy can be a wondrously fluid yet rigorous structure upon which to hang a poem. Seventeenth-century poets, moreover, could draw upon a rich tradition of analogical thinking stretching from Aristotle to Aquinas. In the standard account, however, analogy had lost steam by the eighteenth century, and so it fell to romanticism to revive poetic language, largely by means of metaphor and symbol.[16] For M. H. Abrams, the romantic rejection of analogy marks its decisive break with the enlightenment. For Abrams and others, particularly Earl Wasserman, the romantic overcoming of analogy just *was* an example of secularization, for it signaled the romantics' willingness to strike out on their own rather than rely upon the traditions of the past. Indeed, in the writings of Abrams and Wasserman, analogy keeps showing up as the poetic habit that romanticism kicked. In *The Subtler Language* (1959), for example, Wasserman argues that the eighteenth century witnessed a shift from thinking analogically to thinking *about* analogy; rather than assuming analogy's power, poets felt obliged to demonstrate it. Consequently, analogy becomes mere rhetoric: "The purpose of such poetry is merely to make analogies, not to use the analogy poetically by imposing the patterns of external nature or of the poet's experience with the scene upon merely linguistic syntax and thereby releasing the constitutive possibilities of an extraordinary syntactical system."[17] The "extraordinary syntactical system" that Wasserman calls for is of course romanticism, which he argues *did* invent a new syntax by replacing the passive analogical perception of an alienated consciousness with a perpetually creative act—formalized and externalized as symbol, metaphor, or image—that invents not only the individual poem but also the language in which the poem makes sense. Writing in the middle years of the twentieth century, Wasserman evokes postwar anomie to make the modernity of his romanticism clear: "The condition of man has not changed in this last century and a half; and Wordsworth's predicament is ours" (258). The romantics are modern because, like us, they must make their own meaning.

For his part, Abrams picks up this theme in his classic 1965 essay "Structure and Style in the Greater Romantic Lyric." He argues that eighteenth-century locodescriptive poems are "reduced mainly to the procedure of setting up parallels between landscape and moral commonplaces. . . . The literal belief in a universe of divine types and correspondences, which had originally supported this structural trope, faded, and the coupling of sensuous phenomena with moral statements came to be regarded as a rhetorical device."[18] Once again, romanticism offers an escape from the deadening round of analogy, this time through a dialectical process: a "transaction between subject and object in which the thought incorporates and makes explicit what was already implicit in the outer scene" (102). As in Wasserman's analysis, romanticism's uniqueness is described in terms of the interpenetration creatively carried out by symbol, metaphor, or image, healing through language an ontological breach between subject and object, self and world. Again, too, we see a gesture toward a certain conception of modernity: "The pervasive sense of estrangement, of a lost and isolated existence in an alien world, is not peculiar to our own age of anxiety, but was a commonplace of Romantic philosophy" (96). In sum, romanticism overcomes alienation; analogy is doomed to reinscribe it. In this reading analogy privileges balance within an orderly system; against this logic of similitude, romanticism offers difference, creativity, and energy. And by implication, romantic synthesis speaks to our modern moment, whereas analogical rhetoric, burdened with tradition, rehashes the past.

These analyses manage to naturalize romanticism's triumph as a historical inevitability. In this secularization narrative, romanticism rescues belief—a true or sincere relationship between internal and external—while jettisoning its metaphysical content. Within this progressive narrative analogy is a kind of regression, a refusal or inability to face up to the new day that is breaking in all around. Analogy seems to lack both rigor and originality; it makes nothing happen; it is the province of second-rate poets and derivative thinkers. Unlike symbol or image, analogy is not intrinsic to the poet's language, nor is it anything but a false refuge for the philosopher. Anybody can use analogy—and indeed, pretty much anybody does, because it is a substitute for the hard work of thinking on one's own (that is Kant's complaint) or of making a poem on one's own (that is Stevens's complaint).

To be sure, not every example of analogy in the eighteenth century is a latent argument from design, nor did Blake identify something as specific as the "argument from design" as his enemy. Nonetheless, the analogical mainstream during this period is decidedly theist; and the argument from design, as the age's most widely disseminated theological theme, bases its success largely on the power and persuasiveness of analogical thinking. The romantic rejection of analogy can therefore become, by proxy, an argument for construing romanticism as that which overcomes or secularizes an entrenched religious tradition. For romantic writers such as Blake and romantic critics such as Abrams, tradition functions as a drag or block to a theory of modernization linked decisively to secularization. In this respect, Blake's values become romanticism's values, for just as Blake contrasted the "same dull round over and over again" to "the Poetic or Prophetic character," so Abrams and Wasserman contrast "analogical rhetoric" to an "extraordinary syntactical system." Elevating Blake's contrast between ratios and poetry into a literary critical norm secures romanticism as a site that anticipates the assumed dominance of a modern secular consensus.

The Secret of Secularization

Can opposing poetry to analogy procure for the former a secularizing dynamic and thus a peculiarly modern affect? It is tempting to think so, and certainly many great poems have been written under the influence of such a thought. Deism's reading of natural theology, followed up by a Blakean/romantic reading of deism, proves a powerful combination, producing a romanticism that, by reinvigorating the imagination while jettisoning doctrinal religious content, coordinates attractively with a secularized, humanized modernity.

Yet Blake himself seems ambivalent about this literary history. In *The Visions of the Daughters of Albion* (1793), the character of Bromion represents the deistic confluence of religious orthodoxy and empirical scientism in particularly virulent form. And despite its clear critique of this position, the poem holds out little hope that Bromion's intellectual hold on the world can be broken either by poetry or by actual rebellion. Even the revolutionary, antinomian Oothoon, whose erotic egalitarianism resists Bromion's argument that she is impure because he has raped her, ends by treating women as instrumentally as she herself has been treated when she offers to catch girls in "silken nets and traps of adamant" for her lover Theotormon.[19] Bromion does not only oppress; he refashions the objects of his oppression in his own image.

Bromion's attitude is the limit case of enlightenment reason (which, for Blake, again, includes natural theology, Lockean psychology, Newtonian physics, and deism proper). Enlightenment reason aims to explore, to discover, and to dominate. It bends the world to its will; and when it violates the objects of its knowledge in doing so (as Bromion

violates Oothoon), it blames those objects rather than itself, for it believes that reason is value neutral. The result is an intellectual posture
that perpetually posits new territories to explore:

> Thou knowest that the ancient trees seen by thine eyes have fruit;
> But knowest thou that trees and fruits flourish upon the earth
> To gratify senses unknown? trees beasts and birds unknown:
> Unknown, not unpercievd, spread in the infinite microscope,
> In places yet unvisited by the voyager. and in worlds
> Over another kind of seas, and in atmospheres unknown: (4.13–18)

Scientific and imperial voyaging come together here; both seek to dominate, yet neither recognizes dominance *as* dominance, taking refuge instead in the idea that human reason has an obligation to uncover the
secrets of the world. Bromion believes not only that sense experience
is the only path to knowledge but also that there are general laws that
describe the entire world. That combination licenses exploration and
domination—the positing of more secrets—in the name of those general laws. The deist Matthew Tindal, thinking in his republican way of
the mysterious power of priests and kings, had declared that "there are
no *nostrums*, or secrets" for the deist.[20] Yet in *Visions*, the intellectual posture that Blake calls "deism," far from dispensing forever with secrets
and the structures of power that they legitimate, actually *requires* secrets
so that it can embark on its voyages of discovery. This accounts for the violence of its intellectual project, violence figured here as rape and slavery, violence covered over with layers of reason. Secrets are the hidden
engine—the secret, if you will—of the will to know.

Bromion's voice is the most successful one in *Visions* not because he
has better arguments, but because his opponents accept his claim that
arguments—defined inductively—are what matter. Oothoon, his chief
intellectual opponent, believes that she can argue her lover Theotormon out of his despair by showing that Bromion is wrong; her empiricism has a different aim from Bromion's, but it is still empiricism, which
is why the text insists that only Bromion can hear Oothoon's voice (3.1).
Theotormon has literally bound Bromion and Oothoon together, and
so Oothoon is tied to a set of arguments in which she does not believe
but from which she cannot escape. Indeed, since every attempt to escape must take the form of another argument, each new effort pulls the
chords tighter, for every time she opens her mouth she confirms the
dominance of the attitude Bromion represents.

Thus enlightenment critique binds even its most radical practitioners
to its secret love of secrets. William Godwin's 1794 novel *Caleb Williams*
pursues the motif of binding even further. Here the deistic belief in secrets ripe for investigation turns out to be correct—with devastating

emotional results, as Caleb himself becomes an example of what happens when the secrets in which Bromion trades are let into the open. Bromion, that is to say, does not learn the secret, which means that he can continue to justify his oppression of others intellectually. Caleb enacts a fantasy of liberation when he *does* learn the secret, but that liberation soon twists into something else entirely: a melancholy subjectivity marked by obsessive self-surveillance.

Caleb is clearly taken with the methods of inductive reasoning associated in the eighteenth century with science and natural theology and later (in the nineteenth-century genre that Godwin is inaugurating) with the detective novel. In trying to discover the truth about his master Falkland's past, Caleb employs all the techniques of an empirical reasoner:

I no longer said to myself, as I had done in the beginning, "I will ask Mr Falkland whether he were the murderer." On the contrary, after having carefully examined the different kinds of evidence of which the subject was susceptible, and recollecting all that had already passed upon the subject, it was not without considerable pain that I felt myself unable to discover any way in which I could be perfectly and unalterably satisfied of my patron's innocence.[21]

As he tells us at the beginning of the novel, Caleb is "a sort of natural philosopher" (6); induction is his stock-in-trade. Impelled by his insatiable curiosity, he seeks after the truth about Falkland, the "secret wound" that he bears (114). But he gets more than he bargained for, and Godwin casts Caleb's discovery in language pertinent to the relationship between scientific empiricism and natural theology. Once he discovers that Falkland is indeed a murderer (a discovery that comes about because Falkland admits it, suggesting the hollowness of the Caleb's strictly inductive detective work), Caleb's naïve adulation turns into something darker. Though he "had known Mr. Falkland from the first as a beneficent divinity" (143–44), he is now tormented with a secret knowledge of divine imperfection. Falkland turns from a beneficent deity into a vengeful one: "You might as well think of escaping from the power of the omnipresent God, as from mine!" he tells Caleb (150). This combination of Falkland's vengeful power and Caleb's possession of a secret turns Caleb into an extreme form of the modern subject imagined most memorably by Michel Foucault, poised on the edge of paranoia by the compulsion to monitor himself:

I had made myself a prisoner . . . . Though my prudence and discretion should be invariable, I must remember that I should have an overseer . . . . The vigilance even of a public and systematical despotism is poor, compared with a vigilance which is thus goaded by the most anxious passions of the soul. Against this species of persecution I knew not how to invent a refuge. (144)

In the secularization narrative of *Caleb Williams*, then, no one can leave the sacred world behind. Natural philosophy does succeed in demystifying the sacred universe, but this leads not to freedom but rather to subtler and more characteristically modern forms of constraint. The source of Caleb's "perpetual melancholy" (144) is that Falkland—even the deeply flawed Falkland that Caleb now knows him to be—will always be Caleb's master, and so Caleb is condemned to serve a divinity in whose beneficence he can no longer believe. Here is one rereading of the optimism of the deists: when enlightenment critique meets the belief in a beneficent deity, the result is secularization as perpetual melancholy. The subject can no longer believe, but that loss entails paranoia and a crippling reflexivity rather than a compensatory liberation. Call this "the secret of secularization."

In offering a forceful rejoinder to an enlightened fantasy of intellectual liberation, *Caleb Williams* serves also as a proleptic critique of one prominent strand of romantic criticism. By birth, training, and disposition, Caleb would seem a perfect candidate for the humanist subject of natural supernaturalism, one able to synthesize enlightenment critique and spiritual harmony by bringing the gods down to earth. In rejecting this path, *Caleb Williams* anticipates a development in romantic criticism itself. For with the advent of deconstruction in the 1970s, romantic criticism took on a sort of despondency akin to Caleb's melancholy. Paul de Man's 1969 essay "The Rhetoric of Temporality" displays this tendency perhaps most famously. Noting the pride of place that critics such as Abrams and Wasserman grant to the symbol, de Man counters with allegory: "[w]hereas the symbol postulates the possibility of an identity or identification, allegory designates primarily a distance in relation to its own origin, and, renouncing the nostalgia and the desire to coincide, it establishes its language in the void of this temporal difference."[22] De Man's intervention is well known, and its influence on subsequent romantic criticism considerable. But the force of his distinction between symbol and allegory makes it difficult to see that he shares with his humanist opponents a belief in the necessity of secularization. Like Caleb, though, de Man's version of secularization is melancholy, obsessive, and secretive. Rather than mapping secularization onto a progressive narrative as do his humanist opponents, de Man turns secularization into an individual, anguished possession.

To begin with, de Man cagily follows the literary history established by Abrams and Wasserman, in which the analogical tradition is overcome by being internalized, so that a set of associations between ideas and natural objects turns into a dialectic of subject and object, and that dialectic is in turn registered and perhaps sublated into a higher unity by the poetic symbol. But just at this point de Man parts ways with his precursors. The dialectic of subject and object, he writes, is not a true state of affairs but rather "a temptation that has to be overcome" (204–5). It is a temptation, most particularly, because it covers up the truth that time, rather than space, is language's real constitutive category; the poetic symbol, with its spatial investment in the subject–object dialectic, thus emerges as a denial of death, what de Man calls at various times "an authentically temporal destiny" (206) and an "authentically temporal predicament" (208). Allegory, on the other hand, does acknowledge this "authentic" situation by means of a rhetoric based upon temporal difference itself, since allegory simply points to a preceding sign. It emerges, then, that early romanticism, or what used to be called "preromanticism," glimpsed the true relationship between temporality and language (de Man speaks of the "secularized allegory of the early romantics" [207]), but that high or canonical romanticism soon fled this encounter with time to take refuge in the timelessness of the symbol; humanist romantic critics have followed this pattern, thereby participating in the idealization of a literature that, at its strongest, was resolutely anti-idealist.

It is of course the deconstructive critic, armed against the seductions of symbolic discourse, who can release this anti-idealist, secular literature from its spiritual and symbolic prison. But that liberationist hope quickly runs into the fact than any reading worth the name is endless and never resolves itself or reaches a conclusion. In de Man's world there is no place to escape *to*, no secular beyond against which the mystified present can be measured. There is only the endless process of reading. Thus, having just produced an impressive homology between the degeneration of allegory into symbol and the degeneration of irony into realism, de Man writes that "[t]his conclusion is dangerously satisfying . . . . Things cannot be left to rest at the point we have reached" (222). Such critical restlessness is often remarked as characteristic of de Man's whole procedure, which seeks to return us again and again to the necessary act of reading—reading that always, de Man writes elsewhere, "constantly fall[s] back to nought."[23] It also names the temptation to *stop* reading as the temptation against which all reading must defend itself, for stopping means taking refuge in a timeless fantasy world in which sign and meaning coalesce. That world is indeed "dangerously satisfying," and so de Man must remind even himself to start reading again, to keep pursuing the receding horizon of his authentic temporal destiny.

Like Caleb Williams, de Man believes in the necessity of secularization; divinity can survive neither Caleb's natural philosophy nor de Man's allegory. But also like Caleb, de Man offers a model of criticism in which knowledge does not set us free but rather ties us ever more intimately to the object of critique. For both, the secret of secularization is that it is a lonely and fraught affair, a burden that its apparent necessity does little to alleviate. Having, like Caleb, seen through divinity, the reader cannot go back to naïve belief; but having, also like Caleb, recognized that the pull of divinity is such that he can never fully emancipate himself from it, that reader remains poised between worlds. The only way to resist the spiritual temptation represented by the divine object is to keep reading, but every reading reiterates the reader's commitment to that object, and so the cycle becomes endless, and the reading subject a perpetual melancholic. This melancholy predicament in turn becomes a kind of professional identity, for the reader can believe only in the continued necessity of reading, even if that reading endlessly reveals his or her own naïve investment in the mystifications he or she is seeking to unravel—reveals, in short, the interpretive life as one balanced between blindness and insight.

I have revisited this now-bygone moment within romantic studies in order to make the point that it is really the legacy of the *enlightenment* that is at issue. Is the enlightenment the thing that romanticism must save us from? Or is it the thing that will save us from romanticism? For humanist critics it is the former; for de Man it is the latter. Yet a second point becomes immediately visible: for both kinds of critic, *religion* serves as a stable object of critique against which "romanticism" can be variously positioned. In plotting romanticism as a secularization of inherited theological ideas, Abrams and Wasserman offer it as an alternative to religion, more suitable to an ecumenical and diverse age. Meanwhile, in bringing the "secularized allegory of the early romantics" to bear against later romantic mystification, de Man, like Caleb, finds in the enlightenment the critical wherewithal to resist the spiritual temptations of high romanticism. Both kinds of critic accept an enlightened, which is to say, rational, critique of religion; they differ in how they position romanticism in the aftermath of that critique.

Notwithstanding its powerful contribution, this shared heritage is also something of a liability simply because its own parameters cannot account for the fact that the enlightened critique of religion is not the final word, that modernization has not meant the end of religion, and that many modern people, far from seeking an alternative to religion, have been more or less content with the thing itself.[24] This is to make the rather obvious point that critique alone cannot grasp the reasons for religion's continuing hold: all it can do is reflexively register that hold in the form of critical melancholia, and like de Man demand of itself an ever-more austere reading practice; or it can offer some kind of alternative, like Wasserman's symbol, and immediately thereby risk the charge of proffering a substitute religion.

The tradition that I have called the "argument against design," stretching from deism through Blake and Godwin and on into various strands of romantic criticism that locate the renunciation or refashioning of religion as romanticism's distinctive achievement, is finally just that: an argument. And its faith in arguments—whether in the form of critique or in the form of romanticism's alternative languages—seems here to have produced a dead end, or at any rate a cul-de-sac, where there is room to maneuver but no way to go forward. To find our way into a reading that can account for the multiple ways that religion inflects modernity, we need a different enlightenment legacy. With this aim, the next chapter considers David Hume's emphasis on design as a lived practice.

Chapter 2

Arbitrary Acts of Mind: Natural Theology in Hume's *Dialogues Concerning Natural Religion*

In treating the argument from design as if it were supposed to demonstrate something on its own, those who use the argument either to criticize orthodoxy (the deists) or to defend it (Blackmore) assume from the outset that religious belief is best organized according to the protocols of inductive reasoning. By the end of the century, that assumption looks increasingly implausible—not because the argument has been proved either true or false, but rather because whether it is true *or* false seems irrelevant to understanding religion's hold upon the psyche. The previous chapter's survey of the "argument against design" over the course of the eighteenth century identifies one way in which secularization understood as differentiation follows from treating design as an argument. For whatever one ultimately concludes about the philosophical worth of the argument itself, the decision to treat it *as* an argument positions religion as something over which reason can stand in judgment. Yet such differentiation does not in this case lead to decline, for contrary to the enlightened linkage of reason and emancipation, Blake and Godwin show how critique binds us even more firmly to what we had hoped to escape. Reason may stand in judgment, but this yields only a more symbiotic relationship between differentiated realms of reason and religion.[1]

What, then, if we did not focus upon the validity of the argument from design, but rather upon the things that may have accounted for its influence and power *despite* the kinds of intellectual critique in which the enlightenment was so well versed? To follow out the implications of this question, this chapter departs from the tendency to treat design as an argument—and in so doing, it sets the strategy for the following chapters as well. In this my initial guide is David Hume. Hume's *Dialogues Concerning Natural Religion* is largely remembered for having dealt the intellectual deathblow to the argument from design (Kant, with his arguments against physicotheology in the first and third *Critiques*, is the undertaker, burying what Hume had already killed). But the *Dialogues* also recognize, reluctantly, that the philosophical methods of natural theology are really a secondary issue. Habit and custom, and the power of social networks that behave *as if* the design argument were legitimate: these matter more than the content of the argument itself. Human beings seem to have a built-in "design perception": they pick out patterns, order, and harmony within phenomena. Accordingly, the culture of natural theology (not only sermons and theological treatises but also social networks, polite conversation, and an intellectual milieu in which design simply goes without saying) provides a context in which those design perceptions can be fostered and directed toward their divine origin.

In my reading, the much-discussed final pages of the *Dialogues* ruefully signal Hume's awareness of all of this. The actual burden of the *Dialogues*, as we shall see, is therefore carried by the genre of the dialogue format itself, and Hume's target is the polite sociability that both preserves and is preserved by the form of religious dialogue. This distinction between Hume's sociological contribution and his philosophical one is not of course absolute, for philosophical skepticism, like natural theology, assumes the dialogue format. Nevertheless, rereading the philosophical dimensions of Hume's critique within the context of its social claims highlights how natural theology depends upon a series of affective social bonds in order to hold its world together. Its unraveling, accordingly, will come about not because of something so straightforward as a "loss of belief" but rather because, under the pressures of differentiation, the increasing ungovernability of those social bonds means that design can no longer do its work.

The Argument

Before turning to Hume's treatment of the social bonds that sustain natural theology, however, we need to understand the philosophical argument against which those bonds are posed. *Dialogues Concerning Natural Religion*, published posthumously in 1779, describes a conversation between three people: Philo, a "careless skeptic"; Cleanthes, a rational Christian who defends the argument from design; and Demea, a dogmatic rationalist. It is narrated by Pamphilus, a young student of Cleanthes'. For the majority of the text Demea and Philo are in alliance against Cleanthes. Demea stakes his position early; the nature of God, he declares, is

altogether incomprehensible and unknown to us. . . . Finite, weak, and blind creatures, we ought to humble ourselves in his august presence, and, conscious of our frailties, adore in silence his infinite perfections.[2]

Philo immediately sides with Demea, declaring, "we ought never to imagine that we comprehend the attributes of this divine Being, or to suppose that his perfections have any analogy or likeness to the perfections of a human creature" (44). He concludes his opening remarks by addressing Cleanthes directly: "And it is a pleasure to me (and I hope to you too) that just reasoning and sound piety here concur in the same conclusion, and both of them establish the adorably mysterious and incomprehensible nature of the supreme Being" (45).

In response Cleanthes lays down a classic example of the argument from design:

> Look round the world: Contemplate the whole and every part of it: You will find it to be nothing but one great machine, subdivided into an infinite number of lesser machines, which again admit of subdivisions, to a degree beyond what human senses and faculties can trace and explain. All these various machines, and even their most minute parts, are adjusted to each other with an accuracy, which ravishes into admiration all men, who have ever contemplated them. The curious adapting of means to ends, throughout all nature, resembles exactly, though it much exceeds, the productions of human contrivance; of human design, thought, wisdom, and intelligence. Since therefore the effects resemble each other, we are led to infer, by all the rules of analogy, that the causes also resemble; and that the Author of nature is somewhat similar to the mind of man; though possessed of much larger faculties, proportioned to the grandeur of the work, which he has executed. (45)

Like most formulations of design in the eighteenth century, Cleanthes' argument mixes its several elements together. In referring to the "curious adapting of means to ends," Cleanthes signals his belief in the purposive features of the natural world. Within this teleological framework he draws a comparison between the world as a whole and "the productions of human contrivance." Since these are similar, analogy leads us to infer that the causes are similar as well. As a machine implies a human designer, so the world implies a divine designer. The general strategy of the argument is to build up an *a posteriori* picture of the world as a great contrivance and then employ an analogy between the world and an instance of human contrivance in order to argue that God made the world. Here it is in schematic form:

(1) A machine shows evidence of design.
(2) We know that a machine is produced by a designer.
(3) The world is like a machine in showing evidence of design.
(4) Therefore, the world is produced by a designer whose skills are commensurate with the observed effects.

Like many eighteenth-century theologians, Cleanthes is less than explicit about the third (analogical) step; perhaps, like them, he regards it as so obvious that it scarcely needs mentioning. Indeed analogy itself, which is absolutely central to the entire enterprise, receives little direct attention by natural theologians. Joseph Butler, whose book *The Analogy of Religion* is more conscious than most about the rhetorical status of analogy, nevertheless declares at the beginning of his book that he will undertake no investigation of analogy itself. "Indeed I shall not take it upon me to say, how far the extent, compass, and force, of analogical reasoning, can be reduced to general heads and rules; and the whole be formed into a system," Butler writes. "It is enough to the present purpose to observe," he continues, "that this general way of arguing is evidently natural, just, and conclusive."[3]

Yet the analogy between world and machine is not always natural and conclusive. This, in any case, is Philo's first rejoinder. He notes a familiar rule of analogy: the more remote the analogy between two things, the more hesitant we should be about the inference: "If we see a house, Cleanthes, we conclude, with the greatest certainty, that it had an architect or builder; because this is precisely that species of effect, which we have experienced to proceed from that species of cause. But surely you will not affirm, that the universe bears such a resemblance to a house, that we can with the same certainty affirm a similar cause, or that the analogy is here entire and perfect" (46). The sorts of design and mutual adaptation that the universe exhibits are, in numerous particulars, different from the kind of order exhibited by a human contrivance such as a house. Indeed, anything made by humans is very unlike the universe at large.

The analogy can presumably be shored up by detailing the ways in which the world *is* indeed like a machine. This would require empirical observation of the cause-and-effect relations that characterize the world, and this is apparently what Cleanthes is up to when he speaks of the subdivision of the world into smaller machines. Starting with the "most minute parts" of the natural world, he argues that each one is adjusted with an admirable accuracy; each of these minute parts, in turn, participates by means of relations of cause and effect in a larger grouping of parts, each of which, again, is adjusted to the other—and so on until we have arrived at a world that is one great intricate machine made up of successively smaller machines, all of them tied together by mutual relations of cause and effect. In its production of examples this is a strictly inductive argument, but in picturing a world of smaller machines embedded in larger ones, Cleanthes' argument also shows how the teleological orientation of the argument from design—which is rarely admitted as an actual premise—manifests itself in the sorts of evidence that the argument produces. There is a vector built into the evidence itself as it moves from smaller examples to larger.

Let us assume, for a moment, that the analogy can be rescued by these means. The question then becomes how much it can validly deliver. Not much at all, says Philo in his second argument. Induction, he notes, requires a series of prior experiences in order to work effectively. If I were to come upon a newly built house and wonder how it came to be there, I could reason thus:

(1) Every house has been experienced (by me or by someone I trust) to have been built by a human being.
(2) Therefore, this particular house was (probably) built by a human being.

But it is obvious that such reasoning cannot be transferred to the universe as a whole, because to bring a universe into being is rather dramatically different from building a house. The first is an act of creation, whereas the second is simply a reorganization of existing materials. In order to engage in causal reasoning about the origin of worlds, we would need prior experience of creation *ex nihilo*, which we manifestly lack. "And will any man," asks Philo, "tell me with a serious countenance, that an orderly universe must arise from some thought and art, like the human; because we have experience of it? To ascertain this reasoning, it were requisite, that we had experience of the origin of worlds; and it is not sufficient surely, that we have seen ships and cities arise from human art and contrivance" (51–52). Philo's point is that in naming God as the originator of the world Cleanthes is assuming that he already knows more about God than the design argument can validly deliver.[4] To be consistent, Cleanthes' arguments can only be about the causes of order *within* the universe, not about the causes of the universe itself. So even if the analogy *did* work it would not accomplish what Cleanthes needs it to accomplish, because induction simply cannot deliver a picture of the world that an analogy can validly transfer to the divine creative God consistent with orthodoxy. Our only experience of contrivance is of human designers rearranging existing material. Therefore, by analogy, the only God that a working argument from design delivers is a God who, like a human shipbuilder, works with existing materials, adapting means to ends as best he can within preestablished parameters. The available evidence of the natural world cannot justify more than this.

The middle sections of Hume's book take aim solely at the analogical aspects of the argument from design. Philo notes, for instance, that to determine the excellence of a human contrivance we often compare it to a less successful one; but lacking grounds for comparison, we have no real knowledge that this world works as it was intended to or as it should. So attributing perfection to the world's designer is unjustified. Furthermore, even if we agree that the world is well designed, it does not follow from this that the designer is perfect. One thing we know about human contrivance is that it proceeds slowly and encounters many setbacks; thus if we are to say that the design of the universe is analogous to that of human contrivances, we must consider the possibility that the world may be the lucky contrivance of a divine bungler. Warming to his task, Philo points out that another characteristic of human invention is that it is collaborative, which by analogy suggests not a single unified Deity behind the world but numerous deities working in concert. Clearly relishing the heretical conclusions to which analogical arguments lend themselves, Philo at last concludes: "In a word, Cleanthes, a man, who follows your hypothesis, is able, perhaps, to assert, or conjecture, that the universe, sometime, arose from something like design: But beyond that position he cannot ascertain one single circumstance, and is left afterwards to fix every point of his theology, by the utmost license of fancy and hypothesis" (71).

Cleanthes has a rough time of it after this; indeed, he is on the defensive until the dialogue's last section. But then something dramatic happens. First the alliance between Demea and Philo, struck in the opening pages, abruptly shatters. Philo has made much of the fact that if one were to argue from the perceived perfection of the world to the perfection of its creator, then one would be equally justified in arguing from the perceived imperfection of the world to the imperfection of its creator. Thus strictly inferential arguments, he suggests, land the natural theologian squarely in the problem of evil, and he begins rather gleefully to speculate about the nature of a God who is responsible for making a world full of destruction, pain, and death. This finally alerts Demea to the danger of his ally: "I now find you running into all the topics of the greatest libertines and infidels; and betraying that holy cause, which you seemingly espoused," he tells Philo (114–15). And soon thereafter he departs "on some pretense or other" and never returns.

Once Demea has left, Philo reverses his position and claims to be in complete agreement with Cleanthes. He says that his arguments have been so incautious because he is sure that Cleanthes would never misinterpret his real intent. "[N]o one," Philo says, "has a deeper sense of religion impressed on his mind, or pays more profound adoration to the divine Being" (116). Apparently disregarding his own earlier arguments, he declares that a "purpose, an intention, a design strikes everywhere the most careless, the most stupid thinker; and no man can be so hardened in absurd systems, as at all times to reject it" (116). Cleanthes, who himself seems rather shaken by the vehemence of Philo's earlier arguments, is relieved. "Your spirit of controversy," he tells Philo, "carries you strange lengths, when engaged in an argument."[5]

At length Philo offers this final judgment:

If the whole of natural theology, as some people seem to maintain, resolves itself into one simple, though somewhat ambiguous, at least undefined proposition, *that the cause or causes of order in the universe probably bear some remote analogy to human intelligence* . . . what can the most inquisitive, contemplative, and religious man do more than give a plain, philosophical assent to the proposition, as often as it occurs; and believe that the arguments, on which it is established, exceed the objections which lie against it? (129)

As a confession of faith, notes Keith Yandell, this "comes somewhat short of the Apostles' Creed."[6] Indeed, it is difficult to attribute much content to Philo's version of natural theology: though it excludes a dogmatic atheism (one that would reject the postulation of any principles of divinely instituted order), the theism it offers is attenuated enough to have minimal effect on human conduct. This is precisely Philo's point. If this is all that natural theology amounts to, he seems to suggest, then it's not an enemy worth fighting.

The Situation

The sudden and dramatic shifts of the book's final pages raise two related questions: Who wins the exchange? And who speaks for the author? Until these last pages, the answer to both had seemed obvious: Philo. Midway through the book, in fact, Philo has Cleanthes so thoroughly on the defensive that it seems the game is up: "So great is your fertility of invention," says Cleanthes to Philo, "that I am not ashamed to acknowledge myself unable, on a sudden, to solve regularly such out-of-the-way difficulties as you incessantly start upon me: Though I clearly see, in general, their fallacy and error" (83). He is not any more successful in the second half of the book at describing exactly how Philo's arguments are marred by "fallacy and error."

So it is something of a surprise to find the narrator Pamphilus close out the *Dialogues* by declaring Cleanthes the winner: "upon a serious review of the whole, I cannot but think, that Philo's principles are more probable than Demea's; but that those of Cleanthes approach still nearer to the truth" (130). This single sentence has inspired a great deal of literature on the question of what Hume's "true opinions" about religion actually were.[7] Those inclined to take Pamphilus's judgment as Hume's own note that Pamphilus declares at one other point that Philo is "a little embarrassed and confounded" by Cleanthes' defense of the design argument, and that near the end of the book Philo does say (truthfully or not) that he agrees with Cleanthes. So Pamphilus's closing remarks are not completely out of context.

Most commentators, though, think that Philo's arguments are never adequately countered by Cleanthes. Philo dominates the discussion, especially in the latter half of the book; his words account for 67 percent of the whole, compared to 21 percent for Cleanthes and 12 percent for Demea.[8] Moreover, Philo's arguments are very much in the style of the Hume of *A Treatise of Human Nature*; and his views on religion parallel the views expressed in Hume's *Enquiry Concerning Human Understanding*. Even when Philo famously claims to be in complete agreement with Cleanthes near the end, he in fact gives away very little, for the version of theism to which he assents is severely attenuated. All this suggests that Philo's opinions are closest to Hume's own.[9]

The book's unusual publication history bears out this argument. The *Dialogues* as we know them were basically complete by 1761, but they remained unpublished until 1779, three years after Hume's death. By 1751 he had finished a shorter version and had given it to some of his friends, all of whom apparently urged that it not be published.[10] Hume's friend the Reverend Hugh Blair wrote him from Paris in 1763: "for God's sake let that be a posthumous work, if ever it shall see the light: Tho' I really think it had better not." Hume heeded this advice—in part, it seems, out of a desire not to get his friends in hot water. "Scotland is too narrow a place for me," he wrote to Adam Smith in 1759, "and it mortifies me that I sometimes hurt my friends."[11] But he made every effort to ensure that the *Dialogues* would be published after his death. First he willed them to Adam Smith, with the request that he see them into publication; but just before he died, apparently guessing that Smith was unlikely to publish them, Hume willed the manuscript to his publisher instead, adding the codicil that if they were not published within two and a half years of his death they would become the property of his favorite nephew and namesake, "whose Duty in publishing them as the last Request of his Uncle, must be approved of by all the World."[12] It was this nephew who finally sponsored their publication in 1779.

The concern that the *Dialogues* caused those who were closest to Hume suggests that they all considered the book a threat to prevailing orthodoxy. Since Pamphilus's closing sentences awarding the prize to Cleanthes seem reassuring rather than threatening, Hume's friends and publisher evidently concluded that Pamphilus's final statement obscured rather than revealed the author's true intentions. Certainly Hume's reviewers did not hesitate to identify him with Philo. The anonymous reviewer in the *Edinburgh Amusement* attributes Hume's views to Philo without a second thought; William Rose, in the *Monthly Review*, does the same: "we now proceed," he writes, "to lay before our Readers Mr. Hume's own sentiments in the character of the 'careless sceptic,' Philo."[13] For his readers, apparently, Hume's character as a skeptic was so well known that the identity of his spokesperson was never in doubt. "Mr. Hume," Rose writes, "had been long floating on the boundless and pathless ocean of scepticism" before he wrote the *Dialogues* (354). This latest performance is simply true to form.

Twentieth-century commentators on Hume, then, follow the lead of their eighteenth-century counterparts when they treat as central the question of which character best represents the author's opinion of natural theology. In contrast, I wish to move away from the question of Hume's intentions by focusing on the fact that these are dialogues, and so exert formal and generic pressures on the material that cannot be accounted for by a methodological assumption that Hume has certain beliefs waiting to be elicited by careful commentary. Like natural theology itself, these *Dialogues* are an exercise in reading; they place debates about proper pedagogy within the sociable and shared world of literate men, where the manner in which conclusions arrive are at least as important as the conclusions themselves. Consequently, they demand a kind of interpretive practice that would eventually come to be recognized as "literary."[14]

As Michael Prince has pointed out, most eighteenth-century religious dialogue followed a standard binary structure.[15] In Berkeley's *Three Dialogues Between Hylas and Philonous,* for instance, the conversations take place between a skeptic and a reasonable theist and end with the latter convincing the former. Berkeley explains in his Preface that he seeks to demonstrate how the rules of logic accord with those of religion and government, in contradistinction to "that loose, rambling way, not altogether improperly termed 'Freethinking,' by certain libertines in thought."[16] Prince argues persuasively that this binary format is intended to show that disputants who converse rationally and without the interference of enthusiasm will come to agreement on the fundamental questions of religion. The dialogue's process of bringing order out of disorder may therefore be taken to allegorize natural theology itself, which thus plays a normalizing role within its social and cultural milieu. Yet, as Prince demonstrates, the presence of the rationalist Demea within Hume's *Dialogues* changes the dynamics of the binary dialogue form. By including a third disputant and by making the completion of the dialogue rest upon his banishment, Hume interjects an arbitrary or willful element into this orderly procedure, disrupting what Prince calls the "stable sense of closure" that "enabled orthodox writers to acknowledge the threat of multiplicity" while nevertheless containing it (288). The *Dialogues Concerning Natural Religion* challenge the tradition of thoughtful religious dialogue by distinguishing between social and philosophical triumph. It may not be clear whether Cleanthes or Philo is the best philosopher, but both agree that Demea makes for bad company.

This formal innovation is philosophically foreshadowed when Philo gets Cleanthes to admit to the faith upon which his rational Christianity is built. Philo allows that the mutual adaptation and order of the world could have a causal explanation, but asks why it has to be referred to the order and adaptation of the mind of the divine designer. Why not infer that the designer himself is the effect of an even more fundamental cause? By the same token, why not assume that we could locate a principle of design within the universe itself? "Have we not the same reason to trace that ideal world into another ideal world, or new intelligent principle?" asks Philo. "But if we stop, and go no farther; why go so far? Why not stop at the material world? How can we satisfy ourselves without going on *in infinitum*?" (63). His point is that to rest with the theory of a divine designer of *this* universe is simply to pick an arbitrary stopping point. A world-plus-designer is even more wonderful than the world alone, raising the possibility of a designer of designers. Consistency demands that we commit ourselves to infinite regress or that we search for a principle of order within the material world itself. Cleanthes, temporarily stymied, must admit that purely inductive arguments indeed cannot determine when we have arrived at the true God, and he retreats to the fideism he has so far been avoiding. "You start abstruse doubts, cavils, and objections," he splutters. "You ask me what is the cause of this cause? I know not; I care not; that concerns not me. I have found a Deity; and here I stop my enquiry" (65).

Here Cleanthes verges on terrain more amenable to a rationalist like Demea—and indeed Demea tries to help him out of his predicament by suggesting a retreat to *a priori* arguments. "In mounting up . . . from effects to causes," says Demea to illustrate what he means, "we must either go on in tracing an infinite succession, without any ultimate cause at all, or must at last have recourse to some ultimate cause that is *necessarily* existent" (90).[17] Though its ultimate source is Aquinas, Demea's argument is probably modeled on Samuel Clarke's first series of Boyle lectures.[18] In particular, Demea's argument for a God whose nonexistence is logically impossible echoes Clarke's language, and he follows Clarke in referring to his strategy as *a priori*, although strictly speaking it is not an *a priori* argument. Clarke developed his argument for God as a necessary first cause in response to Locke's well-known cosmological argument in book IV of *An Essay Concerning Human Understanding*. When Hume told James Boswell a few weeks before dying that he "never had entertained any belief in Religion since he began to read Locke and Clarke," he may have meant it as a provoking example of the argument he had made in the *Dialogues*: that there was finally no difference that matters between arguments from necessity and arguments by induction.[19]

Demea's "mysticism," of course, is designed to play badly within the confines of polite discourse: when he violates the dialogue's rules of sociability by leaving in a huff, he reveals the misanthropic nature of his intellectual and religious posture. In sharp contrast to his reasonable companions, Demea finally cannot talk to others who do not already agree with him. Yet Michael Prince shows that by the time Demea leaves Cleanthes has been forced to reveal the dogmatic nature of his own apparently reasonable argument. His desperate assertion that "I have found a Deity, and here I stop my inquiry" comes off as a less sophisticated form of Demea's necessary first cause. Beneath Cleanthes' reasonable façade lurks a fideist, and so by the end of the conversation, Prince concludes, Demea's presence is unnecessary because Cleanthes has adopted his attitude.[20]

In the dramatic structure of the dialogue, Cleanthes has been made to acknowledge that his argument rests upon a preexisting belief. This in itself is not such a huge problem, for as I noted earlier most eighteenth-century design arguments assumed the existence of the God they searched for. Only an unsympathetic commentator would regard this as devastating. The problem for natural theology arises, though, in the way that the revelation of Cleanthes' fideism plays within the world of the dialogue. As the case of Demea demonstrates, dogmatic belief is antisocial; when pushed to justify itself in the course of a conversation, it retreats finally to bald assertion, a way of removing itself from dialogue eventually allegorized by Demea's departure. Likewise, when Philo speculates on the infinite regress to which the design argument seems to commit itself, Cleanthes responds by stopping his inquiry arbitrarily. The implication is not only that dogmatism is the invisible prerequisite for design—more importantly, it is that when dogmatism surfaces it obstructs the polite and elegant context that in earlier dialogues had been rational Christianity's enabling condition.

Such interruptions in the dialogue's flow sit uncomfortably alongside Cleanthes' continued faith in the invisible harmonizing effect of religion. After Demea has left and Philo has given his equivocal assent to the design argument, Cleanthes declares: "The proper office of religion is to regulate the heart of men, humanize their conduct, infuse the spirit of temperance, order, and obedience; and as its operation is silent, and only enforces the motives of morality and justice, it is in danger of being overlooked, and confounded with these other motives" (122). Hume's ironic point, perhaps, is that if religion is so silent and invisible, perhaps it isn't there at all. But in the context of the sudden visibility of dogmatic belief at particular moments in the *Dialogues*, Cleanthes' celebration of strategic invisibility deserves also to be understood as a register of design's vexed hold on its subjects. For Berkeley, religious dialogue produced an elegant philosophical and formal harmony. In place of this, Hume has substituted a clumsy routine: silently and gently design works to bring order out of disorder, harmony out of chaos.

If things get out of hand, dogmatic belief steps in and asserts its arbitrary right to halt the conversation in its tracks, even to the point of disrupting the sociability that design has worked so hard to foster.

An Arbitrary Act of the Mind

Hume introduces the word "arbitrary" when Cleanthes objects to Demea's argument from necessity:

> In such a chain, too, or succession of objects, each part is caused by that which preceded it, and causes that which succeeds it. Where then is the difficulty? But the whole, you say, wants a cause. I answer, that the uniting of these parts into a whole, like the uniting of several distinct counties into one kingdom, or several distinct members into one body, is performed merely by an *arbitrary act of the mind*, and has no influence on the nature of things. (92; emphasis added)

As a defense of the causal chain on which the argument from design rests, this shifts from the cause of the world to the cause of the individual contrivances of the world. The cause of the one, Cleanthes declares, explains the cause of the other. If Cleanthes were to formalize his new argument, it would look like this:

(1) A machine shows evidence of design.
(2) We know that a machine is caused by a designer.
(3) Individual objects and events within the world are like machines in showing evidences of design.
(4) Therefore, a designer whose skills are commensurate with the observed effects must have caused the world.

This is a weak argument: a group of designed items need not itself exhibit design, just as a group of machines need not itself be a machine. It fails to answer Demea's claim that a chain or series of contingent parts is itself contingent and that everything contingent must have a cause. And it implicitly capitulates to Philo's suggestion that natural theology can't follow the chain all the way up to God, but that it must, at a certain point, make a leap from the world to its creator. Now Cleanthes admits it: to get from (3) to (4), from individual instances of contrivance to their divine contriver, demands the agency of an "arbitrary act of mind." A designed world is now analogous to a body or a kingdom: ideas that explain the relationship among diverse parts, not entities inductively derivable from their constituents. If the notion of a designed universe is not empirically verifiable but rather an idea generated by the mind, then, as Demea says, "any supposition which can be formed is equally possible" (91). This is a long way from Cleanthes' initial statement of the design argument, which depended on an analogy between the world ("one great machine") and human contrivance. Where natural theology had traditionally located its penultimate step—the picture of an entire universe of harmonious and adaptive interrelation—Cleanthes substitutes an arbitrary act of mind.

In matters of the psyche, "arbitrary" suggests willfulness or capriciousness; in politics, it connotes monarchical tyranny, perhaps of the sort that would unite different counties into a single kingdom.[21] Arbitrary acts have no place in the religious dialogue as Shaftesbury or Berkeley conceived it. Such acts are antisocial, and their justification by definition falls beyond the boundaries of polite and public discourse. Given these connotations of "arbitrary," Cleanthes' appeal to the analogy of a kingdom seems apposite. At a famous moment near the end of book I of the *Treatise*, Hume had illustrated his philosophical skepticism by conjuring up the tides and wind of a sea voyage:

> Methinks I am like a man, who having struck on many shoals, and having narrowly escap'd ship-wreck in passing a small frith, has yet the temerity to put out to sea in the same leaky weather-beaten vessel, and even carries his ambition so far as to think of compassing the globe under these disadvantageous circumstances.[22]

Here Hume alludes to the common allegorizing of skepticism with the sea and imagines himself driven to skepticism as a result of his philosophical bravery. Whereas the philosopher of the *Treatise* thus takes to the sea out of necessity, as if expelled from home by his own integrity and forced to seek philosophical sustenance in foreign lands, Cleanthes' description of a kingdom as an act of mind rewrites this necessity as both politically arbitrary and socially affective.[23] In the analogy, "each part" of a kingdom exhibits the order that characterizes the whole. Cleanthes has enough confidence in this image to assure his listeners that the seemingly disparate parts of a kingdom hang together through a willed act of mental identification and sympathy. He appeals to the sea lightly, as if confident that he will find something he recognizes at the end of his voyage. The ships that once carried skeptical philosophical adventurers now carry self-assured voyagers, for whom the easy winds of colonial success have replaced the harsher gusts of epistemic doubt.

Pamphilus, it will be remembered, closes out the book with this surprising opinion: "upon a serious review of the whole, I cannot but think that Philo's principles are more probable than Demea's, but that those of Cleanthes approach still nearer to the truth" (130). The verdict is curious because Pamphilus seems to have missed the important action of the final section. Philo has spent the better part of the *Dialogues* showing that the argument from design cannot deliver much in the way of a deity;

when he concludes by affirming the "somewhat ambiguous, at least un-defined proposition, *that the cause or causes of order in the universe probably bear some remote analogy to human intelligence,*" this should hardly be grounds for celebration for defenders of natural theology. Despite hav-ing been present at the entire debate and declaring that "nothing ever made greater impression on me, than all the reasonings of that day" (130), it seems that Pamphilus in fact has not learned very much.

A more likely possibility, though, is that Pamphilus has learned every-thing there is to learn from these dialogues, that he is the best student of all, and that he has taken the conversation so entirely to heart that he has replaced Philo as the "careless skeptic." After listening to the com-batants, he knows that the intellectual posture one adopts has an oblique *rational* relation to the arguments that precede it and try to ex-plain it. Thus his judgment that Cleanthes comes nearest the truth is a conscious choice to accept the historical conclusions of natural theol-ogy, despite their arbitrary nature and their acknowledged intellectual deficiencies. Given that the principles tied to natural theology have throughout the dialogue emphasized unity, affective bonding, and, not least, the opportunities afforded by an expanding empire, Pamphilus's decision seems eminently rational. In this interpretation, the joke is on all of the disputants, *including Philo,* who naively think that truth is more attractive that fiction—and the joke is also on the philosophical reader, who wades through "abstruse arguments" only to discover, in the end, that what mattered was the dialogue itself, not its conclusions. At the end of the day, we think and believe what we were already inclined to think and believe, and for reasons not solely stubborn or self-serving but communal. From the perspective of both the philosophical Christian and the philosophical skeptic, this leaves us in the arbitrary but sociable place of Cleanthes' analogy.

A kingdom is a discursive formation, brought into being by the infor-mation and identities that travel its pathways. Perhaps the truth that nat-ural theology produces is likewise discursive, living only in the pathways of its articulation. The truth of natural theology may not be a thing in it-self gradually uncovered through philosophical disputation, but rather an ad hoc phenomenon created in the very act of disputation itself. Just as the idea of a kingdom coheres around the ships that pass among its parts, so the idea of a designing God is made coherent by the act of coming together to debate its probability. This would deprive truth of its metaphysical character; Pamphilus can choose the arguments he will be compelled by.

If anyone "wins" in these dialogues, therefore, it must be the author himself. In the *Treatise* Hume imagined himself driven inevitably to skep-ticism by his brave determination to discover the limits of thought. The cost of that bravery, as it is for all skeptics, was that he lost the world; it only came back to him under the guise of a dogmatic, if inevitable, faith in the evidence of his senses. Pamphilus's skeptical decision to agree with Cleanthes, in contrast, is stripped of all the melodramatic freight that Hume had packed into that earlier self-description: Pamphilus picks one set of arguments over another without bothering to justify the choice in the language of reason, certainly without portraying himself as necessarily *driven* in one direction or another. It is, of course, virtually unimaginable that Pamphilus would have chosen differently, but such narrative inevitability is hardly a defeat for the author. Quite the contrary, in fact. Because in making his choice, Pamphilus effectively signals that natural theology marches under the banner of a skepticism whose most skeptical or arbitrary act, far from meaning the *loss* of the world, actually *produces* it as a pleasantly familiar home away from home. Thus Cleanthes' "arbitrary act of the mind" concedes what the narrative has been all along suggesting: the truth of the world is not that its designer can be glimpsed through its phenomena, but that those phenomena appear to us only as the result of an idea produced by its iteration and re-iteration. Interpretation after the *Dialogues* does not conform to the depth model on which the argument from design had earlier seemed to depend, which posited a world everywhere connected by threads of meaning. Now it is spread out along the surfaces of things, like a conversation, like ordered discourse, like a map.

Chapter 3

Theory, Practice, and Anna Barbauld

Early in the *Dialogues Concerning Natural Religion*, Philo asks rhetorically: "[w]hen the coherence of the parts of a stone, or even that composition of parts which renders it extended; when these familiar objects, I say, are so inexplicable, and contain circumstances so repugnant and contradictory; with what assurance can we decide concerning the origin of worlds, or trace their history from eternity to eternity?"[1] Here Philo makes the link between epistemological and religious skepticism explicit. A literary historian might be drawn to read this situation as representing too the dead end in which eighteenth-century poetry found itself. No longer able to assume what their predecessors had assumed about the "origin of worlds" (namely, that God made them, with the universe itself as evidence), poets would be given more to shoring up metaphysics than to using it. The consequence might be a static and nontransformative verse. Avoiding this fate would demand a rethinking of poetic language in general and indeed might require the bravery to cut it loose from its theological orientation. Enter romanticism.

As I noted earlier, this version of literary history links secularization to romantic innovation: the religious metaphysics in which design is embedded loses its hold, and the poet must then discover a new and dynamic poetic language. In constructing it as an epistemic shift that anticipated the modernity whose spiritual crises they were themselves observing, romanticism's admirers in the middle years of the twentieth century interpreted romantic exceptionalism as the sublation of modernization theory—as that which both carried it forward and redeemed it.

Without ever fully repudiating the notions of secularization and modernization that gave rise to this construction, romantic criticism has been moving away from it over the past several decades. Increased attention to women writers has been one manifestation of this movement. The conceptual challenge of this inclusiveness has always been the need to read and appreciate formerly noncanonical writers for what they are doing rather than for what they are not doing. If they are not writing Greater Romantic Lyrics, then under what definition do they qualify as

romantics? Faced with this difficulty, the temptation is either to construct an alternative canon (masculine romanticism versus feminine romanticism, for example) or to fold the very idea of romanticism into a
larger conception of period writing. For different reasons, both strategies do a disservice to rediscovered writers and to the supposedly hege-
monic romanticism they are understood to either critique or dissolve.

The effort to pluralize romanticism will remain incomplete so long as
romanticism's own relationship to secularization remains uninterrogated
and unhistoricized. In what follows I offer Anna Barbauld's important
disagreement with the models of progressive secularization that underwrite traditional constructions of canonical romanticism as a place to
begin redressing these shortcomings. As a religious dissenter and publishing intellectual woman, Barbauld stands conspicuously athwart the
dominant trajectories along which religion and gender were understood
in late eighteenth-century England. Within that context, however, her
various engagements with the design argument signal an important
point of connection between dissent and orthodoxy, and place her simultaneously in a complexly dialectical relationship to a burgeoning
romanticism with its own complicated relationship to religious interpretations of the natural world. Unlike the romantics as Abrams understood
them, Barbauld does not take the failure of the design analogy as an excuse to invent a new poetic language. Instead, she employs the kind of
skeptical strategies we have just examined in the previous chapter, which
contextualize Philo's skepticism about design *arguments* within a wider
culture of *practice*. If we take both halves of Hume's argument seriously—
that the analogical argument is fatally flawed *and* that when it comes to
practices such as religion people do not depend on watertight arguments anyway—then it ought to be possible to remain within the general
vicinity of analogical design arguments without depending on their conceptual impregnability. This is Barbauld's dissenting perspective: design
may lose the battle of ideas, but not the battle of practice.

One goal of this chapter is to fold design back into a discussion of romanticism through the auspices of differences marked by gender and religion. Barbauld's poems move consistently between the natural world
and divinity, and yet they do not demand an adequate theory about
God's relation to creation. Rather, they practice design by fostering the
development of a set of mental dispositions and bodily postures in which
it can operate regardless of its conceptual viability. In arguing that Barbauld takes skepticism about the design analogy as an opportunity to engage in a particular poetic practice, I contrast her with a set of powerful
men who take skepticism much more seriously. John Milton, Joseph
Priestley, and Samuel Taylor Coleridge each, in his own way, interprets
conceptual failure as a problem to be solved through an appeal to a

better language. The debate between Barbauld and these men, registered intertextually in her poetry, marks a contrast of intellectual values.
One set of values puts a premium on getting things right; the other set of
values emphasizes getting by. Following the lead of the philosopher
David Burrell, I shall refer to this distinction as the distinction between
"theory-construction" and "doing philosophy"—or as the distinction between theory and practice, for short.[2] Theory construction, says Burrell,
emphasizes the development of a better language in the face of conceptual failure; here I link it to constructions of romanticism derived from
modernization theory, in which the enlightenment defeat of religion demands of poetry a syntax more adequate to a demystified age. Philosophic practice, in Burrell's account, considers failure and success less
interesting than usefulness and illumination: if a language helps us to get
by, its conceptual impregnability is really beside the point.

The most worked-over version of this distinction within romantic
studies is that between imagination and fancy, which in Coleridge's influential formulation marks the difference between an originary and
synthetic power and one that merely reproduces its materials without
transforming them. Rather than contesting this distinction, Barbauld
simply accepts the lesser term; her status as a religious dissenter and as
an intellectual woman is figured rhetorically by a poetics of fancy traditionally excluded from the constructions of romanticism linked constitutively to secularization. Her poetry's most ambitious claim, I argue, is
that the practices and habits of devotion that sustain natural theology
work best from the fanciful position jointly articulated through gendered and religious difference.

If gender marks a difference between Barbauld and her male inter-
locutors, all the figures discussed here are nevertheless religiously heterodox. Religious dissent bears an important relation to secularization
at the institutional level, its vibrancy demonstrating the vulnerability of
the connection between church and state. In classic Whig historical accounts such as G. M. Trevelyan's *A History of England* (1926), religious
dissent, both rational and orthodox, works in sympathy with parliamentary Whigs to form a progressive strand that runs through Georgian England.[3] This ad hoc alliance of Whigs, Low Anglicans, and dissenters
then comes into more visible conflict with a resurgent Tory Anglicanism
during the years of the American Revolution.[4] It is a matter for historians
whether this picture of a nascent two-party system is accurate; at the very
least, however, it does suggest that dissent's support of tolerance and disestablishment is part of a larger-scale historical process of differentiation.
In my analysis, though, dissenting commitment to differentiation sits
oddly with the totalizing theoretical arguments of Barbauld's male in-
terlocutors. Barbauld herself, meanwhile, takes differentiation more

seriously by following out its poetic implications—both its implications for writing poetry and its implications for thinking about what it is that poetry ought to be and do.[5] Unlike the theoretical projects of some of her fellow dissenters, Barbauld is able to resist the urge to reclaim the center. Indeed, she reveals that the theoretical urge to claim the center—to be once and for all *right*—ironically partakes of the very resistance to differentiation that has proved, historically, to lead to religious decline.

In discussing the contrasting values of theory and practice, and the various poetic techniques that accrue to them, my aim is not to celebrate one set of terms at the expense of the other. Rather, I join the effort to foster a sense of "romanticism" various enough to retain its analytic focus while it expands to meet modes of procedure and practice that at an earlier critical moment seemed alien to it. Hence the seemingly anachronistic business of attending again to those influential earlier accounts such as Abrams's that understood romanticism along secular humanist lines. While scholarship of the intervening decades has disputed much that characterized this approach, our failure to attend analytically to the concept of secularization in the course of that critique continues to hamstring efforts to reimagine the romantic canon. The price of an expanded canon is that we lose secularization as we know it, and this demands some careful thinking about our own investment in that category.

Testimony and Retreat

Barbauld's poem "A Summer Evening's Meditation" describes an intellectual and emotional journey to the heavens and back. The poem seems firmly anchored in the argument from design. To begin with, the night sky is a "field of glories" that are

> worthy of the master: he, whose hand
> With hieroglyphics elder than the Nile,
> Inscrib'd the mystic tablet; hung on high
> To public gaze, and said, adore, O man!
> The finger of thy GOD. (31–35)[6]

But the clear reference to Psalm 19 is troubled by the curious decomposition of the divine creator, who begins as a "master," becomes a "hand," and ends as a "finger." This process makes the object of adoration progressively thinner and more abstract, as if the God of the design argument becomes simply a collection of parts. In order to thicken her devotional response, then, the speaker "[t]urns inward" (54) to her own soul. What she finds there is a "stranger"

Of high descent, and more than mortal rank;
An embryo GOD; a spark of fire divine,
Which must burn on for ages. (55–57)

This discovery, coupled with the divine decomposition of the earlier passage, looks like natural supernaturalism. Yet the speaker, unperturbed, continues on a journey that she understands to be firmly orthodox. She sails upward, accelerating quickly past Saturn and other suns, into "the trackless deeps of space" (82) until she is compelled at last to ask:

What hand unseen
Impels me onward thro' the glowing orbs
Of habitable nature; far remote,
To the dread confines of eternal night,
To solitudes of vast unpeopled space,
The desarts of creation, wide and wild;
Where embryo systems and unkindled suns
Sleep in the womb of chaos? (90–97)

The "embryo systems" and "unkindled suns" take up the figures of the "embryo God" and the "spark of fire divine" the speaker had earlier discovered within herself. Here, it seems, the speaker has found what she is seeking: a stable and apprehensible relationship among self, nature, and God.

Already by this time, however, the seemingly fixed correspondences of the speaker's world are supplemented by a series of other possibilities. Throughout the poem's first movement, images of potentiality abound: sparks, unkindled fires, and the more organic embryos and wombs all suggest a latent content capable of development. The poem thus situates itself between a series of static and largely rhetorical correspondences and a more dynamic movement, two impulses curiously brought together in a description of space that is simultaneously "unpeopled" and redolent with the anthropomorphism of the womb. There is moreover some uncertainty about which aspects of the poet are engaged on this journey. The self-contemplating soul begins the action, but immediately before that agency is ascribed differently:

This dead of midnight is the noon of thought,
And wisdom mounts her zenith with the stars.
At this still hour the self-collected soul
Turns inward. . . . (51–54)

Is thought the same as wisdom? Are either of these the same as the self-collected soul? The figure of wisdom rising with stars suggests a perfect

coincidence between mind and nature, but this is undermined by the suc-
ceeding claim that the vehicle of the poem's ascent is fancy ("on fancy's
wild and roving wing I sail" [72]) and thus anything but natural. Fancy is a
familiar eighteenth-century poetic device, its invocation often signaling
the advent of knowingly poetic language; here, the naturalizing ascription
of wings to fancy hardly conceals the poem's self-consciousness about the
artifice of its procedure.

The poem, then, seems conceptually unsure of itself. It throws elements of the design argument together with a developmental, secularizing narrative. It seems confused about the relationship among thought,
wisdom, and fancy, and about whether its insights are products of poetry
or of nature. The crisis that will shortly ensue is thus implicit in the
poem's own language.

That crisis comes suddenly, as the poet's equipment fails her:

> fancy droops,
> And thought astonish'd stops her bold career.
> But oh thou mighty mind! whose powerful word
> Said, thus let all things be, and thus they were,
> Where shall I seek thy presence? How unblam'd
> Invoke thy dread perfection?
> Have the broad eye-lids of the morn beheld thee?
> Or does the beamy shoulder of Orion
> Support thy throne? (97–105)

Only after the halting or interruption to its line of flight does the poem
address the God it has been seeking. The negative power of the event is
registered in the poem's meter when the first two questions ("Where
shall I seek they presence? How unblamed / Invoke thy dread perfection?") are answered with three beats of silence—the broken blank
verse making manifest the gap between self and God that the poet has
just described. The rhetorical questions that follow, whose cadence
and theme recall God's questions to Job, scarcely fill in that silence,
since their implicit answer in both cases is "no." The net effect of these
four questions is to produce a "mighty mind"—no longer merely a
hand or finger—incommensurate with human categories. Barbauld
here comes as close as any of her contemporaries to a genuinely negative theology.

Whether the poem exemplifies a design argument or whether it is an
exercise in natural supernaturalism does not finally matter, then, for in either case its epistemological confidence is unwarranted. This confidence
is eventually exposed as fallacious by the poem itself, which performs its
own disruption at the moment when "fancy droops, / And thought aston-
ish'd stops her bold career." Cognitive failure is a consequence of rhetori-

cal failure, revealing the supposedly intrinsic connection between language and world as a product of the poet's own intellectual ambitions.

What the poem had confusingly pictured as connection is now revealed as fissured. The anti-humanism accomplished by the description of unpeopled space rebounds back upon the poet when God turns out to be a "mighty mind" who speaks a similarly incorporeal "word." The unusual syntax, in which the word in effect says itself ("whose powerful word / Said"), marks God's language as performative and unconditioned. It is fully adequate to its task ("thus let all things be, and thus they were"), in marked contrast to the poet's words, which are now revealed as both inadequate and presumptuous, demonstrably the product of a human mind that has gotten ahead of itself. This recognition is manifest in a critical failure of poetic resources: fancy droops, meter falters. Searching for a confirmation of correspondence, the poet finds a difference that can be bridged only from above, in the form of the creative word whose power resides in its ability to cross from the immaterial into the material.

Throughout his corpus, Hume makes much of the strictly arbitrary nature of the relation between events and our cognizance of them. In the *Treatise* he dwells at length on the habit of mistaking contiguity for causation. In a notorious essay called "Of Miracles," which he left out of the *Treatise* but later published in *An Enquiry Concerning Human Understanding*, Hume suggests that there can be no internal connection between a miracle and the language in which it is described. Testimony to a miracle is "merely . . . external evidence," he writes, for such language must be paradoxically committed to the truth of a thoroughly unlikely event.[7]

As a result the puzzles of skepticism become intractable. When Hume at last confronts this fact near the end of book I of the *Treatise*, he famously recommends a retreat from the rigors of philosophy and a return to life's customary pleasures:

Most fortunately it happens, that since reason is incapable of dispelling these clouds, nature herself suffices to that purpose, and cures me of this philosophical melancholy and delirium. . . . I dine, I play a game of back-gammon, I converse, and am merry with my friends; and when after three or four hour's amusement, I wou'd return to these speculations, they appear so cold, and strain'd, and ridiculous, that I cannot find in my heart to enter into them any farther. (269)

By "nature" Hume means a human tendency to revert to habitual practices as an escape from reason's cold artifice; he thus implicitly invokes the sensuous and bodily dispositions that he will discuss at greater length in book II of the *Treatise*. Epistemological conundrums are now said to be only abstract problems of reason, to which "nature" conve-

niently offers the solution. This is not Hume's most philosophically rigorous moment, but it is an effort—perhaps not fully realized—to shift the
ground of philosophical conversation by reintroducing things that reason tends to sideline, such as passion, feeling, and the body. The effect is
to use custom and habit to reposition philosophy, to move it from the
center to the periphery. If seeking epistemological certainty drives one
to skepticism, then, as Wittgenstein remarks in a similar context, skeptics don't need to be answered. They need to be cured. The cure, in
Hume's case, is a retreat to the practices of sociability.

Like Hume, Barbauld's concluding lines retreat from the aporia that
the poem has staged:

> But now my soul unus'd to stretch her powers
> In flight so daring, drops her weary wing,
> And seeks again the known accustom'd spot,
> Drest up with sun, and shade, and lawns, and streams,
> A mansion fair and spacious for its guest,
> And full replete with wonders. Let me here
> Content and grateful, wait th' appointed time
> And ripen for the skies: The hour will come
> When all these splendours bursting on my sight
> Shall stand unveil'd, and to my ravish'd sense
> Unlock the glories of the world unknown. (112–22)

The poem ends by rejecting the epistemic privilege it had earlier
claimed. The rhetorical failure that dominates the middle of the poem
means that the speaker will return to earth without any knowledge of
God beyond the experience of his distance from her. "Sun, and shade,
and lawns, and streams" are to be enjoyed for themselves, not for what
they point to. The final, virtually apocalyptic, image of the ravishing
God restates again the distance between this world and God's world,
and thereby constitutes a final rejection of its initial argument by similitude. The next world is of a different order altogether, and until God
chooses to reveal it, it will remain a world unknown.

The poem's final lines nicely realize the halting to which fancy is subjected, a moment whose implicit content was, as we saw, one of rupture.
Again, however, the sternness of the message is tempered by the poem's
refusal to abandon organic imagery and the apparent contentment of a
"known accustom'd spot." The tension between rhetoric and nature that
we noted at the beginning of the poem here reasserts itself, manifested
this time in the disjunction between a poet ripening for the skies and a
God who will burst upon her suddenly from above. In this sense the
poem's language remains intact from start to finish. At the beginning
the artifice of fancy is counteracted by a naturalized wisdom mounting
with the stars; in the middle, the negation and halting that marks the

(non) encounter with God is countered by an anthropomorphic projection of God's pity; at the end, the violence of bursting and ravishing is softened by a ripening poet fully at home in the world. For every acknowledgment of rhetorical inadequacy, it seems, the poem produces an organic assurance of connection.

This careful balancing of the rhetorical and the organic, manifested especially in the valuation of the "known accustom'd spot," is difficult to account for. How do we read a poem that offers us a cure instead of an answer? One method would be to read the poem as still too committed to its analogical heritage to produce the imaginative new syntax of romanticism; reversing that emphasis, we might take the poem's failure to produce a match between its language and the world as the implicit recognition of a temporal rather than spatial destiny and thus as evidence of strength, but read its valuation of custom as a weak retreat from the difficult truth that its language glimpses. Neither approach seems to offer an analytic language that can work with both sides of this poem and account for a ripening poet *and* a ravishing God. Yet Hume's own account of custom argues for its philosophical substance, for if custom escapes the problems of reason, it also identifies reason as a producer of pseudo-problems. "A true sceptic," Hume writes in the closing paragraphs of book I of the *Treatise*, "will be diffident of his philosophical doubts, as well as of his philosophical conviction" (273). The retreat to custom is tactical and not conceptually watertight. Hume in fact says that he has put out to sea in a "weather-beaten vessel" (263). Yet the attempt to shift debate beyond the strictly propositional language of philosophy and theology and into a realm generally associated with such notions as pleasure, disposition, and habit—in short, to remind philosophy and theology that they must share space with the body—is a powerful one. God may be only a disembodied mighty mind, but the poet of "A Summer Evening's Meditation" has to live in the world. What does it mean when a poem turns toward that world?

Two Kinds of Philosophy

Analogy orchestrates the carefully controlled tension between likeness and unlikeness, the organic and the aporetic, in "A Summer Evening's Meditation." Here I would like to introduce a distinction between argument by analogy and analogical language. Arguments by analogy are ratios, in the form *a:b::c:d*. This is the way analogy is used in standard arguments from design (watch is to watchmaker as world is to God), and it is the subject of Philo's relentless attack in the *Dialogues*. This is also the analogical form that inspires the poet's initial self-confidence in "A Summer Evening's Meditation," in which God first appears as a divine artist. One important strand of Christian thinking about analogy, which derives from Aquinas's reading of Aristotle, devotes considerable energy to analogical ratios, for its ultimate aim is to show how certain kinds of words ("one," "being," "substance," "good") could be applied to God. What does it mean to say that God is one, or that he has being? When we use such terms we are deriving their meaning from our own human experience; since God is radically different from human beings, such terms can be applied to God only analogically. Analogy is thus a built-in reminder of the difference between God and humanity, but it also gives mortals a way of speaking about God. The ultimate aim here is to stabilize what seems like the absolute pluralism of language. Thus one contemporary representative of this position argues that we need a portrayal of analogy "that construes the superficially chaotic data as the logical outcome of simple linguistic universals."[8]

In contrast to such arguments by analogy, what I shall call "analogical language" is less concerned with stability and ratios than it is with understanding the contexts in which language is practiced. This tradition of thinking about analogy can also find its roots in Aristotle; more recently, it has been influenced by Wittgenstein and ordinary language philosophy. For this second tradition, more concerned with the practice of analogy than with its theoretical stability, analogical statements are not arguments per se, and certainly not claims that can be reduced to a ratio such as *a:b::c:d*, but rather ways of using a language, verbal recommendations whose aim is to illuminate something true about the world. In this tradition the use of words in particular circumstances, rather than their definition, is of primary importance. David Burrell notes that in this way of thinking about analogy, "what turns up is more a way of doing philosophy than a set of conclusions."[9]

Underwriting these two ways of thinking about analogy are the two ways of looking at the philosophical tradition itself that I described earlier as "theory" and "practice." For the former, the history of philosophy is the history of accumulating positions and building upon them. For the latter, philosophy is an activity, and learning to do it means assuming viewpoints rather than accumulating them. In one, philosophy means answers and conclusions; in the other, philosophy means a certain kind of behavior. Burrell takes Socrates, the great practitioner of philosophy who never wrote anything down and whose only method was continual questioning, as an archetype of the latter attitude. The death of Socrates, consequently, represents an attempt to shut down the ambiguities he delighted in opening up, to exchange the fluidity of philosophical practice for the stability of theoretical knowledge. And yet the very presence

of analogous language in philosophical argument, Burrell writes, "testifies to that feature which distinguished philosophy from theory construction, and links learning philosophy firmly with doing it. For theory
construction demands that its key terms remain unambiguous. The formulation must stand still if it is to admit of multiple application. But
analogous terms may usefully be described as 'systematically ambiguous.' It is as though one can never let them out of sight" (5–6). At stake
in these conceptions of analogy, then, is a more general posture toward
what counts as success in the history of ideas. The theoretical side, the
side more inclined to view analogy as an argument, is also the side more
likely to take intellectual defeat seriously. What Burrell calls the "philosophical" side, the side more inclined to view analogy as a linguistic
practice, is also the side more likely to take intellectual defeat lightly
and to recommend retreating to something else when the puzzles become intractable.[10]

Burrell's distinction corresponds very well to Hume's distinction between the lonely contemplation that ends in skepticism and the sociable
games of backgammon that displace skepticism. And yet in the *Dialogues*
Hume cannily makes both Philo and Cleanthes into theorists rather
than practitioners. Philo views natural theology as a theory, and as such
he demands the sort of stability from it that he knows it cannot provide.
His relentless claim that analogy cannot deliver real knowledge indicates that he thinks of analogy as an impossible search for permanence.
Cleanthes, for his part, agrees with Philo's reading of natural theology
as a theoretical construction. Rather than attempting to make his own
position more flexible, he accepts an all-or-nothing interpretation of
their disagreement. And yet, as we saw in the previous chapter, the dialogue form itself and Pamphilus's parting conclusion give the lie to this
shared intellectual posture. It may be, as Hume himself had recognized
in the *Treatise*, that if the only choices on offer are complete skepticism
and arbitrary dogmatism, the best thing to do is to restore one's faith in
common life by playing a game of backgammon with friends. In the case
of the *Dialogues*, the conversation itself functions as a form of backgammon, since it is designed to showcase the fact that the practices of sociability are of greater importance than the reasonings of a theorist isolated
in his study. If this is the correct reading, then the *Dialogues* themselves
(as distinct from the various arguments they contain) would be an example of analogy as a philosophical practice: an activity rather than a set
of conclusions. On this reading, the residue of the *Dialogues Concerning
Natural Religion* is a notion of analogy as language that illuminates the
world.

This is a reading of the *Dialogues* very much against the grain of Philo's interpretation of things and perhaps against the grain of Hume's as well. Hume cleverly writes as if our only choices are between theory constructors such as Cleanthes and theory destroyers such as Philo. But if we are able to see that both Cleanthes and Philo share a conception of what philosophy is, and that there might in fact be another sort of philosophy altogether (perhaps the kind of philosophy that Pamphilus hints at when he arbitrarily awards victory to Cleanthes), then analogy can reenter the picture not as a ratio nor an argument but as a linguistic practice that illuminates truths otherwise unavailable. Thus a poem such as "A Summer Evening's Meditation," which begins in great confidence but ends in humility, may demonstrate the futility of argument by analogy without abandoning analogical language. Indeed, amid claiming that God is unknowable, Barbauld applies concepts to God that make sense only by analogy: God has a "voice," he "looks," and he has a "mind," for instance. The appearance of these words in a poem dedicated to remarking upon the separation between humanity and God may be taken as a performative illustration of something true of language in general: to describe similarity accurately is to acknowledge the fact of difference, and to describe difference accurately is to presuppose a concept of similarity.[11]

The Devilish Enginery of Theory

Barbauld doubtless knew of Hume's skeptical arguments—though not the *Dialogues*, which were not published until 1779.[12] She responds more directly to other writers, chiefly John Milton and her own mentor, the dissenting theologian and scientist Joseph Priestley.[13] Milton's influence can be felt in the language of "A Summer Evening's Meditation," whereas Priestley's spirit shadows many of the poems in Barbauld's 1773 volume. By uncovering the powerful and disturbing presences of these men within Barbauld's poetry, we can reconstruct the manner in which Barbauld portrays them as theorists and herself as a devotee of practice.

Paradise Lost exerts considerable pressure on "A Summer Evening's Meditation." When Barbauld describes "the dread confines of eternal night" and the "solitudes of vast unpeopled space" as a place where "embryo systems and unkindled suns / Sleep in the womb of chaos" (93, 94, 96–97), she echoes Milton's description of Satan and Sin looking out from the gate of Hell:

> a dark
> Illimitable Ocean without bound,
> Without dimension, where length, breadth, and highth,
> And time and place are lost; where eldest *Night*
> And *Chaos*, Ancestors of Nature, hold
> Eternal Anarchy. . . .
> . . . .

> Into this wild Abyss,
> The Womb of nature and perhaps her Grave,
> ....
>   the wary fiend
> Stood on the brink of Hell and look'd a while,
> Pondering his Voyage. (2.891–96, 2.910–11, 2.917–19)

The Miltonic allusions come at the crucial moment of Barbauld's poem, when the speaker pauses to consider whether she will continue her voyage into the womb of chaos; her decision to continue might thus be understood as a Satanic choice. Indeed, *Paradise Lost* links Satan with just the kind of writing in which the speaker of "A Summer Evening's Meditation" engages: the kind of writing that seeks equality with God. Milton describes God's language as performative: "Silence, ye troubled waves, and thou deep, peace / Said then the omnific word, your discord end" (7.216–17). Echoing Milton, Barbauld describes a God "whose powerful word / Said, thus let all things be, and thus they were" (99–100). Satan tries to show that the various feats of engineering in which he engages are equal to this performative power. He creates a palace that imitates the one in heaven, and he leads his hosts into battle confident that the canons he has forged can match heavenly thunderbolts. These canons, described by the narrator as "devilish Enginery" (6.553), resemble a huge, phallic writing instrument: "hollow Engines long and round / Thick ramm'd" that will send forth "Such implements of mischief as shall dash / To pieces, and o'erwhelm whatever stands / Adverse" (6.484–85, 6.488–90). Satan hopes to inscribe this giant phallus pen upon the world in a great act of writing and self-invention.

What is the origin of such Satanic desire in "A Summer Evening's Meditation"? In several other poems from the 1773 volume, Joseph Priestley, the intellectual leader of the dissenters, appears in terms that recall Milton's description of Satan. Though Priestley and Barbauld had a warm personal relationship, his own intellectual ambition, inflected through gender and age differentials, led him to think of her as very much his own project. He reported that Barbauld wrote the lead poem of the 1773 volume, "An Address to the Deity," after hearing a sermon of his. And in his *Memoirs* he declared that "Mrs. Barbauld has told me that it was the perusal of some verses of mine, that first induced her to write any thing in verse, so that this country is in some measure indebted to me for one of the best poets it can boast of."[14] Priestley is overtly present in a number of the poems in the 1773 volume, and his tendency to place himself inside his pupil's work raises the possibility of his implicit presence elsewhere.

A mock epic from the 1773 volume, "A Fragment of an Epic Poem,

Occasioned by the Loss of a Game of Chess to Dr. Priestley, in Consequence of an Unseasonable Drowsiness," pictures the relationship of
teacher and pupil in affectionate but decidedly ambivalent terms. The
opening of the poem is notable for the sexual innuendo embedded in a
friendly but fierce intellectual competition. A "hostile maid" refuses "to
yield, / The honours of the long disputed field;" (1–2); her knightly
opponent "despair[s] by open force to gain / Victorious laurels on the
chequer'd plain" (5–6). Desperate, the knight strikes a bargain with
"Morpheus," allowing Barbauld to satirize Priestley's preaching and
scholarship as guaranteed soporifics. Morpheus puts the maid to sleep,
and the result is devastation. The maid's squadrons are broken, her
pawns "in wild disorder lie," her troops turn pale and give themselves
over to "ruin," "confusion," and "shameful flight." Meanwhile the con-
queror presses his advantage with "ardent hopes" and "a new flush of
more enliven'd red" (44, 45). There is an evident sexual charge in these
lines, with the flushed and ardent knight looming over a maid whose defenses lie in wild disorder and confusion. Since the maid's ardour has
fled with the onset of sleep, the desire is all on the side of the knightly
attacker, who here realizes something like Satan's wish to "dash / To
pieces, and o'erwhelm whatever stands / Adverse" with his masculine
cannon.

   To be sure, the predominant tone of this poem is of a shared satire on
the knight's competitiveness and the speaker's sleepiness. Still, the
Priestley whom Barbauld presents here is one whose competitive ardor
overruns the chivalric code. In violation of his own empirical intellectual orientation he is willing to cut a deal with divinity in order to get
what he wants. The irony in this case, which Barbauld wittily exploits, is
that his victory results not in the orderly production of scientific knowledge but in scattering and confusion. The "Fragment" shows a Priestley
whose desire fails to respect limits, and consequently the mild narcis-
sism on display when Priestley claims credit for Barbauld's poetic career
gets a harder edge here: in the classic rape scene toward which the
"Fragment" gestures, the rake believes that ravishing the maid will instill
in her the sexual desire she has never felt before.

   The desire to make Christianity more palatable to intellectuals inspired both Priestley's scientific and theological interests. His aim, as he
put it in his *Memoirs*, was "to defend Christianity, and to free it from
those corruptions which prevent its reception with philosophical and
thinking persons" (111). He apparently thought that it was up to him
and a few others to save religion by pluralizing and democratizing the
church, but his belief in tolerance coexists with a basic intellectual posture that, following Burrell's terms, we may call "theoretical." Priestley

imagines the consequences of intellectual arguments in the most absolute terms; for him, Christianity will be saved or destroyed at the level of ideas, in a battle of rival systems, Platonic dualism against his own philosophic monism. The belief that only one of these can be right leads to a systematic and very extensive writing program: voluminous political, scientific, personal, and theological writings, elements of the single immense religioscientific system he viewed himself as developing.[15] Priestley's correspondence reveals a similarly bellicose nature: he engaged in lengthy pamphlet wars with his opponents, eventually browbeating many of them into silence.

Priestley was well known for his experiments with electricity, and "lightning" is a word that crops up in several of Barbauld's descriptions of him. In "A Character of Joseph Priestley," also in the 1773 volume, he is

> Champion of Truth! alike thro Nature's field,
> And where in sacred leaves she shines reveal'd,
> Alike in both, eccentric, piercing, bold,
> Like his own lightnings, which no chains can hold,
> Neglecting caution and disdaining art,
> He seeks no armour for a naked heart. (1–6)

The figure of Priestley as truth's champion is an odd one, since the description that follows presents him more as truth's pursuer than her defender. The rapaciousness of his search ("piercing, bold") picks up his behavior in the "Fragment," where the chivalric code similarly served as a screen for an ignoble strategy. Beneath the affection, the poem's implication is that those who make much of standing up for truth are actually making it in their own image; Priestley's "bold[ness]" treats neither nature nor scripture as sites of revelation in the strict sense. In consequence he behaves as a free agent; like lightning, which in its momentary flash of brilliant illumination seems an autonomous phenomenon, Priestley has come unchained from a feminized heart, which is left vulnerable and defenseless when the champion marches off to war with his phallic weapons.

Boasting to his comrades of his newly made cannon, Satan compares them to lightning: "they shall fear," he says of the heavenly host, "we have disarm'd/The Thunderer of his only dreaded bolt" (6.490–91). Satan claims to equal God's power through this cannon; he assumes that good engineering will erase the line between artifice and nature. His entire rebellion, indeed, is premised on the notion that God's claim to priority can be overcome through sufficiently impressive artifice. To control lightning is therefore a paradoxical project, since it depends both on allowing lightning the autonomy that would make it symbolic of absolute power, and on rendering it instrumental, hence adaptable to a specific end. From Milton's perspective this is an incoherent position for anyone but God (who created lightning) to assume; but Satan's skill as a rhetorician manages, for a time, to make this paradox productive rather than debilitating.

Priestley's own belief about his "lightnings" has the marks of Satan's instrumental reasoning. In *The History and Present State of Electricity*, he declares that electricity makes the scientist the "master of the powers of nature."[16] Thomas Cooper, Priestley's most distinguished scientific disciple, writes in the same spirit that "science compels every object around us to contribute, in some way or other, to our pleasure, to our profit, to our comfort, or to our convenience."[17] Barbauld, a much more ambivalent disciple, fills in what such enthusiasm leaves out. In "A Character of Joseph Priestley," lightning is an image of the human mind unchained, and Priestley can convince himself that he controls it only at the cost of leaving his heart behind. Lacking that heart, the explorer ranges over nature as if he owns it; he pushes his way into places he should not go because he persuades himself that he is simply engaged in the neutral activity of replacing error with truth. But, as the knight discovers in the "Fragment," piercing something changes it instead of simply illuminating it. Claiming to own lightning is the kind of thing you do, in short, when you think that the usual rules don't apply to you—or, in Barbauld's figure, when you have left your heart behind. The figure of lightning as it appears in Milton, Barbauld, and Priestley thus reads as a debate about human autonomy that traces itself back to a Satanic blurring of the distinction between human artifice and divine law. When she pauses to ask what unseen hand is pushing her "thro' . . . habitable nature," the speaker of Barbauld's poem is poised on the edge of a theoretical Satanic journey; the hand that pushes her in that direction may well be that of the mentor and friend who himself ranges "piercingly" "thro' Nature's field."

Analogy and the Unknown God

Satan's "devilish Enginery" is difficult to resist, even for those who recognize its dangers. Indeed, for all his condemnation of Satan's ambitions, Milton himself appears to fall prey to it. The invocation of the Holy Spirit at the beginning of *Paradise Lost*, though full of the requisite humility, also registers Milton's sense that he is engaged in a great and original act. His poem will pursue "Things Unattempted yet in Prose or Rhyme" (1.16); it will "assert Eternal Providence, / And justify the ways of God to men" (1.25–26). As many have pointed out, this claim opens Milton to precisely the sort of theological heresies the entire poem seeks to shut down. For to justify the ways of God implies both that God's ways need justifying and that Milton is the man to do it. And these twin notions—a questioning of God's unconditioned status and a subtle elevation of the self—are just the qualities that define Satan within the text of *Paradise Lost.* The entire poem, with its massive assertion of poetic ability, its endless feats of invention, its continual subterranean assertion, like a drumbeat, of Milton's greatness—all this is, in a word, Satanic. When William Blake writes in *The Marriage of Heaven and Hell* that Milton is "of the devil's party without knowing it," he means among other things that Milton's self-righteousness betrays the poem's own antinomian impulses.[18] Milton too employs the devilish enginery of theory when he trades poetic power and ambiguity for final and definitive answers.

The problem with this reading of Milton, as Blake himself came to recognize, is that it commits itself to an interminable battle between freedom and constraint, oppression and liberation. Theoretical closure and antinomian multiplicity turn out to be parasitic upon each other; each becomes the other in a closed system from which there is no exit. We have already seen a version of this in the various Humean debates between skepticism and dogmatism—debates that come to no end for the very reason that though the debaters come down on opposite sides of the issue, they actually share a preconception of what a proper philosophical argument looks like. The way out of this impasse, Hume suggests, is to reenter the social world, play a game of backgammon, change the conversation. In like manner, Barbauld avoids the dramatic Blakean dynamic of subversion and oppression. Though critical of the totalizing logic of theory, she does not commit therefore to a radical multiplicity nor to the ideal of unfettered freedom. Instead, she changes the conversation through a poetic practice whose dominant figures are fancy and analogy.

Analogy appears in a later poem of Barbauld's, "To an Unknown God," which describes a world-weary modern traveler arriving in Athens to view the altars to various gods. They all look much the same, until one, dedicated to "the God unknown," catches his eye:

Age after age has rolled away,
Altars and thrones have felt decay,
    Sages and saints have risen;
And, like a giant roused from sleep
Man has explored the pathless deep,
    And lightnings snatched from heaven.
. . . .
And many a shrine in dust is laid,
Where kneeling nations homage paid,

By rock, or fount, or grove:
Ephesian Dian sees no more
Her workmen fuse the silver ore,
    Nor capitolian Jove.

Yet still, where'er presumptuous man
His Maker's essence strives to scan,
    And lifts his feeble hands;
Tho' saint and sage their powers unite,
To fathom that abyss of light,
    Ah! still that altar stands. (13–24, 31–36)

Refusing the binary of a mysterious religious past and a rational demystified present, this poem works by putting into question the notions of scientific progress through which enlightened Europe claims to master the world. Barbauld's proto-Byronic traveler is not allowed the self-gratification that characterizes nostalgia, namely the pleasure of encountering monuments to the past and thus being reminded that he is part of a superior age even as he mourns the passing of time. Nostalgia is the luxury of progress, a nascently modernizing plotline; in rejecting progress the poem replaces nostalgia with reverence, for when it comes to understanding God, nothing has changed. The poem thus pictures secularization less as the by-product of modernization than as a kind of fatigue that is capable of being reversed by a sufficiently imaginative presentation. If the prevailing ethos of modernity is not optimism but *ennui* with humanity's continual efforts at progress, then another sort of sensibility, such as that inspired by the altar, may begin to have a purchase upon the mind. This is an important and perhaps surprising point, for it suggests that modern scientific rationality opens the door to religious experience.

Once again, the argument is mounted intertextually. In this case, the original scene comes from the New Testament book of Acts, in which the Apostle Paul confronts the philosophers in Athens:

Then Paul stood in the midst of Mars' hill, and said, *Ye* men of Athens, I perceive that in all things ye are too superstitious. For as I passed by, and beheld your devotions, I found an altar with this inscription, TO THE UNKNOWN GOD. Whom therefore ye ignorantly worship, him declare I unto you. God that made the world and all things therein, seeing that he is Lord of heaven and earth, dwelleth not in temples made with hands; Neither is worshipped with men's hands, as though he needed any thing, seeing he giveth to all life, and breath, and all things; And hath made of one blood all nations of men for to dwell on all the face of the earth, and hath determined the times before appointed, and the bounds of their habitation; That they should seek the Lord, if haply they might feel after him, and find him, though he be not far from every one of us: For in him we live, and move, and have our being; as certain also of your own poets have said, For we are also his offspring. (Acts 17:22–28)

Paul claims to know clearly what the altar to the unknown God merely gestures toward, his narrative filling in the blank space marked by the inscription. Yet his presentation needs to be contrasted to Miltonic theodicy. Paul is supremely self-confident; but he is careful to avoid the implication the God needs his help, and he acknowledges the cultural variety that surrounds him. The scene he describes is one of diversity ("all nations") tied to a single point ("one blood") because they all share the same creator, and it is this combination that provides the opening for his notion of evangelism in which all people can "feel after" God. Most interestingly for Barbauld's purposes, Paul adds a codicil regarding poetic language. Even pagan poets have a dim sense of the godly means by which they are tied together with other humans, and this comes through in their own language about divinity, which Paul is happy to quote as evidence. Thus the language of poetry registers what philosophy is unable to understand, namely that all human variety is tied together at the single, shared point of the divine creator.

Now the Athenians should know what Paul is talking about here, for Aristotle himself had made a similar point about poetic language. In the *Categories* Aristotle makes a distinction between two kinds of words. Equivocal words use the same word to refer to entirely different things. Univocal words refer to the same sort of thing. For example (and this is Aristotle's example), if we were to say that a man and a picture are both animals, "animal" here is equivocal, for it is clearly being used with reference to two different sorts of being. But if we were to say that a man and an ox are animals, "animal" is here univocal, since it refers to the same sort of being.[19] One problem with this neat division, as Aristotle himself realized, is that it cannot account for certain kinds of words that are transcategorical, words such as "one" and "being" and "good," which are neither univocal nor equivocal. Thus Aristotle writes in the *Metaphysics*: "there are many senses in which a thing may be said to 'be,' but they are related to one central point, one definite kind of thing."[20] If we say that this book exists and that love exists, we are clearly using the word "exists" in a similar way, though we don't mean exactly the same thing by it, since a book is a physical object and love is not. To account for this sort of thing we need a category that is neither univocal nor equivocal but somewhere in between.

In the *Topics* Aristotle mentions metaphor as a mediating category between univocal and equivocal (158b10). His feelings about metaphor are ambivalent, however, since his philosophic project largely turns on making distinctions, and metaphors often introduce confusion. Thus in the *Rhetoric* Aristotle comes out in favor of "proportional" metaphors— that is, those that display an analogical structure. David Burrell, thread-

ing his way through this exposition, interprets analogy as a category between equivocal and univocal language. Analogy on this reading becomes the expression of the phenomenon that Aristotle had noted in
the *Metaphysics*, in which words used in an obviously different manner
are also "related to one central point, one definite kind of thing."

This is exactly the point that Paul makes to the Athenian philosophers,
and it indicates how Barbauld's poetic project can be described as "analogical." In Acts the Athenians are portrayed as true pluralists, genuinely
interested in any new idea that comes their way but not prepared to
judge the truth of any. The altar to the unknown god is there simply to
cover any gods they do not know about yet, and this is why they are willing to hear Paul out. Surveying this radical variety, Paul tells the Athenians that the language of their own poetic tradition, if they would pay
attention to it, belies their equivocal position. This is not an argument
about the content of religion—Paul is not suggesting that the Greek poets had an intimation of Christian doctrine. Rather, he is making a point
about language itself. Simply by being true to their craft, the Greek poets
expressed about the divine what is also true of the God about whom Paul
is preaching. The poets did this by analogy—that is, they chose words
that, though clearly differing in meaning and context from the way Paul
employs them, do not differ radically enough to count as the sort of
equivocation that the pluralist Athenian philosophers are mistakenly celebrating. A second and related analogy resides in the act of creation itself, for the poets who wrote of the gods perform analogously to the God
who made all human beings of one blood. This analogical reading of the
pagan poets allows Paul to grant them legitimacy without subscribing to
the relativism of the Greek philosophers to whom he speaks.

Although Barbauld is considerably more cautious than Paul, she models her own poetic discussion of the Unknown God on his example. Her
poem criticizes the joint logic of spiritual nostalgia and technological
progress, but it carefully avoids both an equivocal pluralism (in which
all religious expressions amount to the same thing) and a univocal confidence (which would replace the unknown god with a known one). "A
term belongs to different sciences," writes Aristotle in the *Metaphysics*,
"not if it has different senses, but if its definitions neither are identical
nor can be referred to one central meaning" (1004a23). That is, words
belong in different categories only if they carry with them incommensurate conceptual schemes, such as Blake's categories of Heaven and Hell.
In Paul's reading of the situation, which I am arguing is also Barbauld's,
human creation and divine creation do not belong to "different sciences," for their distinct context-dependent renderings of the very idea
of divine being are tied up to a central point. It is therefore not incoherent for Barbauld to describe the blankness of the altar *and* refer to the

Unknown God as her maker. Such predication is not the same thing as claiming to know God. It does, however, mean that the poet does not put the Unknown God at the same level as all the other gods, as the Athenians do. Rather, it means that whatever *is* said about him has already been recognized, beforehand, as inadequate. This poem is an explicit meditation on the representational adequacy of language, and it establishes for itself an analogical space between the univocal attitudes of Satan and Priestley, on the one hand, and the equivocal attitudes of Blake and the Greek philosophers, on the other.

It is clear, then, that "theory" as I have described it can be either univocal or equivocal. Both take seriously an intellectual history that gives pride of place to tenable arguments; they search for a new and better language, which is what keeps them writing. Though they disagree on what is right, the univocal and the equivocal positions share the belief that getting it right is what matters. But people who believe that will never be satisfied—that is why Wittgenstein waggishly suggests that they need to be cured of their belief. A cure might mean simply changing the conversation: that is what Hume recommends when he retreats from solitary thinking to sociability and to pleasant games of backgammon. A cure can also mean deciding that when it comes to divinity, arguments don't matter as much as finding a language that enables habits and practices of devotion.

Fancy and Imagination

The "theoretical" version of the design argument that we have been tracing so far is given an influential restatement by Samuel Taylor Coleridge, who began his own intellectual and literary career as a disciple of Priestley. Characteristically, Coleridge is all over the map when it comes to design, but there is a basic (and familiar) pattern to his thinking that moves from enlightenment radicalism through canonical romanticism to late conservatism. Thus in the 1795 *Lectures on Revealed Religion,* a youthful Coleridge sounds like Archbishop Tillotson, mocking an atheism that supposed the universe came about by a lucky accident, "even as you may easily suppose," writes Coleridge, "a vast number of Gold & Brass Particles accidentally commoved by the Wind would after infinite Trials form themselves into a polished and accurate Watch or Timepiece!"[21] In focusing on the corruptions of revealed religion, the young Coleridge adopts Tillotson's established reasonableness and adds a radical, revolutionary-era inflection. In his hands the design argument reveals its origins in an enlightenment culture shared by a variety of intellectuals, from deists to natural philosophers to orthodox theologians. In his later phase, though, Coleridge construes things somewhat differently: "Assume the existence of God,—and then the harmony and fitness of the physical creation may be shown to correspond with and support such an assumption;—but to set about *proving* the existence of a God by such means is a mere circle, a delusion."[22] Critiques of design such as Hume's have had their effect, apparently; now Coleridge is arguing that belief in God comes from somewhere else, from an "assumption" that, to refer to Cleanthes' own analogy, must appear as arbitrary within the parameters of strictly rational argument. Like Pamphilus, though, Coleridge thinks that this arbitrary assumption is not much of problem.

Coleridge's two arguments, separated by nearly forty years, seem to map the changing fortunes of design onto a familiar narrative of romantic political apostasy, in which trading an enlightened idea of what the design argument can accomplish for a more chastened sense of its limits figures the abandonment of enlightenment radicalism for proto-Victorian conservatism. In the remainder of this chapter, however, I would like to disentangle the religious narrative from the narrative of personal apostasy and conservatism. Inflected through gender difference, Coleridge's chastened sense of design in 1834 was for Barbauld in 1773 an important means of *claiming* agency, not surrendering it. Her celebrations of habit, discipline, analogy, and fancy variously figure God not as an object of knowledge but as the recipient of a set of practices. In this respect her use of design is importantly antidevelopmental, dedicated to modes of agency focused on repetition rather than innovation.

I turn first to the relationship between gender and fancy. Between the bookends of the radical enlightenment Coleridge and the conservative Victorian Coleridge comes the figure we can name the "romantic Coleridge," author of these famous lines from the *Biographia Literaria*:

The IMAGINATION then I consider either as primary, or secondary. The primary IMAGINATION I hold to be the living Power and prime Agent of all human Perception, and as a repetition in the finite mind of the eternal act of creation in the infinite I AM. The secondary I consider as an echo of the former, co-existing with the conscious will, yet still as identical with the primary in the kind of its agency, and differing only in degree, and in the mode of its operation. It dissolves, diffuses, dissipates, in order to re-create; or where this process is rendered impossible, yet still at all events it struggles to idealize and to unify. It is essentially vital, even as all objects (as objects) are essentially fixed and dead.

FANCY, on the contrary, has no other counters to play with, but fixities and definites. The Fancy is indeed no other than a mode of Memory emancipated from the order of time and space; and blended with, and modified by that empirical phenomenon of the will, which we express by the word CHOICE. But equally with the ordinary memory it must receive all its materials ready made from the law of association.[23]

This influential discussion of the imagination elevates unity over diversity and synthesis over separation. For Coleridge there is a single ideal language toward which poetry strives, an ideal that mirrors divine creation. Against this theoretical ideal he poses fancy, which is a kind of nontransformative practice.[24]

In the context of the rest of book 13 of the *Biographia Literaria*, however, the distinction between fancy and imagination begins to seem less secure. Indeed, the chapter as a whole may be taken to deliver a message exactly opposite to the one communicated by this well-known excerpt, for Coleridge is unable to support the distinction that he marks out. The chapter begins with a philosophical discussion whose somewhat confused point is that Kant's transcendental deduction can be modified so as to demonstrate the necessity of the imagination as that which overcomes the opposition between two incommensurate forces. Having gotten this far, Coleridge interrupts his own text in order to reproduce a letter from a friend, who claims to have read the chapter in its entirety, and who advises Coleridge to withdraw it. He gives two reasons. First, "you have been obliged to omit so many links, from the necessity of compression, that what remains, looks . . . like the fragments of the winding steps of a ruined tower" (302–3). Second, the friend worries that Coleridge will alienate his audience:

This Chapter, which cannot, when it is printed, amount to so little as an hundred pages, will of necessity greatly increase the expense of the work; and every reader who, like myself, is neither prepared or perhaps calculated for the study of so abstruse a subject so abstrusely treated, will . . . be almost entitled to accuse you of a sort of imposition on him. For who, he might truly observe, could from your title-page, viz. "My Literary Life and Opinions," published too as an introductory to a volume of miscellaneous poems, have anticipated, or even conjectured, a long treatise on ideal Realism. (303)

Coleridge declares himself convinced by this letter, and so ends by stating simply the "result" of the chapter, namely the distinction between fancy and imagination quoted previously.

The friend is fictitious, of course, but Coleridge's anxiety is very real. Chapter 13 aspired to a grand unified theory; instead of admitting his inability to deliver it, Coleridge introduces friendly objections whose terms innocently reveal the failed project that confronts the reader. The issue of readerly deception here is crucial. Theory ("ideal Realism") is expensive, and its potential to inflate the cost of the volume is all the more worrisome because it appears under false pretenses by masquerading under the sign of practical literary criticism. According to the friend, theory should come labeled as theory—this would prevent it from being a hidden cost that drives up the price of the work. But to make this argument is to return the reader to the very Kantian distinction between pure and practical reason that the theory of imagination was supposed to overcome. The failure of chapter 13, then, is not simply the failure to follow through on a promise; it is rather an implicit ac-knowledgment that the problem it addresses is built into the project's very language, so that the divide between theory and practice, pure and practical reason, subject and object, will *necessarily* return to haunt any achievement that claims to have transcended it. To recur to Coleridge's own monetary analogy, the cost of theory will always outrun the ability of the public to pay for it. Imagination's perpetual and self-authorizing ability to create, like the fabulous resourcefulness of capital itself, re-quires an initial borrowing from fancy whose standing as imagination's condition of possibility means that the loan can never fully be paid back.

Indeed, the self-conscious exhibition of failure, the capitulation to the world of objects, the inability to seize upon material and transform it—these are the characteristics of fancy. This means that the entire exercise that chapter 13 performs, particularly in its invention of the practical friend, is an extended flight of fancy that, for all its stated ambition, hasn't managed to combine opposites but rather remains a testament to their continued distinctiveness. If this is the case, then imagination appears only under conditions drawn up by fancy, the dis-tinction between fancy and imagination is produced by fancy itself, and imagination's idea of itself as radically unconditioned is a case of self-deception.

In Hume's *Dialogues*, Philo's argument against the analogy of a human designer to a divine designer is that humans merely rearrange existing material, whereas the God of orthodoxy creates *ex nihilo*. Because we have no experience of such divine creation, when we compare the de-sign of the world to the design of a house, all that the analogy can validly deliver is a God who rearranges existing materials. We are free, of course, to believe in an unconditioned God, but we do so not because analogical reasoning has led us there inevitably but because we have leaped over the inherent limitations of analogy and, in an "arbitrary act of the mind," produced a God who transcends his materials and is in fact the condition of their possibility. Coleridge's distinction between fancy and imagination nicely parallels this argument. Like a carpenter who merely rearranges existing materials, fancy must receive its materi-als "ready-made." And like a God who creates *ex nihilo*, the secondary imagination brings something new into the world. Where Philo had regarded the differences between a carpenter and God as devastating for the design argument, however, Coleridge understands things the other way around: the arbitrary act that allows the mind to leap into the pres-ence of divinity is relabeled "imagination" and set up as the ideal toward which poetry itself strives. Humean skepticism about traditional ways of narrating the connection between creator and creation becomes an op-portunity for a new theory of language that claims for humanity what had before been the preserve of the divine. In this way a secularization narrative underwrites the contrast that romantic criticism of the twentieth century would institutionalize when it opposed analogy to romanticism's "new poetic syntax" of image and symbol. In this interpretation, fancy is a poetic mode that cannot do other than reiterate its role as that which is determined by its materials, and it thus becomes, like analogy, an example of poetry locked in tradition.

Yet the elaborate textual maneuverings of the *Biographia Literaria* here indicate that by 1817 Coleridge was well aware that a truly unconditioned language was not a possibility for him, and that imagination would always fall back into fancy. The *Biographia*'s natural supernaturalism is not a confident narration of smooth historical progress from tradition to modernity; it feels instead like a desperate and probably failed leap into modernity, with tradition (as fancy) still tugging at the leaper's heels. Perhaps, though, the opposition of tradition to modernity, like that of oppression to freedom, actually distorts the historical process. Rather than a mode that blocks a natural development toward modernity, fancy might be one way of *becoming* modern.

This will be true only if we lift the burden of modernization from this passage, and that is where gender becomes crucial. For Coleridge's *Biographia* passage not only depicts imagination as decisively modern; it also genders modernity as masculine. In the eighteenth century fancy and imagination had been used more or less interchangeably and were generally associated with the feminine in opposition to masculine reason. In distinguishing imagination from fancy, then, Coleridge masculinizes one poetic faculty at the expense of another. The ground had been well prepared for him in this regard, since by the end of the eighteenth century fancy had been firmly linked to the domestic, diminutive, and decorative aspects of the feminine and the energetic and productive aspects of the mechanical.[25] More generally, fancy is insubstantial, airy, and artificial in the sense of being fabricated, a vehicle or staging that offers a lot of movement but little change. Linking mechanism and domesticity, William Cowper had declared in *The Task* that fancy, "like the finger of a clock, / Runs the great circuit, and is still at home."[26] Notwithstanding fancy's apparent freedom, it never escapes its temporal conditions of possibility.

In "A Summer Evening's Meditation" it is on "fancy's wild and roving wing" that the speaker undertakes her journey, and it is fancy's limited staying power that is made explicitly to contrast with the unconditioned creative word of God. Like Coleridge in the *Biographia*, Barbauld imagines an encounter with God's creative word, and like him she recognizes the vast distance between that word and her own human words. But where Coleridge tries to bridge the gap with a theory of imagination, Barbauld does not: she stops, turns around, and goes home.[27] Fancy offers the salutary reminder that language too has material conditions. The temptation to transcend them never goes away, of course, and so fancy also acts as a structural reminder of the impossibility of such transcendence; as a poetic vehicle that by definition simply tinkers with its materials, it reminds the poet of the conditioned status of her language. To speak of a poet's "choice" of fancy or imagination may seem misleading, however, for these choices are decisively gendered. Imaginative enfranchisement is implicitly masculine, in contrast to the constrained or determined "choice" of feminine fancy. In this sense Barbauld does not in fact have a choice when it comes to a poetic vehicle, for women in the later eighteenth century can hardly be poets of the imagination. As Julie Ellison puts it, fancy is "an allegory of women's literary ambition" in both its aims and its built-in failure.[28]

The poem itself, however, demonstrates the freedom to be found within this nonchoice, freedom unavailable to the notion of autonomy to which Coleridge ties his theory of imagination. Fancy's status as a gendered poetic mode that rearranges a given script offers means for living with the possibilities that adhere to a marginalized and nontransformative poetics. Its circumscribed movement is oriented not toward liberal conceptions of freedom but toward a self trained in an active, anticipatory waiting. By the same token, this is not a simple reversion to tradition; fancy's ambition for a disciplined knowledge is very real and seems specifically designed for the modern position in which Barbauld's speaker finds herself at the end of "A Summer Evening's Meditation."

Read this way, fancy resists the modernization narrative embedded in the *Biographia*, and resists too the "failed modernization" of Coleridge's own radical-to-romantic-to-conservative trajectory. Concomitantly, fancy resists the temptation to interpret a poem's acts of recognition as victories of an enfranchised self. When the speaker of "A Summer Evening's Meditation" implicitly recognizes the "hand unseen" as Satanic desire, this might appear a triumph of the poet's own autonomy over the devices of those who would influence her. Yet if this were indeed the case, it would mark Satan's victory rather than his defeat, since it would suggest that Satan's picture of the world, which dramatically pits servility against freedom, is the right one. In this case Abdiel offers a response to Satan that might be Barbauld's own: "Unjustly thou deprav'st it with the name/Of *Servitude* to serve whom God ordains" (6.174–75). Satan himself is not free, Abdiel continues, but is simply subject to another kind of bondage: "Thyself not free, but to thyself enthrall'd" (6.181). Fancy is Barbauld's defense against such enthrallment, for it helps the speaker resist the temptation to claim credit for the poem's insights. This is why the speaker ascribes her actual turning around not to her own triumphant resistance to coercion, but to the generic limitations imposed, from the outside, by fancy itself.

Gender, Repetition, and Agency

It may be that our ingrained intellectual habits make it difficult to recognize the fanciful agency I have just described as agency at all. Certainly it is possible to read the speaker's constrained choice of fancy as an example either of false consciousness or of what Judith Butler has called "an attachment to subjection,"—that is, the subject's passionate bond to the power that has produced it.[29] By contrast, "A Summer Evening's Meditation" asks us to conceptualize agency as produced by a reiteration of the structures of authority that inhere in generic expectations. It locates agency in the way fancy works to *uphold* a religious norm. When imaginative emancipation beckons, fancy calls the speaker back by producing epistemic modesty as a condition of possibility for the active waiting with which the poem concludes.

Repetition—particularly repetition undertaken with the aim of more firmly entrenching an already established subject position—has not fared especially well within a liberal theoretical tradition that tends to validate freedom, autonomy, and originality. For this tradition, human agency has meant the capacity to realize one's desires over and against repressive structures (of class, gender, religious hierarchy, and so on); choosing to subsume desires within those structures looks from this perspective like a failure of agency. Poststructuralist accounts of repetition, meanwhile, while critical of liberal notions of agency as the free enactment of desire, have tended to locate agency in the slips and gaps between reiterative self-performances. Thus Gilles Deleuze, in *Difference and Repetition*, argues that far from being an anomaly, variation is in fact the condition of possibility for repetition; difference thus frustrates simple repetition's identitarian logic.[30] And Butler, in her influential discussion of the sex / gender distinction in *Gender Trouble*, likewise identifies variation as that which contests naturalized gender norms: "all signification," writes Butler, "takes place within the orbit of the compulsion to repeat; 'agency,' then, is to be located within the possibility of a variation on that repetition."[31]

To be sure, Butler's claim that gender is "[l]ess a radical act of creation" than a "tacit project to renew a cultural history in one's own corporeal terms" is very useful for thinking through the relationships among agency, fancy, and gender in Barbauld.[32] By focusing upon the agentive possibilities that reside within norms, Butler opens up a promising avenue for theorizing the various kinds of marginalization that Barbauld performs. Yet as Saba Mahmood has emphasized, Butler's analysis remains problematically tied to liberalism insofar as the agency that she locates within variation remains bound to a dialectic of compulsion and subversion. Such a dialectic has strong affinities, as we have seen, with the Blake of *The Marriage of Heaven and Hell.* Pushing Butler's analysis of performativity beyond this dramatic scenario, Mahmood stresses the "variety of ways in which norms are lived and inhabited, aspired to, reached for, and consummated."[33] This focus on religious subjectivity, particularly the cultivation of piety among female participants in the Egyptian mosque movement, makes Mahmood's analysis especially relevant here. The pious female subjects of the mosque movement, she argues, reveal the limitations of Western feminist theory precisely at the moment that this theory reaches for a demystifying analytic when it encounters women who actively desire to uphold religious norms. In a similar manner, Barbauld uses "fancy" to link a display of religious humility to the reiterative performance of a set of gendered norms. A learned behavior, fancy's goal is here to build up a certain kind of pious subject through the adoption and inculcation of a set of habits, dispositions, and bodily postures.[34]

Barbauld calls the learned behavior activated by fancy "meditation." The implication of her title, therefore, is that this particular summer evening's meditation is not a unique event but part of a series—a series whose purpose is to help the speaker live simultaneously in the present moment's flight of fancy and in the retrospective futurity of the poem's end. If she has been here before, she knows that her fancy will fail, but she departs on the journey anyway because its point is not to make some new discovery but rather to reinforce, with each journey, the subject's status as a radically conditioned being who must learn to live simultaneously both here and in the hereafter.[35]

At the close of "A Summer Evening's Meditation," the speaker describes the natural world to which she returns as a mansion. Such inhabitation may be taken as a figure for the meditative disposition that the poem is designed to instill. Living in a home demands repetitive practices and requires that they become matters of course rather than objects of cognition. As an analogy, the mansion conforms not to a ratio (carpenter is to house as God is to world) but rather to the looser sense of analogy consistent with a fanciful poetics. Thinking of the world as a mansion illuminates what the poem has discovered to be true, namely that when we call God a builder we mean it neither in the same sense nor in a completely different sense than we do when we call a carpenter a builder. The point is that houses are for living in, not for theorizing about.

One of the most difficult of the temptations represented by skepticism is the desire to defeat it. From fancy's perspective, any theory (including a theory of the imagination) falls victim to this temptation; it thinks of history as a process of finding new languages and better arguments. A poetry of fancy and analogy represents an alternative to this dominant discourse. In this alternative, originality is less important than repetition, progress less important than stability. As my analysis of fancy's gendered agency suggests, however, these different values do not map onto a distinction between modernity and tradition. Rather, the self-consciousness with which fancy is deployed, and the way it is embedded within a repetitive pedagogy, makes fancy one example of the multiple ways in which tradition and modernity dynamically interact.

Chapter 4

Natural Designs: William Paley, Immanuel Kant, and the Power of Analogy

The controversy over deism largely drove religious debate in England for the first half of the eighteenth century. By claiming to follow the principles of science and rationality all the way to their logical outcome, deism left no room for supernatural agency and thereby forced orthodox theologians to define their relationship to reason with greater care. The various arguments against miracles, from Thomas Woolston in 1727 to Hume in 1748, likewise proceeded under the principle of natural uniformity that the deists had deployed so effectively, and this is one reason that Hume's contemporaries frequently and mistakenly labeled him a deist. In this climate, most midcentury defenses of miracles appealed to the authority of scripture. Yet by 1790, when William Paley entered the fray, the tone of the debate had changed, for Paley did not try to establish the trustworthiness of miracle stories.[1] Instead he relied upon a refashioned argument from design to underwrite both revealed religion and human ethics. Orthodox natural theology had grabbed the momentum back from its deist competitor.

If Paley encountered difficulties, they were posed not by deism but by his own methodology. He proceeded as if the largely inductive procedures of the argument from design were methodologically neutral, but this was hardly the case. If you think there is a God, the natural world will offer evidence that this is so; if you don't think there is a God, it's unlikely that design will compel you to believe. An unsympathetic commentator (such as David Hume) might therefore accuse natural theology of assuming what it sets out to prove; he might write as if natural theology is fatally torn between matters of reason and matters of faith. As I noted earlier, most discussions of the *Dialogues* accordingly concentrate on which of the three characters best represents Hume's own view of natural theology. But this is to treat belief as the central issue, when in fact belief—in the sense of assent to propositional statements—was not natural theology's primary concern. Hume, indeed, is best read as actively forcing religion onto this narrower and more intense terrain, creating the conditions within which natural theology will be compelled to acknowledge its own reliance upon preexisting "belief."

Faced with this situation, we can search for a public language more adequate to a world of increasingly privatized beliefs. Such a language might serve as a repository for spirit, but it can no longer be a carrier for specific doctrinal content. This is the strategy of a romanticism coordinated with secularization. A second possibility, as I argued in the previous chapter, is to accept Philo's critique but seek to develop fanciful strategies for living with it rather than searching out a new poetic syntax. Antidevelopmental and nonlinear, this tactic stands in important opposition to the critical plotting of romanticism as secularization. The present chapter explores a third possibility. My extended assessment of William Paley's *Natural Theology* (1802) aims not simply to resurrect this book as an object of study but also to demonstrate that by deploying the resources of the design argument in a novel way, Paley offers an original response to Philo's criticism. In its overt concerns about social stability, that response is symptomatic of its historical moment, as the discussion of Jane Austen in the next chapter intimates.

Insofar as Paley offers an answer to Hume, it is revealing to place him alongside Immanuel Kant, Hume's greatest philosophical respondent. I therefore conclude the chapter with a discussion of Kant's analysis of teleology and analogy in the *Critique of Judgment*. Placing Kant next to Paley allows us to see what is at stake among various attitudes toward analogy: Kant's suspicion of it characterizes one persistent strand of modernity's relation to religion, whereas Paley's celebration of it comprises a resourceful, though largely unnoticed, response to that modern suspicion.

Instructor of Millions

William Paley may not have been the age's most original or inspiring thinker, but he was one of its most ubiquitous and, among the educated classes at least, influential. Every university-educated man would have encountered Paley's works at least once during his career; many who did not encounter his thoughts directly came under their influence indirectly, since virtually every orthodox clergyman during the romantic era would have turned to Paley, in sermon or pamphlet, for a defense of natural theology, of practical biblical ethics, and of miracles.

Born into a middle-class household in 1743, Paley spent his formative intellectual years at Christ's College, Cambridge, first as a student in the early 1760s, then as a lecturer from 1766 to 1775. His closest friends at Cambridge were a group of latitudinarians known as the Hyson Club.

These included John Jebb, who campaigned actively for reform at Cambridge and in 1775 became a Unitarian; John Law, who would become bishop of Killala in 1787; and Richard Watson, Regius Professor of Divinity from 1771 and later, under Whig patronage, the bishop of Llandaff (the same bishop to whom Wordsworth's famous letter is directed). Jebb and Law were also deeply involved in the effort to repeal the 39 Articles during the 1760s and 1770s. The first attempt at repeal culminated in the Feathers Tavern petition, which was signed by over 200 Cambridge divines (though not by Paley); the House of Commons defeated the ensuing bill in February 1772 by a vote of 217 to 71. Later bills were defeated in 1787, 1789, and 1790. Watson was one of only two bishops to speak in favor of repeal in 1787, and as late as 1812 he was still advocating for repeal and for Catholic emancipation, earning the displeasure of George III in the process. In general, then, Hyson Club members subscribed to a pragmatic and tolerant faith. They shared the conviction that religion should be based on empirical testimony and subject to the disinterested scrutiny of reason; they were for the most part suspicious of "enthusiasm." Like virtually all eighteenth-century clergymen, they were heavily invested in the argument from design; and they believed that evidence of God's design in adapting means to ends provided substantive support for a generally optimistic outlook. Thus Paley was part of a middle-class Whig environment at Cambridge, plainspoken in manner, latitudinarian in theology, and committed to limiting the role of the Crown in public affairs.[2] It is important to establish these credentials because today he is generally viewed as the spokesperson for a staid orthodoxy and an apologist for a repressive state apparatus. This is an opinion passed on to us both by the invectives of romantic-era writers such as Coleridge and Hazlitt and by our own unexamined sense of the status of traditional theology in the late eighteenth century. These views are not entirely wrong—Paley's theology was accommodationist in numerous ways—but the relation among religious beliefs, theological arguments, and political opinions cannot be simply mapped onto a conservative / progressive distinction.

In 1775 Paley left Cambridge for the Rectory of Musgrove in Cumberland. He would spend the rest of his life as a clergyman: as archdeacon of Carlisle from 1782 to 1795 and, then, newly famous for the *Evidences of Christianity* of 1794, in Durham and Lincoln from 1795 until his death in 1805. His modest rise through the ranks of the church hierarchy was accompanied by a growing rapprochement with the status quo. Although in *Principles of Moral and Political Philosophy* (1784) he had spoken approvingly of Locke's idea that the people had a right to revolution if the government abdicated its responsibilities, Paley's moderate views, like those of many in the British church and intelligentsia, did not survive the events in France. It is reported that when he unexpectedly happened upon a copy of *The Rights of Man*, he threw it angrily into the fire. In 1792 he published a reply to Paine called "Reasons for Contentment," which praised the industry and moral rectitude that went along with poverty and repeated familiar arguments about happiness not being dependent upon rank or station. Then in 1802, near the end of his life, he published *Natural Theology*, the work he regarded as the crowning achievement of his career. In the *Principles* Paley had attempted to establish the basis of Christian morality; in the *Evidences* he had attempted to establish the credibility of revelation, especially the miracles of Christ. But *Natural Theology* was the cornerstone of his system, for there he argued that the existence and attributes of God could be seen in the works of nature and apprehended by human reason. Without the arguments of *Natural Theology*, Paley declared, the arguments of his other works were ineffective, for everything else he wrote presupposed the existence of a divine and benevolent creator. *Natural Theology* was therefore an effort to establish the preconditions of all practical Christian philosophy, and in this regard Paley was typical of his natural theological heritage, which came increasingly to build its claims about revelation and ethics on the ability of reason to establish incontrovertibly the existence of a benevolent creator.

It is difficult to overestimate Paley's influence on British moral and religious thought in the late eighteenth and early nineteenth centuries. The *Principles of Moral and Political Philosophy* became a required text at Cambridge by 1786, within two years of its publication, and retained this status well into the nineteenth century. The *Evidences of Christianity* had even greater success; it went through twenty-four editions by 1816 and became a required text for all second-year students at Cambridge from 1822 until 1920. These facts alone mean that a good portion of the British clergy cut their theological teeth on Paley's works. Reflecting on Paley's corpus in 1859, Richard Whately wrote that "it has laid the foundation of the Moral Principles of many hundred—probably thousands—of Youth while under a course of training designed to qualify them for being afterwards the Moral instructors of Millions."[3] As for *Natural Theology*, it had gone through twenty editions by 1820—more than one per year. In this book Paley passed on to the nineteenth century a relatively unified and very famous version of the heterogeneous mass of eighteenth-century rational theological thought. In its pages he tried to capture the essence of eighteenth-century natural science and to place within the covers of a single book the most compelling evidence for the existence of a divine designer. Its impact made Paley a subject in his own right, a representative to future generations of eighteenth-century theology itself. He thereby also provided a convenient target for those who regarded the eighteenth century as a long exercise in reactionary logic chopping and murdering to dissect. As Shelley writes in the Preface to *Prometheus Unbound*, "For my part I had rather be damned with Plato and Lord Bacon, than go to Heaven with Paley and Malthus."[4]

The Reproducing Watch

Natural Theology opens with a famous analogy:

In crossing a heath, suppose I pitched my foot against a *stone*, and were asked how the stone came to be there: I might possibly answer, that, for any thing I knew to the contrary, it had lain there for ever; nor would it perhaps be very easy to show the absurdity of this answer. But suppose I had found a *watch* upon the ground . . . when we come to inspect the watch, we perceive (what we could not discover in the stone) that its several parts are framed and put together for a purpose, e.g. that they are so formed and adjusted as to produce motion, and that motion so regulated as to point out the hour of the day. . . . [T]he inference we think is inevitable, that the watch must have had a maker: that there must have existed, at some time, and at some place or other, an artificer or artificers who formed it for the purpose which we find it actually to answer: who comprehended its construction, and designed its use.[5]

The natural objects of the world, Paley will say over and over again, are like this watch. Like the watch they bear the marks of contrivance and artifice; like the watch they entail the existence of a designer behind the design, a being who comprehended their construction and designed their use.

The whole argument of *Natural Theology* is here in this single analogy— and yet the ellipses in the quotation eclipse the primary burden of the book. For in those ellipses Paley records, with painstaking care, the attributes of the watch: it has a coiled elastic spring, a cylindrical box, a flexible chain, a "series of wheels, the teeth of which catch in, and apply to, each other" (2) and a glass face. And it is only after listing these properties, and describing their importance within the overall design of the watch, that Paley will confidently declare that the inference "is inevitable." This is the true spirit of *Natural Theology*: listing, often for pages upon pages, the precise attributes and functions of various mechanical and natural objects. Most of this long book, in fact, is an exhaustive catalog of the current state of the natural sciences, with chapter titles such as "Of the Muscles," "Of the Vessels of Animal Bodies," "Of Insects," "Of Plants," and "Of the Elements." Only in the relatively short chapters near the beginning and end does Paley offer the argument that God has made this massive collection of stuff. And even there he cannot resist the impulse to take an inventory of the natural world. In the middle of the third chapter (rather disingenuously entitled "Application of the Argument"), we are treated to a twenty-page disquisition on the eye: eyes of birds, eyes of babies, eyes of fishes, and eyes of eels, with special attention to the lids and membranes of eyes. Even the watch analogy seems to get out of Paley's control: it continues for some seventeen pages during which Paley entertains the possibility that the watch might possess "the unexpected property of producing, in the course of its movement, another watch like itself" (5–6). "The thing is conceivable," he notes defensively. Where there was once a single watch we must now picture multiple watches, each of them containing the same intricate mechanisms; each of them in turn subjected to Paley's inexhaustible listing (springs, wheels, boxes, chains, faces); and each of them bearing an analogical relation to each of the thousands of other natural and mechanical objects that make their appearance within the pages of *Natural Theology*. Watches are like bird's wings are like the eyes of fishes are like telescopes are like intestines are like the muscles of the foot. And so it goes.

Another rhetorical impulse in *Natural Theology*, equally strong, also takes its cue from the opening watch analogy. This is Paley's persistent use of mechanical language. "To some," he writes, "it may appear a difference sufficient to destroy all similitude between the eye and the telescope, that the one is a perceiving organ, the other an unperceiving instrument. The fact is, that they are both instruments. And, as to the mechanism . . . this circumstance varies not the analogy at all. For observe, what the constitution of the eye is" (13). He then inserts a lengthy description of the various mechanical contrivances of the eye, concluding on the next page by declaring that "[t]he lenses of the telescope, and the humours of the eye, bear a complete resemblance to one another, in their figure, their position, and in their power over the rays of light" (14). Here, as in virtually every analogy that he draws, Paley gives pride of place to mechanical descriptions of organic objects. This strategy certainly procures the full endorsement of the *Edinburgh Review*, which gave Paley a lengthy notice soon after the book appeared. "All our ideas of intelligence being derived from the consciousness of its existence in human creatures," writes the *Review*,

it is plain that the analogical argument for its existence in the Author of the universe is more close, and more irresistible, when his works bear some obvious and undeniable analogy to the products of *our* power, industry, and skill; when we comprehend the end, and are able to judge of the efficacy and adaptation of the means. For this reason, Dr. Paley has, with great judgment, selected the *mechanical* functions and contrivances in organized bodies, as proofs of design.[6]

Paley's own justification for this technique is that "It is only by the display of contrivance, that the existence, the agency, the wisdom, of the Deity, *could* be testified to his rational creatures. This is the scale by

which we ascend to all the knowledge of our Creator which we possess"
(26). For the same reason, he considers the more impressive works of
God's creation less powerful proofs of design, for they are apt to overwhelm the mind. "My opinion of Astronomy has always been," he declares, "that it is *not* the best medium through which to prove the agency
of an intelligent Creator" (249), an opinion the *Review* notes approvingly. Rather, God is found in the smallest of mechanical details, for
such details are best adapted to human capacities.

To some degree, the practical rhetoric of mechanism runs against the
teeming plenitude of Paley's book, its endless production and exhibition of objects. Mechanical rhetoric reduces natural objects to human
categories: the eye is really only a complicated telescope, the world a
complicated watch. By contrast, the fecundity of the natural world that
Paley describes tends to outrun the mechanical analogy, lending him
the wide-eyed enthusiasm of the amateur naturalist. Consider this extraordinary passage:

> The air, the earth, the water, teem with delighted existence. In a spring noon, or
> on a summer evening, on whichever side I turn my eyes, myriads of happy be-
> ings crowd upon my view. "The insect youth are on the wing." . . . Other species
> are *running about*, with an alacrity in their motions, which carries with it every
> mark of pleasure. Large patches of ground are sometimes half covered with
> these brisk and sprightly natures. If we look to what the *waters* produce, shoals of
> the fry of fish frequent the margins of rivers, of lakes, and of the sea itself. These
> are so happy, that they know not what to do with themselves. . . . Suppose, then,
> what I have no doubt of, each individual of this number to be in a state of posi-
> tive enjoyment; what a sum, collectively, of gratification and pleasure have we
> here before our view! (300–301)

Describing this joyful, teeming world in mechanical language is the
chief rhetorical challenge of *Natural Theology*, one Paley negotiates only
partly successfully. Throughout, one senses a persistent tension between
the cataloging of manifold objects and the functionalist language of
mechanism and contrivance. Such tensions lend the book as a whole a
slightly uneasy quality, as if its competing impulses of mechanistic reduction and naturalistic expansion are never quite brought into harmony.

Some of this unease gets deflected into a general tendency toward
excessive description and detail. Nothing within the pages of *Natural
Theology* maintains a discrete and limited existence: analogies reach un-
gainly proportions; descriptions of muscles and valves go on for pages.
The problem of too much detail confronts Paley throughout the book,
and he never quite masters his impulse to tell his readers everything he
knows. As the *Edinburgh Review* delicately notes, in *Natural Theology* "more
anxiety is shown that nothing necessary shall be omitted, than that all superfluity should be excluded" (288). This tendency appears in the book's

opening pages when the reader confronts the image of a reproducing watch:

Suppose, in the next place, that the person who found the watch, should, after some time, discover, that, in addition to all the properties which he had hitherto observed in it, it possessed the unexpected property of producing, in the course of its movement, another watch like itself (the thing is conceivable): that it contained within it a mechanism, a system of parts, a mould, for instance, or a complex adjustment of laths, files, and other tools, evidently and separately calculated for this purpose; let us inquire, what effect ought such a discovery to have upon his former conclusion.

I. The first effect would be to increase his admiration of the contrivance, and his conviction of the consummate skill of the contriver. (5–6)

It is hard to avoid the suspicion that this strange passage is operating as an allegory for *Natural Theology* itself. In a text that will continually court the possibility of sinking under the weight of its own proliferating details, this little thought experiment attempts to head off the implication that the pure accrual of objects will start to achieve a life of its own. Instead, the inevitability of "admiration" and "conviction" implies that the reproducing watches simply produce in their viewer a more firmly entrenched affective response.

Yet Paley's strategy remains a delicate one, as often the evidence appears to be accumulated simply for its own sake, bursting the seams of a well-focused argument. So many objects in the world, each of them bearing the marks of divine design, means that there is just *too much evidence* to fit into a single book. The upshot is theology as a festival of productivity, a seemingly endless display of natural objects in which the message is always the same: "only God could have made this." Because he makes this point on the very first page, Paley could conceivably have cut his examples short and retired from the field. The fact that he does not, but instead draws the argument out at ever-increasing length seems to make this book, which purports to be a demonstration of God's existence, simply a register of the surfeit of its own subject matter—its excess mirroring the overabundance of the world it purports to describe.

Paley's apparent fascination with the abundance and mechanical intricacy of individual objects, and his tendency to describe these qualities *ad nauseam*, leads Isabel Rivers to call *Natural Theology* "the fullest, most laboured and most banal account of the argument from design."[7] Here she follows in the footsteps of the *Edinburgh Review*, which is sure that the entire genre suffers from such banality: "On the subject of Natural Theology, no one looks for originality, and no one pretends to discovery. . . . No thinking man, we conceive, can doubt that there are marks of design in the universe; and any enumeration of the instances in which this design is manifest, appears, at first sight, to be both unnecessary and impossible" (289). Natural theology, in other words, is common sense, and its familiarity raises serious questions about the necessity of a book such as Paley's. "It may at first site appear to have been superfluous," continues the *Review*, "for Dr. Paley to come forward with a new work upon a subject in itself so simple, and already so learnedly discussed" (291). The formal excessiveness of the text thus reflects the potential irrelevance of the argument itself. The book risks, that is, becoming part of the very superfluity it both describes and tries to manage. It may become just one more object in a world already too full of them.

Hume's Shadow and the Argument from Perception

That an intellectually ambitious theologian such as Paley should devote so much time to an argumentative procedure that Hume had apparently demolished some twenty years earlier may seem surprising. And indeed Paley is regularly scolded by historians of ideas for failing to take account of the *Dialogues Concerning Natural Religion*. Yet Hume's seeming preeminence is largely a retrospective judgment: in his own day Paley's arguments (and indeed the bland assurances of the *Edinburgh Review* that design was everywhere in the universe) dwarfed Hume's final work. Reviews of the *Dialogues* generally contented themselves with extensive quotations from the book interspersed with *ad hominem* attacks and worries about the effects of Hume's arguments on the lower classes. Paley, when he came to write his magnum opus, could have ignored Hume altogether. In fact, though, the material proliferation that characterizes *Natural Theology*, and Paley's staging of it in the passage about the reproducing watches, actually addresses Hume's argument by continually pressing upon the one place where Philo's skepticism seems vulnerable.

This vulnerability appears quite early in the *Dialogues*. Cleanthes, the supporter of the design argument, declares: "Look round the world: Contemplate the whole and every part of it: You will find it to be nothing but one great machine" (45). He then applies the familiar analogy of natural theology: we know that machines are designed; the world is like a machine in its intricacy; therefore, the world is also designed. The skeptical Philo offers his objections, namely that the dissimilarities between world and machine outweigh the similarities and that the analogy delivers only an explanation for the causes of order *within* the universe, not an explanation of creation *ex nihilo*. Cleanthes is so stymied by Philo's attacks that he finally declares in frustration that evidence of design is simply too obvious to be denied: "Consider, anatomize the eye: Survey its structure and contrivance, and tell me, from your own feeling, if the idea of a contriver does not immediately flow in upon you with a force like that of sensation" (56). This is the only point in the *Dialogues* where Philo appears to be flustered. "Here I could observe," writes the narrator Pamphilus, "that Philo was a little embarrassed and confounded" (57).

In one sense Cleanthes has not given much of an argument at all; it seems more like an assertion. But it has a certain rhetorical power. Because belief in design strikes us with extraordinary force every time we consider the eye, Cleanthes seems to argue, it is natural and instinctual to accept this belief. In fact, to reject design is effectively to close our eyes to the truth, obscuring, as he says, our "natural good sense by a profusion of unnecessary scruples and objections." He rejects the arguments of a skeptic such as Philo simply because they need to be "summon[ed] up" over time, whereas the "obvious conclusion" is the one that strikes immediately, and with "force" (28). Call this an "argument from perception."

Paley employs this argument from perception in *Natural Theology* constantly, as it is the best means he has for marshaling all his evidence into an argument. Thus, he describes the several "contrivances" of a particular natural object and then asks, as he does after the early discussion of the eye, "Can any thing be more decisive of contrivance than this is?" (18). The technique is to pile up the evidence and so make it all but impossible to answer the rhetorical and tautological question negatively. Like Cleanthes, Paley stresses the natural ability, even the inclination, of his readers to *feel* in a certain way when presented with evidence—or, in Cleanthes' lovely phrase, to be "ravished into admiration" by the intricacy of the natural world. Paley's use of the rhetorical question thus enters the debate at the only place where Philo appears vulnerable, following an option that was opened up by Cleanthes.

The strategic importance of Paley's technique becomes clear when we remember that Cleanthes' apparent defeat in the *Dialogues* comes about because Philo forces him to adopt an impossibly weak form of the design argument:

(1) A machine shows evidence of design.
(2) We know that a machine was caused by a designer.
(3) Individual objects in the world are like a machine in showing evidence of design.
(4) Therefore, the world is caused by a designer.

Philo's point is that the step from (3) to (4) is in fact an unjustified leap from the objects in the world to the world itself. Yet, in his use of the rhetorical question, Paley accepts this weaker form of the argument precisely because its emotional impact is more readily exploited. He concentrates almost all of his energy on step (3), rendering every natural object he can think of in mechanistic terms. The reiterative quality of the examples thus serves a philosophical function, because the more natural objects Paley can show to be mechanical, the greater the likelihood that objects he does *not* consider are also mechanical. Once (3) is sufficiently established, he abandons induction altogether and makes the jump from (3) to (4) by means of the emotional strength of his argument from perception. Unlike Cleanthes, Paley never claims that the entire world, considered as a whole, is like a machine. The muscles of the foot are efficient, elegant, and mutually adapted one to another—can anything be more decisive of contrivance than this? Apparently only the unnatural skeptic could resist Paley's answer.

At one point Paley is very explicit about his technique: "The proof," he writes, "is not a conclusion which lies at the end of a chain of reasoning, of which chain each instance of contrivance is only a link, and of which, if one link fail, the whole falls; but it is an argument *separately supplied by every separate example*" (51; emphasis added). Unlike Cleanthes, who wants to compare the entire world to an instance of human mechanism, Paley sticks exclusively to the humble parts of creation. He does not build up a total picture of the world but simply compares the parts of it. "I know no better method of introducing so large a subject," he writes, "than that of comparing a single thing with a single thing: an eye, for example, with a telescope" (12). Comparing single things is very different from the procedure of the natural theologians depicted by Hume, who gradually build up an image of a designed world, starting from the minutest parts of the world and ending with the greatest. In Paley's version, each instance of design is now a complete argument unto itself, and the task of the natural theologian is simply to collect as many of these arguments as possible. Paley's willingness to produce concrete mechanistic descriptions of the world's objects thus limits the skeptic's ability to go on listing analogical dissimilarities and helps him maximize the argument's emotional potential, allowing its power to flow in upon the reader "with a force like that of sensation."

Of course something is lost here. Indeed, this might be the end of the *argument* from design, for in its immediacy and its reliance on emotional force it is hardly an argument at all. Consider this version of it: "we find that the eye of a fish, in that part of it called the crystalline lens, is much rounder than the eye of terrestrial animals. What plainer manifestation of design can there be?" (12–13). The emphasis is on minute observation and the speed of the transfer from observation to conclusion. It assumes that human beings are innately impressed by marvelous engineering in the natural world. And it is the very opposite of the "slow and deliberate steps of philosophers" that Philo advocates in the *Dialogues*.[8]

Despite the opening watch analogy, therefore, *Natural Theology* is really not an argument by analogy at all. With few exceptions, Paley avoids analogical ratios of the sort *a:b::c:d*. He concentrates instead on securing analogies between natural and mechanistic objects, and lets the argument from perception do the rest.

Kant and the Persistence of Analogy

Paley's argument from perception identifies and exploits a certain flexibility within analogy. The persistence of such analogy complicates a history of ideas in which analogy has run its course by the end of the eighteenth century. Concluding his important study of literary analogy, for instance, Earl Wasserman remarks that in the eighteenth century "there is to be found the last significant vestige of the myth of an analogically ordered universe."[9] Wasserman is thinking of analogy as a static scaffolding for the neo-Platonic system of correspondences popular during the Renaissance, and so far he is correct. But he is wrong to assume that the neo-Platonic tradition represents the entire spectrum of analogical thinking. Of course, one might expect that analogy would appear in Paley; it is more surprising to find it in the thought of Immanuel Kant. Yet Kant's critique of natural theology is itself a failed attempt to keep analogy out of philosophical reasoning—and that failure, which Kant understands to be a necessary one, tells us something of analogy's persistence.

Kant's critique hinges on a rigorous separation of teleology and analogy. Strategically this move makes great sense, for it allows Kant to reckon with the ubiquity of design in our everyday lives.[10] Design arguments of one kind or another are almost impossible to avoid, for we reason according to design's precepts all the time. If I asked someone whether a fishhook or a shovel were better for catching fish, it is unlikely that the question would be taken seriously. One *could* enumerate the various reasons why fishhooks are more effective than shovels for catching fish, but listing those reasons seems to miss the point. The two objects are so obviously designed to perform different functions, and the differences between them are so evident, and that anyone with an adequate grasp of reality can "just see" that fishhooks are the proper equipment for fishing. We make these "design judgments" all the time, and we make them so rapidly that they scarcely qualify as judgments. In this sense design is simply built in to our perceptions; the ontology of a world without design is quite literally unimaginable.

Both Hume and Kant are sensitive to this. Both recognize that we cannot *not* make design judgments, and both try, in consequence, to limit the confusions that such judgments might cause if they got out of hand.

The chief confusion, they agree, is the habit of extrapolating from the teleology of everyday objects all the way up to the origin and cause of the universe itself. It is one thing to say that a watch is designed by a specific maker in order to perform a specific function; it is quite another to say this about the universe. Thus what Hume and Kant and many subsequent philosophers criticize is not design *per se* but rather its tendency to hook itself up to analogy. We know, without having seen him do it, that a watchmaker made the watch. Does it follow that God made the world?

In Chapter 2 we traced Hume's argument against analogical inferences in some depth. Kant's argument is more subtle and technical. Like Hume, Kant acknowledges that human beings inevitably make design judgments (Kant calls these teleological judgments). But he is somewhat clearer than Hume that analogy, too, is an inescapable part of human perception. Both teleology and analogy, Kant thinks, are relatively harmless in themselves, as long as we remain clear about their limitations and as long as we keep them apart. Kant gets uncomfortable when they join forces, for in combination they lead to such things as the argument from design and to speculative theology generally. Of course, teleology and analogy are in considerable formal tension anyway: a tension between resolution and separation, or between fulfillment and distinction. Taking advantage of this tension, Kant will try to uncouple teleology from analogy. But, as we shall see, analogy will haunt this very effort.

Kant had addressed the argument from design already in the *Critique of Pure Reason*, criticizing it on the Humean grounds that it delivered only an architect, not a creator, of the universe. Since this is quite an effective argument in its own right, why does Kant take up design again in the *Critique of Judgment*? The short answer is that the third *Critique* is concerned largely with aesthetic judgment, and Kant is concerned that teleological and aesthetic judgments will look the same to an insufficiently attentive observer. That would confuse judgments of taste, which Kant thinks are made freely, with the sorts of judgments still tied to religious modes of thinking, which for Kant are by definition not free. Kant will thus argue that aesthetic purposiveness is an internal or purely formal matter whereas teleological purposiveness posits a series of external relations and distributions and is thus far from disinterested. Yet the very fact that Kant feels compelled to revisit material he had already dispatched within the first *Critique* indicates his awareness that he must carve his aesthetic theory out of a territory dominated by religion: the feeling that an object is made for a purpose is a sensibility owned by the argument from design. And indeed, the well-known distinction between the sublime and the beautiful in the first part of the book risks recapitulating the distinction between aesthetic and teleological purposiveness more generally, since the beautiful seems to reference an object world whereas the sublime refers to the world within the subject. Accordingly, to head off the objection that his discussion of purposiveness in aesthetic judgments has smuggled religion in by the back door, Kant's strategy is to show that pure teleology, which is a kind of judgment associated with religion, differs from the purposiveness characteristic of aesthetic judgment.

Aesthetic judgment refers us to *a priori* categories within the mind, whereas teleological judgment refers us to nature. Yet nature is not an intelligent being and so cannot be said to have purposes. Although teleology in nature is not legitimately an *a priori* principle, then, neither is it easy to see how it can be an empirical one, since to judge nature teleologically is to find purpose where there is none, "slip[ping]," Kant says, "the concept of a purpose into the nature of things." Still, he continues,

we are right to bring teleological judging into our investigation of nature, at least problematically, but only if we do this so as to bring nature under principles of observation and investigation by *analogy* with the causality in terms of purposes, without presuming to *explain* it in terms of that causality.[11]

Thus we may legitimately employ teleology to aid our investigation of nature, so long as we refrain from thinking that it provides an explanation of natural objects. In fact, Kant thinks of us as compelled to make such judgments because it is the only way we can make sense of the world—his goal is merely to keep us from thinking that teleological judgments are the same as knowledge. Teleology always involves us in an act of critical bad faith, since when we use it we "borrow . . . causality from ourselves" (§61); that is, we make an analogy between nature and our own capacity for producing purposive objects.

The incompleteness of teleological judgments recalls Kant's analysis of aesthetic judgments in the first part of the *Critique of Judgment*. There, Kant had argued that aesthetic judgments were also incomplete— indeed, that they were necessarily so. Some critics have argued that Kant's analysis of beauty exemplifies an aesthetic ideology because it encourages feelings of completion and fulfillment. Separated from the social world, withdrawn into itself, the beautiful object seems to nurture a feeling of order and design but refuses to locate it specifically or participate in its actual creation or maintenance.[12] In fact, though, Kant does not associate beauty with fulfillment. True, he thinks that we experience the beautiful object as an end in itself because it elicits in us a principle of inner organization, what he calls a feeling of "purposiveness without a purpose" (§15). Yet aesthetic judgment is always marked by incompletion. Like epistemological and moral judgment, aesthetic judgment attempts to understand the object in terms of an *a priori* concept. But in the case of aesthetic judgment, that attempt is defeated by the inscrutability of the object itself, and as a consequence the notion of purposiveness that aesthetic judgment seeks to deploy cannot be exactly stated. Kant writes: "We do call objects, states of mind, or acts purposive even if their possibility does not necessarily presuppose the presentation of a purpose; we do this merely because we can explain and grasp them only if we assume that they are based on a causality that operates according to purposes. . . . Hence there can be purposiveness without a purpose" (§10). Beautiful objects reside somehow beyond the mind's grasp, sketching the limits of its conceptual range so that the relevant concept (purposiveness) remains purely formal, an always-about-to-be-filled potential that is forever on the way but never quite arrives.[13] Rather than delivering ideological closure, the aesthetic is a space in which the possibility of closure is presented but never brought to fulfillment.

At this point aesthetic judgments and teleological judgments are running roughly in parallel. They are alike in that they both rely for their formulation upon an analogy to more absolute forms of knowledge. Aesthetic knowledge is *like* transcendental knowledge, but the purposiveness of the aesthetic object eludes conceptual grasp. For its part teleological judgment is *like* empirical knowledge of the natural world, except that it can only approximate nature, not explain it. The lack or necessary incompleteness shared by teleological and aesthetic judgments means that they are structured by an impossible desire for completion. In failing to provide an adequate conceptual basis for theology, for instance, teleology produces a *desire* for theology that must remain unfulfilled: "Physical teleology does induce us to look for a theology; but it cannot produce one, no matter how far we take our empirical investigation of nature" (§85). Thus both teleology and the aesthetic frame out an impossible dream—a dream to be contrasted with theology and with transcendental knowledge, respectively, which complete thought by matching object and concept. Unlike those logics of identity, aesthetic judgments and teleological judgments remain tantalizingly close to but rigorously distinct from their objects.

Thought, as Kant portrays it here, wants to complete itself, and alongside this desire comes a temptation: to force a theology into existence by conveniently forgetting the fact that when we reason teleologically we are reasoning by analogy. To deal with this potential confusion, Kant finds himself in the strange position of emphasizing the very concept—analogy—that he had originally set out to banish. Note the passage quoted previously: "we are right to bring teleological judging into our investigation of nature," writes Kant, "but only if we do this so as to bring nature under principles of observation and investigation by *analogy* with the causality in terms of purposes." At this point the third *Critique*, which is partially motivated by Kant's wish to limit analogy's range, in fact becomes a site for analogy's replication. Teleology, which Kant had tried to decouple from analogy so as to render it harmless, now becomes useful only when understood analogically.[14] Thus analogy returns as a name for the impossibility of completing a teleological judgment.

Paley and the Persistence of Analogy

If Kant discovers that analogy persists amid the very argument that had been designed to limit its reach, Paley too testifies to the ubiquity of analogy. The argument from perception moves as fast as a single rhetorical question; combined with Paley's lack of faith in the external order of the chain, this grants the objects of the world an autonomy rarely seen in the tradition of natural theology. The natural tendency to leap from a minute object all the way up to God does not respond to a sense of the grand ordering of the cosmos but rather resides within the mind itself, by means of a feeling for design conceived as a natural possession of the human subject. Thus teleology begins to be located in the relation of the mind to its objects; eyes and gallbladders begin to communicate a sense of their own ends and purposes. By ignoring the external relations among objects, Paley implicitly grants each enough autonomy to escape from the orderly distribution of the scientific table—what need have they of an external order if they can, in their internal arrangement, point to God?

In a social world based on carefully monitored external distinctions, a strategy such as this one is not without political ramifications. At first glance Paley's text offers support for Michel Foucault's account, in *The Order of Things*, of the moment when the representational power of the scientific table begins to lose its hold. No longer subject to an order imposed by a system of external bonds, Foucault writes, things come into full possession of their own modes of being: "Withdrawn into their own essence, taking up their place at last within the force that animates them, . . . [things] turn in upon themselves, posit their own volumes, and define for themselves an *internal* space."[15] In *Natural Theology*, too, the difficulties of the argument spring from the inner organization and sheer number of the objects, which combine to make them resistant to the process of external ordering.

Foucault's account of this dramatic epistemic break depends upon the premise that the fixed order of nature associated with the Great Chain of Being is the dominant tradition in the eighteenth-century enlightenment. We have seen that Paley is suspicious of the Great Chain's fragility. But even one hundred years before Paley, John Ray's *Wisdom of God in the Creation* had moved away from the Great Chain when it comes to describing the relation among species. Paley's struggles with classification, then,

are best understood not as examples of a Foucaultian epistemic break
but rather as a continuing problem within the design tradition of how to
account for change.[16] Foucault's description of the sudden autonomy
and internalization of things has more purchase, however, as a description of how religious orthodoxy struggles with the various pressures of
modern differentiation, of which the scientific classification of species is
one example. Like the things described by Foucault, religion itself turns
inward and begins to cultivate its own domain. Paley's argument from
perception participates in this process. If design is part of our perceiving apparatus, then we carry it around inside us, and it is activated not
in response to institutional prompting nor to inherited ways of looking
at things, but simply through openness to the natural world. Indeed,
this is how Paley pictures himself: as simply bowled over by the design
that everywhere presses upon him the minute he steps outdoors.

The inwardness of Paley's argument from perception is, however, a
rhetorical effect, as his pamphlet "Reasons for Contentment" (1792) reveals. In the pamphlet Paley declares that manual laborers take pleasure
in the "exercise of attention and contrivance, which, whenever it is successful, produces satisfaction."[17] Contentment is the equivalent of the
maintenance of the division of labor, and so according to Paley the poor
should not agitate for a better life. This blunt argument in favor of the
status quo sits rather uneasily next to the more capacious and flexible
world of *Natural Theology*; the ten-year gap separating these two documents therefore deserves consideration. In 1792 England's counterrevolutionary government was gearing up for war abroad and repression at
home; the year 1802 offers a quite different political scene, as it marks
the beginning of the brief cessation of hostilities between England and
France known as the Treaty of Amiens, which lasted from 1802 to 1803.
Neither war nor peace, a truce such as that accomplished by the Treaty
of Amiens is a necessarily limited moment, time held in suspension. As
Jerome Christensen describes it, "[b]ecause truce has no grounding in
anything but convention, it is a peculiarly rhetorical time."[18] To read
Natural Theology as a book characterized by truce rather than war is to
uncover what is "peculiarly rhetorical" about Paley's endeavor, its effort
to stretch the rhetoric of analogy to answer to a time suspended between
past and future.

Following out Christensen's suggestion, we can read the contrast between "Reasons for Contentment" and *Natural Theology* as a contrast between a clear-eyed rendering of natural theology as a form of ideology
dedicated to preserving the privileges of those already in power, and
a rendering of natural theology in which rhetorical force limns the
utopian historical possibility of autonomy and freedom made possible
by religious differentiation. One piece of anecdotal evidence supports

reading *Natural Theology* as a differentiated truce-time document. Paley suffered increasingly debilitating attacks of kidney pain near the end of his life. The Reverend Robert Lynam, who wrote the biographical sketch of Paley included in the 1825 collected *Works*, calls it a "violent nephralgic disorder." Lynam continues: "the moments allowed him by every intermission of pain, he cheerfully devoted to the completion of his last work, his Natural Theology" (xxxvi–xxxvii). Lynam then quotes one "Dr. Fenwick, of Durham," who in his 1806 book, *Sketch of the Professional Life and Character of John Clarke, M.D.*, seems, under the impression that he was presenting a biographical interpretation, to have offered the first allegorical reading of *Natural Theology*.[19] Dr. Fenwick writes of Paley: "That truly eminent man was then engaged in finishing his Natural Theology; but the completion of that great undertaking was frequently interrupted by severe accessions of a painful disorder, under which he had long laboured, and which has since proved fatal. . . . When it is considered that the twenty-sixth chapter of his work was written under these circumstances, what he has said of the *alleviation of pain* acquires additional weight" (xxxvii). In the twenty-sixth chapter of *Natural Theology* we read:

Pain also itself is not without its *alleviations.* It may be violent and frequent; but it is seldom both violent and long-continued; and its pauses and intermissions become positive pleasures. It has the power of shedding a satisfaction over intervals of ease, which, I believe, few enjoyments exceed. A man resting from a fit of the stone or gout, is, for the time, in possession of feelings which undisturbed health cannot impart. They may be dearly bought, but still they are to be set against the price. (327)

Paley's comparison reads as an allegory of the contrast between war and truce, and thus by implication interprets the relation between "Reasons for Contentment" and *Natural Theology*. The hard-line approach of 1792 is justified retrospectively as a posture that gives greater value to the 1802 intermission, whereas *Natural Theology* and its truce-time context are changed from a merely negative into a positive pleasure. Religious ideology is the precondition of the more utopian kinds of freedom embedded in *Natural Theology*.

This "peculiarly rhetorical" context of *Natural Theology* simply reflects the nature of analogy itself, which must actively manufacture the similitude that so impresses the natural theologian. To dwell on Paley's analogies for any length of time is to be reminded that they are moments when language encounters the world. And Paley's language does some strange things. Rather than compare a telescope to an eye, for instance, Paley compares an eye to a telescope, reversing the expected order and thereby focusing attention on the manner in which his argument *produces* the designedness it claims merely to reveal. In the case of the eye, the miraculous adjusting of means to ends that inspires such admiration in the observer cannot of itself convey designedness without the introduction of the telescope, an object that already exhibits this value. The eye, the presumptively natural object, assumes its place in the argument only with the aid of a mechanical analogy for vision. Thus the perception of design is the *result* of the analogy rather than something that adheres in the object itself; when Paley asks, "What could be more decisive of contrivance than this?" the very question reveals how the world itself is disclosed by acts of language.

The counterintuitive relationship of eye and telescope reveals the degree to which Paley's argument actually works to denaturalize vision: without the presence of mechanism, the work of the eye in showcasing design remains invisible and unreadable. Though it is an image of immediate access and of the immediacy and force of the argument from perception, the eye is in fact made understandable within the argument only through the introduction of the telescope, and thus Paley's invocation of a natural world that points to its contriver depends upon the very contrivances that the argument from perception had seemed designed to short-circuit. Contrivance is always there before nature because the creation itself is not autonomous but radically contingent. And even though that is the postulate that Paley sets out to prove, what we actually get is an analogy for it, an endless reiteration of human contrivance visiting itself upon the natural world, making it intelligible. In place of an argument by analogy, Paley gives us a world disclosed only via analogy, in which a mechanical object haunts every natural object that comes under analysis and a machine lurks inside nature like a ghost.

At this point the comparison of Paley and Kant gains some added depth. For Paley, analogy is a source of possibility: it allows him to see likenesses everywhere, and to confer likeness through the power of language itself. Kant, meanwhile, sees things the other way around; he thinks analogy is an inherently unstable form of reasoning because it always tempts us to forget its rhetorical status, always invites a cognitive slip between showing that one thing is *like* another and thinking that one thing *is* another. The desire here is to delineate the space of free autonomous judgments, and since for Kant religion offers the most powerful competition for such judgments, he strives to limit the influence that religion can have on human cognition.

Both Paley and Kant therefore understand analogy as a rhetorical activity whose effects are unpredictable. For Kant, this means acknowledging that the teleology he needs for his description of aesthetic objects is contingent upon analogy—the very concept he had tried to divorce from teleology in the first place. And for Paley, this means acknowledging that the rhetoric of analogy itself confers designedness upon the objects of the world. This shared understanding of analogy suggests that in this case the dispute is not over the truth or falsehood of a particular set of religious beliefs. No beliefs are being contested in a discussion of analogy; rather, the issue turns on the proper category under which to subsume a persistent habit of thought.

Finally, the basic agreement over analogy's slipperiness, combined with differing attitudes toward that slipperiness, once again identifies differentiation rather than content as the source of religious disagreement. Kant tries to distinguish reason from religion in order to carve out an autonomous zone for reason against which religious "belief" will stand as fundamentally nonrational activity of the heart. Paley's *Natural Theology*, meanwhile, imagines a differentiated zone of religious perception that *includes* Kantian reason within a more capacious and visceral mental universe. Historically, Paley's kind of differentiation has lost out, whereas Kant's has prevailed—though never perhaps with quite the authority that Kant himself imagined.

Paley and Secularization

In concentrating on the object at the expense of the chain in which it participates, Paley's natural theology defines for itself a newly specific field of inquiry. The microscope of the careful scientist, comparing "single things with single things," replaces the generalized and expansive view of the natural theologian who takes in the world at a single glance. Cleanthes, with his faith in the impact of a general survey of the landscape, represents this other view. "Look round the world," he tells Philo. "Contemplate the whole and every part of it: you will find it to be nothing but one great machine" (45). Here Cleanthes echoes Alexander Pope's *An Essay on Man* (1734):

> Look round our World; behold the chain of Love
> Combining all below and all above.
> . . . .
> Nothing is foreign: Parts relate to whole;
> One all-extending, all-preserving Soul
> Connects each being, greatest with the least;
> Made Beast in aid of Man, and Man of Beast;
> All serv'd, all serving! nothing stands alone;
> The chain holds on, and where it ends, unknown.[20]

What holds the world together, in Pope's view, is a divinely ordered chain that "connects each being, greatest with the least." To perceive this chain, of course, requires a broad and comprehensive view, the ability to "look round our World" in a single, easy glance.

In making Cleanthes appeal to Pope here, Hume cannily mixes Platonic with Aristotelian arguments. The teleological orientation of design puts it in the Aristotelian tradition, whereas the *Essay on Man* depicts a version of the Great Chain of Being that Pope probably learned from Lord Bolingbroke and that Bolingbroke himself derived from neo-Platonism. According to Arthur Lovejoy's magisterial history of the Great Chain of Being, the principle of plenitude upon which the Great Chain was built develops toward autonomy over the course of the seventeenth and eighteenth centuries. Gradually, writes Lovejoy, each link in the chain was understood to exist "for the sake of the completeness of the series of forms, the realization of which was the chief object of God in creating the world." The notion of a universe so arranged that each being might manifest itself fully, already present in the eighteenth century, prepared the way for romanticism, which according to Lovejoy transformed the latent autonomy of the chain into full-blown diversification. By contrast, in Lovejoy's account the Aristotelian argument from design was directly opposed to this Platonic plenitudinousness, for it "rested in great part upon the supposition that all other created beings exist for man's sake." Against such reasoning, writes Lovejoy, "the logic of the conception of the Chain of Being worked potently."[21]

There is indeed something heterodox about the Great Chain, as indicated by those of Pope's contemporaries who worried about the poem's deistical tendencies. But in constructing romanticism as a logical culmination of a secularizing and democratizing set of ideas—the principle of plenitude inherited from the Platonic tradition—Lovejoy makes romanticism modern by splitting it off decisively from design, which appears in his analysis as a retrograde form. He narrates this history of ideas retrospectively, from the viewpoint of the modernity of which he wishes himself to be a product. In this respect Hume anticipates and indeed calls into being interpretations such as Lovejoy's when he deliberately confuses the philosophical terrain by making Cleanthes turn to Pope for guidance. If at moments of stress natural theology reverts to Platonism, then the game is up and mainstream theology is already well prepared to be superceded by a secularizing romanticism.

The trajectory stretching from Hume to Lovejoy, which in effect diverts analogical thinking into a Platonic stream amenable to secularization, can thus serve as a powerful apologia for a romanticism conceived as the inheritor of its variety. Yet the Platonic world had been breaking up for a long time when romanticism arrived on the scene, whereas the Aristotelian and teleological tradition, far from disappearing, had been creatively adapting. Thus in "An Anatomie of the World" (1611), John Donne, considering the effects of the new cosmology being developed by Galileo and Kepler, anticipates Paley by almost two centuries when he laments that "'Tis all in pieces, all cohaerance gone."[22] Paley's similar judgment that astronomy and similar sciences are "not so well adapted, as some other subjects are, to the purpose of argument" (249) marks his distance from the neo-Platonic tradition into which Cleanthes inadvertently falls and that already seems retrograde by the middle years of the eighteenth century. If Donne, however, is unable to imagine an alternative, Paley is eager to use this opportunity in order to build order upon new foundations. Perhaps the entire world, taken together, cannot be shown to be one great coherent system, but this can have little material effect on the natural theologian who is more interested in finding God in the eye of an eel than in the starry heavens. Paley questions the utility of the broad view taken by the Renaissance cosmologists, by Pope and by Cleanthes, devoting himself instead to his microscope and to detailing the suddenly inexplicable internal networks of what had seemed familiar objects. The argument from design is in this respect a product of and conspirator with scientific modernity; refashioned as an argument from perception, design contributes to what Charles Taylor terms the "modern social imaginary" organized instrumentally around the idea of mutual benefit and a contingent, rather than necessary, distribution of social functions.[23]

If one takes the Platonic tradition as the norm, then it will seem clear that by the late eighteenth century religion—even the tradition of the Book of God—has little to offer to modernity. Indeed, as Donne understood, cosmology's integrative ability was already breaking up in the early years of the seventeenth century. From this perspective, the assumption that science and religion were mutually constitutive is desperately out of touch. Eager to be counted as men of science, eighteenth-century clergymen were according to this interpretation willing to accept enlightenment's terms and allow science to organize their understanding of knowledge.[24] However, if Taylor is correct in emphasizing the contribution of instrumental rather than intrinsic order to the modern social imaginary, then design's continued popularity is no longer a mystery. The habit of looking for God in the details of natural phenomena rather than in the majesties of heavens was not only effective science; it also allowed the observer to see the principle of mutual benefit in action. From this perspective, it should not be surprising that as late as 1802, William Paley—and, if the *Edinburgh Review* is to be believed, most of his readers—hews consistently to a picture of the world in which all things, including the eye of the eel, point to the glory of God.

Chapter 5

Mansfield Park and the End of Natural Theology

In the previous chapter I argued that, appearances to the contrary notwithstanding, Paley's self-conscious use of rhetoric to ground his argument made him something of an original within the tradition of natural theology. Still, there is an obviously conventional side to his argument, manifested most clearly in his concern for social order. The argument's rhetorical nature accounts for this conventional side of things as well. For if the division of labor cannot simply be referred to the natural ordering of the world but must rather be demonstrated instrumentally at the level of the individual, then there is always the danger that someone might fail to be persuaded. "Could anything be more decisive of contrivance than this is?" Paley asks. And what if someone says, "Actually, that doesn't seem very decisive to me. Not at all"? If social cohesion rests not in the nature of things but in an act of perception that everyone agrees to regard as inevitable, such dependence upon convention and mutual benefit is always susceptible to the person who declares that he or she simply does not find the convention compelling.

In Jane Austen's 1814 novel *Mansfield Park*, Mary Crawford in effect says just that. Since Mary is the foil for the heroine, Fanny Price, and since the narrator summarily banishes her for her willfulness, Mary's insensibility to natural theology may not be wholly unexpected. More surprising, however, is that Fanny Price, in her own quiet way, is similarly insensible. Mary and Fanny, that is, mark out two distinct but related responses to design's persuasive power. Mary's response seems quite secular, while Fanny's is overtly pious; but both women are unconvinced by design and put their trust instead in feelings distinct from its shaping discourse.

In demonstrating the autonomy of feelings, Mary and Fanny thus underscore something that was already present in Hume's *Dialogues*, when Cleanthes scored his biggest victory at the moment he departed from traditional inferential arguments and simply asserted that the fact of design was overwhelming and irresistible. At the far side of Cleanthes' assertion, we can place the following report of a dying Charles Darwin, as recounted by the duke of Argyll:

> I said to Mr. Darwin, with reference to some of his own remarkable works . . . and various other observations he made of the wonderful contrivances for certain purposes in nature—I said it was impossible to look at these without seeing that they were the effect and expression of Mind. I shall never forget Mr. Darwin's answer. He looked at me very hard and said, "Well, that often comes over me with overwhelming force; but at other times," and he shook his head vaguely, adding, "it seems to go away."[1]

In their various ways Hume, Paley, and Darwin each register the presence of a world in which feelings, including the feeling that one is in the presence of design, have an increasing tendency to go their own way—or, as Darwin suggests, simply to go away altogether. The "overwhelming force" that Cleanthes had posited as inevitable becomes unpredictably occasional. The *content* of belief is not the issue; Darwin is not describing a crisis of faith but rather an event that takes place at a deeper emotional and visceral level. Strikingly, too, Darwin is alone; abandoned to the inconstant gusts of emotion and to the inevitability of death, there is no surrounding apparatus or discourse upon which he can draw.

Though neither Mary Crawford nor Fanny Price comes to such melodramatic ends, my argument here is that their own fates anticipate the world in which Darwin dies, where the feeling that the world was made by a divine designer comes—and then, just as suddenly, disappears.

Austen and Religion

The question of religion in Jane Austen's novels has been on the critical backwater since John Henry Newman declared in 1837 that she had "not a dream of the high Catholic ethos."[2] Like Newman, critical tradition has assumed that there is little to say about the subject beyond rehearsing Austen's Anglican traditionalism. This is partly due to the lack—one might even say avoidance—of religion in her novels. If she is indeed the brilliant observer of everyday life that most critics declare her to be, why do her characters rarely go to church or talk theology or pray or read the Bible?[3] Indeed, the matter of religion is one of several instances in which Austen's reputation as a realist has served her poorly: if there's little religion in her novels, there must be little religion in her soul—at least "religion" of the sort that Newman would recognize. Such critical disinterest in religion, along with its more sophisticated equivalent, namely the assumption that whatever of it there is in Austen is wholly normalizing, takes its cue from Richard Whately's 1821 review of

Northanger Abbey and *Persuasion.* Whately praised Austen in the *Quarterly Review* for presenting fictions both natural and probable, something not before achieved in the novel. She thereby elevates the genre "in some respects at least, into a much higher class." And he goes on to laud her handling of religion: "Miss Austin [sic] has the merit (in our judgment most essential) of being evidently a Christian writer: a merit which is much enhanced, both on the score of good taste, and of practical utility, by her religion being not at all obtrusive. . . . The subject is rather alluded to, and that incidentally, than studiously brought forward and dwelt upon."[4] The strands of Whately's approval coalesce: the utility and good taste of Austen's Christianity are of a piece with the probability of her fictions generally and hence with her elevation of the genre itself. Austen's novels are exemplars of religious tolerance, in return for which the novel itself is elevated. This is, in embryo, a Whig history of the novel. One thinks, for instance, of those hardworking middle-class latitudinarian divines of a generation earlier, men such as Richard Watson and William Paley, neither republican nor Tory, who benefited from the mechanisms of Whig patronage and were consequently elevated—in Watson's case, all the way to a seat in the House of Lords.

The most distinguished contemporary inheritor of this argument is Marilyn Butler, whose 1975 book *Jane Austen and the War of Ideas* elegantly revives the terms of Whately's review while reversing their political valence. Countering several generations of critics who had supposed Austen uninterested in social and political matters, Butler's book freed Austen to participate in a vibrant and ever-changing series of debates about politics, religion, the French Revolution and the ensuing war, industrialism, and the rise of evangelicalism.[5] Yet by inserting Austen into the war of ideas, Butler also entrapped her there. "Jane Austen's novels belong decisively to one class of partisan novels," she writes. "Intellectually she is orthodox."[6] The Austen who emerges from this account is a Tory conservative who repeats the conservative tenets with which she has been indoctrinated. As she is furthermore distinguished in Butler's reading by her sharply realistic eye, the success of her conservative intervention is effectively linked to what Whately had termed the "probability" of her fictions generally. This affiliation comes to the fore when Butler turns her attention to religion, which not surprisingly plays an entirely consolidating role and moreover in a manner that would win Whately's approval, though Butler draws the opposite conclusion. Like Whately, Butler declares that although Austen does not dwell specifically on religion, her manner as a novelist is "broadly that of the conservative Christian moralist of the 1790s; . . . she continues to write as a Christian, with minor modifications only to accord with the prevailing manner" (164). In thus collapsing the novel's religious and moral lessons into a single whole, Butler produces an Austen who wishes to enter cultural debate so that she can regulate it.

On the basis of such a reading, Butler constructs a genealogy of the novel that imports the polarized terms of the French Revolution debate back into the years of the 1688 settlement. She associates Anglican latitudinarians such as Tillotson with the view that humans are naturally good and reasonable beings; this individualist view is then coordinated with the kind of political liberalism celebrated by the eighteenth-century novel; Austen's novels consequently become conservative responses to these sentimental and liberal trends, implicitly critiquing the latitudinarian religious legacy handed down through literary figures as diverse as Goldsmith, MacKenzie, Edgeworth, and Radcliffe. Austen aims to rescue the novel from its tendency to dwell on individual perception (whether cast as reason or as sentiment) by making the moral maturity of her characters rest on their ability to discern and submit to the social norms around them.

This is a powerful and persuasive interpretation, particularly in its focus on genre. I have dwelt on it here, however, because in assigning a strictly regulative function to the novels' treatment of religion it tends to obscure the very real paradoxes at the heart of mainstream theology during the eighteenth century. For Austen the relevant sources of contention are indeed the events of 1688 and their immediate aftermath. The tradition of natural theology in England is partially designed to stabilize the meanings of 1688, but as the ensuing years made clear, that task was vexed both politically and conceptually. *Mansfield Park*, I shall argue, engages the various debates engendered by 1688 in a spirit of criticism rather than of consolidation. In particular, it reads 1688 in light of those who, more than 100 years later, are the inheritors of its various meanings. Rather than Austen herself reforming the meanings of 1688, *Mansfield Park*'s Edmund Bertram undertakes this task, and the novel then subjects his attempt to a thoroughgoing critique. Butler is right to see these years as crucial for the religious vision of the novels, but she oversimplifies Austen's relation to them. Rather than being a simple repudiation of latitudinarianism, Austen's discussion of religion in *Mansfield Park* shows her to be a critical reader of her own religious history. History, or more properly a sense of historical*ness*, functions in this novel as an absent cause in Althusser's sense, the elsewhere that conditions the textual present.[7]

"There Is Nothing Awful Here"

In *Mansfield Park* discussions of space encode the historical consciousness of the principal characters. Even the novel's most apparently "readable" spaces render up ambiguous meanings. Here is Fanny's first impression of the chapel at Sotherton:

Fanny's imagination had prepared her for something grander than a mere, spacious, oblong room, fitted up for the purpose of devotion—with nothing more
striking or more solemn than the profusion of mahogany, and the crimson velvet
cushions appearing over the ledge of the family gallery above. "I am disappointed,
cousin" said she, in a low voice, to Edmund. "This is not my idea of a chapel.
There is nothing awful here, nothing melancholy, nothing grand. Here are no
aisles, no arches, no inscriptions, no banners. No banners, cousin, to be 'blown by
the night wind of Heaven.' No signs that a 'Scottish monarch sleeps below.' "[8]

The chapel to which she had so looked forward reminds her of a comfortable drawing room, with the solemn "profusion of mahogany, and
the crimson velvet cushions" recalling the "shining floors, solid mahogany, and rich damask" of the rest of the house (71). But this response is hers alone; the Rushworths, who own Sotherton, apparently
do not mind that their chapel looks like a drawing room, and the Crawfords have no response to sacred places whatsoever. Even Edmund, soon
to be a clergyman and generally an ally of Fanny's, completely misses
her sentiment here. "You forget, Fanny," he tells her, "how lately all this
has been built, and for how confined a purpose, compared with the old
chapels of castles and monasteries. It was only for the private use of the
family. They have been buried, I suppose, in the parish church. *There*
you must look for the banners and the atchievements" (72). Either Edmund is missing the point, or he is just not bothered by Fanny's palpable sense of loss. He judges that the decor of churches should match
their functions, and thus that a private chapel should not strive to look
like the old chapels of castles and monasteries, or like the pseudo-
medieval sanctuaries of the gothic novel. In making this judgment he
not only fails to enter sympathetically into Fanny's response but also actually mistakes her meaning: she is looking for symbols of holiness; he
makes historical distinctions.

In *The Idea of the Holy*, the twentieth-century theologian Rudolf Otto
offers a descriptive language for Fanny's sensibility. Otto defines holiness as a nonrational moment residing amid the rational. It is best figured by an *ideogram*, he writes, "a sort of illustrative substitute for a
concept." Though the holy is "in its nature fundamentally non-rational,"
Otto continues, the mind recognizes it in the experience of ideograms,
those "obscure and inadequate symbols which are its only expression."[9]
We can think of Fanny's disappointment at Sotherton as defined by an
absence of the sort of holiness Otto describes: it is something she can
feel, but to which she cannot give clear conceptual expression. The wish
for arches, inscriptions, and banners is a desire for the symbolic expression of an ideal that resists conceptualization.

Fanny's desire, though, is thoroughly mediated by the romance history of Walter Scott, whose poem *The Lay of the Last Minstrel* provides her

with her dramatic material. Given Austen's generally low opinion of romance, critics have assumed that Edmund has the novel's endorsement when he criticizes Fanny on historical grounds. In accusing her of wanting "the old chapels of castles and monasteries," Edmund repudiates the romance of British history and so positions Fanny as someone led astray by an unrealistic and nostalgic conception of worship. At the same time Edmund figures himself as the inheritor of a modern history marked by a distinction between public church and private chapel and, it seems, comfortable with the domestic environment and the domestic God that Sotherton's chapel delivers.

Yet while Edmund labels Fanny's romance history unrealistic, her response implicitly comments upon the inability of his modern history to understand holiness. The emotional failure of the chapel is also a theological failure, for it lacks that ideogram of the holy necessary for a space to *be* a chapel. Fanny's romantic desires for chivalry and heroism point out the inadequacies of Edmund's response, suggesting that his history, and the history that has given rise to someone like him, is susceptible to critique.[10]

The formative moment of this history is 1688. This becomes clear when Mrs. Rushworth narrates the history of the chapel, placing Edmund's defense of it within a historical setting whose specificity is unusual for Austen:

This chapel was fitted up as you see it, in James the Second's time. Before that period, as I understand, the pews were only wainscoat; and there is some reason to think that the linings and cushions of the pulpit and family seat were only purple cloth; but this is not quite certain. It is a handsome chapel, and was formerly in constant use both morning and evening. Prayers were always read in it by the domestic chaplain, within the memory of many. But the late Mr Rushworth left it off. (72–73)

The chapel in its present form is about 130 years old—though it may have been in use for much longer, since the house itself is Elizabethan. Before it was "fitted up" it was more austere, with wainscot (oak) pews and purple cloth; its transformation into a more domestic space by means of cushions and mahogany is tied to a time of religious turmoil in England, when parish churches became sites of resistance to James's attempt to convert the nation to Catholicism. Apparently the family withdrew from such turmoil by fitting up its chapel for private use. Thus when Edmund tells Fanny that she has forgotten "how lately all this has been built, and for how confined a purpose," he invokes a founding moment of the eighteenth century's interpretations of worship and belief, as the contested legacy of James's reign and the 1688 settlement altered for good how the nation viewed the intersections of culture, politics, and religion.[11] The chapel becomes, in effect, a repository of the religious history of the eighteenth century. Understanding this history, not merely as context but also as internal to the aesthetic object—both chapel and novel—will allow us to uncover how that history has materially altered the text's theological discourse.

After the failed campaigns of Monmouth and Argyll in 1685, the political tone in England shifted from mutual toleration between a Catholic king and his Protestant subjects to mutual mistrust.[12] James began manipulating parliamentary elections to favor dissenters and Catholics.[13] Though he did not try to convert the nation itself to Catholicism, his policy of filling governmental and civil posts with Catholics meant that eventually he would have been able to transform England into a nation whose political and social structure was Catholic, even if its official religion remained Anglican. Anglicans fought back in a number of ways, often using chapels to stage anti-Catholic agitation. In October of 1688 a Jesuit preacher at London's Lime Street chapel was pulled from his pulpit by a mob. In early November chapels in Bristol, Oxford, Worcester, and Suffolk were attacked. It was common for Protestants to enter Catholic chapels during mass and make a commotion or to occupy the chapels so that Catholics could not get in. This is the environment in which the Protestant family at Sotherton would have stopped worshipping at the parish church and begun worshipping in its private chapel. Under the pressure of such events, the 1688 settlement would be asked to refashion the nation's religious imagination.

According to J. G. A. Pocock, there were two contemporary interpretations of the events of 1688. One saw Parliament and the legal system remedying Parliament's own predicament; in this interpretation England was a constitutional state marked by continuity of government. The most famous inheritor of this conservative Whig interpretation is Edmund Burke. The other interpretation of 1688 belongs to those whom Pocock calls "radical Whigs," who viewed 1688 as a struggle to limit the monarchy still further and achieve a genuine republic in England.[14] Many radical Whigs had been in Holland with William, like John Locke, or had keenly felt James's attack on the Anglican establishment, like the divines John Tillotson and Gilbert Burnet.[15] On such men fell the early burden of interpreting and justifying the 1688 settlement, especially as it applied to the religious polity of the new administration. Under their influence a remarkable religious and political consensus began to emerge. Politically, it was republican; religiously, it was Anglican, latitudinarian, and tolerant; intellectually, it valued reason and free inquiry over blind faith and enthusiasm. It was suspicious of absolute authority in both temporal and eternal matters. Under Locke, Tillotson, and Burnet, and with William's benevolent support, the events of 1688 came to represent a consolidation of the Anglican hold over national affairs—more specifically, of the hold of a particularly Whiggish, latitudinarian, and anti-Catholic Anglicanism.

One of Locke's chief claims concerning religion, for example, is that the Christian faith is sufficiently supported "by its own beauty, force and reasonableness," and therefore that "external force is not necessary" for it to take hold of the human imagination.[16] Locke's dislike of state coercion is clearly an argument against James's effort to impose Catholicism on England and a defense of William's tolerant regime, as Locke opposes the authority of state religion to a Church brought voluntarily together by the internal authority of Christianity itself. "A Church," he writes in the first *Letter Concerning Toleration,* "I take to be a voluntary Society of Men, joining themselves together of their own accord, in order to the publick worshipping of God, in such a manner as they judge acceptable to him, and effectual to the Salvation of their Souls."[17] The way to salvation is plainly revealed in the Scriptures and requires no external authority or force to interpret it. In *The Reasonableness of Christianity* Locke rejects the "unnecessary mysteriousness" of certain doctrines— the Trinity, transubstantiation, and vicarious atonement—as mystifications intended to enslave the believer to the state. Complicated doctrine subverts the ideal of the Church as a voluntary society structured around freedom of conscience; while articles of belief and creed are subject to endless dispute, everything important in Christianity boils down to a single, self-evident message. This reduction of dogma to a single tenet is an attempt to hold Anglican orthodoxy together in the aftermath of 1688, when its newly reconstituted hegemony is almost immediately threatened by the competing influences of Calvinism on the one hand and deism on the other. Reasonable Christianity often tries to find a middle ground by invoking the specter of Catholic dogmatism and arbitrary power. It is thus set against, in Locke's words, "stately buildings, costly ornaments, peculiar and uncouth habits, and a numerous huddle of pompous, fantastical, cumbersome ceremonies."[18]

The resolute nonmysteriousness of the chapel at Sotherton has something in common with Locke's rejection of stately buildings and fantastic ceremonies. The dominant interpretations of 1688 would certainly have approved of a chapel that refused to cloak itself in mystery and indirection. Burnet thought that the cathedral of Milan had "nothing to commend it of architecture, being built in the rude Gothic manner," whereas Locke himself urged parents whose children showed a taste for poetry to have it "stifled and suppressed as much as may be."[19] Sotherton chapel has nothing "rude" or gothic about it and is certainly no place for poetry, as the Scott-quoting Fanny recognizes. Both chapel and latitudinarian theology reject substantive debates about doctrine, appealing instead to the self-evident clarity of the Scriptures and to a history that constitutes truth as linear and progressive. Such lowest-common-denominator faith abjures the paradoxes of orthodox doctrine in the name of intellectual consistency. For its part, the chapel's lack of banners and arches suggests a deliberate representational poverty: in banishing such ideograms the chapel rejects paradox as unnecessarily mysterious. It is only what it appears to be.

For *Mansfield Park* this refusal of figuration has serious consequences. In the walk through the Sotherton grounds that succeeds the chapel scene, Mary tells Edmund he should choose another profession: "Men love to distinguish themselves, and in either of the other lines [the law and the military], distinction may be gained, but not in the church. A clergyman is nothing." Edmund replies that clergymen have "charge of all that is of the first importance to mankind" and notes their influence too upon morals and manners. Mary objects that Edmund has overestimated the amount of good a clergyman can do, but he holds fast to his claim that clergy set the example for their parishioners:

"The *manners* I speak of, might rather be called *conduct*, perhaps, the result of good principles; the effect, in short, of those doctrines which it is their duty to teach and recommend; and it will, I believe, be every where found that as the clergy are, or are not what they ought to be, so are the rest of the nation."

"Certainly," said Fanny, with gentle earnestness.

"There," cried Miss Crawford, "you have quite convinced Miss Price already."

"I wish I could convince Miss Crawford too."

"I do not think you ever will," said she with an arch smile; "I am just as much surprised now as I was at first that you should intend to take orders. You really are fit for something better. Come, do change your mind. It is not too late. Go into the law." (77–79)

Most critics see Edmund's argument as traditional Tory, but its heritage is equally latitudinarian Whig. Edmund draws on the latitudinarian effort to keep Anglicanism together by deemphasizing doctrine and preaching a Christianity of morality, social order, and natural religion. Tillotson, the greatest spokesperson for this strand of latitudinarianism, famously declared that "the great design of the Christian religion" was "to restore and reinforce the practice of the natural law or, which is all one, of moral duties."[20]

In using this defense of the clergy, Edmund reflects the theological training he would have received at Oxford early in the nineteenth century.[21] The requirements for achieving the bachelor's (BA) and master's (MA) degrees included training in classics, logic, and natural law. To earn a BA, the minimum for ordination, candidates had to pass exams in spoken Latin, in "the Sciences" (logic, geometry, and grammar), and in three classical authors of their choosing. To achieve ordination after the BA, a candidate had to pass a deacon's examination, which called for knowledge of Latin and of the Scriptures sufficient "to defend the tenets of the Church of England against papists, sectaries and enthusiasts."[22] Undergraduate reading lists suggest that Oxford colleges did little to make up for the university's lack of theological instruction: the only authors who appear there with any consistency are Locke and Newton. Since Edmund is ordained partway through the novel, he is probably preparing himself for such examinations during the time of the Sotherton visit. Mary subjects him to her own examination when she raises her objections to the clergy and to Edmund's impending ordination. His answering appeal to morals and manners perhaps prefigures the sort of answer he is likely to give at his deacon's examination.

The futility of this conversation demands attention. Though Mary and Edmund are beginning to fall in love, neither shows the least inclination to budge from his or her position. Edmund repeats his argument about the social importance of the clergy three times, and three times Mary declares this representation false and urges him to choose another profession. When it comes to religion, if not love, this has been an undialectical exchange. The novel needs us to interpret Mary's unwillingness to be persuaded as evidence of her selfishness, and Edmund's unwillingness to be persuaded as evidence of his sturdiness, but it is not clear that their conversation lends itself to such an understanding. In the chapel Edmund had positioned Fanny's desire for banners and inscriptions as retrograde, but it may be Edmund who is out of touch. In the aftermath of James's reign the Anglican Church had spent most of the eighteenth century worrying about excesses of religious feeling and training its clergy to do battle with papists and sectarians, for which a heavy diet of classical logic and rhetoric perhaps fitted them well. But now, in the early years of the nineteenth century, Anglican theology seems caught unawares by people like Mary, who have little religious sensibility of any kind. Like the chapel he defends, Edmund is confident of his social and moral authority but mute on matters of theology and emotion. Trained to identify and curb excess feeling, he does not find it in him to champion his vocation by appealing to sentiment rather than to social norms.

When Edmund defends the Sotherton chapel by appealing to the ecclesiastical history of the eighteenth century and defends the clergy by describing them as central to social cohesion, he behaves as if the 1688 settlement is still the primary reference point of such discussions. But the fact that he cannot satisfy Fanny about the chapel, and cannot satisfy Mary about the clergy, suggests that his response no longer has sufficient purchase in the early years of the nineteenth century. We may see the evidence for this in the twin responses of Whately and Newman to Austen's novels. Whately praises Austen for her religious circumspection and the consequent class mobility this makes possible. Although such a response might make sense for middle-class latitudinarians like Richard Watson, for whom religious tolerance represents a rather brilliant career path, it makes little sense for Edmund, who is already the son of a peer. To Mary, who views it as a mundane career, the Church has little to say beyond rehearsing its own claim to social importance—which merely confirms her belief that the Church is *only* a social institution, and a rather shabby one at that. Meanwhile, Edmund's defense of the tolerant, bourgeois Sotherton chapel invites responses such as Newman's dismissive comment that Austen has "not a dream of the high Catholic ethos." By the early nineteenth century latitudinarianism had overcome its early prejudice and reached out to Catholics, but under the banner of liberality and tolerance. Catholicism refashioned under the terms of liberal Anglicanism is anathema to Newman, as indeed it is to Fanny's quasi-Catholic aesthetic sensibility. Thus the Whig latitudinarian consensus to which Whatley still subscribes, fashioned to hold the nation together in the aftermath of 1688, cannot now encompass either the "liberal" reaction of Mary or the "conservative" reaction of Fanny.

Though Fanny's and Mary's reactions appear polar opposites in terms of their attitudes toward religion, they are actually the same reaction in that each woman treats religion as a matter of personal choice that resides primarily in the feelings. A platform of religious tolerance that deemphasizes public displays of doctrine works as long as religion remains a coherent ground of social choice rather than one social choice among others. But tolerance works by privatizing belief and thus removing religious dispute from the public arena, and this opens the door to the sort of world that Fanny and Mary between them lay out, in which personal conviction is at the center of things. In this new world, Edmund's adherence to an earlier language is largely ineffective.

Second Nature

If the distance between 1688 and the early nineteenth century renders Edmund's position largely incoherent, we can trace two related reasons for this development. The first, as I have already suggested, is the development of latitudinarianism itself, whose search for a lowest common denominator in the name of peace and tolerance necessarily constrains the sphere in which religion can operate. The second reason is not gradual but sudden: the French Revolution and most especially the various English responses to it in the context of 1688. Here we return to Pocock's second, "conservative Whig" set of interpretations of 1688, particularly that of Edmund Burke. Critics who wish to find in Austen a critique of Lockean liberalism sometimes align her with Burke. Yet

Mansfield Park demonstrates that despite its language of tradition and continuity, Burkean conservatism contributes to social differentiation just as much as does Lockean liberalism.

Burke's interpretation of 1688 is an explicit rejection of the radical Whig wish to limit the monarchy and turn England into a republic. Freedom, Burke argues, is grounded in the state, in the capacity of the constitution to pass along to each successive generation the freedoms traditionally enjoyed by its citizens. Burke traces this idea backward through 1688 to the Magna Carta, and beyond that to the "still more antient standing law of the kingdom." The Glorious Revolution was therefore not a true revolution at all, but rather an event "made to preserve our *antient* indisputable laws and liberties," an organic reaffirmation of principles inherent in the body politic itself. The English, Burke writes, can feel the power of these principles on their pulses; custom and tradition are a "Second nature" to them. Burke's methodology thus validates both the constitution and its history of persistence: "We wished at the period of the Revolution, and do now wish, to derive all we possess as *an inheritance from our forefathers,*" he writes.[23]

Few of those who lived through the tumultuous years of James's reign, and through the threats of violence during the interregnum, regarded 1688 as simply an exercise in continuity.[24] Burke's appeal to antiquity therefore smoothes out a real and ultimately inconclusive debate about exactly what the 1688 revolution *did* mean. Burke's interpretation thus bequeaths a paradoxical legacy to the anti-Jacobin cause. If the anti-Jacobins want to claim 1688 as a vital part of their English heritage, and if the chief intellectual defenders of 1688, men such as Tillotson, Locke, and Shaftesbury, are also the founders of a liberal tradition of political and religious thinking, then British conservatives must powerfully revise their own material in the act of deploying it.[25] Burke thus gives voice to a process through which the Lockean consensus, forged in an era of religious toleration as a defense of the 1688 settlement, has been remade into a traditionalist argument for English gradualism and social order, defined against the French Revolution and French atheism—an argument that works primarily on historical ground, distinguishing 1688 from both France in 1789 and England itself in 1649.

Edmund Bertram follows the example of Edmund Burke, accomplishing a similar kind of historical revision at the Sotherton chapel when he tells Fanny that she forgets "how lately this has all been built, and for how confined a purpose." He stresses the connection between historical process and physical object, positing the chapel as a natural result of historical development. Yet, like Burke's interpretation of 1688, Edmund's explanation must work upon latitudinarian raw material, and here lies the paradox of the argument. Sotherton is an enlightenment chapel, a product of the Whig consensus gathered around William, in which the old drapery has been torn off and replaced with the bourgeois cushions and anthropomorphized God that made up the enlightenment's own ideological interior. Fanny may sense a radical discontinuity between her idealized religious history and the interior of the chapel, but in Edmund's eyes the chapel is the inevitable result of a history implicitly posited as continuous. Like the anti-Jacobin novels of the postrevolution retrenchment, Edmund transforms the lexicon of 1688 liberalism into that of 1790s conservatism. He stands at the end of a long eighteenth-century narrative about the fate of the Whig latitudinarian consensus, which gradually remade an argument for toleration into an argument for tradition.

The presence of 1688 within the novel thus creates problems of interpretation for the characters themselves. In Sotherton chapel, debates over the meaning of the historical legacy one inherits are revealed as part of that process of inheritance. Consequently, there is no easy distinction between the "real" history to which Edmund appeals and Fanny's romance history. For all its talk of continuity and its appeal to "our records" and "our acts of Parliament," the Burkean line is highly selective when considering its own retrospective history; moreover, it comes with a powerful naturalizing apparatus in the form of a tradition and a constitution that passes on "our *antient* indisputable laws and liberties." The very notion of "second nature" means that one understands convention as natural, a paradox illustrated when Burke asks himself why he is so affected by his own description of Marie Antoinette's suffering: "Because," he answers, "it is *natural* I should; because we are so made as to be affected at such spectacles with melancholy sentiments."[26] Burke here appeals to a self that can learn to appreciate the virtues of tradition and custom through training and experience. Weeping for Marie Antoinette, though clearly marked as part of the literary convention of the man of feeling, is also *natural.*[27] In like manner, Edmund's defense of the chapel turns on a historical fiction (call it tradition) every bit as powerful and seductive as Fanny's historical fiction—perhaps more seductive and powerful, insofar as it appears stamped as natural and does not, like Scott's romance history, wear its fictiveness on its sleeve.

The debate over the meaning of 1688 that is covered over by Burkean tradition is in fact embedded in the very language of the settlement itself, for James's recent attempt to impose Catholicism on the nation had made it pertinent for Parliament to recall and to formalize the church's wonted subservience. To the coronation oath requiring William and Mary to maintain the true profession of the Gospel, Parliament added the sectarian phrase the "Protestant Reformed Religion established by law."[28] The phrase suggests anti-Catholicism and also serves as a reminder that the Church of England was the result of a process of differentiated secularization, when Henry VIII transferred large tracts of church land to private ownership, thereby limiting the role it was able to play in public administration and political negotiation. Most church livings were consequently subject to the whims of private landholders— something Jane Austen knew all too well. The coronation oath is therefore full of the continuity terminology that was so important to the Burkean understanding of the revolution, but this continuity guarantees the Church's subservience. Thus the Whig version of 1688 reduces the Church to a second-class political player even as a revolution is ostensibly being enacted over its preservation.[29] In his defense of the chapel, Edmund unwittingly dramatizes the developing incoherence in the Church's language of self-justification.

The sign "1688" betokens a certain imagination of history. In the chapel it masquerades in the guise of historical fact, which obscures but does not dispel its essentially imaginative character. Later, when Edmund appeals to the social and moral example set by the clergy, he reproduces the only religious language that the historical imaginary of the coronation oath allows. He cannot offer a description of the Church as something that might be attractive on its own terms because the "Protestant Reformed Religion," by legal definition, does not *have* its own terms. Mary's playful suggestion that he "go into the law" may be more serious than it appears. A careful study of the law and its history might reveal to Edmund the legal constraints of the institution he is about to join.

Out of the conversations, impressions, and arguments that circle around the Sotherton scenes, we can therefore construct a prescient critique. The tolerant latitudinarianism of 1688 offers the church little with which to respond either to Fanny's search for holiness or to Mary's disdain. Addressing this inadequacy by rereading 1688 as continuity recapitulates the problems it seeks to escape. Conceptually, moreover, 1688 cannot appear as a singular historical value. Not only is Edmund's history every bit as fictional as Fanny's, but his effort to distinguish the two histories reveals the performative nature of the distinction between reality and fiction, which appeals to a presumably self-evident difference even as it constitutes that difference in the architecture of the chapel itself. Just as there is nothing natural about Burke's second nature, so there is nothing natural about Edmund's historical explanation of the chapel, or about the history of the church of which this explanation is an implicit defense.

An Alternate History: The Seven Bishops
and the Anglican Revolution

When she was sixteen Jane Austen, in collaboration with her sister Cassandra, wrote *The History of England, from the Reign of Henry the Fourth to the Death of Charles the First.* Conceived as a burlesque of standard textbook histories, it also reveals in the young author a prickly relationship with the received history of her country. The association of the House of Tudor with England's historical destiny, familiar from Goldsmith's *History of England,* is conspicuously missing from this narrative. Invariably, Austen prefers Catholics to Protestants, Stuarts to Tudors. "My principal reason for undertaking the History of England," she writes, is "to prove the innocence of the Queen of Scotland . . . and to abuse Elizabeth."[30] One does not want to lay too much weight on the lighthearted productions of a clever sixteen-year-old, but at the very least Austen's sense that "Englishness" is a constructed rather than a natural category suggests a kind of historical skepticism, and there is no reason to think that she has lost this skepticism by the time she writes her novels. Indeed we might say that her early *History* reveals an especially keen eye for just the moments when historical contingency gets naturalized as destiny—for just those kinds of histories upon which Edmund relies, and upon which progressive secularization narratives rely.

I have already proposed that the Sotherton chapel scene be read as a critique of the religious histories available to Edmund. Lurking in the margins of that scene, however, is a different religious history, a possible history rather than the probable history celebrated by Whately.[31] This history also begins in the tumultuous years of James's reign; it involves men who became known as the seven bishops, who went along neither with James's attempt to transform England into a Catholic nation nor with the latitudinarian dispensation that followed. They refused both of these histories in the name of an independent Anglican Church, and although their efforts were largely buried by the Whig hegemony that came to dominate eighteenth-century religious life, they represent nevertheless perhaps the last, futile effort to restore comprehensive religious authority to a differentiating world.

Faced with an increasingly recalcitrant Parliament and the stubborn Anglicanism of his subjects, James tried to pressure the Anglican establishment by extending civil and religious tolerance to Protestant dissenters. In 1687 and again in 1688 he issued a declaration of indulgence, which suspended all penal laws in ecclesiastical matters and exempted officeholders from the Test Acts (which required allegiance to the 39 Articles). Moreover, James demanded that the 1688 declaration be read on two successive Sundays in every cathedral and parish church. This was anathema to most clergy, for it required them to extend tolerance to religious groups they regarded as heretics, and to do so from their very pulpits.[32] Among those who resisted the order were seven bishops, who sent a formal protest to the king. They were charged with seditious libel for denying his dispensing power and, on refusing bail, were sent to the Tower.

These bishops quickly became national heroes. Even Goldsmith's Whiggish *History* cannot resist the language of heroism and martyrdom:

As the reverend prisoners passed, the populace fell upon their knees; and great numbers ran into the water, craving their blessing, calling upon Heaven to protect them, and encouraging them to suffer nobly in the cause of religion. The bishops were not wanting, by their submissive and humble behaviour, to raise the pity of the spectators, and they still exhorted them to fear God, honour the king, and maintain their loyalty. The very soldiers by whom they were guarded kneeled down before them, and implored their forgiveness.[33]

The bishops' acquittal in late June was widely perceived as a repudiation of James. Certainly it represented a rejection of his dispensing power, on which the declaration of indulgence had been based. In this sense the acquittal reaffirmed the power of divine law over the king's law.

Some historians call this event the "Anglican Revolution." Mark Goldie, for example, argues that the acquittal of the seven bishops formalized a process already underway in England, in which the Anglican Church gradually took the upper hand and established a thoroughly Anglican Tory state with James as king.[34] The principles of this Anglican Revolution were precisely those of divine right and passive resistance to which the bishops had given voice on the river. Their appeal was mild, even submissive; they strongly dissociated themselves from the language of revolution and insubordination and never so much as hinted that James was not the rightful heir. This revolution combined a strongly royalist and conservative politics with an allegiance to divine law; when the two were not aligned, the Church followed its mandate by passively resisting the sovereign while respecting his divine right.

In the context of this slowly progressing Tory Anglican Revolution, with its powerful joint command to "fear God [and] honour the king," William's invasion becomes a *second* revolution, this time dominated by Whigs and latitudinarians. Most Tory Anglicans resisted: along with the 400 clergy who resigned around the time of William's ascension, five of the seven bishops refused to acknowledge his claim to the throne and were deprived of their livings; they would not accept, writes Pocock, that "secular power could change the Supreme Governor of the Church of England even when that governor was an aggressively Popish successor" (279). William's appointment of latitudinarian Whiggish bishops, fifteen in all, and his promotion especially of Tillotson and Burnet, suggests an effort to influence the prevailing interpretation of 1688, to consolidate the union of Whiggism and Anglicanism around a joint rejection of James—a successful effort to silence the royalist voices of the Anglican Revolution, so recently ascendant.

The tradition of the Anglican Revolution would have given Edmund another sort of language to use at Sotherton, one not beholden to the differentiation entailed by the 1689 coronation oath. When James demanded that the second declaration of indulgence be read in every parish church, adherents of the Anglican Revolution refused on the grounds that he had demanded something that contradicted the clergy's oath to defend the Church against heresy. The bishops resisted James as Anglicans publicly, as demonstrated in that extraordinary scene on the Thames. To withdraw from the parish church to a privately fitted-up chapel looks, from this perspective, like cowardice; that Edmund, about to become a representative of the Anglican establishment, defends the chapel's "confined purpose" suggests that the latitudinarian Whigs have won the battle for the interpretation of 1688, as his language tacitly acknowledges that the terms of the contest have already been set by Locke, Tillotson, and the simplified religious language of the chapel. The linearity of his narrative aligns itself effortlessly with the artlessness of the chapel.

At Sotherton, the only alternative to that narrative is the degraded language of romance to which Fanny appeals. The novel codes the disjunction between Fanny's and Edmund's responses to the chapel as a choice between fantasy and reality, naïveté and understanding, but as we have already seen, this construal supports Edmund's way of viewing things. Interpreting Fanny's language as naïve is structurally necessary to Edmund's instrumental matching of means to ends. Thus the turn to Scott is underdeveloped and undervalued in the text because, if taken seriously, it would jeopardize Edmund's attempt to reorganize historical material into a rational and progressive narrative.[35] The narrator has in effect decided beforehand that a particular interpretation of 1688, namely the Whiggish one, will be granted the status not of an interpretation but of disinterested truth, against which all other interpretations will be judged. Thus the form of Fanny's appeal—its reliance on a debased genre—has been determined by the linguistic regime handed down by the 1688 settlement. We can read its nostalgia as symptomatic of a latitudinarian language regime tolerant of everything except what hinders "progress." Faced with the chapel's own refusal of figuration what can desire do but become romance?

In this context, Fanny's appeal to Scott is an allegory of how to read differently than Edmund. In implicit contrast to his "defense" of the

Sotherton chapel, the lines from *The Lay of the Last Minstrel* that surround those Fanny quotes depict Saint Michael defending the faith:

> Full in the midst, his Cross of Red
> Triumphant Michael brandished,
> And trampled the Apostate's pride.[36]

In the poem, this image of Saint Michael is in the center of a stained-glass window, surrounded by "many a prophet and many a saint." The moonlight, shining through the window, projects Michael's red cross onto the chapel's floor. Thus romance history is cast into the physical space of the chapel, formalizing an influential relationship between past heroics and the actions of present characters.[37] Indeed, with its complex layering of historical and religious material, *The Lay of the Last Minstrel* models such historical understanding on a broader scale. Its nineteenth-century readers hear the story of its sixteenth-century events as narrated by a minstrel who has survived Cromwell and whose audience is Anne, duchess of Monmouth and widow of the same duke of Monmouth executed for leading the rebellion against James. *The Lay of the Last Minstrel* thus artfully mediates the confrontation of past and present with an array of possible futures.

So to the question "what has happened to the seven bishops and the possible history they represent?" we can answer: they live now as Fanny's nebulous desire that the chapel were otherwise. History that is not part of official history becomes fantasy. Given the chapel's own history ("fitted up . . . in James the Second's time"), the most appropriate historical referent of Fanny's fantasy history is the seven bishops' public resistance to James's state coercion. Thus the invocation of Scott may be understood as a coded way of setting Edmund's propensity to accommodate against the kind of principled resistance practiced by his forbears.

This comparison of Edmund and the seven bishops gains depth during the later staging of *Lover's Vows*, when Edmund is prevailed upon to act the part of the clergyman Anhalt, despite his reservations about acting itself and about this particular role. In the novel's moral economy we are meant to take Edmund's capitulation as a kind of fall, to be set against his later success in resisting Mary's charms. Some time afterward, when Mary recounts her happiest days at Mansfield, she chooses overpowering Edmund's scruples against acting as the very pinnacle: "[F]or I never knew such exquisite happiness in any other [time]. His sturdy spirit to bend as it did!" (297). Mary's language requires that a moral reading of these events be supplemented with a historical one. In the context of 1688, with sturdiness as the defining characteristic of the Anglican Revolution, Edmund is a weak inheritor of his own religious history. In accepting the part of Anhalt, he agrees to play the sort of clergyman who pleases others by reading out a script already prepared for him.[38] Here the contrast to the seven bishops gains its greatest definition, since their resistance to James centered around their *refusal* to read out a script, namely the declaration of indulgence, that had been prepared for them. Bishop Trelawny said he would rather be "hanged at the doors" of his cathedral than read the indulgence. Like the shadow of Michael's cross cast into the chapel in *The Lay of the Last Minstrel,* the shadow of the seven bishops is cast forward into the text of *Mansfield Park* in these scenes, suggesting that in just over a hundred years a possible though unlikely history organized by undifferentiated religious authority has been rewritten as an impossible, fantastic, and absent history.

"Indeed I Cannot Act"

The discussion so far has made Austen into a critical reader of her own religious history by uncovering a debate about the work of historical imagination that is 1688. But this criticism is undertaken, through the mediation of Scott, from the vantage point of the seven bishops—itself an instance of historical and religious imagination. Like most readers of *Mansfield Park*, we have in the process taken Fanny Price as the novel's chief moral spokesperson and interpreter. The virtues of sincerity, integrity, and self-transparency that seem to win her the role of moral arbiter in the novel rely for their effectiveness upon a larger series of oppositions between the natural and the artificial scattered throughout *Mansfield Park*. The novel's condemnation of acting turns on this opposition, with Fanny lined up on the side of the natural and true. "[I]ndeed I cannot act," she declares (122), describing not a lack of skill but a quality of character. In this schema the protean Crawfords, their love of acting standing for their ultimate bad faith, are foils to Fanny's stability and transparency.

Recent work on the novel, however, has destabilized Fanny as its authentic voice. Critics have shown that acting and artifice are actually conditions of possibility for the natural and true, not simply their opposites. On closer inspection, Fanny's supposedly authentic self turns out to be a product of something like Burkean second nature, a naturalized construct exposed by events as a product of the will. Second nature is culture naturalized and has the further advantage of always having been naturalized before one inherits it. The improvement of the landscape, a textbook case of such naturalization, is overtly critiqued in the novel; the case of acting is more complicated because Fanny persists in the fiction that she is not acting. Yet the plot of *Mansfield Park* forces Fanny to act and hence participate in the play of appearances that she purports to reject: her sincerity turns out to be as much an act as Henry's machinations.[39]

On occasion Fanny, who supposedly cannot act, actually acts rather well—the most important example being her ability to deceive everyone in the novel about her feelings for Edmund. Here Fanny's words and actions are at odds with what the reader is assured are her "true" feelings—yet these true feelings, and Fanny's moral status as the only character who has consistent access to such feelings, have been grounded all along in her refusal to play the game of appearances, a refusal that the plot often forces her to betray. This is important not only for those scenes in which acting is the chief thematic concern but also for the moral economy of the novel as a whole. If authenticity cannot be consistently distinguished from the appearance of authenticity, then Fanny is mistaken when she assumes that she has immediate access to her own thoughts and desires. Romantic antitheatricality such as Fanny's is still theatrical because it rests on the performative deployment of a self subsequently troped as natural and authentic.

Witness Fanny's conversation with Henry when he asks for her opinion about a tenant of his:

"When you give me your opinion, I always know what is right. Your judgment is my rule of right."
"Oh no!—do not say so. We have all a better guide in ourselves, if we would attend to it, than any other person can be."[40]

Henry is clearly acting, for his words are chosen for their effect on his audience, and Fanny, in appealing to the moral guidance available to the private self, is clearly resisting Henry's invitation to join the act. This conversation may be taken as an example of Fanny's unique ability to think for herself, but this assumes that her true self can be easily located, and it fails to reflect upon what her words imply: that we have easy access to the truth of our desires; that, while prey to the devices of others, we are incapable of self-deception. To the contrary, the thematic importance of acting within the novel suggests that we ought to be especially skeptical of those moments when we think we are being sincere. As she does when she offers the nonexplanation that she "cannot act," Fanny here expertly performs her role as the allegory of sincerity; in her conversation with Henry she naturalizes sincerity as a given, handed down from a traditional moral selfhood whose historical origins are appropriately clouded in mystery.

If the amateur theatricals highlight Fanny's susceptibility to a certain kind of naturalization, improvement relies on a similar process, to which she is equally susceptible.[41] Most critics agree that *Mansfield Park* satirizes the improvements proposed at Sotherton and condemns characters temperamentally given to improvement. Raving about the Reptonian improvements undertaken by his friend Smith, Mr. Rushworth declares: "I never saw a place so altered in my life. I told Smith I did not know where I was" (45). He intends this as a compliment, but the weight of the novel pulls in the opposite direction; we are generally meant, like Fanny, to regard a statement such as "I did not know where I was" with extreme suspicion, for it is precisely when the characters of *Mansfield Park* lose their sense of where they are that they get into moral difficulty. Mrs. Norris, the least likable character in the novel, turns out to be not only an enthusiastic proponent of improvement at Sotherton but also quite an improver herself: "We made [the parsonage] quite a different place from what it was when we first had it," she declares proudly. If it had not been for her husband's illness, she says, "we should have carried on the garden wall, and made the plantation to shut out the churchyard, just as Dr. Grant has done" (46). In a novel so concerned with the role of clergy in a community, putting a wall around the parsonage can only be a symbol of selfishness and misapplied energy. Mrs. Norris refuses to recognize the source of her livelihood, abandoning both economic and spiritual obligations for the sake of aesthetic ones. In an improved estate, one literally does not know where one is, where one stands in relation to the rest of the world. Like acting, improvement transforms a certain artificial arrangement into a natural one so that it can be appealed to as already given. *Mansfield Park* ruthlessly exposes this sort of ideology.

The novel's sharp eye for naturalization on this level makes its apparent blindness for a more global naturalization all the more surprising. I refer to the economic base of Mansfield Park itself: Sir Thomas owns a plantation in Antigua and manages its affairs offstage for most of the first volume.[42] An English estate supported by slave labor is the ultimate version of cutting the parsonage off from the churchyard or the commons off from the private park: in each case material reality is divorced from aesthetic ideal. Yet although the novel critiques the tendency among improvers to cut a house off from its economic bases and responsibilities, it is strangely reticent about slavery. Indeed, by focusing on Fanny's reaction to Mansfield, the novel seems to participate in the forgetfulness perpetuated by a colonial state, for Fanny is very susceptible to the naturalizing discourse that Mansfield employs so well. When she visits the Portsmouth home of her biological parents, for instance, she "was almost stunned. The smallness of the house, and thinness of the walls, brought every thing so close to her, that, added to the fatigue of her journey, and all her recent agitation, she hardy knew how to bear it" (317). The contrast with Mansfield could hardly be stronger, as Fanny is soon led to reflect: "At Mansfield, no sounds of contention, no raised voice, no abrupt bursts, no tread of violence was ever heard; all proceeded in a regular course of cheerful orderliness; every body had their due importance; every body's feelings were consulted" (325). Fanny here repeats the very illusions that Mansfield itself seeks to perpetuate: calm ease, order, spaciousness, and a wealth whose source nobody has to contemplate. No "raised voice" or "tread of violence" is heard at Mansfield because those things take place far away on Antigua. As readers we know that Sir Thomas is a slaveholder, but the novel tends to turn aside any effort to integrate such knowledge into our understanding of it. This is largely because Fanny's own reading of the situation is so poor: she knows Sir Thomas is a slaveholder, and she knows that the slave trade has been newly outlawed, but she fails to connect that knowledge to the actual space of Mansfield Park. Prompted by Fanny, our knowledge of slavery remains dissociated from our interpretation of *Mansfield Park*, residing simply at the level of fact. The novel emerges from the context of slavery precisely by not articulating the richness of that context.

Fanny's reaction to Portsmouth thus reveals a knot at the heart of the novel's attitude toward improvement. For here we find her thinking of Mansfield in remarkably Reptonian terms. At Mansfield, that is, one is not constantly reminded of the means of production that support the establishment; rather, it is a place of "elegance, propriety, regularity, harmony—and perhaps, above all, [of] peace and tranquility" (325). Mansfield itself has been improved, its means of production shunted off to a distant land, out of sight and (mostly) mind. Moreover this improvement, because it seems to Fanny an already established fact, can be contrasted to clumsier modes of improvement such as those undertaken by Mrs. Norris and Mr. Rushworth. Their fashionable improvements are condemned because the mechanisms by which they effect their transformations are clunky and obvious; in them, ideology lies too close to the surface. At Mansfield, however, the process of improvement via slavery has been so fully naturalized as to become almost invisible. The awkward silence surrounding slavery is the very thing that structures the novel's presentation of improvement, and the vigorous debates over improvement are, in effect, a surrogate for the debate over slavery that does *not* happen.[43] Mansfield Park thus perfects a performance of naturalness that sinks its own artifice into invisibility, disguising itself so completely that its final realization becomes the moment of its disappearance, when act and truth can no longer be distinguished.

The End of Natural Theology

The result is that we cannot always count on Fanny to tell us the truth about Mansfield, for she is susceptible to its discourse of naturalization. What does this mean for the novel's religious discourse, and particularly for natural theology? Like acting, improvement, and slavery, natural theology relies upon a process of naturalization—so by implying that naturalness is always a performance the novel does not so much criticize the philosophical worth of the arguments for natural theology as question the project of a *natural* theology by casting doubt on what such a theology must presuppose: if the "natural" in *Mansfield Park* turns out to be not a given category but a series of performances or acts, then what status are we to assign any discourse that depends for its legitimacy on the naturalness of the natural world? In this way *Mansfield Park* reveals the degree to which natural theology is always a matter of rhetoric. This is something that we have been tracing throughout this book, as a sort of undercurrent to the more obvious concern about whether the argument from design is true—but its presence here is of particular interest because it allows us to leave behind a philosophical question ("is the argument from design a good, verifiable, argument?") in order to replace it with a rhetorical or literary question: "is the argument from design compelling?" The short answer that *Mansfield Park* offers to this second question is "no."

One result of the natural world's uncertain status is that whenever love of nature is the topic, human desire derails the conversation. Consider Fanny's enthusiasm for natural variety:

The evergreen!—How beautiful, how welcome, how wonderful the evergreen!—When one thinks of it, how astonishing a variety of nature!—In some countries we know the tree that sheds its leaf is the variety, but that does not make it less amazing, that the same soil and the same sun should nurture plants differing in the first rule and law of their existence. (174)

For Fanny, the natural world is at once diverse and harmonious, meticulously ordered yet teeming with variety, and so her response draws on a theological description of the world as an orderly, interconnected mechanism. The "astonishing . . . variety of nature," amazement that the same earth could nurture plants "differing in the first rule and law of their existence"—these are the sentiments of natural theology, whose rapturous exclamations showcase the world's harmony and suggest the benevolence of its designer.

Mary, to whom Fanny's words are addressed, replies: "I see no wonder in this shrubbery equal to seeing myself in it" (175). She is referring to her surprise at how much she enjoys living in the country, but her choice of words betrays a tendency to project herself onto the natural world. These sentiments may seem merely new instances of the self-centeredness that will eventually get her banished from Mansfield altogether, yet her lack of response to the greenery also suggests that some people are simply unmoved by the discourse of natural unity in variety that is the backbone of the argument from design. Here, recognizing design in the natural world turns on one's ability to *feel* in a certain way, and hence there is no structure in place to reconcile the antithetical feelings of the two women. Both remain as they were: Mary is still "untouched and inattentive" (174), while throughout the narrative Fanny makes little effort to understand Mary. Many readers have wondered at Fanny's persistent dislike of Mary, and although the moral plot that requires Mary's eventual banishment demands it, this exchange about the evergreen suggests another, more immanent explanation for their failed friendship, namely an inability to feel in common. Little wonder that soon after Fanny's appeal to the evergreen their conversation lapses into silence. Animation returns only when Edmund approaches, for he is the one object for whom Mary and Fanny *do* have a shared feeling. Unable to jointly love the natural world for itself, the two women love the theologian instead.

Edmund himself, who as a prospective clergyman ought to be most receptive to Fanny's enthusiasm for God's creation, often fails to respond as expected. Earlier in the novel Fanny and Edmund stand by a window, looking out at a moonlit scene, while Mary plays the piano. Fanny offers another enthusiastic response to nature:

Fanny spoke her feelings. "Here's harmony!" said she, "Here's repose! Here's what may leave all Painting and all Music behind, and what Poetry only can attempt to describe. Here's what may tranquillize every care, and lift the heart to rapture!"

Edmund replies:

I like to hear your enthusiasm, Fanny. It is a lovely night, and they are much to be pitied who have not been taught to feel in some degree as you do—who have not at least been given a taste for nature in early life. They lose a great deal.

They discuss going out on the lawn to look at the stars. "It is a great while," says Fanny, "since we have had any star-gazing."

"Yes, [replies Edmund] I do not know how it has happened." The glee began. "We will stay till this is finished, Fanny," said he, turning his back on the window; and as it advanced, she had the mortification of seeing him advance too, moving forward by gentle degrees towards the instrument, and when it ceased, he was close by the singers, among the most urgent in requesting to hear the glee again. (94–95)

Edmund turns his back not only on Fanny but also on the outdoor scene itself, so recently the subject of their joint enthusiasm. She has just declared, with his concurrence, that the scene "leave[s] . . . all Music behind," but he soon turns around and chooses music over moonlight. Fanny's contrast between art and nature would make the natural scene appear as a given alongside the obvious artifice of poetry, music, and painting. This contrast depends, for instance, on our forgetting that she is looking through a window, an invisible framing device that presents and shapes the landscape. In choosing the unembarrassed artifice of the glee over the naturalized artifice of the outdoor scene, Edmund signals that Fanny's performance fails to carry the requisite emotional weight. He knows that one must be "taught to feel" for nature; like poetry, music, and painting, it is a taste that requires cultivation, not something that arises naturally from within. Moreover, Edmund's choice inadvertently reveals the contingency of Fanny's own feeling for nature, since once he leaves she "sigh[s] alone at the window till scolded away by Mrs. Norris's threats of catching cold"; her melancholy belies her own earlier claim that there would be less sorrow in the world "if the sublimity of Nature were more attended to" (95). Human love wins again.

Perhaps we can hear in Fanny's rejected invitation for star-gazing an echo of Paley's 1802 pronouncement that "astonomy . . . is *not* the best medium through which to prove the agency of an intelligent Creator." Still, this conversation, like that of Fanny and Mary, is only obliquely connected to the design argument. What both conversations clearly indicate, however, is that nature itself plays a limited role in organizing the desires, feelings, and conversations of the novel's characters. In both cases the encounter ends with the characters wanting what they wanted before. And so it is within the context of such failed dialogues that we can return to the conversation that Mary, Edmund, and Fanny have in the wilderness at Sotherton. Much like the scene in which Edmund abandons Fanny at the window, this may be read as a scene of temptation, a symbolic threat to Edmund's virtue and steadfastness. Yet its most compelling theological associations come by way of a very concrete examination of the persuasive power of natural theology, whose tropes are in play throughout the conversation. While Mary pursues and celebrates a winding path, Edmund seeks to measure with his watch the wilderness where they are walking. Mary claims they have walked a mile; Edmund avers that it is less than a half mile:

"We have been exactly a quarter of an hour here," said Edmund, taking out his watch. "Do you think we are walking four miles an hour?"
"Oh! do not attack me with your watch." (80)

We are meant to take this as further evidence of Mary's willfulness, but Edmund's insistence on measuring the wilderness with his watch revisits the most familiar analogy of natural theology, recently given a famous formulation, as we know, in the opening paragraph of Paley's *Natural Theology*:

In crossing a heath, suppose I pitched my foot against a *stone*, and were asked how the stone came to be there: I might possibly answer, that, for any thing I knew to the contrary, it had lain there for ever; nor would it perhaps be very easy to show the absurdity of this answer. But suppose I had found a *watch* upon the ground, and it should be inquired how the watch happened to be in that place.[44]

When he appeals to his watch, Edmund, like Paley before him, signals his participation in a culture that is gradually secularizing time. By the late seventeenth century London produced more watches and clocks than any other European city, and historians have noted the link between the rationalization of time and the increase in watch production. Monastic time, though regular, was uneven because its units varied according to daylight. But commercial time demanded greater regularity and rationalization in order to bring an increasingly complex world into harmony. By 1700 the minute hand had made its appearance, and it is to this that Edmund appeals when he corrects Mary's irregular conception of time.[45]

When Edmund produces his watch, he also reproduces the paradox we explored in Chapter 4, namely, that a *mechanical* object is supposed to reveal something characteristic of the *natural* world. Edmund claims, of course, to reveal only what is already true of the wilderness. But Mary immediately calls attention to the watch's performativity. "A watch is always too fast or too slow," she continues. "I cannot be dictated to by a watch" (80). In effect Mary recasts Paley's rhetorical question ("suppose . . . it should be inquired how the watch happened to be in that place") and answers it by declaring that the watch ought *not* to be in this place. She thus resists the watch's naturalizing tendencies by refusing to accept its claim to be merely a cipher that displays nature. Like all the mechanical analogies of natural theology (and like Fanny's window), the watch actually shapes and orders the natural world it claims simply to display, and in noting this Mary identifies the same performative structure that we traced in the discourses of improvement and of acting. She thus exposes the presupposition embedded in Edmund's appeal to his watch, namely that a mechanical object deserves epistemological priority over human judgment and desire—that mechanisms are somehow more "natural" than emotions.

Putting Mary's point in a more abstract idiom, we might say that she unmasks the watch's claim to procedural neutrality by suggesting that watches, too, have interests. To the extent that the watch stands here for Edmund's general habits of mind and of argument, Mary's counterclaim could be taken to mean that the reasonable and empirical procedure that he advocates in fact attempts to arrange things beforehand by smuggling its own notions of truth into the conversation under the guise of impartiality. From the perspective of Edmund's watch, Mary looks willful, naïve, unrealistic—she looks, that is to say, just as Fanny had looked in the chapel, when, faced with another putatively neutral discourse, she took refuge in gothic fantasy. Meanwhile, from Mary's perspective during this walk, just as from Fanny's perspective in the chapel, Edmund's notion of truth and reasonableness looks forbiddingly thin and austere. Thus, although Mary and Fanny differ markedly in the content of their beliefs, their philosophical positions turn out to be surprisingly congruent. Who, they in effect demand, would want to live in a world where watches and mahogany cushions were the only standards of measurement?

The narrator seems willing to grant Mary more license than she had granted Fanny, perhaps because she is already building the case here for Mary's eventual banishment. In any event Mary's rejection of Edmund's watch at this juncture is troubling because she is allowed to win this little exchange, getting the better of her earnest companions in both intellect and wit. She also manages to get Edmund to herself for a full hour, further cementing her rejection of his penchant for measurement. For though they had begun this walk with the express purpose of "determin[ing] the dimensions of the wood by walking a little more in it" (81), when they return the watch has vanished from the scene: "[i]t was evident that they had been spending their time pleasantly, and were not aware of the length of their absence" (87). Moreover, their wandering proceeds during the supposed discussion of Sotherton's prospects for improvement—a conversation that itself deteriorates into an inappropriately intimate encounter between Henry Crawford and Maria Bertram. So the novel's longest religious discussion, which is framed by a standard analogy of the design argument, is contrapuntally linked to improvement, the most thematically overt instance of naturalization within the novel. Improvement becomes an excuse for erotic dalliance, and the watch for a jaunt into what Austen, with the Eden story in mind, terms the "wilderness." Like improvement and acting, the discourse of design, instead of channeling enthusiasm for nature into religious wonder, serves as a screen behind which human desire may slip the bonds of naturalized convention.

At Sotherton as by the window, human desire trumps the discourse of nature, and Edmund abandons Fanny for Mary. In the window scene, Mary is clearly representing artifice, but in acknowledging that nature, too, is an acquired taste, both Edmund (explicitly) and Fanny (implicitly) subvert the novel's governing opposition between natural and artificial. At Sotherton the situation is more complex, for it features a three-way contest between the overt naturalization of improvement, Mary's anthropocentric relationship to nature, and the notion, symbolized by Edmund's watch, that accuracy is the same as truth. The watch's argument, so the Sotherton scenes demonstrate, is the hardest to sustain, because it must convince us that right measurement will so impress us that we will wish to stay on the path rather than brave the wilderness.

In these scenes desire is not subject to design's control, but has broken free to become an autonomous domain in its own right. Where nature was once deployed to bend strong feeling upward toward the divine, we now see feeling escaping into a social realm ungoverned by design, and the human protagonists into an ambiguous, post-Edenic wilderness. As we have seen throughout this book, design turns on a number of paradoxes, the most fundamental of which is that it proceeds inductively but takes for granted not only the existence of the God it seeks but also the desire to seek him. It was Hume's rhetorical triumph, I argued in Chapter 2, to make this situation appear question begging— a judgment that virtually all modern commentators have accepted but that presupposes a modern split between faith and reason. The irony of this history is that it is Edmund who, all unknowingly, has adopted Hume's position by reducing the notion of reasonableness to ascetic neutrality. When the watch is aligned procedurally with the chapel, this completes a process of transformation in which paradox drops out of rational procedure and lends its energy to the subterranean space below reason that generates, among other things, the various inappropriate encounters at Sotherton.

The failed dialogues scattered throughout *Mansfield Park* pick up on the failure inaugurated by the *Dialogues Concerning Natural Religion*, in which the participants continually talk past each other. If Hume seemed to be unfairly forcing the issue, *Mansfield Park* suggests that perhaps he was simply ahead of his time. Certainly Sotherton fails as a religious dialogue. Not only does desire consistently escape control, but religious discourse throughout this novel is static rather than flexible. Edmund, Fanny, and Mary engage in friendly and spirited conversation and then withdraw without learning much about each other, without coming to a new understanding or revising a previous one. As many critics have noted, Mary refuses to be changed by her experiences. She cannot bring herself to give up either her preconceived notions of the clergy or her desire for a fashionable and urban life. Yet if she refuses to learn from Edmund, he too refuses to learn from her. Though fascinated by Mary, he misses the implications of her ability to cast doubt on his vocation, his inability to answer her questions to her satisfaction, and her refusal to be compelled by the reasons he does offer. Austen's readers sometimes lament that if Mary could overcome her selfish desire for distinction and marry Edmund, then Fanny would marry Henry and the novel would have a more romantically satisfying ending. But the novel's rejection of this more symmetrical series of unions—a symmetry anticipated, indeed, by Mrs. Norris and by Mary herself, the two women whom the narrator summarily banishes—might equally be blamed on Edmund: if he were able to convince Mary of the worth of his vocation, the same happy outcome would ensue. In fact, Edmund can ally himself only with Fanny, who is already convinced.

The Book of Nature and Human Books

In this novel religion seems insufficiently aware of the rhetorical nature of its own arguments. When functioning at its best, design not only assumes the existence of the God it seeks but also accomplishes a strategic blend of the natural and the artificial. One is "taught to feel" for nature, and these lessons often involve an appeal to an explicitly mechanical object, like a watch, but the feeling that arises must be coded as an entirely natural one, so that it seems like human nature to believe that intricacy manifests the presence of a divine creator. All this is encapsulated in the figure of the watch itself, as Paley's *Natural Theology* makes clear. But Edmund refuses to allow such a complicated blend full play, insisting instead on the watch's complete transparency rather than acknowledging that, indeed, a watch might be too fast or too slow. He thus loses the potential for a real dialogue and sets the watch up for the absolute rejection that Mary quickly achieves. Fanny employs that same absolutism when she draws an inaccurately sharp distinction between nature and art in the window scene; by forgetting her own reliance on performance, Fanny misses a moment of potential communication, and mutual pedagogical training, between music and moonlight. And Fanny's stubborn insistence that she cannot act, though everywhere exposed by the novel itself, attests to a similar inability to recognize the potential strength and flexibility that comes when artifice and nature are blended. Such absolutism, to which Fanny and Edmund are variously susceptible, gradually comes to dominate the voice of the novel itself, as the narrator takes it upon herself to demonstrate the Crawfords' perfidy—gratuitously, in the case of Mary. As such, the novel follows in the footsteps of the *Edinburgh Review*, whose discussion of Paley's *Natural Theology* had reduced the inherent paradoxes of the dialogue format to a static opposition: "The great book of the universe lies open to all mankind; and he who cannot read in it the name and titles of its Author, will probably derive but little benefit from the labours of any commentator."[46] Either one feels design or one does not. In acknowledging more or less explicitly that there are some who "cannot read" the book of nature rightly, *Mansfield Park* inhabits the less flexible world hailed by the *Review*, a world split between the uncertain legitimacy of the sentiments of those still taught to feel for nature and those who wish not to be taught at all.

Religious dialogue had been a foundation of rational theology in the eighteenth century. Its polite format both governed the social world and grounded individual belief by legitimating rational investigation of nature as a means to study God's revelation. But the religious dialogue of *Mansfield Park* identifies not a world of amiable social ordering but a steadily less governable realm of feeling that cannot be adapted to the traditional dialogue's generic limits, chiefly because feelings in this novel cannot be rendered public. Edmund's arguments, which effectively collapse the different traditions represented by the chapel and the watch, meet with immediate and heartfelt rejection: "I cannot be dictated to by a watch," says Mary; "I am disappointed," says Fanny. Both responses come not from the discourse of nature but from somewhere else. Without natural theology's social engineering to govern the meeting place of personal and social, individual expressions of desire become detached from the structures that previously gave them meaning. Here religion surrenders its claim as a discourse that shapes desire, becoming henceforth a discourse shaped *by* desire. For some, like Fanny, this leads to a deeply felt quest for holiness; for others, like Mary, it licenses other sorts of desire. Both are private experiences and therefore can be communicated only to those who already agree.

Perhaps Cardinal Newman was right, and there is no "high Catholic ethos" in Austen's novels. But if that is so, it is not, as Newman seems to think, because Austen lacked the imagination for it. *Mansfield Park*, rather, interrogates the conditions under which the felt need for such an ethos comes into being. Above all, this means the privacy of the desiring self. Here, ironically, a critical tradition that has remained largely silent about religion in Austen (or, in the manner of Whately, deduced religion from Austen's silence) duplicates the problem set forth in the novel itself: religion, as much as slavery, is a conversation stopper in this novel. This makes *Mansfield Park* the heir of Hume's *Dialogues*, as the novel cannot finally present an identifiably religious discourse that is not itself private and *sui generis* and, hence, like Demea, subject to rejection instead of engagement.

Near the beginning of this chapter, I turned to Rudolf Otto's notion of the holy in order to give shape to Fanny's response to the Sotherton chapel. Otto, working with a post-Kantian language of rationality, theorizes holiness as a unique and thoroughly private *feeling*. Using Otto to understand Fanny is therefore symptomatic of the theorization of the religious within this novel. Otto's world, Fanny's world, and Newman's world are very much of a piece: in each case, they stand at the end of a long process that has effectively removed the religious from public conversation and located it in private and interior spaces. This is our world, as well—which is one reason it is difficult to go very far beyond Whately when it comes to the question of religion in Austen. Religious dialogue, and design's important place within that genre, mark one effort at saying something more, but the closing down of conversation accomplished in the pages of *Mansfield Park* suggests that such efforts have run up against their historical limits.

What is left to do, though, is historicize this process—something Austen, though not her narrator nor Otto nor Newman, invites us to do. The invitation is registered most clearly in the Sotherton chapel. The chapel is the result of a process that began with the creation of the Church of England itself and its literal institutionalization of secularization; that was reinvigorated by William and Mary's confirmation oath in 1689; and that was consolidated over the course of the eighteenth century until it became simply the voice of reason and good sense. Against this, Fanny has only a sensibility picked up through her reading. Her conception of what religion ought to be comes to her mediated by a book and so too does the possibility of critique that inheres in her response to the Sotherton chapel. The hope that things might have turned out otherwise is everywhere blunted and undermined by its suspect genealogy. It is no wonder, then, that this novel cannot imagine a different religious vision except under the guise of romance. For such an imagination depends upon the triumph of a private self that can be said to *possess* its needs, aspirations, and desires, religious and otherwise. In its celebration of reading over acting, of silence over speech, the novel formalizes its ambivalence about Fanny by linking her to the private and silent reading self. Fanny's critique of the chapel draws its energy from a book, which means that despite its critical tone it shares with the chapel Locke's belief that religion is ultimately a private affair.

And that, of course, is where our own critical energy derives: from a book. We too are reading. The narrator, fully conscious of this, announces her hasty denouement with the following words: "I purposely abstain from dates on this occasion, that every one may be at liberty to fix their own. . . . I only intreat every body to believe that exactly at the time when it was quite natural that it should be so, and not a week earlier, Edmund did cease to care about Miss Crawford, and became as anxious to marry Fanny, as Fanny herself could desire" (387). As several critics have pointed out, this is an assertion of the novelist's right to tie up her fictional loose ends in any way she pleases; yet the fact that such knowing artifice proceeds under the label of the natural, however ironically intended, should lead us back to those other places in the text where nature plays such a decidedly central role. The playful invocation of nature implies that every reader knows for him or herself just how long a "natural" time is, knowledge upon which the narrator will not impose by assigning names and dates. Such "natural" knowledge, while it implies universality, is also in this instance isolating, for it marks the moment in which the putatively public discourse of the novel gives way to the private speculations of its readers. It is, one might say, the final rejection of theatricality, and the possibility of shared experience that the abortive theater at Mansfield represents, and that its religious dialogues equally fail to sustain: a rejection that, not accidentally, validates the private reading subject. In conceiving of its choices in such polarized terms, the novel registers the end of religion as a public discourse that shapes private desire to its own providential and inductive ends; now, desire changes its objects at a pace that the novel itself declares to be formally undecidable. The playful language of the conclusion thus admits to what we had suspected before: from here on lives must be narrated from the inside.

Seemingly deprived of its ability to shape subjectivity, design remains at the end of this novel as a force of regulation and consolidation. In the previous chapter I noted two tendencies within Paley's *Natural Theology*: on the one hand, an unconventional identification of inwardness with rhetoric; on the other, a conventional worry about social order, given new impetus by the privacy of feeling built into the argument from perception. If the manner in which the novel gives way to the private experiences of its readers explores this first tendency, the authoritarian and repetitive close of the novel itself exemplifies the second. Thus the narrator turns deliberately away from the possibility that Edmund might wed Mary and that Fanny might marry Henry, and in so doing turns away from a utopian rapprochement with difference in which a marriage of opposites might produce a new series of human possibilities. The novel opts instead for a return of the same: cousins marrying cousins is as close as the marriage plot can come to substituting an incestuous logic of similitude for a logic of difference. Indeed, incest is the first narrative possibility that the novel considers, for when Sir Thomas is wondering whether to bring the ten-year-old Fanny to Mansfield, "He thought of his own four children—of his two sons—of cousins in love, &c." (7). Mrs. Norris immediately objects: "do not you know that of all things upon earth *that* is the least likely to happen; brought up, as they would be, always together like brothers and sisters?" (7–8). The narrator herself seems to abandon the possibility after this, at least until Fanny's brother William visits Mansfield, which prompts the narrator to reflect: "Children of the same family, the same blood, with the same first associations and habits, have some means of enjoyment in their power, which no subsequent connections can supply." In sum, "even the conjugal tie is beneath the fraternal," and indeed, "Fraternal love" is "sometimes almost everything" (195). By the time, finally, that a marriage of cousins reappears as a narrative possibility at the end of the novel, it has been both strengthened—Edmund is, as Mrs. Norris predicted, essentially Fanny's brother—and purged of its taint. In marrying Edmund, Fanny is thus able to combine the "conjugal tie" and the "fraternal." And so Sir Thomas's final judgment on the matter "formed . . . such a contrast with his early opinion on the subject when the poor little girl's coming had been first agitated" (388–89). Things work out remarkably well for Sir Thomas, in fact, as Fanny's marriage to Edmund initiates a series of repetitions and substitutions that he finds immensely gratifying. Susan Price takes Fanny's place at Mansfield, "with every appearance of equal permanency":

In her usefulness, in Fanny's excellence, in William's continued good conduct, and rising fame, and in the general well-doing and success of the other members of the family, all assisting to advance each other, and doing credit to his countenance and aid, Sir Thomas saw repeated, and for ever repeated reason to rejoice in what he had done for them all. (389)

This, of course, is the outcome that Fanny has been hoping for all along, and the fact that she has had to keep it secret for so many years has been the chief reason for her silence, solitude, and intense inwardness—for the very romantic antitheatricality that has come to define her.

What remains here is one half of Paley's argument. Design is a normalizing logic of similitude that endeavors to bring about just the sort of conclusion Sir Thomas so happily contemplates, in which things change precisely in order to stay the same. This is the phenomenon Mrs. Norris calls "*that,*" and which the narrator manages to transmute into "fraternal love." The incest form, apparently abandoned by the novel in its opening pages, seems from this perspective to have been invisibly shaping the narrative throughout, operating silently through Fanny's subjectivity until it can reemerge at last as a consummation devoutly to be wished. In tying its success so intimately to a form of love that is more mirror than lamp, *Mansfield Park* preserves the intimacy of conjugal love under the auspices of literary convention: "cousins in love, &c.," as Sir Thomas puts it to himself.

The cost of preserving convention by hooking it up to human desire in this manner is that desire won't always be so amenable. Thus, the novel has to acknowledge that the world is full of Mary Crawfords who have little interest in being interpellated quite so thoroughly as Fanny and Edmund are. To be sure, *Mansfield Park* does seem nostalgic for a world in which religion still saturates social space, what Marcel Gauchet aptly characterizes as a "system of dispossession, inheritance, and immutability."[47] Dispossession, inheritance, and immutability are exactly what we get at the end of *Mansfield Park*. But in such a world, there would have been no possibility of opting out, and so in such a world Mary would have found Edmund's defense of the clergy compelling. Thus, at the level of plot, the novel has a vested interest in a more modern world, one in which Mary can go her own way and so make room for Fanny. In this way the novel in fact depends upon Mary, or rather upon a world in which Mary is a possibility: a modern world, in short, in which, as Gauchet writes, "faith became an option with no further hold on collective organization" (164). Beneath the narrator's flippant last lines, therefore, we can read a certain anguish. She wishes to reward Fanny, but this is possible only if Mary is given her freedom, and the result is that Fanny's victory is both contingent and partial. It looks like a total victory if one remains, as the punning final sentence tells us, "within the view and patronage of Mansfield Park." But the narrator herself, like her readers, lives in a bigger world, according to whose protocols she has given us no compelling reason to choose Fanny's way over Mary's. Indeed, she cannot, for when it comes to ideas of happiness, as Mary herself observes, "every one may be at liberty to fix their own."

Chapter 6
Wordsworth: The Shape of Analogy

In the case of Jane Austen the problem is the author's relative silence about religion; in the case of Wordsworth, the problem is the opposite. He not only says too much, but what he says in unclear, vague, even contradictory, and often changing. Like many of the major male romantic poets, Wordsworth seems to be perpetually bordering on religious terrain without ever quite entering it, especially in the poetry written during his so-called "Great Decade" (1797–1807). Not only are the methodological hurdles legion, but the very concept of "religion" as it relates to Wordsworth is so slippery that it may seem hopeless to begin with it. I will aim for specificity by concentrating on design—though that too has the alarming tendency to slip through our fingers and, like Proteus, appear as something else. That "something else," I shall come to argue, is "literature," in its modern form.

My approach here can be distinguished from two recent books that treat the topic of Wordsworth and religion.[1] Deeanne Westbrook's *Wordsworth's Biblical Ghosts* is simultaneously an extensive survey of the range of Wordsworth's biblical allusions and a meditation on intertextuality. Intertextuality here is not simply allusion but what Westbrook calls a "presence" as "pervasive and subtle as white noise and at the same time invasive as a haunting by a not-altogether-congenial ghost."[2] The subtle and informative readings that issue from this notion of intertextuality are, however, put in the service of a familiar Wordsworth, one who experiences the disjunction of the aesthetic and the religious and tries to give expression to it in language. This methodological thread ties Westbrook's study to influential earlier readings of Wordsworth by M. H. Abrams, Harold Bloom, and Geoffrey Hartman; the implicit premise is that Wordsworth faces a spiritual crisis that he tries to solve by means of poetry. For these critics, the characteristic pressure and tension registered in that poetry is symptomatic of the failure of Wordsworth's attempted solution, even as it also makes that poetry recognizably modern.

Wordsworth's own intentions figure centrally in this account, something that becomes clear when Westbrook turns to the poet's famous meditation upon language from the *Essays Upon Epitaphs*: "Language," Wordsworth writes there, "if it do not uphold, and feed, and leave in quiet, like the power of gravitation or the air we breathe, is a counter-spirit, unremittingly and noiselessly at work to derange, to subvert, to lay waste, to vitiate, and to dissolve."[3] Whereas a generation of deconstructive critics found in such statements ample evidence for the way that language escapes the intentions of the poet, Westbrook finds here a poet who wields words, who understands the high stakes of the (intertextual) contest in which he is engaged.[4] When intertextuality in turn gets linked to religion, the result is to bring intentionality back into the picture as a means for getting at the poetry's religious content. Although Westbrook wisely eschews any speculation on Wordsworth's own religious beliefs, her methodology leads her to claim that recognizing the pervasive presence of the Bible in Wordsworth's poetry requires the sort of intentional reading practices that her sophisticated discussion of intertextuality had sought to displace.

If Westbrook approaches intentionality ambivalently, William A. Ulmer, in *The Christian Wordsworth, 1798–1805*, embraces it enthusiastically. He aims to "examine the poetry in light of Wordsworth's consciously held private convictions as they evolved from 1798 to 1805."[5] Wordsworth never traveled very far from Christian orthodoxy, Ulmer argues, and even the early poetry, while not "religious poetry," is shaped by a "displaced Christianity" (x). Ulmer admits, however, that "the faith of the poet and the religious vision of the poetry do not fully coincide" (ix), and this immediately complicates the relation of the poet's private convictions to his literary text. For if one makes much of this lack of coincidence, it becomes difficult to argue for Wordsworth's Christianity. If almost any poem written in late eighteenth-century England will contain religious allusions, as Ulmer acknowledges in his discussion of "Tintern Abbey," then how are we to know when the poet standing behind the poetry is a quasi-orthodox Christian such as Wordsworth or an atheist such as Percy Shelley? In order to make his claim for a Christian Wordsworth, then, Ulmer must turn to biographical matters. Wordsworth's religious allusions are different from Shelley's religious allusions, in Ulmer's reading, because Wordsworth's own private beliefs positioned him within the orbit of Christian orthodoxy, whereas Shelley's private beliefs took him outside that orbit. Yet establishing the nature of a poet's private convictions in this way will have analytic yield only if one assumes beforehand that religion is a private affair, and that public statements are vehicles for expressing prior beliefs. This formulation builds a substantive theory of religion—that its essence is private belief—into its premise.

My focus on design seeks both to lighten the weightiness that attaches itself to Wordsworth's poetry in studies such as Westbrook's and to displace the question of Wordsworth's own beliefs that Ulmer considers. My claim is not that design is the key that will unlock Wordsworth's poetry. That would be overly ambitious. Nor is my claim merely that design is "relevant" for understanding Wordsworth. That is not ambitious enough. Wordsworth's own opportunism as a poet, his ability to use whatever comes to hand, would in any case obviate both claims.[6] Instead, my focus on design seeks a different approach to the question of intentionality itself. Rather than interpreting the poet's intentions as a cipher for the poem's religious content, I argue that design allows us to understand just why it is that intentionality and religion seem so indissolubly linked in the first place. It is not accidental that romanticism—and Wordsworthian romanticism perhaps most of all—has always seemed to verge upon the spiritual *and* that it has had an uneasy relationship to the kind of anti-intentionalist reading practice that was canonized by W. K. Wimsatt, Jr., and Monroe Beardsley in their essay "The Intentional Fallacy." Design itself is a theory of intentionality; I propose that we can explain Wordsworth's spiritual affinities by reading the presence of design in his poetry as figuring the complexities of intentionality.

Virtually every reader has felt the presence of intentionality in Wordsworth—most insistently, of course, in his autobiographical epic *The Prelude*—but agreeing on what that intentionality *is* has proved more difficult. My own approach is to make a virtue of precisely this fact. Wordsworth's interest, I will argue, is in intentionality *itself*—more specifically, in creating the feeling that the reader is in the presence of intention without being able to say just what that intention is. What I will call Wordsworth's "literary effect" is just this: a recognition, keyed to his sense of the poet's complex professional status, that through the auspices of design, literature can be the means for carrying forward a consciousness of intentionality into an increasingly differentiated social world.

My reading of Wordsworth ends with the ascent of Snowdon in book 13 of *The Prelude*, a passage that does not exhibit the tensions that critics have read as symptomatic of Wordsworth's divided loyalties (divided between tradition and modernity, religion and poetry) precisely because those loyalties are no longer divided but have been displaced into a newly differentiated and recognizably "literary" domain. Taking my cue from Mark Schoenfield's claim that Wordsworth was "the most methodically professional of the major romantics," I link Wordsworth's sense of professional vocation to the literary effect his poetry produces as it differentiates itself from theological renderings of design.[7] Thus *The Prelude* offers itself as an example of literature as an entity set apart, something that carries its own special form of knowledge. If this is right, then the Snowdon passage is not a denial of or retreat from modernity, but rather an embrace of its multiple forms.

To get to this point, however, we need to trace how Wordsworth uses the design analogy in order to specify literature's differentiated status. Of course, much of Wordsworth's early verse treats the theme of poetry's emergence either directly or allegorically. From longer narratives such as "The Thorn" and "Michael" to shorter lyrics such as "Old Man Travelling" and "Simon Lee," Wordsworth relentlessly narrates not simply the genesis of poetry but also the genesis of a particular *kind* of poetry that needs to be read in a particular kind of way. *Peter Bell* and *The Ruined Cottage* draft of 1797–98 both tell this story through reference to analogy, however; and this allows us to link their concerns with the culmination of this narrative in book 13 of *The Prelude*, in which analogy at last becomes the vehicle through which intentionality is made the solution to the difficulties of modern differentiation.

What should emerge is a relationship of differentiation to literary reading that contrasts decisively with that pictured in *Mansfield Park*. Recall, for a moment, the way that in Edmund's public reading of the Sotherton chapel, any paradox that might be linked to a "sense of the holy" drops out completely and can be revived only through Fanny's counterreading, which is at once private and, as Edmund says, fantastical.[8] In contrast to Edmund, Fanny is the sort of "literary" reader who would win the approval of Cleanth Brooks, for she values ambiguity and mystery as gestures toward an integrated and holistic universe. In *Mansfield Park*, however, that literary sensibility is decisively split off from design, whose increasingly deracinated reiteration hails what I called "the end of natural theology." In contrast to this distinction between literary reading and design, the Wordsworth poems I discuss here narrate literary reading *as* a reading of design: design's negotiation of the question of intentionality models a kind of literary reading that can bring together intentionality and the secularization that attends modern differentiation.

Peter Bell: Selfhood

Peter Bell may seem a strange place from which to begin tracing the genesis of literary reading. Indeed, the poem is one of Wordsworth's clunkier efforts. Yet *Peter Bell* also showcases the demise of an orthodox hermeneutic, a demise that will eventually require the emergence of the literary domain within Wordsworth's own understanding of a poetic career. To begin with, Peter Bell is a figure whose difficulties occupied Wordsworth in the later 1790s, a figure who shows up, in various forms, in poems such as "Simon Lee," "Michael," and "Resolution and Independence." The chief difficulty for these characters, as Wordsworth describes it in the letter to Charles James Fox that he included with the manuscript of "Michael," is the effect of industrialization on the rural poor: "It appears to me," Wordsworth writes to Fox, "that the most calamitous effect, which has followed the measures which have lately been pursued in this country, is a rapid decay of the domestic affections among the lower orders of society." The "measures" to which Wordsworth refers are "the spreading of manufactures," "the heavy taxes upon postage," workhouses, "Houses of Industry," and the drop in real wages. The cumulative results of these changes, he continues, affect the family most directly, specifically in the form of alienated labor: "parents are separated from their children, and children from their parents; the wife no longer prepares with her own hands a meal for her husband, the produce of his labour; there is little doing in his house in which his affections can be interested, and but little left in it which he can love."[9] In "Michael" and "Simon Lee" Wordsworth examines this situation through figures who are remnants of an earlier time. Both Michael and Simon are virtuous men and from their deserving flows the pathos of their stories.

Peter Bell, too, depicts the rise of industry and the breakdown of family. But instead of responding virtuously to such exigencies, Peter is one of those members of the lower orders whose domestic affections have calamitously and rapidly decayed. He has not learned economic or sexual self-denial. In an emerging middle-class order built around restraint, the ability to sacrifice present desire for a future object is the guarantor of both economic stability (in the form of increased consuming power) and the social and moral order represented by the family. Malthus's *Principle of Population* (1798) makes the link between sexuality and economics starkly clear: self-discipline was the glue that held both sexual morality and economic prosperity together, and those who failed to restrain their sexual appetites were in effect choosing to be poor. Peter is a Malthusian nightmare: his incessant wandering allegorizes desire's hold on his psyche, for he seems to move through the countryside more or less at random; his twelve wedded wives, a preposterously exploded family structure, invert the governing notion of family as the locus of economic and sexual stability. He is a "woodland rover," but his itinerary reveals an attraction to industrial settings as well as rural ones: Pembroke, Exeter, Kent, Dover, Nottingham, York, Carlisle, Aberdeen, Inverness, Cheviot, Yorkshire. "Sure never man like him did roam!" the narrator concludes[10] (217, 245).

Peter is also a savage, as the narrator tells us twice, but some of this savagery is due to Peter's experience of industrialization rather than to anything "natural." He is a hybrid of "solitary Nature" (307) and "whatever vice / The cruel city breeds" (309–10), a combination that visits itself upon his very body, for we soon learn that his wrinkled, dangerous-looking physiognomy is a blend of economic calculation and the harsh glare of the sun. The signs of savagery (wrinkled face, a "long and slouching" gait, and a tendency toward superstition) are thus consequences of modernity rather than its opposite. Peter, in short, is a modern problem dressed up in primitive garb. Or—putting the matter more polemically—Peter is a figure through whom modernity represents its problems to itself under the sign of savagery.

The poem avoids a direct confrontation with the savagery of which Peter might be capable by transforming his potential for violence into the violence that he directs at an Ass whom he discovers during his roaming:

> Upon the beast the sapling rings,—
> Heav'd his lank sides, his limbs they stirr'd;
> He gave a groan—and then another,
> Of that which went before the brother,
> And then he gave a third: (476–80)

Though the narrative purpose of the Ass is to reveal the presence of a dead man in a nearby stream, the beating itself is the central event in the poem's production of meaning. And yet the poem thematizes the beating of the Ass as a moment of incomprehensibility. In fact, the narrator begins his tale with it:

> All by the moonlight river side
> It gave three miserable groans;
> " 'Tis come then to a pretty pass,"
> Said Peter to the groaning Ass,
> "But I will *bang* your bones!" (196–200)

The listeners immediately protest that they have no idea what the narrator is talking about because, as Mistress Swan puts it, "You've got at once into the middle" (MS 162). Chastened, the narrator hastens to provide a context for this rather shocking beginning to his tale, and he does this chiefly through the character delineation noted here. Yet it is unclear how much this helps; specifically, it is unclear what the beating of the Ass *means*, and this opens onto the issue of how the poem asks to be read.

Peter Bell certainly comes supplied with its own interpretive directions. To begin with, the story proceeds under the sign of allegory. Peter, on a journey, leaves the clear path in search of a shortcut and immediately finds himself, much like Dante, in a "thick wood." Soon thereafter the shortcut ends in the "yawning fissures" of an abandoned quarry. Instead of admitting his mistake and turning back to the path, Peter obstinately presses on. In case his listeners don't catch the allegorical significance of paths, wandering, and shortcuts, the narrator casts the Squire's earlier demand for more explanation in the form of a biblical lesson:

> Sure as Paradise
> Was lost to us by Adam's sinning,
> We all are wandering in a wood,
> And therefore, Sir, I wish you would
> Begin at the beginning. (MS 166–70)

When Peter's wandering from the path appears in the narrative itself, then, we have already been prepared to link its allegorical value to the redemption of the poem's audience: like Peter, they are wandering in a wood. Yet the Squire's confusion raises this interpretive maneuver to the level of a problematic; his protest at the narrator's method suggests that without the narrative context of motivated action, the redemptive value of the story itself is threatened. When, in response, the narrator offers the description of Peter's savagery and the story about his ill-fated attempt to take a shortcut, this does not resolve the issue: the internal demands of narrative and allegory are not necessarily congruent, which is why the poem as a whole seems to rest uneasily between the two. Allegory ought in principle to be understandable without the kind of background that the Squire demands; indeed the elaborate delineation of character, not to mention the historical contextualization of industrialism and rural poverty, seems out of place altogether in an allegory—or rather, it is an application that the listeners ought to have been able to make for themselves. We may read all of this in the Squire's initial demand. "We are all wandering in a wood" means, as narrative, "we do not understand what you are saying" and means, as allegory, "we are a postlapsarian people; wandering is the condition of our life." The demand to "begin at the beginning" seems to take on both of these meanings, to say, in effect: "If we do not understand Peter as a character, we will not be able to grasp the larger significance of his story and thus, like him, make our way home."

In this respect *Peter Bell* both relies upon and significantly modifies a traditional biblical hermeneutic. As Frederic Jameson has discussed so influentially in *The Political Unconscious*, medieval exegetes developed a method of linking the Old and New Testaments by means of four successive levels: the *literal* events of the Old Testament are to be understood *allegorically* in the life of Christ, then *morally* in the life of the individual believer, and finally *anagogically* in terms of the destiny of humanity itself. Consider Israel's bondage in Egypt:[11]

Table 1.

4. Anagogic	meaning of history; destiny	time on earth before Christ comes again
3. Moral	psychology of individual believer	individual's thralldom to sin and worldliness
2. Allegorical	Christ's life (interpretive key)	descent into Hell after death on the cross
1. Literal	historical referent or event	captivity of the people of Israel in Egypt

Prepared by the Squire's reference to post-lapsarian wandering and Wordsworth's somewhat labored emphasis on Peter's own wandering and shortcut taking, we are set up to read *Peter Bell* within this hermeneutic schema, filling in the blanks ourselves:

Table 2.

4. Anagogic	universal meaning	Wandering is not permanent, for the heart is a holy thing.
3. Moral	Peter's psychology	Savagery and sin are overcome by love and sympathy.
2. Allegorical	Adam's life (interpretive key)	Condemned to wander, Adam is not abandoned by God.
1. Literal	Peter's life	Wandering and violence are followed by eventual reformation.

But, crucially, when the listeners protest that they don't understand a story that begins *in medias res*, they signal an alteration in this formula: namely the primacy of character (level 3). What they recognize, in other words, is that *Peter Bell* is first of all a story about someone's subjectivity; the literal events serve as an illustration of psychological truth, to be interpreted *in light of* Peter's psychology rather than the reverse. That is why the Squire protests that he will not be able to understand the meaning of the story unless the narrator begins at the beginning.

Peter Bell is, thus, a sacred story offered within a context in which the expected method of interpreting sacred stories no longer holds because individual psychology (level 3) has gained precedence over the literal truth (level 1) as the fundamental ground of interpretation. The "meaning" of the poem (the fourth level) remains the same: Peter takes his place in a productive social network presided over by the humanized heart. Yet it is not exactly clear how one arrives at such a meaning if one begins with the self. Thus the listener's confusion. Thus also the unsatisfying ending, which appears to wrench meaning from the events of a story whose meaning is not entirely clear:

> And now is Peter taught to feel
> That man's heart is a holy thing;
> And Nature, through a world of death,
> Breathes into him a second breath,
> More searching than the breath of spring. (1121–25)

If the traditional allegorical hermeneutic that *Peter Bell* references has been disrupted by the demands of individual psychology, how do we get to this point? The poem needs a way to make allegory real in the form of historical destiny so that it can arrive at a general truth even though it begins in utter confusion, but that task is complicated because the poem does not appear to provide any principle that will transform allegory into a felt relationship with the social system. The literal truth of this story, that is to say, simply *is* the truth of the self; the conviction carried by the meaning of the poem (level 4) depends on the transformations that interpretation can work upon that truth.

Modernity and Poetic Growth

How does the poem modulate from allegory to meaning if it begins with the individual? If "Adam" is the allegorical key that unlocks Peter's psychology, and if the poem can therefore figure the landscape through which Peter wanders as specifically post-Edenic, then it needs some representational structure to move from there to the transpersonal redemption that Peter's own redemption accomplishes. Putting it this way suggests that the primacy of the individual, which we saw earlier was the chief formal problem of the poem, must also be its solution. Peter will be asked to play a split role, one that correlates with levels 1 and 3 in the hermeneutic table. There is still a literal truth that must be experienced (level 1), but there is also the personal interpretation of that experience (level 3) to be accomplished. Unlike traditional allegory, neither of these tasks can be subcontracted out to another time, another place, or another person. In short, Peter is a modern subject. He must reform himself.

Not surprisingly, the moment when Peter beats the Ass, already thematized as a site of incomprehensibility, is the crucial event in this self-reformation. A moment of literal as well as allegorical blockage (since it refuses to move), the Ass points beyond itself while remaining stubbornly material. What it points *to* is the poem's second mystery: the dead man in the river. The connection between these two signs is simply that both inflict pain upon Peter. When Peter beats the Ass, he also punishes himself, for "Each blow the arm of Peter stings / Up to the elbow and the shoulder" (MS 469–70). Likewise, when Peter pulls the dead man out of the river he "feels some ugly pains / Across his liver, heart, and reins / Just like a weaver's shuttle pass" (MS 658–60). One of the poem's projects, however, is to transform this physical pain into psychological pain, which it begins doing by making the dead body in the river a site for a fantasy of corporal punishment:

> Is it the shadow of the moon?
> Is it the shadow of the cloud?
> Is it a gallows there pourtrayed?
> Is Peter of himself afraid?
> Is it a coffin or a shroud? (MS 531–35)

This progression of questions rewards careful scrutiny. The link between the gallows and Peter's self-induced fear, cemented by the rhyme ("pourtrayed," "afraid"), elides an important shift in the relationship between the narrator and Peter. The first three questions of the stanza, we assume, are Peter's own thoughts rendered in the narrator's voice. But the fourth question is clearly the narrator's own, a kind of metaquestion that is also an interpretation of the previous questions. By casting the matter as one internal to subjectivity ("Is Peter of himself afraid?"), the narrator not only pokes fun at Peter's superstitious mind but also exposes the fact that the objects of the first two questions are not in fact the objects themselves but their shadows, ghostly projections that suggest their origins only in the shape of absence. The spectral nature of the objects in these first questions is subsequently reinforced and modified by the third question: "is it a gallows there *pourtrayed?*" begins the work of internalizing the object by suggesting that the epistemological issue depends on representation. This internalization is completed by the metacommentary of the fourth question, so that by the time we get to the coffin and shroud of the final question the absent object has been completely internalized as self, and thereby linked both figuratively and psychologically to death. Crucially, however, the mechanism works through the mediation of the question about the gallows, with its representation of punishment giving meaning to the pain that Peter had inflicted on himself when he beat the Ass. The presence of the gallows here is perhaps why death arrives in the final question not through an evacuation of the ego but through an internalization of the very symbol of punishment itself. From being a virtually uncontainable savage, Peter beats himself into a disciplined subjectivity in which interiority is indistinguishable from death.

Such scenes are not uncommon in the poetry Wordsworth was writing during this period. Within a few years, in *Prelude* passages such as the drowned man episode and the gibbet mast "spot of time," he was able to recast such materials into examples of internal growth. In those scenes, of course, death and corporeal punishment occupy a memorial time distinct from that of the narrative. Their purpose is to discover in prior events a renovating virtue and to memorialize, as Wordsworth shortly says, such moments "for future restoration."[12] In retrospective adulthood, trauma and violence are internalized as essential to the development of the self, and the consequent visionary moment becomes a register of growth.[13]

Here we confront a regulation central to the formation of a Wordsworthian poetic self. Influential studies of romantic selfhood in relation to such regulation have generally followed the lead of Michel Foucault, whose book *Discipline and Punish* analyzes the transformation of punishment from a largely external to a largely internal affair. Foucault tells us that in early modern Europe the torture of criminals was a public spectacle, a means for displaying the body of the criminal as a visible sign of penal power. The tortured body of the criminal as well as the public spectacle of the scaffold offered themselves to public interpretation:

Hence the insatiable curiosity that drove the spectators to the scaffold to witness the spectacle of sufferings truly endured; there one could decipher crime and innocence, the past and the future, the here below and the eternal. It was a moment of truth that all the spectators questioned: each word, each cry, the duration of the agony, the resisting body, the life that clung desperately to it, all this constituted a sign.[14]

Cast this description of the scaffold into the psyche and it would beautifully gloss *The Prelude*'s gibbet mast scene. Like the prisoner, the boy experiences agony and fear when confronted with the scaffold; like the spectators, the mature poet discovers in those things signs of the eternal. Observing this connection, Alan Liu has proposed that the birth of the poetic self in *The Prelude* comes when, through an act of memory, the subject fulfills the roles of both spectator and prisoner.[15] Such internalization or privatization is precisely the shift remarked by Foucault as characteristic of modern punishment, when the imagination or expectation of torture replaces its literal manifestation.[16]

Yet Peter and his Ass are no spot of time, for here violence and its anticipation have not yet been imaginatively fused. The poem's machinery clanks on; its protagonists do not live in the poetic, memorial time of *The Prelude* and are therefore unable to take their place immediately in a story that transforms violence into selfhood through the ministrations of memory. Peter's gallows fantasy has had its effect, however, for when he thinks of the dead body some time later, the physical pain that he had earlier felt returns: "And once again those ugly pains / Across his liver, heart, and reins/Just like a weaver's shuttle pass" (MS 923–25). Importantly, the 1819 version of the poem makes the internalization here even more explicit: "And once again those darting pains, / As meteors shoot through heaven's wide plains, / Pass through his bosom—and repass!" (783–85). Unlike the gibbet mast of *The Prelude*, where torture is recast as the poem's prehistory, *Peter Bell* thus replays and displays corporal punishment once more before documenting its transformation, during Peter's ride, into an internal discourse of the heart. And once the heart's journey is underway, the conclusion is inevitable. Peter's body, disciplined by the imagination of torture, becomes available for the depths of memory and of feeling that will signal his redemption—becomes available, that is, for the psychological depths we associate with Wordsworth's greatest poetry. The heart begins its journey at the moment of the imagination of punishment, and ends when Peter "feel[s] / The heart of man's a holy thing" (MS 1312). "Feeling comes in aid of feeling," as Wordsworth would put it in *The Prelude*, accomplishing an uninterrupted supervision of the process of self-production. Once feeling has become a matter of habit, its literal sources—pain, dead bodies—disappear, replaced by a sensibility whose location is, simply, deep.

Peter Bell's journey allows us to see that secularization is the condition of possibility for this trauma *and* its transformation. The poem's negotiation of its allegorical material reminds us that, though Peter's story needs to be heard, it cannot be heard within the sacred structures that would have given it meaning in the past. The listeners in *Peter Bell* are poised between interpretive worlds, and in this respect Peter's story is designed to usher them fully into a hermeneutic driven by character rather than tradition. Yet that hermeneutic must produce the same meaning that its sacred antecedents did, rescuing the audience from their post-lapsarian condition and inserting them into a redemptive narrative. Literary understanding, as this poem presents it, thus presupposes the very modern world that it would narrate away. To "begin at the beginning" is to offer a history of the modern self as a traumatized subject and also to reembed that subject into a network of significance whose continued viability is belied by his presence. From now on, the subject must save the system that gives him meaning.

Growth in *The Ruined Cottage*

In *The Ruined Cottage* (1797–98), traumatic events likewise fall suddenly upon exposed and vulnerable figures. And again, literary interpretation is forced to make sense of the interpretive difficulties such events necessarily entail. The model for such interpretation is the advice given to the narrator by the Pedlar: "no longer read / The forms of things with an unworthy eye." The play on "form" makes it obvious, if we hadn't realized it before, that the lesson is applicable to both Nature and Art. In fact, since this is a message delivered to an apprentice poet by a man associated with a proper reading of Nature, its claim might be put more strongly: to read Nature rightly is to participate in poetic creation. Nature does not have to be wrenched into Poetry; instead, Poetry arrives as the gift of Nature itself. Since this is *The Prelude's* principle article of faith, as well as its frequent object of demonstration, *The Ruined Cottage* may be understood as helping to effect an important transition into a familiarly Wordsworthian understanding of vocation in which the poet realizes, by examining his own memory, that Nature has all along been ministering to him and preparing him for the task of writing.[17]

One thing that has to be in place for this transformative poetics to take hold, however, is a reading technique able to turn the raw materials of nature into images of spiritual truth. This is a task in which *The Ruined Cottage*, especially its treatment of the eye, plays a central part. "No longer read the forms of things with an unworthy eye" is a lesson in reading that is also a lesson in seeing: with a proper reading of the forms of things, the worthy eye transforms the sad human story of Margaret and Robert into an image of tranquility. The Pedlar demonstrates this transformative process in his lengthy "reading" of the spear-grass at the poem's end:

> "My Friend, enough to sorrow have you given,
> The purposes of wisdom ask no more;
> Be wise and chearful, and no longer read
> The forms of things with an unworthy eye.
> She sleeps in the calm earth, and peace is here.
> I well remember that those very plumes,
> Those weeds, and the high spear-grass on that wall,
> By mist and silent rain-drops silvered o'er,
> As once I passed did to my heart convey
> So still an image of tranquillity,
> So calm and still, and looked so beautiful
> Amid the uneasy thoughts which filled my mind,
> That what we feel of sorrow and despair
> From ruin and from change, and all the grief
> That passing shews of being leave behind,
> Appeared an idle dream that could not live
> Where meditation was. I turned away
> And walked along my road in happiness."[18]

When he speaks these words the Pedlar has just finished telling the story of Margaret's slow demise after her husband, Robert, first loses his job as a weaver and then, desperate for money, departs for the army. The Poet, his auditor, is the recipient of both this story and its moral.[19] The poem thus rehearses a scene of poetic instruction, in which the Poet, who enters the scene toiling across "a bare wide Common" with "languid feet which by the slipp'ry ground/Were baffled still" (19–21) is instructed in the art of worthy seeing and worthy reading by the Pedlar. The play on feet at the poem's beginning, like the play on form at its end, sets up the ensuing transformation: the Poet will exchange his "baffled" feet for a "worthy" eye. In other words, as technique is absorbed into form, poetry will be revealed as the product not of toil but of tranquility. The Pedlar will manage this exchange by teaching the Poet what he knows, thereby transmuting the truths that repose in Nature into the knowledge delivered by Art.

This is the hesitant emergence of a differentiated literary domain, structured by its own habits and pedagogies of reading. But this domain remains constitutively linked to the poet himself, as both a figure and a historical personage. "Wordsworth," that is to say, is intimately tied to the production of "literature," simultaneously inviting and complicating a biographical interpretation of the text. We have the man himself to thank for this; many years later he told Isabella Fenwick that the Pedlar was "chiefly an idea of what I fancied my own character might have become in his circumstances."[20] The attraction of the Pedlar's life is obvious when we compare it to the Poet's toiling, impeded feet, or to the frustrations of the speaker in *The Prelude*, who declares in "measured strains" (1.57) his desire to write a great poem but whose mind, in yet another play on poetic feet, refuses to cooperate: "where'er she turns she finds/Impediments from day to day renewed" (1.140–41). Yet if poetry represents distance from the Pedlar's world—the inevitable distance allegorized by the post-lapsarian setting of *The Prelude*—it will also be the solution to that distance. In *The Ruined Cottage*, the Pedlar's story is not only preserved but also transformed by the vocation of poetry itself, which generalizes the Pedlar's lessons on proper seeing and proper reading, interpreting tranquility by way of the feet and forms of poetic craft.

That worthy method of reading, though, must be distinguished from an equally meaningful but dangerously static method. This becomes clear in a draft passage about the Pedlar that Wordsworth eventually moved to *The Prelude*:

> To every natural form, rock, fruit, and flower,
> Even the loose stones that cover the highway,
> He gave a moral life; he saw them feel
> Or linked them to some feeling. (*Ruined Cottage* MS B, 80–83)

The lines revise themselves: "he saw them feel" looks like unabashed animism, while "linked them to some feeling" asserts that feeling arises from the conscious subject, not the natural world itself. Because these lines describe a sensibility that will be held up as a model of what the reading eye can do, the internal revision betrays some anxiety: is the poet a crude animist or a sensitive man of letters?

When he moved this material to *The Prelude* and turned it into a self-description, Wordsworth added some contextualizing lines.[21]

> A track pursuing not untrod before,
> From deep *analogies* by thought supplied
> Or consciousness not to be subdued,
> To every natural form, rock, fruit, or flower,
> Even the loose stones that cover the highway,
> I gave a moral life—I saw them feel,
> Or linked them to some feeling: (3.121–27; emphasis added)

The new context changes the character of this self-revision. The retrospective mode of *The Prelude* version blunts the earlier anxiety by placing it at an early moment in an autobiographical epic, so that the possibilities represented by animism become of historical interest only: "And here, O friend, have I *retraced* my life" is how Wordsworth begins the next verse paragraph (3.168, emphasis added). In *The Elementary Forms of Religious Life*, Emile Durkheim describes animism as a kind of dreaming that confuses the worlds of sleeping and waking.[22] The *Prelude* lines revise such animism into a more stable relationship to objects that relocates dreams within the boundaries of the wakeful mind by casting them as an exercise in retrospective retracing, the narration of a progression from darkness to light, from being mastered by an animistic world to mastering that world through the intensities of feeling. In short, this is the arc of Wordsworthian "growth" itself, in which the poet achieves his mature, conscious vision after awakening from his animistic dreams.

The added lines about analogy and consciousness likewise contextualize animism's appeal. Reflecting a familiar distinction between tradition and autonomy, analogies originate somewhere else ("by thought supplied"), while consciousness arises from within ("not to be subdued"). Though the manifest purpose of the passage is to demonstrate that analogy and consciousness lead to the same place, its grammar belies that claim by linking analogy not only with tradition but with primitivism: "analogies . . . or consciousness . . . saw them feel, / Or linked them to some feeling." On one side, then, we have analogy, tradition, and feeling rocks; on the other, consciousness, autonomy, and a "feeling" method of reading.

By moving these lines from *The Ruined Cottage* to *The Prelude*, in short, Wordsworth describes both the growth of the poet and the growth of a reading method that can understand him. Similar growth narratives pass by with extraordinary economy and beauty in the famous "spots of time" passages. Here, though, the revisionary attention that Wordsworth gives to the cluster represented by analogy / tradition / animism offers a glimpse of the anxiety that attends growth, an anxiety harder to locate in the spots of time, with their mature consciousness so eager to offer us the appropriate interpretation of their trauma.

What we can easily miss in those spots of time is the appeal of the static world from which the narrative of growth must extract itself. Primitivism is the "other" of Wordsworth's developmental narrative precisely because it does represent, if only briefly, an alternative that disrupts and halts the series of transformations upon which the developmental narrative depends. *The Ruined Cottage* makes this alternative explicit in the figure of Robert, who begins as model husband and rural laborer, but is reduced by circumstance to random and unproductive labor:

> Ill fared it now with Robert, he who dwelt
> In this poor cottage; at his door he stood
> And whistled many a snatch of merry tunes
> That had no mirth in them, or with his knife
> Carved uncouth figures on the heads of sticks. (161–65)

Forced to exchange his loom and "busy spade" for whistling and carving, Robert regresses from forward-looking industriousness into fetishistic equilibrium. Floating free of the seasonal activities that had structured his life, he is incapable of redeeming his enforced leisure time. The figures that he carves find their mirror image in the poet's own animistic temptation regarding the feeling stones, for in each case progress is replaced by a primitive complacency unredeemable by poetry. If rocks really *do* feel, after all, the world doesn't need poets.

This does not mean that animism and fetishism are the same thing. Rather, it identifies in each a threat to the narrative of professional progress to which the poem is committed, and which the Pedlar's literary reading of the spear grass simultaneously secures and generalizes as the privileged method for worthy reading. For progress to resume, and for the narrative of poetic maturity to continue, tendencies toward animism ("I saw them feel") need to be made to appear not as primitive but as early forms of sensibility ("linked them to some feeling"). And tendencies toward fetishism ("uncouth figures on the heads of sticks") must be revised into a spiritualized reading of objects (the spear grass in which the Pedlar reads the poem's lessons). These revisions are of paramount importance: upon them depend the coherence of a "poetic career," with its narrative of growth from thralldom to self-consciousness. The poet's journey is thus the converse of Robert's; while Robert devolves into stasis and primitivism, the poet progresses from a state of subjection to a maker of meanings. He learns to explain the workings of the external forces that had bound him and he thus overcomes and subsequently internalizes that which had held him in its power.

Secularization and Primitivism

In *The Disenchantment of the World,* Marcel Gauchet offers a theory of secularization that helps explain why the primitive exerts such power for Wordsworth. Gauchet begins with an anthropological postulate derived from Durkheim: that religion is essentially a process of subjectification in which humans give up autonomy in exchange for stability. This agreement is obtained in its purest form in the primitive world. The development of monotheism signals a fundamental break in this schema because it introduces the idea that there is a higher principle toward which growth is possible. For the first time, the idea of a future enters a form that had been oriented toward the past, and once this decisive break has been made, it is only a matter of time before the development of what Gauchet terms the "religions for exiting religion" (Judaism and Christianity), which in confining the holy to God alone eventually empty the world of meaning. Gauchet emphasizes, however, that this is not a progressive narrative; the shifts from polytheism to monotheism to modern differentiation are not to be understood as "purifications" of religion. Secularization is not the unfolding of a latent potentiality but rather a long crisis, a series of breakdowns in the original totalizing vision.[23]

Gauchet's analysis targets the presuppositions of developmental secularization narratives in which the vector runs toward modernization and demystification. "[H]umanity is not oriented in only one direction," Gauchet writes. "The human race undoubtedly has a stubborn tendency to increase its power and objectify its freedom, . . . [b]ut hidden in the depths of time is another humanity whose secret has been lost, and needs to be rediscovered, one that found a way to be at one with itself in its accepted dependency and its passive relation with the world" (7). The only way to rediscover the "humanity whose secret has been lost" is to lift the burden of modernization from that other humanity. Gauchet's primitive is not a modern subject waiting to be liberated but has rather found a way to be at one in his passivity. But the secret of that contentment has been lost, covered over by the teleological orientation of our modernization and secularization stories.

Here then, is a reading of the power of the primitive in Wordsworth. The primitive world is completely saturated with meaning, with the pure religion of polytheism. That meaning-rich world is attractive in part because it moves according to mythic time rather than historical time. But that is also its limitation, for it is a static world, predicated upon changelessness. Growth becomes possible only with monotheism, with the idea of a future. To engage in forward movement, however, means losing the richly meaning-saturated world, purchasing knowledge with loss of power. If history is the history of breakdowns, poetry must redeem history by transforming it into progress. Thus the narrative of growth that structures so much of Wordsworth's early poetry is in fact an attempt to overwrite an alternative narrative predicated on the loss of meaning. The narrative of growth is so powerful because it recapitulates at the level of the individual a progressive modernization narrative: meaning is gradually elicited and released from a natural world gradually discovered to be benevolent rather than hostile, and then purified by a consciousness whose genesis is itself natural. The alternative to this narrative appears as a traumatic rupture in the smooth surface of historical time, a deviation from business as usual, an accident in which primitivism emerges suddenly like the drowned man of Esthwaite, who "bold upright / Rose with his ghastly face" (5.471–72). Or, as we observed already, the alternative can appear as a blockage or resistance, like Peter's savage beating of the Ass, like Robert carving his uncouth figures, or like the "uncouth shape" (4.402) of the discharged soldier in *The Prelude*, with his "ghastly mildness" (4.493).

This secret humanity, uncouth and ghastly, is the "other" against which Wordsworth's narrative of personal growth must define itself. It does this through a method of reading that turns that secret humanity into what the Pedlar calls a "secret *spirit* of humanity." That is, it rereads an anthropological story as a story of the human spirit, updating the religious totality of primitivism into something more familiarly modern, more amenable to the transformations of content that growth must achieve. So Peter learns to read his adventures from the perspective of the humanized heart, and the Poet is taught to trace the "secret spirit of humanity" encased in the dilapidated scene before him, and the narrator of *The Prelude* learns to read the terror of the drowned man with his inner eye. Modernity, these examples suggest, *just* is the management of trauma and backwardness, their transformation through reading and memory into something that can be used.

From Peter Bell's savagery to feeling stones, uncouth carvings, murderers, drowned men, and deep and gloomy breathing places, the attraction of primitivism is that it allows the poet to have it both ways, to get the primitive's richly meaningful relationship to the world without sacrificing progress and growth. Thus *The Ruined Cottage* follows Gauchet's recommendation when it delves into a past marked by passivity and equilibrium in order to redeem it. Gauchet writes of "another humanity whose secret has been lost, and needs to be rediscovered" (7) as an antidote to progressive theories of religious transformation. But by transforming passivity into activity and discovering the hidden meaning of the past, reading in *The Ruined Cottage* inscribes that other humanity within the very progressive narrative of modernity against which it apparently stood. In this poem, one cannot read primitivism because, by definition, to read primitivism is to overcome it by putting it to use in a developmental narrative. In these passages, Wordsworth shows himself less sanguine than Gauchet about our ability to divorce ourselves from progressive narratives of secularization.

In moving now to a discussion of analogy in *The Prelude*, I will argue that in analogy Wordsworth finds an alternative to the twin poles of primitivism and progressive secularization between which *Peter Bell* and *The Ruined Cottage* oscillated. That alternative will be a model of secularization as differentiation rather than progress.

The Prelude and the Pathway of Analogy

To get a sense of how differentiation and analogy modify a narrative of growth and transformation, we need to begin by remarking upon the extraordinary facility with which *The Prelude* does indeed transform trauma and blockage into visionary imagination. In a variety of ways, both celebratory and critical, this facility is also at the heart of Wordsworth commentary. Critics note, for instance, that *The Prelude*'s traumas often depend upon chance or upon an outright mistake that is then transformed into a spiritual necessity. Sometimes this contingency gets literalized as a faulty or absent guide. So in the gibbet-mast episode in *The Prelude*, "some mischance" separates the boy from his comrade (11.284), and the boy's subsequent "visionary dreariness" is the result. The crossing of Simplon Pass in book 6 foregrounds this theme, as the speaker's party meets another group of travelers, and "making of these our guides,/Did we advance" (6.497–68). These guides eventually leave them behind, however, and the speaker's party follows but fails to overtake them. When a peasant finally informs them that they have taken the wrong path and that they must retrace their steps, the consequence is the famous apostrophe to the Imagination:

> Imagination!—lifting up itself
> Before the eye and progress of my song
> Like an unfathered vapour, here that power,
> In all the might of its endowments, came
> Athwart me. I was lost as in a cloud,
> Halted without a struggle to break through,
> And now, recovering, to my soul I say
> "I recognize thy glory." (6.525–32)

Geoffrey Hartman, whose reading of this scene is paradigmatic, remarks that imagination stops the poet in his tracks, forcing him to attribute to it the glory that his eye had earlier attributed to nature. Hartman calls this an "apocalyptic" moment: "there is an inner necessity to cast out nature, to extirpate everything apparently external to salvation."[24] The eye, associated since *The Ruined Cottage* with progress, poetic development, and a proper reading of nature, is here overcome by a moment beyond nature, whose source is internal and unworldly. In Hartman's reading, language orchestrates imagination's usurpation of nature; poetry is relieved from its burden of accurately representing the world. This appears to be the achievement toward which Wordsworth's narrative of growth has been tending all along: imagination is at last set free of the world and dialectical progress becomes spiritual rather than linear. Through the agency of language the mind now experiences itself in its own perpetual act of creation and transformation.

This is such a remarkable moment and has received so many memorable critical readings that it is difficult not to think of the Simplon Pass episode as the highpoint of *The Prelude* itself. Yet its power comes at a cost, for it presents the speaker with a version of the division between tradition and modernity that structures modernization theory. The speaker must choose: either he remains stuck in the past or he enters the lonely but glorious world of vision. The end result of this conception of poetic growth is the kind of theoretical and political emancipation that Wordsworth later describes as "a stride at once / Into another region" (10.240–41), an intellectual revolution in which the solitary self suddenly grasps its separation from the movement of history. And that decisive stride will lead, as book 10 documents, into *The Prelude*'s most sustained crisis, during which the speaker "Yield[s] up moral questions in despair" (10.900).

In contrast to the Simplon Pass episode, with its referents (variously displaced) to the French Revolution and England's subsequent war, Wordsworth returns at the end of *The Prelude* to the path from which he had so abruptly departed. In book 13 he describes his ascent of Mount Snowdon in northern Wales, an event that far from being a stride into "another region," follows in a familiar path. The speaker and his companion seek out a conductor, "the shepherd who by ancient right / Of office is the stranger's usual guide" (13.7–8). No one will get lost on this trip. On Simplon Pass and in the spots of time, imagination's arrival depended upon a surprise or shock that was the result of a vanished path or a poor guide, and the ensuing trauma descended suddenly upon the exposed self. In the crisis of book 10, likewise, various intellectual guides such as William Godwin lead the speaker astray. In book 13, though, the track is clear and the guide is reliable: many people have been this way before, and the shepherd's office is "ancient." This is a somewhat labored way of emphasizing that the vision atop Snowdon comes to the poet by way of tradition rather than as condition of abandoning it.

The vision itself turns upon the mist that covers the ocean and so appears as a second sea:

> Meanwhile, the moon looked down upon this shew
> In single glory, and we stood, the mist
> Touching our very feet; and from the shore
> At distance not the third part of a mile
> Was a blue chasm, a fracture in the vapour,
> A deep and gloomy breathing-place, through which
> Mounted the roar of waters, torrents, streams
> Innumerable, roaring with one voice.
> The universal spectacle throughout
> Was shaped for admiration and delight,
> Grand in itself alone, but in that breach
> Through which the homeless voice of waters rose,
> That dark deep thoroughfare, had Nature lodged
> The soul, the imagination of the whole. (13.52–65)

Despite the sublime apparatus, many readers experience this passage as a disappointment when compared to the address to the Imagination in Simplon Pass. Whereas in book 6 mind and nature battled for supremacy, book 13 aims for synthesis, claiming that mind and nature reflect each other, making the natural scene before the poet a "perfect image of a mighty mind" (13.69). Wordsworth has apparently moved from being a poet who casts out nature to being a poet *of* nature, and so influential readers of Wordsworth have interpreted this scene as a retreat from his most daring poetry.[25]

Simplon Pass and the spots of time, whose insights are predicated upon confusion, misrecognition, and blockage, exhibit linguistic pressures that seem to mark them as authentically modern experiences. In an astute analysis of Snowdon's difference from these other moments, David P. Haney writes that "[i]n the Snowdon episode, the disappearance of language into the 'deep and gloomy breathing place' should be even less readable [than in the spots of time], but through the miracle of reflection . . . the scene is completely readable."[26] This "miracle of reflection," he continues, is a figure for the miracle of the incarnation. I agree with Haney about the difference between the spots of time and Snowdon, but I do not think that it is a "miracle" that makes the Snowdon event legible. Quite the opposite, in fact: what makes Snowdon readable is the language of the design analogy that has structured Wordsworth's presentation of Snowdon from the beginning. Rather than the special revelation that Haney finds here, I find general revelation: the always available reading of nature as God's Book.

This is so because analogy plays such a crucial role in organizing the speaker's response to the scene. Indeed, Wordsworth himself attempted an analogical interpretation of this event: 140 lines, generally known as the "Analogy Passage," composed in the early spring of 1804. The passage announces an "analogy betwixt / The mind of man and Nature," for both transform their objects and "to one life impart / The functions of another."[27] Wordsworth offers several such analogies: a rainbow over Coniston, unmoved in the midst of natural chaos, "With a colossal stride bridging the whole vale"; a motionless horse, "a living statue or a statued life," which the poet and his companion leave "With all his functions silently sealed up"; the voyagers Columbus and Gilbert, who remain calm even when nature threatens their lives; and the anticipated deaths of the explorers Mungo Park and William Dampier. The passage loses energy by the time it gets to these voyages, perhaps because Wordsworth is quoting extensively from travel books. Gilbert in fact seems to drown in a book, sitting "In calmness, with a book upon his knee— . . . The ship and he, a moment afterwards, / Engulphed, and seen no more" (101, 104–5). At this point the passage becomes the experience of a textuality whose meanings are externally imposed.

The manuscript (MS.W, DC MS.38) shows that Wordsworth gave the passage considerable attention prior to dropping it entirely, shortly before the five-book version of *The Prelude* reached its final form around March 10, 1804.[28] Yet excising the Analogy Passage apparently failed to satisfy him, for soon after telling Coleridge and Thomas De Quincey that the poem was virtually done, Wordsworth decided to expand it; and by the end of March 1804 he was beginning to think of it in the form that we know as the thirteen-book *Prelude*, completed by May 1805. Wordsworth's writing of the Analogy Passage, his rejection of that passage, and his reconceptualization and expansion of the entire poem, therefore, all take place within a couple of weeks.

This textual history invites speculation about Wordsworth's intentions, and Joseph F. Kishel has accordingly provided a remarkably coherent biographical interpretation of the Analogy Passage and Wordsworth's reasons for rejecting it. Kishel remarks that in the spring of 1804 Wordsworth was anxious about finishing *The Prelude* and turning to the massive, Coleridge-imposed burden of *The Recluse*.[29] During early March, probably with his inability to tackle *The Recluse* in mind, he was composing the despairing passage in *The Prelude* in which, blaming his own "over-anxious eye," he described himself "Unprofitably traveling towards the grave, / Like a false steward who hath much received / And renders nothing back" (1.269–71). The other piece of the five-book *Prelude* that Wordsworth was working on at this time was the Analogy Passage: an attempt to explain how the Snowdon event confirmed him as a good

steward, able to turn a profit with poetry's gifts by writing a great philosophical poem. In Kishel's account, then, the Analogy Passage must justify
Wordsworth's own sense of professional vocation—a burden that neither poem nor poet could sustain. Then Coleridge left for Malta, and
Wordsworth decided to drop the Analogy Passage and expand *The Prelude*. Kishel proposes that Coleridge's departure relieved the pressure to
turn immediately to *The Recluse*, and, with that burden lightened,
Wordsworth was able to see that the Analogy Passage was not adequate
to the task of justifying his worthiness to undertake "a work that should
endure." He started writing at a terrific pace.[30]

    In contrast and complement to this intentional reading, I interpret
the Analogy Passage as an allegory of intentionality itself—that is, of the
poet's attempt to force meaning upon his material by means of analogy.
The difference between the Analogy Passage and the verses that eventually made it into the 1805 *Prelude* is the difference between a series of
analogies imposed from the outside and an analogical meditation presented as rising from within the speaker. Rather than coming from the
"somewhere else" of tradition and history, analogy in the 1805 *Prelude*
emerges simultaneously as a "meditation" within the mind (13.66) and
an intrinsic power of Nature. The power "which Nature thus / Thrusts
forth upon the senses, is the express / Resemblance . . . of the glorious
faculty / Which higher minds bear with them as their own" (13.85–87,
13.89–90). Just as Nature transforms the landscape by covering it with
mist, so, by analogy, the imagination transforms "all the objects of the
universe" (13.92) upon which it bends its power.

    By book 13 analogy arises intrinsically, generated by its material
rather than being imposed upon it. It seems free of orthodox theological content, as it links human creation to nature without making reference to a divine creator. Divinity, meanwhile, has come to reside in the
mind itself, as Wordsworth shortly concludes: "The sense of God, or
whatsoe'er is dim / Or vast in its own being" is an "under-presence" of
the "mighty mind" that the natural scene has bodied forth (13.72–73,
13.71, 13.69). Such familiar natural supernaturalism arrives here only
because intentionality, figured as extrinsic analogy, has been recognized as yet another false guide. In the previous chapter, discussing
Burke's invocation of historical continuity and England's "*antient* indisputable laws," I observed that Burkean tradition in fact presupposes the
differentiated world it claims to combat. In book 13 Wordsworth makes
a similar observation about the shepherd's "ancient right / Of office."
In trading the extrinsic analogies of the Analogy Passage for the intrinsic analogies that appear in *The Prelude*, Wordsworth acknowledges that
analogy is the carrier of differentiation rather than tradition. In a differentiated world, the strong intentionality of the Analogy Passage cannot

be sustained, for the conditions to which it speaks and responds no longer obtain. Dropping the Analogy Passage means dropping intentionality as an overt principle of poetic composition. Henceforth, poetic meaning will arise from within, just as the meditation rises within the speaker in book 13, and the mist rises off the ocean, and the reading of the spear grass rises from within the Pedlar's own meditation. Only once poetry is no longer analogical can it become truly analogical: only when analogy is no longer understood as a vehicle of intentionality will poetry arise naturally—that is, on analogy with nature. Thus does the Snowdon passage retain the aura of design within a differentiated universe.

Intentionality and Literary Effect

Once the intentionalism of external analogy no longer shapes the Snowdon experience, a new kind of reading practice, intimated already in *Peter Bell* and *The Ruined Cottage*, can take its appointed place as the privileged interpretive method. Like the literature it interprets, this method does not produce meaning through the application of an external analogy but rather reads deeply in the text itself. Together, this literature and its privileged reading make up Wordsworth's "literary effect": a nonintentional practice of writing and reading so constructed as to retain the "power" (13.84) of the older, intentional modes of writing and reading from which the poem has differentiated itself. Appositely enough, Wordsworth calls this power a "function" (13.74), namely, the ability to make the "grossest minds" (13.83) see, hear, and feel the "domination" of this new domain and its characteristic effects (13.77). Thus the natural supernaturalism of the Snowdon passage, which seems to accord with a progressive secularization narrative, is here shown to depend upon a functional differentiation felt powerfully even by the dull-witted. Moreover, the literary domain establishes its domination—and thus legitimates Wordsworth's vocation—by retaining the power of analogical reading. For if the literary arises as if by nature, but nature must still be read analogically if we are to feel the power of that literature, then design and the intentionalism it encodes remain a curious presence within this newly nonintentional poetics. The idea that nature is structured analogically remains, but the paradoxical result of the poem's special literary effect is that an analogical reading of nature now seems to come *from* a nature severed from its divine creator, just as a meaningful reading of poetry seems to come *from* a poem severed from the intentions of the poet.

In thus relying upon design's aura while referencing it only obliquely, Wordsworth fastens upon an aesthetic sensibility buried within design arguments. Recall one of Cleanthes' formulations of design in the *Dialogues*, the version I have called the argument from perception:

Consider, anatomize the eye: Survey its structure and contrivance; and tell me, from your own feeling, if the idea of a contriver does not immediately flow in upon you with a force like that of sensation. (56)

Cleanthes does not say that the idea of contri*vance* will flow in upon the observer; he assumes that contrivance is a given and appeals immediately to the supposed contriv*er*, the agent behind the scenes whom he assumes to possess desires, aims, and intentions. The idea that design necessarily carries with it the implication of intentionality is as much an aesthetic as an epistemological judgment, and indeed it does not take a great deal of imagination to perceive the analogy between theological discussions of design and aesthetic discussions of it.[31] Intentionality is always a religiously inflected story of origins.

Accordingly, discussions of intention within literary study try to sophisticate Cleanthes' naïve assumption that he has access to the intentions of the creator. Thus in "The Intentional Fallacy," W. K. Wimsatt, Jr., and Monroe Beardsley try to distinguish a properly critical reading practice from the naïve belief that knowing the author's intentions will unlock the literary object.[32] Debates such as those instigated by Wimsatt and Beardsley bear interestingly upon theological discussions of design, for both cases employ the same logical structure: the intentions of a creator are said to be inferred from the evidence of the artifact, and yet in practice other kinds of knowledge are generally smuggled in: biographical and historical knowledge, in the case of an author; theological doctrines or prior beliefs, in the case of a divinity. Indeed, it is just this smuggling that inspires Wimsatt and Beardsley to label intentionality a "fallacy" in the first place, just as Hume and Kant had objected to the way that natural theologians smuggled positive theories of God into an apparently inferential procedure. In this respect the attempt by Wimsatt and Beardsley to declare intentionality off limits correlates with earlier efforts to police and critique design arguments.

Because Wimsatt and Beardsley used their critique of intention to make literary study an autonomous discipline with its own objective criteria, moreover, their project in "The Intentional Fallacy" meshes with a differentiated model of secularization. Thus the anticlerical impulse of their closing thought experiment, in which they imagine a hypothetical critic writing to the still-living T. S. Eliot in order to ask him what he had in mind with a particular line from "The Love Song of J. Alfred Prufrock." "Critical inquiries," they write, " are not settled by consulting the oracle"(18). In order to cut literary criticism free of its thralldom to authorial intentionality, we must free ourselves from religious habits of deference to authority. Literature must be differentiated from theology so that criticism may be differentiated from literature. In both cases, "intention" names the cord that must be cut.

Wordsworth, though, is a tricky place to make this cut. Indeed, Wimsatt and Beardsley write that "It is not so much a historical statement as a definition to say that the intentional fallacy is a romantic one" (6). The reason: a distinction between the conditions of a poem's creation and the critical evaluation of the poetic object itself is central to the notion of the intentional fallacy. And in apparent opposition to this doctrine, *The Prelude*'s most ambitious claim is that the conditions of its creation *are the same thing* as the criteria against which it must be evaluated.

Yet what if we understood those conditions as a narrative of professional differentiation rather than personal development? In that case, a new model of literature that *does* yield itself up to an anti-intentionalist, professional reading practice could emerge. Concomitantly, this would differentiate poetry from similar professional callings—most importantly, given Wordsworth's own career choices, that of the clergy. As Brian Goldberg has noted, Wordsworth's deliberations about his own poetic vocation coincide with a gradual historical shift from a "status" to an "occupational" model of professionalism itself. In Goldberg's judgment Wordsworth tries to accommodate both, presenting the poet as simultaneously born to his task and worthy of his title only after "long, tough hours of preparation."[33] Those hours of preparation, the necessary training of the future professional poet, appear in *The Prelude* as a narrative of crisis and renewal that revolves around the question of intentionality; beginning with the thwarting of intentionality on Simplon Pass, the latter half of *The Prelude* works to recover a model of intentionality that keeps its religious forms at arm's length and therefore does not compromise the status of the literature created by a professionalizing poet. Wordsworth's professionalism is thus organized by secularization, understood not as a progressive narrative but as a complicated negotiation between intentionality and differentiation.

Intentionality and Differentiation

In the Simplon Pass episode, the speaker finds his intentions thwarted. The spiritual vision called imagination interrupts his overwhelming eagerness to see a beautiful natural vision. The power of this scene turns, then, upon anti-intentionalism: the best things come when the speaker is not searching for them. Like the criticism celebrated by Wimsatt and Beardsley, the experience of the imagination in book 6 is both internal and public: internal because it is presented as intrinsic to the poem;

public because unlike the factual details of the walk, its meaning can be discovered simply though the act of reading. The reader does not need to know the exact geography of Simplon Pass in order to know what Imagination feels like when it appears suddenly "Like an unfathered vapour" (6.527). The ensuing "thoughts / That are their own perfection and reward" (6.545–46), meanwhile, are equally contextless; for having survived imagination's usurpation, they become an example of a consciousness newly aware of its own "greatness" (6.536). The commonplace analogy of artistic creation and divine creation, therefore, will not work for the Simplon Pass episode. For the analogy to hold, God's intentions must be derivable from his creation, and the poet's from his. That is manifestly not the case in this passage, which narrates the defeat of intention by something—the imagination—subsequently identified with the very essence of poetry itself.

One consequence of imagination conceived as radically autonomous in this way, however, is that the mind falls out of correspondence with the movement of human events. This is perhaps the most notorious effect of the model of critical reading that Wimsatt and Beardsley propose: their rigorous exclusion of intention must also exclude the more general and contextual tide of human affairs usually gathered under the shorthand "history." A substantial portion of *The Prelude* between books 6 and 13 is devoted to understanding the effects of this exclusion. Those effects are chiefly psychological, as the cost of having been forcibly removed from history in the name of Poetry begins to make itself felt. In particular, the series of crises to which the speaker falls victim in book 10 is the poem's most dramatic depiction of the isolation consequent upon the kind of autonomy achieved in the Simplon passage. Witness his experience of revolutionary Paris:

> I crossed—a black and empty area then—
> The square of the Carousel, few weeks back
> Heaped up with dead and dying, upon these
> And other sights looking as doth a man
> Upon a volume whose contents he knows
> Are memorable, but from him locked up. (10.46–51)

Unable to read the scene in France,[34] the speaker is equally out of step with the situation in England. When France declares war on Britain he experiences a "shock / . . . that might be named / A revolution" (10.233, 10.236–37):

> All else was progress on the self-same path
> On which with a diversity of pace
> I had been travelling; this, a stride at once
> Into another region. (10.238–41)

This other region, characterized by "A conflict of sensations without name" (10.265), recalls in its turn the speaker's directionless time in France, marked by Louvet's "irresolute friends" (10.103) and the "indecision" (10.113) that hamstrung all who supported the Revolution but opposed Robespierre. Godwinian philosophical investigations, too, become a correlative for a French history that looks increasingly like a history of misplaced energy; the speaker tells us that he "took the knife in hand" to probe "The living body of society / Even to the heart" (10.872, 10.875–76). As a cure, of course, this is worse than the disease. When he can't read for intentions, then, the speaker can't read at all: everything is closed up, indecisive, or murderous. There is no evident design in the course of events, no way to narrate "history." This is differentiation ("another region") as modern trauma.

In an influential reading of *The Prelude*'s crisis narrative, James Chandler shows how Edmund Burke's antirevolutionary writings silently shape Wordsworth's depiction of the French Revolution in the 1805 *Prelude*, and hence the narrative of crisis and recovery that dominates books 9–13. "Burke's comments [on the revolution] may seem to anticipate Wordsworth's crisis so completely simply because Wordsworth used Burke's terms to reconstruct it," he writes.[35] As Chandler narrates it, then, the corrective return to Nature that Wordsworth prescribes for himself after his revolutionary fling is underwritten by Burke's own powerfully ideological invocations of "second nature" as a counter to revolutionary action.

Chandler is right to note that the key to the poem's success is Wordsworth's ability to rewrite his political crisis as simply a mistaken journey away from Nature. I would add, however, that the speaker's political crisis is itself cast in terms of a *professional* crisis dominated by the difficulties of intentionality. The social and political world that Wordsworth encounters in books 9 and 10 remains unreal and unreadable ("black and empty") because, having experienced the thwarting of intention in book 6, he remains cut off from the inner springs of human affairs. Imaginative apocalypse casts out intentionality in general, threatening not only Wordsworth's political identity but also his ability as a poet to understand and narrate the events he is witnessing—to produce, that is, the very autobiography that will sketch poetry's occupational logic and professional legitimacy. Moreover, the poet intoxicated by revolutionary possibility may have abandoned intentionality in order to pursue imagination, but the political actors whom he observes on both sides of the Channel have taken the opportunity offered by the sudden advent of the revolution's "other region" to place control of the state in human hands. Their version of differentiation severs the analogy between the state and the divinely created natural world, so that social connection and cohesion must now come about, in Godwinian fashion, as a result of human rather than divine intention. Rather than becoming anti-intentionalists, they have become secular intentionalists.

How then will Wordsworth recover a world redolent with intention and purpose without also committing himself to the secular intentionality of the revolutionary cause? Through a corrective return to a Nature, a process of spiritual restoration narrated in the last four books of the poem that describes a return to intentionality and culminates in the intrinsic analogies of Snowdon. The speaker's claims will stand or fall based on how convincingly he can narrate his own success as an acknowledgment that he participates in an intentional universe. This return must skirt the secular political intentionality that had led to the crisis narrative of book 10, *and* it must avoid falling back into the "ancient" intentional universe, for in that universe there is no place for the professional poet as Wordsworth is coming to understand that vocation. The only way to bring *The Prelude* to a successful conclusion is to recover intentionality without historical consequences—to recover it, that is, as a purely literary event.

In these terms, the last half of *The Prelude* narrates an elaborate move away from design and then a subsequent return, a journey completed in the Snowdon passage, which presents itself as a postpolitical return to Nature but whose real professional purpose is to refashion analogy into a power whose precise source can no longer be identified. This means that not only the Snowdon passage but also the whole series of changes narrated in books 6 to 13 describes a process whereby the "function" of design is shifted into a domain that future readers would recognize as literary. By overtly casting off analogy and then recovering it as an inner phenomenon, the poem preserves the feeling that one is in the presence of intentionality but also manages its material so that only an unsophisticated reader would try to discover the content of those intentions. Thus the poem's "literary effect": a work redolent with purpose and meaning that nevertheless endures beyond the reaches of a single intention. Design is everywhere—but, as a force that rises from within, it is also nowhere in particular.

Much of *The Prelude* wrestles with the apparent incommensurability of intentionality and differentiation. In a universe presided over by divine intentions, meaning is automatic and flows from a single source. Differentiation, on the other hand, offers multiple sites of authority, those "other regions" into which one might stray. Conversely, however, a differentiated world makes possible the autonomous professional calling of the poet, while a world of divine intentionality allows only poetic creation on the order of an analogy to divine creation. To feel the ambivalence that subtends these developments is simply to feel what it means to live in the modern world. This is why Wordsworth's attempted solution is both so ambitious and so hard to measure. For by making analogy intrinsic to the perceiving mind in book 13, Wordsworth tries to make differentiation (in the form of professionalization) the condition of possibility for the preservation of intentionality (in the form of design).

The result is that we can never say just *what* the intentions are, nor *who* has them. Like Hume's *Dialogues*, *The Prelude* preserves design as a form of acknowledgment rather than argumentation. When Cleanthes asks Philo whether the idea of a contriver does not immediately flow in upon him "with a force like that of sensation," he proposes not a philosophic analogy but a state of receptiveness toward the feeling that one is in the presence of design. The only reason that Philo cannot acknowledge that feeling, according to Cleanthes, is that he has allowed his mind to become distracted by skeptical arguments. Cleanthes is not looking for agreement; he simply wants Philo to acknowledge that the mind's natural state is one that recognizes the general provenance of design and intention within the universe. The only way to understand Philo's continued obtuseness, accordingly, is as a Fall: corrupted by skepticism, he thinks that finding design means finding specific instances of it. On this argument, what Philo fails to understand is that design is a movement of the mind, a movement acknowledging and mirroring, as by analogy, the designs and intentions it perceives to imbue nature in general.

In the literary domain, that acknowledgment is called "reading"—a professional activity that nevertheless retains enough vague intentionalist affinity with its object to preserve meaning and therefore make the activity seem worthwhile in the first place. When Raphael instructs Adam to "read [God's] wond'rous works" in *Paradise Lost*, his pupil had merely to go outside in order to find a text to read. By contrast, *The Prelude* is less interested in reading the world than in representing what it means to *try* to read the world. The poem forces its readers to concede that there is an intentionality to be grasped, but that by definition no reading will be able to produce it. Reading comes into its own only when it gives up on intentionality in favor of the representation of intentionality. And so, unlike Adam, Wordsworth's literary readers will be looking less often at the Book of God and more frequently into the pages of a book.

Chapter 7
Reading with a Worthy Eye:
Secularization and Evil

Is there a special relationship between Wordsworthian romanticism and secularization? The previous chapter suggested that we can find that relation in the creation of the differentiated domain of literature itself and its construction of specialized reading strategies. If this is right, then the relationship is not the sort postulated by modernization theory: the romantics are not partially liberated versions of us. If we replace modernization theory with the concept of multiple modernities, however, we can see how certain romantic texts register the presence of religion in a characteristically modern manner without turning that observation into a progressive theory of historical change. On a "multiple" reading, romanticism does not lead to us, and yet we share with it a set of unresolved preoccupations.

In this chapter I address the way in which Wordsworth's *The Ruined Cottage* participates in the constitution of a characteristically modern cultural project: how we manage the presence of evil. Though design arguments do consider the problem of evil—Paley worried that evil disrupted the order of the natural world upon which his argument rested, and Hume's Philo has good fun describing the misery he observes in the world—my concern here is only secondarily with design and primarily with how *The Ruined Cottage* inflects the problem of evil in a differentiated modern world. It does so, I argue, in a startlingly proleptic way. First, though it cannot find satisfaction in theological explanations for evil, it cannot entirely escape those explanations. And second, the shift in emphasis that occurs when Wordsworth incorporates *The Ruined Cottage* into *The Excursion* documents a crucial transformation in religion itself, as the poem in effect withdraws its earlier claim to be a comprehensive interpretation of the world, with all its ambiguities, in favor of an intensified but narrow version of religious faith.

The Problem of Evil

There are actually *two* problems of evil. The first is a theological and perhaps ontological one, involving the question of how God could allow suffering; this is the familiar issue of theodicy. The second involves the question of why human beings do awful things to each other. This is a moral question, and it is also primarily a modern one.

Susan Neiman has remarked on the centrality of this distinction to the story that philosophy tells about itself.[1] Philosophers writing about evil today generally use Kant's analysis of evil (particularly in *Religion Within the Limits of Reason Alone*) as their touchstone, as Kant articulates most influentially the transition from a metaphysical to a moral conception of evil. Kant held that all theodicies failed because speculative knowledge of God was impossible; consequently, evil was a matter to be considered under the categories of human freedom and human agency. This strategy makes Kant, according to some commentators, the first major philosopher to discuss evil without finally having recourse to the attributes of God.[2] One result of this intervention is that we now try to come to grips with evil from what might be termed a "postmetaphysical" perspective; we tend to rule out of bounds discussions of evil that have recourse to theological concepts or that identify evil with mystery. (Hannah Arendt's *Eichmann in Jerusalem* is perhaps the most well known of such attempts.)

Because the events of the twentieth century have focused our attention on instances of moral evil, postmetaphysical discussions of evil feel intuitively correct. But such accounts also feel intuitively correct because they help to align the history of philosophy with a progressive version of the secularization thesis that underwrites intellectual legitimacy. One feels the pull of modernization theory here. Moderns must face evil squarely without having recourse to theological justifications, and thus the fading power of theology becomes the condition of possibility for philosophical maturity.

In contrast to this standard story, Odo Marquard has argued that the problem of evil in fact marks a point of historical transition. Far from fading with the advent of modernity, argues Marquard, theodicy is central to it; indeed, theodicy becomes necessary only once it becomes possible to ask questions about the meaning of suffering. Only when issues of divine benevolence have become sufficiently disembedded does suffering no longer seem inescapable; and once this is the case its continued presence demands explanation.[3] Theodicy thus registers the presence of differentiation. In the book of Job, for instance, Yahweh does not answer Job's challenge on its own terms, but rather reveals himself as the sort of being who renders Job's anthropomorphic questions of justification inappropriate. In that account, it is nonsensical to demand that Job's suffering have a reason. Once earthly life begins to make sense on its own terms, however, Yahweh's response seems like a way to avoid the issue rather than contextualize it. Evil *becomes* a problem only at the precise moment that we separate ourselves from Job's world sufficiently to feel that God must be called to account when things go wrong.

In the common story, we now consider evil from a postmetaphysical perspective; references to divine authority or intention seem inappropriate attempts to evade the issue rather than confront it. Marquard's revision of this story, however, contests the distinction between metaphysical and postmetaphysical understandings of evil and the understanding of modernity in which the distinction is embedded. If the problem of evil actually becomes a problem only as a result of modernity, then theological answers to that problem are not attempts to avoid modern clear-sightedness but actually demonstrations of the mutually informing nature of the relationship between modernity and tradition.

Suffering and *The Ruined Cottage*

The Ruined Cottage shows us both of these reactions to suffering. Both center upon the Pedlar's consolatory conclusion near the poem's end:

> "She sleeps in the calm earth, and peace is here.
> I well remember that those very plumes,
> Those weeds, and the high spear-grass on that wall,
> By mist and silent rain-drops silver'd o'er,
> As once I passed did to my heart convey
> So still an image of tranquility,
> So calm and still, and looked so beautiful
> Amid the uneasy thoughts which filled my mind,
> That what we feel of sorrow and despair
> From ruin and from change, and all the grief
> The passing shews of being leave behind,
> Appeared an idle dream that could not live
> Where meditation was. I turned away
> And walked along my road in happiness." (512–25)

A familiar criticism of these lines is that they make the tragedy of Margaret and Robert the condition of possibility for a visionary reading of the spear grass.[4] There is something compelling and inescapable about this objection, and the reason is that it is a restatement of one classic solution to the problem of evil.

The particular resonances of this criticism have been brought out most fully by Cleanth Brooks's commentary on this very passage:

Is Wordsworth saying here that, seen in the full perspective of nature, seen as a portion of nature's beautiful and unwearied immortality, Margaret with her sorrows is simply one detail of an all-encompassing and harmonious pattern? One can, for example, look at the rabbit torn by the owl in something like this fashion, and the rabbit's agony, no longer isolated and dwelt upon in itself, may cease to trouble us when understood as a necessary part of a total pattern.[5]

There is a Darwinian inflection to Brooks's language here. But his objection to a reading that focuses upon the "total pattern" at the expense of individual suffering picks up on a response to suffering at least as old as Augustine. "I no longer wished for a better world," writes Augustine in the *Confessions*, "because I was thinking of the whole of creation, and in the light of this clearer discernment I had come to see that though the higher things are better than the lower, the sum of all creation is better than the higher things alone."[6] What appears to be evil will ultimately, with the proper perspective, be revealed as part of a larger good. In *Natural Theology* Paley tries out a version of this Augustinian argument:

The two cases which appear to me to have the most of difficulty in them . . . are those of *venomous* animals, and of animals *preying* upon one another. . . . From the confessed and felt imperfection of our knowledge, we ought to presume, that there may be consequences of this economy which are hidden from us; from the benevolence which pervades the general designs of nature, we ought also to presume, that these consequences, if they could enter into our calculation, would turn the balance on the favourable side. (308)

Paley must cede a bit of ground when he admits to the imperfection of his knowledge, but the Augustinian argument basically satisfies him. Brooks, however, is not at all satisfied. Following his own summary of the problem, he declares: "One shrinks from concluding that such an interpretation as this is Wordsworth's own" (386). This "shrinking," a kind of ethical distaste, is worth meditating upon because it marks the distance between Paley's age (which is also Wordsworth's age) and our own. Brooks is objecting, I think, on two different counts. He objects to the Augustinian argument that apparent evil will turn out to be part of a larger good when viewed from the proper perspective. And he objects to the assumption that Margaret's suffering is an instance of natural evil, like that of the rabbit. He wants to make it a question of moral evil, which means removing it from the realm of theological explanations such as Paley's. For Brooks, Margaret's suffering cannot just be a part of the way the world works; it is, rather, something excessive and aberrant. That is why it demands a postmetaphysical explanation. Brooks responds to evil in such a way that the visceral impulses of moral feeling— one *shrinks*—achieve autonomy from theological explanations. Faced with a gap between what the poem says (evaluating suffering is a matter of proper perspective) and what he wants it to say (suffering is an absolute), Brooks bridges the gap through his own sensitive reading practices, producing a kind of moral shudder that becomes an index to the distance between Paley's age and our own.

For all that, Brooks like Paley is working within the confines of theodicy. Both men are contemplating the power of attempts such as Augustine's to reembed the problem of evil within an argument about total perspective and therefore make the problem disappear *as* a problem. The poem itself takes the problem and tries to embed it in a different discourse altogether, one that goes under the name of reading. As I noted in the previous chapter, *The Ruined Cottage*, like most of Wordsworth's other poems of this period, is a progressive narrative: from a state of subjection to outside forces, the poet learns to explain their workings and so overcomes and subsequently internalizes that which had held him in its power. The problem of evil (that is, Margaret's apparently pointless suffering) sits right in the middle of this narrative of growth and thus obstructs the poem's developmental arc and, by implication, the construction of Wordsworth's own literary career. If the poet or his readers get caught by the enormity of Margaret's suffering, they may simply be stuck there, unable to continue along the path toward worthy reading, victims of the same stasis that claims Robert and eventually Margaret herself. Continued growth, therefore, requires that the poet get himself and his readers from one side of the problem of evil to the other, and not become blocked by a suffering whose enormity seems in excess of any possible meaning.

There are two choices here. Either pointless suffering *is* in fact the condition of growth, in which case Augustine is right and Brooks will "shrink" and the poem's readers remain, happily or unhappily, in the realm of theodicy. *Or* some creative act must take place that neutralizes the problem of evil itself. The Pedlar tries the second of these, and his term for the creative act is "reading." I call this a creative act because we don't know the future, so we don't know, at this point in the poem, if the apprentice poet will indeed learn to read with a worthy eye.[7] Moreover, reading in the manner prescribed by the Pedlar rules out of bounds the very question many readers want to ask, namely whether the poem's consolatory conclusion, with its impressive interpretation of the spear grass, is worth the price of Margaret's suffering. As I have said, this is a question of theodicy and hence, like Brooks's shrinking, substantially continuous with the religious narrative it takes itself to be critiquing. The poem *itself*, however, achieves a break with theodicy by doing exactly what it has often been accused of doing, namely refusing to take Margaret's suffering as an event that requires special attention. The Pedlar's command to read differently aims to terminate any questions we might ask about the meaning of suffering by refocusing our attention on the acts of reconstructive self-improvement in which both Pedlar and Poet engage.

The "reoccupation" theory of secularization that Hans Blumenberg offers in *The Legitimacy of the Modern Age* helps to clarify this counterintuitive situation. Like several others discussed already in this book, Blumenberg criticizes theories of secularization that understand it as the transformation of religious content. In so doing he distinguishes between the function of particular ideas and their contents, arguing that it is not the case that the content of ideas gets transformed, but rather that the function of an idea changes. For instance, nineteenth-century theories of progress are not "secularizations" of Christian eschatology. Rather, the two poles of creation and eschatology determine the meaning of Christian history; modern thinkers, still compelled to answer the question of the meaning of history, consequently developed the idea of progress. Thus "progress" is not a secularization of a religious idea but rather an attempt to reoccupy by different means a position originally staked out by Christianity. Blumenberg proposes that such "reoccupations" are typical of modernity.[8]

This process of reoccupation leads to intellectual distortions, and among those distortions is the very idea of secularization as a transformation of content. At this point Blumenberg's thesis becomes reflexive: though progressive theories of secularization are false as historical explanations, they have historical truth as evidence of the very desire *for* meaningful explanations of modern phenomena, since the roots of that desire go back to the theological explanations whose demise progressive secularization takes itself to be narrating. Although secularization as a transformation of religious content is only the appearance of secularization, writes Blumenberg, that appearance nevertheless "has a real foundation, a demonstrable role in a historical logic" (64). In other words, the appearance of secularization performs at the level of function what it claims to be performing at the level of content, since the compulsion to answer by modern means questions that arose against a different set of background conditions responds to a deeply felt need. Blumenberg does not develop this theme quite as thoroughly as one might wish, but his most succinct formulation of it is quite rich: "the reoccupation that is the reality underlying the appearance of secularization," he writes, "is driven by the neediness of a consciousness that has been overextended and then disappointed in regard to the great questions and great hopes" (89). This proposal serves as an eloquent gloss on Brooks's reaction to *The Ruined Cottage*. When Brooks writes that he "shrinks from concluding that such an interpretation as this is Wordsworth's own," that reaction means, in effect, "I hope Wordsworth thinks as I do about suffering," and as such it is driven by a need doomed to disappointment.

Suffering seems to demand an explanation, and this felt need surfaces in paradigmatic moments such as that of Brooks's "shrinking" (and also in Alan Liu's elaborate historicization of the poem, a reading constructed on the scaffolding of Brooks's moral discomfort[9]). We do,

after all, want to know what all that suffering really means, and this desire generally takes the form of a moral imperative. This return of the
question of the meaning of suffering may present itself as being too
hardheaded about religion to gain solace from its assurances. But if Blumenberg is right, then this question is not in fact evidence of secularization but is rather the distorted return of a question about the meaning
of suffering that was originally broached under a set of background circumstances that we don't all share anymore. Brooks, specifically, doesn't
share them with Paley, and he's worried that he doesn't share them
with Wordsworth, either, which is precisely the source of his difficulty.
Brooks's reaction embodies a particularly modern anguish: that human
beings differ not simply over specific visions of the good life but also
over the first premises from which those visions derive.

Apologetics and Hermeneutics

Shrinking is an understandable though obfuscating reaction to the end
of *The Ruined Cottage*. It obscures a perhaps surprising convergence between the two other reactions to the poem. The Augustinian tradition
emphasizes that understanding evil is a matter of achieving the proper
perspective on it. But so too does the Pedlar's creative institution of reading as a way to overcome questions about the meaning of Margaret's suffering. Augustine learns to read the world differently; so too does the
Poet in *The Ruined Cottage*. What matters is not *whether* one reads, but
how one reads. The command to "no longer read the forms of things
with an unworthy eye" takes it for granted that the Poet is already reading; the only question is whether he reads "worthily" or whether he allows his sentimental concerns about Margaret's suffering to overwhelm
him. Only the reader who shrinks persists in the idea that reading can be
escaped. The poem, that is, seems to recognize that whether its gambit
works or not, we are inevitably within the realm not of apologetics but of
hermeneutics. Or, to put it in the terms I have used throughout this
book, both kinds of reading are examples (though different examples)
of differentiation.

This matters because the problem of evil was usually presented in the
eighteenth century as an empirical problem. Of course it *may* be posed
as a logical difficulty, as if the existence of evil were incompatible with a
beneficent God. Liebniz's theodicy, with its appeal to possible worlds,
springs from this perspective. But for the most part, the problem of evil
was posed in empirical rather than logical terms: the undeniable existence of various evils seemed evidence against the proposition that the
world was made and is still watched over by a beneficent and omnipotent creator. Such evidentiary arguments retain their force today. In an

influential paper, the philosopher William Rowe gives a version of this argument that focuses on "pointless suffering." His example: "Suppose in some distant forest lightning strikes a dead tree, resulting in a forest fire. In the fire a fawn is trapped, horribly burned, and lies in terrible agony for several days before death relieves its suffering."[10] It seems clear, Rowe concludes, that an omnipotent and omniscient creator could have prevented the fawn's suffering without thereby losing a greater good or permitting a worse evil.

An Augustinian response to Rowe's argument would counter that, despite appearances, there is indeed a greater good at work in this situation, though given our limited cognitive capacities we are unlikely to grasp it. Rowe, considering this argument, admits that we cannot *know* for sure that the fawn's suffering is pointless, but argues that it is nevertheless *rational to believe* that it is. "We are often in the position," he writes, "where in the light of our experience and knowledge it is rational to believe that a certain statement is true, even though we are not in a position to prove or to know with certainty that the statement is true" (130). This probabilistic argument should seem familiar to readers of this book, for it is the very one that Hume employed to such effect across a range of issues, from epistemology to theology. Against it the Augustinian must simply reassert his claim that sufficient knowledge (perhaps not attainable on earth) will demonstrate that there is no such thing as pointless suffering. Paley appeals to this Augustinian argument in *Natural Theology*. Yet because Paley shares Hume's evidentiary and inductive approach to philosophical matters, his appeal to Augustinian ignorance makes for an aporia within *Natural Theology*. At this point, Paley seems to imply, one must simply choose what to believe. In a surprising twist, however, Paley is joined in this argument by Pamphilus, the narrator of Hume's *Dialogues*, whose actions suggest that he takes fully to heart Cleanthes' inadvertent admission that rational arguments eventually reduce to "arbitrary acts of the mind."

The Augustinian argument from ignorance often takes an eschatological form by arguing that God will redeem suffering at the end of time. But the very notion of eschatology is external to the more restricted debate about whether or not God exists. So if, in trying to answer the problem of evil, the Augustinian appeals to the idea that God acts redemptively in a manner beyond our understanding, he is appealing to a certain understanding of God for which he has not argued. Hume's Philo notes that this is characteristic of eighteenth-century design arguments in general. In trying to meet this objection, Paley appeals to an argument from perception, but that argument, as we saw in Chapter 4, itself assumes that the appearance of design in the world is such that a thoughtful and unprejudiced reader will "just see" that the world must have been designed. In making his case, therefore, Paley appeals to a set of background beliefs that tilt the playing field in his direction and yet appear methodologically neutral.

As it turns out, though, Philo's evidentiary argument runs into the same difficulty. When Rowe, following the technique developed by Hume's Philo, argues that the suffering of the fawn does not appear to be mitigated by any greater good, he like Paley is appealing implicitly to a set of background beliefs that he thinks do not require justification. Rowe thinks that a thoughtful and unprejudiced reader, on considering the evidence, will "just see" that the fawn's suffering is pointless.[11] But Rowe's "just see" argument works only if one has already decided beforehand to bracket the question of God's existence, and hence the possibility that there may be an unknown eschatological scheme afoot that explains the fawn's suffering. Rowe's argument, therefore, cannot be methodologically neutral, for it places the burden of proof entirely upon the theist. Like Paley, Rowe appeals to a set of background beliefs that he presents as simply common sense but which in fact builds its conclusions into its premises.

In their final recourse to premises that reside outside the parameters of the dispute, therefore, Augustinian arguments such as Paley's and skeptical critiques of it such as Philo's and Rowe's turn out to be philosophical fellow travelers, as each, pursued far enough, reverts to a "just see" argument. This means that although both sides in the debate behave as if they are arguing the apologetic question of God's existence, in fact neither is doing so. The contested terrain is actually not apologetics at all but rather hermeneutics: the actual issue under discussion is what resources each side brings to bear upon the empirical fact of suffering. Or, in the language of *The Ruined Cottage*, the issue is one of reading. What looks initially like a question of apologetics—can God be justified, given that evil exists?—transforms under the pressure of the evidentiary argument into a question of understanding: *how* can a particular God coexist with evil? Can the theist give an adequate explanation of the sorts of goods that God might employ to overcome suffering, or not?

To understand the problem of evil as a matter of hermeneutics rather than of apologetics means that the relevant issue becomes not the *existence* of God but the methods one uses to *understand* the copresence of God and evil, and whether those methods appear to be adequate. This shifts attention away from questions of justification and epistemology and toward questions of discipline and training: by what means does one acquire the skills to read in one way or in another way? As the example of Augustine suggests, this question has long been at the heart of the matter, but that fact can be hidden by enlightenment-era preoccupation with proofs for God's existence. Both the proponents of the argument from design and its philosophical opponents tend to behave as if God's existence were at stake—and thus that some agreement could be reached based upon shared, rational, first principles. Thus the moral distaste with which a reader such as Brooks approaches *The Ruined Cottage* in effect treats a matter of hermeneutics as if it were one of apologetics. Most of us, I suspect, are likewise *prima facie* suspicious of the claim that suffering can lead to greater understanding because, under the influence of arguments such as Philo's, we tend to view the question of evil as a matter of justification rather than of understanding. But in fact the question is one of reading: of understanding and interpretation, and thus dependent upon principles that derive from elsewhere and are hence potentially incompatible. If we can see Brooks's reaction to Margaret's suffering for what it is, namely a reaction that misrecognizes its own moral sensitivity as evidence of secularization, then we can correct this methodological distortion by returning the question of suffering to the place where it belongs: the place of reading and interpretation, and thus to the role of practices of pedagogy and discipline that train readers to view things in a particular way. To say this more boldly: the problem of evil is a literary problem, not a philosophical one. The secularization that the poem documents is simply the fact of a differentiated world in which literature can claim for itself the authority to wrestle with the problem.

Attaining Belief in *The Excursion*

If indeed the chief contest of *The Ruined Cottage* is a contest of reading, then its most important debate revolves around pedagogy: how does one learn to read in one way and not in another? The important point on which Augustine and Wordsworth's Pedlar agree is that understanding evil is a matter of perspective, of how one learns to view the world. They differ on what that perspective should be: how it is to be appropriated, understood, and articulated. This underscores the importance of proper training. Learning to read correctly is like learning to put evil in perspective: both require that one practice a certain stance toward one's object. How one learns that stance, and internalizes it, becomes a question not of reason or argument but of pedagogy and desire. We want to read with a worthy eye (whatever we decide that means) for reasons quite remote from evidentiary considerations of God's existence.

The Ruined Cottage offers no distinct answer to the question of *how* one learns to read worthily. The Poet, who is the poem's first reader, grapples with the meaning of the spear-grass image. The Pedlar gently instructs him, but these maneuvers do not address the full task of how one might come to proper judgments. Fulfilling the command to read worthily makes up its methodology as it goes along, for the background conditions of an image-laden reading technique remain implicit until they are activated by the image itself, and this means that one seems to be continually constructing both the interpretation and its conditions of possibility.

Wordsworth never published *The Ruined Cottage* on its own.[12] He chose rather to incorporate it into the first book of *The Excursion* (1814), in which Margaret's story and the Pedlar's final speech are framed by an explicitly eschatological, Christological narrative. Here is the Pedlar's revised speech, with the new lines in italics:

"My Friend! enough to sorrow have you given,
The purposes of wisdom ask no more:
Nor more would she have craved as due to One
Who, in her worst distress, had ofttimes felt
The unbounded might of prayer; and learned, with soul
Fixed on the Cross, that consolation springs,
From sources deeper far than deepest pain,
For the meek Sufferer. Why then should we read
The forms of things with an unworthy eye?
She sleeps in the calm earth, and peace is here."[13]

Such revisions are generally understood as part of Wordsworth's apostasy, both political and artistic. Particularly when measured against modernization theory, Wordsworth's later work inevitably looks like a throwback to an earlier era, "conservative" in the specific sense that it backs away from its own most forward-looking impulses. If we rewrite secularization as differentiation, rather than decline and loss of belief, however, then a different reading of Wordsworth's later career becomes possible. In this reading, Wordsworth's appeal to Christ's atonement is not a return to some earlier age of orthodoxy but rather a remarkably accurate register of the very conditions that shape modern religious belief.

A contemporary account of evil and suffering by the theologian Diogenes Allen offers insight into this later phase of Wordsworth's career. In an essay entitled "Natural Evil and the Love of God," Allen suggests that suffering can enrich one's relationship to the material world. He argues that suffering reorients the human subject, helps him shed the narcissistic and immature demand that he be well cared for, and thereby creates experiences otherwise unavailable: "Indeed in our humbled and more realistic condition we can see the glory of the entire world-order and be grateful for our capacity to yield ourselves to it courageously and magnanimously even when we are caught in its workings."[14] Though it is open to various objections, this argument has the analytic benefit of highlighting the expectations we bring to the world. Slavoj Žižek, considering a similar phenomenon, quotes G. K. Chesterton: "If Cinderella says, 'How is it that I must leave the ball at twelve?' her godmother might answer, 'How is it that you are going there till twelve?' " "The function of the arbitrary limitation," Žižek comments, "is to remind us that the object itself, access to which is thus limited, is given to us through an inexplicable arbitrary miraculous gesture of divine gift, and thus to sustain the magic of being allowed to have access to it."[15] In Žižek's analysis this apprehension of and consequent gratitude for limitation is the central paradox of orthodoxy that pushes the subject beyond egocentricity. From Allen's perspective too there is something petulant and childish about Philo's demand that the natural order take better care of him. Suffering, in this analysis, helps us to grow up.

We grow up, Allen continues, when we realize that despite appearances we live in a well-ordered world. Suffering "can enable a person . . . to see that the order of nature is glorious, not odious, and that we have ample reason to be grateful for it" (195). Allen admits, though, that recognizing natural order does not necessitate theism; the next step in his argument therefore supplements the apprehension of orderliness with religious belief. He recommends that humans learn to experience God's love amid suffering—something, he continues, that "can be performed only by a person who believes in a loving God and who also has the humility of the stoic" (196). In this argument, then, the perception of the world's harmony is a necessary but not sufficient condition; the belief that allows one to experience God amid suffering must come from elsewhere—and about the origins of that belief Allen is mute. The identifiably "religious" content in his argument thus comes by way of a *belief* independent of the rational, mature sensibility that has learned to recognize divine control even in a seemingly chaotic world.

Allen's two-part schema—the perception of natural order contextualizing suffering, then belief giving it meaning—nicely matches the version of *The Ruined Cottage* that appears in *The Excursion*. The image-driven apprehension of the world's fundamental harmony remains in *The Excursion*, but in this instance it is not asked to do the heavy lifting that it must do in *The Ruined Cottage*, for now it is a typological reading of Christ's suffering that gives meaning to Margaret's affliction. *The Excursion* also matches Allen's schema from a formal perspective. The apparent lack of fit between the poem's aesthetic elements (the "image of tranquility," the command to read with a "worthy eye") and its Christological ones (soul "fixed on the Cross") parallels the copresence in Allen's argument of natural harmony and theistic belief. The transition between these elements drops from sight completely, as though they occupy two distinct spheres of argument. This perhaps is what the Pedlar knows: if experiencing or just encountering suffering helps us to grow up, what is to prevent us from entering a new world freed from religious commitments? The only possible answer is that belief arrives to push us into a different trajectory—the trajectory of *The Excursion* rather than of *The Ruined Cottage.* Yet neither the Pedlar nor Allen can say where that belief comes from, nor why it arrives. This unmoored conception of belief is the true register of the poem's modernity. From this point, all one has to do is to follow Philo in declaring teleology out of bounds, thus isolating "belief" as the content of religion, and Wordsworth's so-called apostasy follows inevitably; for *The Excursion* narrates the return of an orthodoxy that, like the Pedlar's abrupt Christology, appears as the imposition of a belief that originates outside the world of the poem. We already know, from the fate of Demea in the *Dialogues,* that such dogmatism cannot be engaged but only dismissed.

What is seldom remarked in this apostasy narrative is the great weight that belief, now unsupported by the evidence of the world, must bear. As differentiation reduces the scope and range of religion, and as a new class of readers, trained by the Pedlar and his kind, comes to understand the natural world in nondevotional terms, belief compensates by claiming greater autonomy for itself—in the case of *The Excursion*, even, the autonomy to rewrite a poem's apparent conclusion and thus, retrospectively, a poetic career.[16] But its range is narrowed. "Religion" comes to mean the cultivation of an interior space distinct from other domains of knowledge—in particular, from the literary "knowledge" into whose world it can come only as an uninvited, and sometimes rude, guest.

Chapter 8
Religion Three Ways

Wordsworth's revisions of *The Ruined Cottage* between 1798 and 1814 compactly encompass a much longer process within the history of Western Christianity, during which religion comes to be understood as a largely inner phenomenon.[1] In general terms, this means that a world organized through a central Church and structured by the idea of a participatory universe slowly breaks up and fragments: increasingly, the construction of meaning becomes the task of individuals rather than of a corporate body. This is a long and complex story of gradual change within Western Christianity, and one might adduce numerous reasons for it: intellectual historians point to the development of modern individualism; political theorists note the rise of a functionally secular nation-state that depends upon religious tolerance; religious historians refer to the Protestant emphasis on correct belief; sociologists emphasize the rise of social differentiation, which reduces the role that religion plays in everyday life. Together, and despite their important differences, these varying approaches suggest that one of modernity's most profound changes is the transformation of "religious culture" into "religious faith."[2]

This does not mean, of course, that there were not forms of religious inwardness in earlier eras. The point is rather that the notion of religion as an *essentially* internal phenomenon is a modern one, encapsulated in the common distinction between "faith" and "reason." John D. Caputo describes this development very evocatively when he considers the fate of Anselm's famous ontological argument for the existence of God. Though the proof follows the dictates of logic, it begins and ends in Anselm's experience of God and thus moves in a big circle: "Had someone suggested to Anselm that he break out of this circle and start from scratch, from some neutral point outside the circle, Anselm would have thought him mad (or a fool). For Anselm, outside the circle there is no light and nothing happens."[3] The suggestion that one needs to start from a neutral point, however, does characterize a later age, when Anselm's ontological proof and other proofs were asked to stand on their own as demonstrations of God's existence. The surrounding apparatus of a religious experience and of a self oriented toward and nourished by the very God whose existence the proof was trying to demonstrate could no longer be admitted. Here is Caputo again: "[B]y the time it gets to Kant, Anselm's argument for the being whose bountiful excess Anselm experiences daily, in prayer and liturgy, in community and everyday life, has been transplanted to a different world where it is transformed into an argument about whether existence is a predicate" (44). Kant held that existence was not a predicate, which is why belief in God was a "belief" in our current sense of the word: something to be distinguished from knowledge based on facts.

If it is to survive in the post-Kantian world, religion must be creative. Without the assurance that the general cultural milieu sustains and mirrors the internal state of the subject, that very internal state must become the ground and source of meaning. Under modern conditions, Marcel Gauchet notes, religion assembles a coherent whole at the level of the subject rather than at the level of the collective.[4] What counts as religion under these new conditions? The three categories under which I consider religion here—those of belief, ideology, and discipline—are not intended to be exhaustive. The first two, however, are prevalent, often in unconscious ways, among scholars working outside the field of religious studies—particularly, perhaps, among literary scholars. The idea of religion as a discipline, meanwhile, will perhaps seem less familiar to such readers. As I hope to suggest, however, understanding religion as a form of discipline helps us to see how it can function creatively under the conditions of modernity.

Religion as Belief

By "religion as belief" I mean the idea that religion is a set of propositional statements and their associated doctrines, and the corollary idea that one's salvation hinges on the acceptance of such statements. The association of religion with individual belief (as distinct from culture, practice, habit, and so on) seems to be particularly indebted to the Christian tradition. Elaine Pagels, for instance, has traced the centrality of belief to John's Gospel.[5] The various Christian creeds are another early instance, especially the Nicene Creed and the debates surrounding the Council of Nicea in the fifth century. Such examples suggest that uniformity of belief is often important for social and institutional cohesion, as the examples of the Catholic Counter-Reformation and the Test Acts in England attest. Although the tendency to think of religion in terms of belief may always have been present within Christianity, then, that tendency manifests itself in remarkably diverse ways. A particularly important transformation away from the collective and toward matters of individual belief occurred in the aftermath of the crisis of authority in the Western Church marked by the Reformation, the Renaissance, and the seventeenth-century wars of religion. In response to these various crises, notes Peter Harrison, the concept of religion as we understand it today emerged: an "abstracted, depersonalized system which w[as] intended to represent in propositional terms the sum total of the religious lives of other peoples."[6] "Religion" became an outsider's term, a way of signaling that the phenomenon could be objectively studied in the same way that the sciences were learning to study the natural world. The chief tool in this new analysis of religion was its reconceptualization in terms of belief or saving knowledge. "The truth or falsity of a religion had become a function of the truth or falsity of the propositions which constituted it," Harrison writes. "True religion was not genuine piety, but a body of certain knowledge"(26).

This distinction between piety and knowledge, suitably updated to the early years of the nineteenth century, structures the religious debate of Austen's *Mansfield Park*. When Fanny Price seeks fantasy and mystery in the Sotherton chapel, Edmund responds with a Lockean compromise in which reason determines the lowest common denominator of religion. Popular contemporary publications such as *Religion for Dummies* show the continued relevance of Edmund's attitude. After an opening section on "Religion Basics," which itself opens with the enlightened project of "Defining Religion," *Religion for Dummies* moves successively through sections on religious belief, religious ritual, and ethics. The assumptions behind this format are clear: "Every religion has a belief system," write the authors, while, tautologically, a belief system makes "any religion what it is."[7] Ritual, in turn, does not have determinate content itself but is rather the "physical form" of belief. This makes ritual an interesting but nonessential part of religious experience, an attitude that seems to accord with Edmund's dismissal of banners and inscriptions as necessary for a chapel. According to *Religion for Dummies*, ritual provides a religious tradition with a distinct identity, but an analytic focus on belief suggests in Lockean fashion that religions have much in common, if only they could be brought to recognize it. (In this spirit, the authors provide a helpful chart of the central beliefs of the major world religions that emphasizes their common elements.) Not surprisingly, sacred texts do not enter the discussion until a final catchall section of the book—apparently because an emphasis on particular scriptures would distract from the universalist thrust of the book. For a modern reader, of course, there is nothing at all remarkable about this presentation, which, in moving from belief to ritual, from universal to particular, aims to unite its readership around a shared understanding of religion as a set of beliefs that can be abstracted from their particular contexts, studied, and thereby understood as participating despite their manifest differences in a shared human experience. In this sense the title *Religion for Dummies* is particularly apposite: its search for a lowest-common denominator conception of religion marks it as an heir of the early modern project of promoting tolerance and peace, and coming to terms with religious diversity, by securing a minimalist, "dumbed-down" definition of religion.

One manifestation of this long history is the split between reason and revelation. John Montag notes that this split is grounded in a certain way of conceptualizing the difference between the natural and the supernatural, in which the former denotes the world of physical matter whereas the latter implies a breaking of physical laws. Montag contrasts this modern understanding to that found in Aquinas, for whom "nature" does not mean the physical world but is rather a word denoting the kind of thing that a thing is. A supernatural event, accordingly, is not a violation of physical laws but a sign that all natural things are open to a realm beyond themselves. Revelation, Montag concludes, "has to do primarily with one's perspective on things in light of one's final end. It is not a supplementary packet of information about 'facts' which are around the bend, as it were, from rational comprehension or physical observation."[8] Revelation in this sense is not a thing at all but instead a process, something that engages the interest of humans who are themselves both natural and oriented toward a realm beyond nature.

In contrast to this Thomist understanding, Montag identifies a modern conception in which the content of a revelation is distinguished from its authorization. In this conception, revelation comes to mean the exposure of a hidden reality; it is conceived of as *having* a content rather than *being* a process. Revelation, on this new understanding, does not disclose God but rather pieces of information.[9] This matches nicely with the demands of what we know today as "science," as Michel de Certeau has pointed out:

> The experiment, in the modern sense of the word, was born with the deontologizing of language, to which the birth of a linguistics also corresponds. In Bacon and many others, the experiment stood opposite language as that which guaranteed and verified the latter.[10]

Together, Montag and de Certeau point to a grammatical transformation, in which, first, revelation comes to be understood as a proposition (as content rather than process) and in which, second, propositional statements themselves come to require some external guarantor of their truth. Since there can be no guarantor of the "truth" of a revelation on those terms, supernatural events are construed as matters of faith, whereby "faith" itself is strongly distinguished from reason. Hume masterfully exploits this situation, in the *Dialogues* and even more directly in his earlier essay "Of Miracles." Since, he suggests there, a miracle is by definition not susceptible to empirical proof, the only alternative is that it must reside solely in the domain of faith. And Hume professes himself happy to grant religious faith such autonomy. Under the guise of this generosity, then, Hume makes religion an inner and unverifiable phenomenon. He thus advances the trend remarked by Montag in which empirical science regulates public presentations of religious phenomena.

The process I have just sketched is an example of differentiation. But, because it posits "belief" as the content of religion, it is easy to confuse that differentiation with a narrative of religious privatization and perhaps decline. Shorn now of both institutional support and the language of reason, religion as the revelation of a saving knowledge looks vulnerable to modernity. Thus A. J. Ayer's *Language, Truth, and Logic* (1936), which was for many years the standard introduction to logical positivism, picks up on the differentiated model of religion in order to render it wholly irrational. "What is not so generally recognized," writes Ayer,

is that there can be no way of proving that the existence of a god, such as the God of Christianity, is even probable. Yet this also is easily shown. For if the existence of such a god were probable, then the proposition that he existed would be an empirical hypothesis. And in that case it would be possible to deduce from it, and other empirical hypotheses, certain experiential propositions which were not deducible from those other hypotheses alone. But in fact this is not possible.[11]

The key here is the idea that were the existence of a god probable, "the proposition that he existed would be an empirical hypothesis," whereby "empirical hypothesis" means, of course, a hypothesis susceptible to verification. Within the context of an intellectual field arranged like this, religion becomes an inward and unverifiable belief. "Thus we offer the theist the same comfort as we gave to the moralist," Ayer concludes. "His assertions cannot possibly be valid, but they cannot be invalid either. As he says nothing at all about the world, he cannot justly be accused of saying anything false, or anything for which he has insufficient grounds" (116).

What I wish to stress here is the ease with which a descriptive account of religious transformation becomes a normative account of why religion bears no relation to the modern world. Yet it is just in this movement from description to norm that so much twentieth-century analysis went awry, proving itself unable to account for the worldwide religious resurgence of the last quarter century. The scientific study of religion, whose intellectual origins in the seventeenth century are described by

Harrison, remains committed to an empirical approach because it effectively divides the public space of scientific analysis from the private phenomena of religion. Again, this entails a substantive theory of religion
and hence risks tipping over into a theory of religious decline. Steve
Bruce, the most important defender of the secularization thesis writing
today, puts the matter bluntly: "Although it is possible to conceptualize
it in other ways, secularization primarily refers to the beliefs of people."[12] The norm governing this approach owes a great deal to Ayer's
empiricism: "the usefulness of any conceptualization depends not upon
who makes the distinctions it entails but upon their success in the
explanatory endeavour in which they are deployed," Bruce writes.[13]
Here Bruce associates himself with a scientific program that holds fact
and value rigorously apart. At the end of the day it does not matter who
formulates the concepts in question, but rather whether those concepts
explain the data better than any competing concepts, wherein such
explanation is construed along empirical lines. For Bruce, knowledge
and power are two different things. There is something of Ayer's attitude here in the effort to define empirical research in such a way that it
is both free from the subjective realm and able to stand in judgment
over it.

Bruce's rigorous separation of fact and value is unlikely to be popular
among scholars in the humanities, for many of whom knowledge and
power are thoroughly entangled. For us, in other words, it is of paramount importance who formulates the concepts, what their motivations
are, and what their status is vis-à-vis the data under consideration. And
yet when we treat religion, explicitly or implicitly, as a matter of belief, we
unintentionally subscribe to the methodological preconceptions shared
by Hume, Ayer, and Bruce—preconceptions whose own origins can be
traced back to the gradual redefinition of religion beginning in the
early modern period. To be sure, there is no solution to this dilemma,
for those preconceptions are in play whenever we deploy or analyze "religion." But some consciousness of that term's historical contingency
may prevent us from taking as the truth of religion something that came
about only at a specific time, in a specific way, and under a specific set of
circumstances.[14]

Religion as Ideology

Once religion has been equated to belief, two things become conceptually possible: like George Eliot and other Victorian intellectuals, one can
"lose" one's belief; alternately, or in addition, like Feuerbach and Marx,
one can criticize religious belief as false consciousness. In *Genealogies of
Religion*, Talal Asad lays out the connection between belief and ideology:

"[T]he suggestion that religion has a universal function in belief," he writes, "is one indication of how marginal religion has become in modern industrial society as the site for producing disciplined knowledge and personal discipline. As such it comes to resemble the conception Marx had of religion as ideology—that is, as a mode of consciousness which is other than consciousness of reality, . . . expressing at once the anguish of the oppressed and a spurious consolation."[15] Religious beliefs relate to the real world in an illusory way; they obstruct the subject's relationship to reality, and thus become obvious targets for ideological critique. The redefinition of religion as belief is in this respect a crucial precondition of the development of ideology critique itself.

For a straightforward, popular version of such materialist critique of religion, we can turn to a recent biography of the British film star Ewan McGregor. Apparently young Ewan was quite religious, but it didn't last long:

The scales fell from his eyes one night at a church lecture on the evils of sex, when the boy looked up and saw that the chief speaker was a quick-with-his-fists local who regularly beat up his own offspring. "And I just saw right through it," Ewan recalls. And that was that.[16]

Not being a philosopher, McGregor doesn't tell us what he saw through to. More interesting, however, is the presence of the visual metaphor: "scales fell from his eyes," "boy looked up," "just saw right through it." As a coming-of-age story, this one turns upon the notion of seeing clearly.

Our most influential account of ideology likewise depends upon vision:

If in all ideology men and their circumstances appear upside-down as in a *camera obscura*, this phenomenon arises just as much from their historical life-process as the inversion of objects on the retina does from their physical life-process.[17]

This passage, from Marx and Engels' *German Ideology*, has been important in part because it describes the utopian hope of critical analysis so appealingly: turn the world right side up, and the mystifications of ideology will disappear like so many shadows. Yet as Althusser and others have noted, the analogy between criticism and clear sightedness also implies a consciousness hovering somewhere in the background and supervising the inverted image.[18] Marx's analogy, that is, takes it for granted that there is someone there to do the seeing, and that this someone can *already* see clearly. This assumes that vision is more natural or accurate than the camera obscura, but because we know nothing about the influences upon that vision, we are unable to evaluate such an assumption. Ideological critique becomes a "just so" story: as with

young Ewan McGregor, one day "the boy looked up," and everything
changed.

Considering Marx's analogy of eye and camera in his book *Iconology*,
W. J. T. Mitchell notes that the analogy treats the camera as a "scientific
invention that simply mirrors the timeless, natural facts about vision.
But suppose," Mitchell asks, "we reversed the stress, and thought of the
eye as modeled on the machine? Then Vision itself would have to be
understood not as a simple, natural function to be understood by neutral, empirical laws of optics but as a mechanism subject to historical
change."[19] With this imaginative reversal Mitchell aims to help materialist criticism recognize how its critical tools and images are themselves
part of the historical process. The eye of criticism, in this case, cannot
be simply treated as a neutral benchmark against which to measure the
distortions of the camera obscura of ideology. Thus, Mitchell concludes,
reversing the standard analogical relationship between eye and camera
keeps ideological criticism from naturalizing the eye and consequently
saves it from thinking that criticism can turn the world right side up
again.

Because Ewan McGregor's secularization story naturalizes its visual
figure in the very way that Marx does, neither McGregor nor his biogra-
pher feel the need to spell out the argument. They assume that, like
Ewan himself, the reader will "just see" how the argument goes. From
Mitchell's perspective, this is the moment that the visual metaphor becomes uncritical. For if McGregor were to offer an argument, it would
be a weak one: this man is a hypocrite; this man represents religion;
therefore religion is hypocritical. Just as I "see through" this man, so
I can "see through" religion as a whole. As an exercise in logic this is
hardly compelling, since it depends upon making a single individual
stand in for a much larger entity and provides no reason for doing so.

Because the argument turns upon hypocrisy, however, we can follow
Mitchell's recommendation and historicize the tools of critique. The relationship of religion to hypocrisy changed decisively in the early modern period. C. John Sommerville, who has written persuasively about the
religious changes of the early modern period in England, notes that
"[o]ne of the puzzles for modern students is to find that [sixteenth-
century] contemporaries were more shocked by married priests than by
fornicating ones." Sommerville continues:

When Robert Barnes wrote the first justification of clerical marriage in English
(1534) he asked his readers whether it made sense to treat priests who were married more harshly than those who kept concubines. Why were the former executed, when incontinent priests were not even transferred? Whether one saw
things Barnes's way depended on whether one found holiness primarily in the
sacraments or in a moral life.[20]

Because the focus of religious devotion for most sixteenth-century Christians was the Eucharist, the individual failings of those who administered it seemed irrelevant. By contrast, if one's primary relationship to religion comes by way of a sermon, the character of the priest delivering the sermon becomes newly relevant, for the worshipper's relationship to the source of grace is now mediated by a particular individual rather than a sacramental institution. Why should parishioners follow the guidance of someone whose own life was not admirable? Religious hypocrisy, then, only becomes "hypocrisy" in a modern sense (recommending holiness while living carnally) as the result of a series of religious transformations, among the most salient of which is a personalization of the source of religious grace itself, from the sacrament of the Eucharist to the internal life of the individual. Ewan McGregor's secularization story, though presented as simply an objective realization about religion, in fact builds into its analysis a particular, historical understanding of religion itself. For young Ewan to "see through" it, religion must already have come to be understood as a personal relationship to a divine moral order, mediated through individuals themselves understood as exemplary.

To reiterate, my claim is not that ideology critique is wrong but rather that it is historically partial. Materialist analysis stands in need of a self-critical dialectics when it encounters religion—at precisely the point, that is, where it tends to flatten out into a one-dimensional critique of false consciousness.

How might such a dialectical account proceed? In a famous section of *Capital* Marx produces the fetish as an example of how the commodity tricks human beings into naturalizing social and historical contingency. The fetish serves Marx as a useful heuristic for exploring what he coyly terms the "metaphysical subtleties and theological niceties" of the commodity precisely because he can assume that the religious object is already demystified.[21] If ideology is like a camera obscura, the fetish is the object that the camera produces; revealing the fetish character of the commodity, then, gives the critic the power to reverse the camera obscura and set the world right side up again. In this example, religion is the materialist's privileged object of critique, yet because its ideological strategies are so obvious, that critique barely needs unpacking. Like many of the secularization theorists discussed in this book, Marx works to bring about secularization while simultaneously presupposing that religion is intrinsically incompatible with modernity.

We might ask the same question about Marx's fetish, however, that we asked about his camera obscura: who is the clear-sighted viewer who recognizes the fetish *as* a fetish? In this case, the privileged subject here is the anthropologist, trained in the enlightenment critique of religion, able to recognize a fetish when she sees one because she is working from the comparativist perspective achieved by the early modern transformation of religion into belief. But once we have placed the critical subject in this way, it becomes clear that her presumptively universalist view is partial, for the very same reasons that the figure of the camera obscura is partial. Vision is not timeless but historical, and so too is the critic's anthropological viewpoint.

In order to help materialist criticism remember this, Mitchell proposes modeling the eye on the camera, rather than the reverse. It so happens that in *Natural Theology*, Paley proposes a similar reversal when he models the eye on a telescope. I argued in Chapter 4 that this technique revealed a peculiarly rhetorical dimension to Paley's argument, in which the eye assumes its place in the argument from design only when placed there through comparison to a mechanical object that already exhibits designedness. We can now see how this rhetorical quality, like Mitchell's imaginative reversal, might trouble an ideological reading of religion modeled upon the presumptive clear-sightedness of the critic or the anthropologist. The hope expressed by this "rhetorical" argument is not a definitive or accurate reading of religion but rather the development of historical reflexivity. When the Pedlar in *The Ruined Cottage* describes Robert's descent into fetishism, and then uses that descent as foil for a progressive narrative of growth that transforms fetishism into a "secret spirit of humanity," he prefigures a critical tradition that likewise takes modernization to be the definitive demystification of religion. Even those more sophisticated critics who reveal the "secret spirit" as itself evidence of a romantic ideology presuppose the initial transformation of religious content from primitive, mythic saturation into humanizing spirit.

Religion as a Discipline

In *Genealogies of Religion* Talal Asad contrasts religion as a form of belief with a medieval conception of religion as a site of personal discipline. He argues that the seemingly commonsense question of what religious adherents "believe," and how those beliefs influence actions, behaviors, or aesthetic productions, misconstrues medieval religious dispositions. These dispositions invariably turn not on the beliefs of autonomous agents but upon the production of disciplined knowledge within institutional settings. By contrast, the focus on belief that characterizes postenlightenment religion also makes it possible to conceive of religion as something that the modern subject can sympathetically evaluate without entering. Sometime around 1800, Asad remarks, we witness, "the construction of religion as a new historical phenomenon: anchored in personal experience, expressible in belief-statements, dependent on private institutions, and practiced in one's spare time."[22]

Wordsworth's sonnet "Nuns fret not at their Convent's narrow room" (written 1802, published 1807) records the transformation that Asad describes. A complex meditation on the interrelations of religion, discipline, and form, the poem also registers the historical transition whereby such forms of disciplined knowledge give way to the new historical phenomenon of a modern religion practiced in one's spare time.

> Nuns fret not at their Convent's narrow room;
> And Hermits are contented with their Cells;
> And Students with their pensive Citadels:
> Maids at the Wheel, the Weaver at his Loom,
> Sit blithe and happy; Bees that soar for bloom,
> High as the highest Peak of Furness Fells,
> Will murmur by the hour in Foxglove bells:
> In truth, the prison, unto which we doom
> Ourselves, no prison is: and hence to me,
> In sundry moods, 'twas pastime to be bound
> Within the Sonnet's scanty plot of ground:
> Pleas'd if some Souls (for such there needs must be)
> Who have felt the weight of too much liberty,
> Should find short solace there, as I have found.[23]

We might call this sonnet an exercise in religious studies. Straightforwardly a meditation on the solace to be found in the externally imposed rules of the sonnet, it articulates, largely by analogy, a nonmodern understanding of freedom as that which is realized *through* constraint rather than *over against* it. Yet to choose the sonnet as a temporary abode, as the speaker does at the end of the poem, is quite different from the various postures of devotion with which the sonnet opens. The nun's narrow room, if not entirely involuntary, is more the product of calling than of choice. To write from a comparativist viewpoint, as Wordsworth does here, presupposes that constraint (religious or otherwise) has already been produced as an object of knowledge.[24] To put the matter another way, the speaker's self-conscious entry into the limitations of the sonnet form pictures modernity as marked by the freedom to *choose* constraint. In effect, the speaker gives up his freedom without giving it up.

In order to prepare for this conclusion, the sonnet offers a familiar secularization narrative. If nuns and hermits exemplify traditional religious devotion in their submission to artificial constraint, the subsequent analogies—from student to maid to weaver to bee—progressively humanize and then naturalize the comparison, so that by the time we arrive at the rules of the sonnet, constraint has been rendered natural: the poem has become like nature itself, which manages its paradoxical

commitments to freedom ("the highest Peak of Furness Fells") and order ("murmur by the hour in Foxglove bells") so elegantly that both become sources of delight and harmony: whether soaring to the peaks or
murmuring within the long, tubular blossoms of the foxglove, the bee is
carrying out its appointed task of pollination. Indeed, this is a labor so
self-delighted that it loses itself in its own pleasure: it is labor that does
not recognize itself *as* labor. The process by which the religious discipline of the cell is naturally subsumed into the orderliness of nature
finds its linguistic correlative once we observe that bees store their
honey in cells; the discipline and boundedness of the hermit's cell is
thus carried forward and transformed into nature's gentler ministrations. Once the nun has, through this series of verbal substitutions, allusions, and implications, become a bee, the move into the limitations of
the sonnet form seems perfectly natural. Choosing the constraint of the
sonnet is here rendered as a natural culmination of the process of secularization enacted by the transformation from nuns into bees.

If the sonnet manifestly moves within a modern conception of religion, however, the pressures of language and of form begin to question
the comparative framework that is its enabling condition. To begin with,
the various analogies do not accomplish an organic transformation so
much as depend upon a logic of substitution. The stable distancing of
analogy, whose self-conscious artifice both invites and blocks the identification of the poet with his chosen examples, registers a certain ambivalence that seems characteristic of modernity's vexed relationship to
forms of life it finds both necessary and slightly distasteful. In its desire
both to coincide and not to coincide with the past, that is, this sonnet is
a fine example of the now-familiar criticism that modernity is parasitic
upon forms of life that it cannot account for within its own presuppositions. The final lines secure a minimal contract between writer and
reader through the offices of the traditionalists enumerated in the
poem's opening, and in performing this bargain so self-consciously, the
poem makes available for analysis the precise nature of its comparison
between nuns and bees. Rather than the natural redescription of supernatural ideas that it first seems to be, the comparison in fact rings
rhetorical changes upon a single theme: the paradoxical freedom to be
found when constraint is experienced as an aspect of the self. The
speaker cannot construct his final meeting ground without obsessively
reminding us of those forms of life that fall out in the very process of
construction.

We can observe, therefore, a certain muted aggressiveness directed at
those forms of life. Most strikingly, the poem registers this aggressiveness when the sestet encroaches upon the series of analogies that make
up the poem's octave. The poem's rhyme scheme is that of a standard

Petrarchan sonnet, but at the level of content, the turn comes a line early: "In truth, the prison, unto which we doom / Ourselves, no prison is."[25] This early turn in effect splits the poem in half, so that it consists of two groups of seven lines rather than the eight lines followed by six of common Petrarchan form. This modern preoccupation with fairness and equality at the level of content is undercut somewhat by the resolutely traditional form of the rhyme, and the consequent tension between modernity and tradition is registered in the rather clumsy assertiveness of the lines themselves. This belies any larger claim on the poet's part about the naturalness and gentleness of secularization's triumph. The lines that initiate the turn—"In truth, the prison unto which we doom ourselves / No prison is"—present themselves as simply a summing up of the preceding lines, but in fact they actively revise those lines, as the concept of the prison is both introduced and quickly put aside. Because the rejection of the prison metaphor comes at the expected spot for the turn in a Petrarchan sonnet, the air of natural generosity the poem achieves depends upon our not noticing that the language of the prison has been as it were slipped into the octave precisely so that it can be magnanimously superceded in the sestet. Not only, then, does modernity depend for its stability upon forms of life that its minimalism cannot sustain, but its assumption that traditional forms of life can simply be redescribed in another language suggests a willful, if necessary, misunderstanding of what such forms of life entail. Underneath its air of generous neutrality, the sonnet arranges things beforehand in order to achieve its desired outcome.

Although he apparently lives in a world of varied religious expression, the speaker of "Nuns fret not" seems unconcerned by religious pluralism. He has no problem being tolerant; in fact, tolerance is something he does whenever the mood strikes him. As Asad says, this is religion "practiced in one's spare time"—as a literal pastime, with its connotations of both leisure and nostalgic indulgence. Religion is rendered intelligible *as* religion only once it has been disembedded from its disciplinary context and held up as an object of knowledge. This is a secular habit of mind, not because it is "unbelieving," for belief is not the issue here. It is secular, rather, because it is able to imagine religious discipline as a pleasant respite from the business of wrestling with modern freedom, and from the pressures of a professional career as a writer of autobiographical epics in blank verse.

And yet, as the poem itself attests, this transfer of power—from disciplined knowledge to optional pastime—is anything but smooth or ideologically neutral. If the apparent naturalness and ease of the poem's achievement is really the result of modernity's muted aggression toward forms of life upon which it depends, then it becomes possible to imagine a scenario in which those traditional forms of life are freed from the burden of sustaining a history aimed toward modernity. In their work on multiple modernities Charles Taylor and Benjamin Lee remind us that while convergence theories of modernization pose (religious) tradition against (secular) modernity, thinking of modernity as multiple removes this teleological burden, allowing tradition to interact dialectically with modernity. In the case of Wordsworth's poem, the very act of transforming discipline into a modern form aligns the rules of the sonnet with instinct, disposition, and confinement, thereby sketching a meeting ground between writer and reader that is neither idea nor belief but an affective and bodily posture. On this reading, life devoted to God is little different, in its form, from a life of learning or spinning or weaving—in short, an activity or vocation demanding certain skills and certain dispositions.

In her discussion of the women's mosque movement, Saba Mahmood considers the multiple ways in which traditional forms of religious discipline interact with and help to shape Egyptian modernity. In the course of her investigation she offers an analogy that resonates powerfully with Wordsworth's sonnet. A virtuoso pianist, she notes, can achieve excellence only by submitting herself to a rigorous program of drills, lessons, and exercises; the freedom of expertise, accordingly, is not the freedom of an autonomous will but rather the freedom of mastery—the mastery of a certain set of habits, skills, dispositions, or bodily postures.[26] In like manner, the sonnet's speaker imagines that both poet and reader will submit themselves on a regular basis to the rigors of the sonnet form. In this kind of expertise, a certain discipline becomes so ingrained that the self empties out into pure activity; the forms of life enumerated in the sonnet's octave, accordingly, renounce being in favor of doing, striving to become verbs rather than nouns.

To be sure, the speaker remains ambivalent about this form of discipline. Overtly respectful of the octave's traditional forms of life, he nevertheless cannot escape viewing them chiefly as useful ways to image his own more modern choices. It is therefore apposite that this poem offers the domain of the literary as the privileged space in which to negotiate the very relationship of modernity to tradition. On the one hand, literature appears to offer itself as the site of a reconstituted culture. That the literary form under discussion is here said to model itself upon an older and explicitly religious set of institutions accordingly positions literature as the inheritor of the social function formerly carried out by religion. On the other hand, this apparent teleology is countered within the sonnet itself, which reveals that the seemingly natural process by which sonnets replace nuns is not natural at all but rather contingent, the result of modernity's partial and self-interested reading of forms of life it would seek to replace. Thus the poem itself presents the reader with incommensurate conclusions. On the one hand, we observe a very modern solution to modernity: the contemplative freedom to be gained from a shared and willed submission to the sonnet's form. On the other hand, we observe a model of subjectivity produced through discipline and training, in which the reiterative experience of literary form produces neither a belief nor a ritual but a technique.

*　*　*

In its own highly condensed fashion, Wordsworth's sonnet registers the variety of possible outcomes that attend the meeting of modernity with traditional forms of life. In so doing, it reminds us that "modernity" is not the single object sometimes posited by modernization theory; it is, rather, multiply refracted and contested. It may be chosen, resisted, or accommodated, and its meaning varies with each of these possibilities. The aim of this book has been to demonstrate that within the framework of this multiple modernity, religion too becomes a multiple object, demanding in its turn a careful delineation of the various meanings attached to the term "secularization." That it can register these varieties with such nuance and power is one of the pleasures of the literature we call romantic.

Afterword

Intelligent Design and Religious Ignoramuses; or, the Difference Between Theory and Literature

> *Ira Flatow: Why do you think that . . . other countries don't have as big a problem with that idea [of evolution]? Why in this country does there seem to be such a hue and outcry in some places?*
>
> *Richard Dawkins: I think the difference is that although we have creationists in Britain, we don't have any in political power. Something's gone wrong with democracy in this country such that—how can I describe it?—religious ignoramuses somehow managed to hijack local school boards and maybe even higher political offices.*
>
> —Science Friday with Ira Flatow, *National Public Radio*, November 19, 2004

It is not clear why Ira Flatow would think that an Oxford don had light to shed on the present American cultural situation. In producing the predictable mixture of frustration and hostility that has characterized the scientific community's reaction to the current controversy over evolution in the United States, Dawkins certainly sheds no light. His answer is nevertheless revealing, for he immediately makes the issue a matter of political power rather than of cultural analysis. He might have paused to consider why elected officials who look like ignoramuses to him look appealing to a significant portion of the American electorate. But he does not do this. Instead he moves immediately to the political arena by suggesting that democracies that elect ignoramuses are hardly democracies at all, because, tautologically, electing ignoramuses means that "something's gone wrong" with them. Moreover, his hijacking metaphor, though probably unintentional, signifies ambiguously but powerfully in post-9/11 America. Religious fanaticism hijacks airplanes, but it also hijacks school boards; in an indirect riposte to the Bush administration, which has sought to link its "war on terror" to an interpretation of American history indebted to a moralizing evangelical Christianity,

Dawkins suggests that defending democracy will mean protecting it from creationist hijackers. Politics, in short, should be conducted without the interference of religion. And, so goes the implicit corollary, should science.

Dawkins's claim has history behind it, but only fairly recent history, for his distinctions among politics, science, and religion depend upon the various divisions of knowledge that have come to structure modernity. Once the intellectual landscape has been thus divided into separate disciplinary territories, attempts to breach those divisions can be described as inappropriate interference or worse.

When I began thinking about the design argument almost a decade ago, it seemed inconceivable that it would be one of *the* hot-button issues of the early twenty-first century. Whether the current controversy over so-called "intelligent design" has the staying power of other divisive cultural issues such as abortion is doubtful; still, its current status is a surprise for those intellectuals and academics who had thought religion too marginalized to trouble science any more. After percolating below the surface for a number of years, the intelligent design movement has erupted into popular consciousness. It has figured for several years in debates about the science curriculum in Kansas public schools and even more recently in school board elections in Dover, Pennsylvania. But beyond these local and perhaps short-lived manifestations, the debate over evolution has entered public middlebrow discourse in venues far removed from Kansas and rural Pennsylvania. The *New York Times* covered the movement extensively in the summer and fall of 2005; *Time* magazine gave it a cover story; even *The New Yorker* sent a correspondent to Dover to cover a lawsuit against the school board mounted by opponents of intelligent design (the lawsuit was successful).

Intelligent design's target has from the beginning been Darwinian evolution. Its partisans claim that there are explanatory gaps that only the postulation of a divine designer can fill; defenders of evolution, meanwhile, claim either that there are no such gaps or that science is slowly filling them in. This focus on evolution obscures the fact that the debate over design predates Darwin. Indeed, it revisits a collection of issues that were already venerable philosophical topics when design became a cultural flashpoint in the eighteenth and early nineteenth centuries. Hans Blumenberg's "reoccupation theory" of modernity seems especially apt when it comes to design: the questions of meaning—of how we got here, of what it means to live well, of whether history has a direction or purpose—are more or less constant. Design and its attendant issues quite precisely capture the cultural and personal anxieties behind those questions, and so it is not surprising that the topic should crop up from time to time, albeit under different historical conditions. Modernity,

Blumenberg proposes, simply *is* the repeated act of reoccupying old questions of meaning dressed up in new languages.

To be sure, Darwin offered the first positive alternative to a simplistic design hypothesis and thereby shifted the balance of power by putting theism on the defensive for the first time. In the United States, in particular, debates about divine interaction with creation have been filtered almost exclusively through evolution, a process helped along by the way that the Scopes trial of 1925 and its aftermath produced a culture of marginalization, fear, and bitterness among America's religious traditionalists.[1] Yet if we read this important shift as evidence of "secularization," we will wind up as confused as Richard Dawkins about the reemergence of design in the twenty-first century. Neither Darwin's intellectual importance nor evolution's powerful cultural symbolism in twenty-first-century America should prevent us from placing intelligent design in a history of design debates, a history that itself can be understood as a repeated attempt to address basic questions of meaning, purpose, and intention.

Science and Religion

The tendency to portray the issue as a conflict between science and religion obscures the historical dimensions of the current debate over design. In an August 2005 story on intelligent design, *Time* magazine's cover text puts the matter starkly: "The push to teach 'intelligent design' raises a question: Does God have a place in science class?"[2] By framing the issue as a matter of classroom pedagogy, *Time* reveals how powerfully differentiation has shaped the debate and reveals too why that debate has become largely an exercise in defense of disciplinary boundaries. When Kansas removed the phrase "natural explanations" from its state science guidelines, for example, many scientists immediately interpreted this as a religiously motivated attack on methodological naturalism itself.[3]

Yet despite this rhetorical focus on the status of science, older versions of the design debate continue to structure current discussions of intelligent design. Any reader of Paley, for instance, should be struck by the following passage, from an account of the Dover trial in the *New York Times*:

Scott A. Minnich, an associate professor of microbiology at the University of Idaho, testified for the defense on Thursday and Friday, likening intelligent design to seeing a watch and implicitly knowing that it had a designer—the argument the plaintiffs' lawyer called "a meager little analogy."[4]

At stake here is the question of whether analogy counts as scientific reasoning. And as readers of this book will immediately recognize, this little exchange recapitulates a moment in the self-definition of science by evoking the debate between Hume and Paley. Hume's attack on analogy depends upon an implicit distinction between science and religion; once that distinction becomes explicit, as it clearly is in this courtroom scene, it can be used as a weapon against analogy, which suddenly is made to appear "meager." Caught in this historical time warp, Minnich offers a version of Paley's argument from perception. The phrase "implicitly knowing" tries to formulate the perception of design as an internal, intuitive, phenomenon. In effect, it rewrites the teleological dimension of design arguments in phenomenological terms.

As Paley himself understood, this intuitive sensibility has long been design's strongest suit; it matches well with the characteristically modern definition of internal religion discussed in the last chapter. What the intuitive argument tends to downplay, however, is what in Chapter 4 I called "rhetoric"—that is, the degree to which intuition's seeming naturalness and spontaneity is the result of training and education. Behind a phrase like Minnich's "implicitly knowing" stands a pedagogy of enculturation and habituation; Paley's seemingly interminable reiterations of his argument, most particularly its formation as a rhetorical question—"could anything be more decisive of contrivance than this?"—constitute a kind of catechism of design whose effects were, and are, remarkably powerful.

Daniel Dennett, writing in the *New York Times* op-ed page, acknowledges the continuing power of this catechism: "If you still find [the design intuition] compelling, a sort of cognitive illusion that you can feel even as you discount it," he writes, "you are like just about everybody else in the world; the idea that natural selection has the power to generate such sophisticated designs is deeply counterintuitive."[5] Here Dennett sounds surprisingly like his religious opponents, for he implicitly acknowledges that science is a discipline; it takes training to resist the cognitive illusion of design, training that must take place within the context of a scientific culture that gives it meaning. In his formulation we may hear, too, the pathos of a modernity in which the distinction between emotion and cognition has come to structure subjectivity, and in which the price of entry into rational discourse is the rejection of feeling and intuition. In Hume's *Dialogues*, Cleanthes had attacked Philo on the same ground: why corrupt your natural good sense with complicated arguments, Cleanthes asks, when intuition tells us that the world has been designed? Little wonder that, more than two centuries later, many continue to choose their intuitions over a scientific discipline that must be built up over time.

Both design *and* evolution, in sum, depend upon pedagogical strategies. Describing the current controversy as a conflict between science and religion obscures such potential points of contact between those two hypostatized terms and distorts the nature of the actual controversy. When partisans sign up on one side or the other of the current debate, they are not signing up for an abstraction ("science" or "religion") but rather for the cultural orientations in which those abstractions are embedded. As I argued earlier in this book, this is something that Hume understood very well when he had his narrator Pamphilus declare at the end of the *Dialogues* that, even after witnessing Philo's impressive performance, he nevertheless still agreed with Cleanthes.

The twin pieties of intelligent design and evolution are created through organizational and personal logics that go well beyond this particular debate. As Saba Mahmood notes about the pious subjects of the Islamic mosque movement, our standard analytic practices seem ill equipped to deal with the variety of ways in which character is practiced, performed, and instantiated in the modern world.[6] Could we replace the language of religion versus science, which structures the matter as a dispute between tradition and modernity, with a descriptive language that recognizes both evolution and design as examples of the multiple problematics of meaning that characterize modernity itself? Getting to such language would require of each side the epistemic humility to admit that its conclusions are compelling only from within the larger cultural formations to which those conclusions give expression.

Just a Theory

In 2002 the school district of Cobb County, Georgia, approved a motion to place stickers on high school biology textbooks that read, in part: "This textbook contains material on evolution. Evolution is a theory, not a fact." This awkward distinction between theory and fact has proved popular among partisans of intelligent design, many of whom assert that evolution is "just a theory," that intelligent design is an alternative theory, and that schools ought to "teach the controversy" generated by these competing theories. President George W. Bush has even endorsed this approach.[7] The assumption behind this strategy is that there is a real scientific debate about whether evolution or some other theory best explains the complexity of the natural world. Here the intelligent design movement finds itself in a strange alliance with a relativistic tradition within philosophy of science, whose most radical practitioners sometimes write as if science itself can be reduced to its cultural conditions.[8] Intelligent design's alliance with this postmodern temperament is unstable, however, and immediately complicated by what can only be called the movement's scientism—that is, its fetishization of science and its attempt to ground its claims in the scientific method.[9] Pro-evolutionary scientists, meanwhile, betray their frustration with both the postmodern and the scientistic strains of the intelligent design movement, insisting that evolution's opponents have willfully misunderstood the epistemic status of scientific theory: evolution, they note, is accepted by the overwhelming majority of working scientists and has an admirable track record for explaining complexity. Intelligent design can claim neither of these, so it is not a "theory" in the sense that evolution is a "theory."

But pointing out the conceptual confusion that characterizes the intelligent design movement is clearly not enough to make it go away. To see why this is so, we can remember that the version of the design argument prevalent in the eighteenth century was similarly poised between its teleological orientation and its commitment to an inductive procedure. Eighteenth-century design proceeded empirically, that is to say, but its empiricism was undergirded by the presupposition that the only reason to be empirical in the first place was that the firmament declared God's handiwork, that nature was the Book of God and human beings were its readers.

Modern defenders of evolution sometimes write as if ideas behave in the world just as they behave in laboratories and in the pages of scientific journals. In those contexts, variables are controlled or eliminated, and better ideas win out over worse ideas. But in the real world, people sign up for ideas for a whole host of reasons, only some of which can be described in the language of reason. Most importantly, people tend to sign up for the worldview presupposed by an idea before signing up for the idea itself—not the other way around. The teleological end of the design argument, in other words, is where the meaning lies. If something like 50 percent of Americans have hesitations about evolution, that is not because they are stupid, any more than Pamphilus was stupid.[10] Rather, it is because they would prefer to live in the world presupposed by design than in the world presupposed by evolution.

For what design offers is a world ruled over by intentionality. In Chapter 6 on Wordsworth, I argued that the design analogy was the hidden engine of the closing sections of *The Prelude*, enabling Wordsworth to describe a world of generous purpose whose intrinsic organizing principles correlated with and validated his own professional calling. At the center of Wordsworth's literary effect, then, is his extraordinary ability to place his readers in a world brimful of a purpose that can be felt but not pinned to a particular purposive agent. Because design is at the root a theory of intentionality, and because, inversely, intentionality is itself a religiously inflected story of origins, design is the perfect vehicle for the Wordsworthian transformation of an intentional consciousness into a consciousness *of* intention.

If this is one romantic attempt to solve the problem of intentionality by dissolving it, we witness critical dissatisfaction with that attempt whenever intentionality crops up as a flashpoint in literary studies. In my discussion of *The Prelude* I referred to the New Criticism and the "intentional fallacy" debate of the 1950s; in the early 1980s Steven Knapp and Walter Benn Michaels revived that debate again, this time from a pragmatist direction, in their essay "Against Theory." In this essay Knapp and Michaels define theory as "the attempt to govern interpretations of particular texts by appealing to an account of interpretation in general"; the theoretical enterprise always fails in the same way, they argue, because it consistently misrecognizes the particular as the general.[11] And their chief exhibit is intentionality. Both intentionalists and anti-intentionalists are wrong, they argue, for the simple reason that both camps put a premium on getting the relationship between author and text correct. But in fact, "once it is seen that the meaning of a text is simply identical to the author's intended meaning, the project of *grounding* meaning in intention becomes incoherent. Since the project itself is incoherent, it can neither succeed nor fail; hence both [intentionalism and anti-intentionalism] are irrelevant."[12] In making their case, Knapp and Michaels have recourse to what they call the "wave poem," an example that came to dominate subsequent debate about their essay. I quote the example in full, for I will return shortly to its language:

Suppose that you're walking along a beach and you come upon a curious sequence of squiggles in the sand. You step back a few paces and notice that they spell out the following words:

A slumber did my spirit seal;
I had no human fears:
She seemed a thing that could not feel
The touch of earthly years.

This would seem to be a good case of intentionless meaning: you recognize the writing as writing, you understand what the words mean, you may even identify them as constituting a rhymed poetic stanza—and all this without knowing anything about the author and indeed without needing to connect the words to any notion of an author at all. . . . But now suppose that, as you stand gazing at this pattern in the sand, a wave washes up and recedes, leaving in its wake (written below what you now realize was only the first stanza) the following words:

No motion has she now, no force;
She neither hears nor sees
Rolled round in earth's diurnal course,
With rocks, and stones, and trees.

One might ask whether the question of intention still seems as irrelevant as it did seconds before. You will now, we suspect, feel compelled to explain what you have just seen. (727–28)

My explanation of this phenomenon, say Knapp and Michaels, will take one of two forms. Either I will ascribe these marks to an intentional agent (perhaps I decide that the sea itself has intentions), or I will decide that the marks are the accidental, and hence nonintentional effects of some heretofore unknown natural or mechanical operation (erosion, for example). In either case I will be amazed at what I have seen, but amazed for different reasons. In the first case, I will be amazed to discover that the sea is an intentional agent; in the second, I will be amazed to discover that what looks like poetry is in fact the result of accidental processes.

If I decide that the marks on the sand *are* actually the result of an accidental process, then the wave poem is not actually a poem at all, because it isn't language. Knapp and Michaels are especially emphatic about this point, for it goes to the heart of their case against theory. The mistake that makes theory possible, they argue, is to imagine that such a thing as intentionless meaning is possible; we wrongly think that the encounter with language involves a moment of decision about whether to treat language as originating in an intentional agent. But in fact, to recognize something *as* language is *already* to treat it as intentional; if it weren't intentional it wouldn't be language but only a series of marks or utterances that *resemble* language. This is why there can be no such thing as intentionless meaning. "In debates about intention," Knapp and Michaels conclude, "the moment of imagining intentionless meaning constitutes the theoretical moment itself. From the standpoint of an argument against theory, then, the only important question is whether there can in fact be intentionless meanings. If our argument against theory is to succeed, the answer to this question must be no" (727). So much for theory.

In a different register, "intentionless meaning" is an excellent description of the natural world that Darwinian evolution asks us to imagine. According to its defenders, evolution produces such extraordinarily intricate solutions to the problem of survival that those solutions look for all the world like the result of some behind-the-scenes designer. But in fact that impression is really the result of a series of accidents whose cumulative effect over billions of years is to produce the appearance of intention where there is none at all. In the language of "Against Theory," then, evolution "constitutes the theoretical moment itself"—that is, the attempt to distinguish between intentionality and meaning and thereby raise the possibility that the accidental process of natural selection can give a meaningful shape to the world.

When its opponents claim that evolution is "just a theory," this looks initially like an attempt to knock evolution from its epistemic throne; "theory" is a synonym for "opinion." But the much stronger definition of theory that Knapp and Michaels offer is in fact more relevant to the cultural stakes of the debate. For evolution is indeed a theory in the sense of an "attempt to govern interpretations of particular texts by appealing to an account of interpretation in general," where the "text" is the natural world itself.

Framing the issue in this way helps us to see that the relevant conflict here is not between science and religion but between differentiation and intentionality. "Against Theory" was an attack on a whole way of doing business, which the authors labeled "theory" but which can be more accurately described as a model of professional literary study that derived its authority by systematically downplaying the author's intentions (even when author's intentions were granted, they were granted as a result of theoretical investigation rather than the simple pragmatics of reading). In like manner, the claim that evolution is just a theory is in fact an attack on a differentiated model of science that derives its authority from systematically downplaying the role of a divine author and proposing its own, intentionless, models of understanding. Whether the object in question is a poem or a bacterium, the positing of intentionlessness marks the denial or denigration of authorship. And this is why both "Against Theory" and intelligent design mount their attack in the name of a recovery of intention as the best or only way of ascribing meaning to the object. Both attacks pose implicit or intuitive knowledge against the artifices of theoretical knowledge: by recognizing a poem as a poem, we have already granted intention; when we recognize an eye as an eye, we already know that it has been designed. And finally, because the presupposition of intentionlessness undergirds a professional formation (theory, evolution), both attacks play intentionality off against the sort of differentiation that has allowed those professions to behave as autonomous disciplines.

Against theory Knapp and Michaels pose the *practice* of literary criticism, which automatically grants intention rather than mistakenly trying to distinguish it from meaning. In this book we have traced a similar opposition between theory and practice, whereby theory came to be identified with an autonomous epistemological stance that was implicitly secularizing even when its aim was religious, whereas practice came to be identified with a celebration of intrinsic habits and dispositions for which design and its theory of divine intentionality became a figure. When Knapp and Michaels counterpose theory and practice through the offices of a debate about authorial intentions, then, they are unknowingly replaying a debate that has its roots in a positing of divine intentionality that goes by the name of the argument from design. Even more particularly, they inherit a version of the design argument inflected though romantic-era literature: not only Wordsworth's ruminations on what it means to be conscious of intention but Barbauld's meditations on design as a distinctive set of practices. All literary interpretation of the sort that Knapp and Michaels approve partakes of the intuitive structure that characterizes design: in treating a poem as a poem, rather than a series of marks that resemble a poem, we have already assigned intention automatically, without thinking. Indeed, we observed such a pragmatic approach already in John Tillotson's sermon "The Wisdom of Being Religious," considered near the very beginning of the book, whose rhetorical questions nicely amalgamate divine intentionality, the intentions of the artist, and the pragmatics of reading: "How often might a man after he had jumbled a set of letters in a bag, fling them out upon the ground before they would fall into an exact Poem, yea so much as make a good discourse in Prose? And may not a little *Book* be as easily made by chance, as this great *Volume* of the world?" (15). For Tillotson as much as for Knapp and Michaels, to acknowledge the power of these rhetorical questions is already to step outside the realm of theory and into "practice." To do theory, on the other hand, is to resist Tillotson's questions, to do what Cleanthes accuses Philo of doing, to do what intelligent design proponents accuse evolutionists of doing: obscure the natural, intuitive good sense that adheres to practice by inventing theoretical distinctions (between meaning and intention, between purpose and cause) where there are none to be found. That intuition and practice are themselves not natural but rather must be built up over time goes unremarked. That is the basic Humean insight that both design advocates and its opponents conveniently forget.

The parallel between "Against Theory" and design arguments turns uncanny when we consider two scenes of reading. The first is the excerpt from Knapp and Michaels quoted previously, which places us on a beach and asks us to interpret what we find there. Here is the second scene, which places us on a heath and asks us to interpret what we find there:

In crossing a heath, suppose I pitched my foot against a *stone*, and were asked how the stone came to be there: I might possibly answer, that for any thing I knew to the contrary, it had lain there for ever; nor would it perhaps be very easy to show the absurdity of this answer. But suppose I had found a *watch* upon the ground, and it should be inquired how the watch happened to be in that place: I should hardly think of the answer which I had before given—that, for any thing I knew, the watch might have always been there. Yet why should not this answer serve for the watch as well as for the stone? . . . For this reason, and for no other, viz. that, when we come to inspect the watch, we perceive (what we could not discover in the stone) that its several parts are framed and put together for a purpose.[13]

"Suppose that you're walking along a beach and you come upon a curious sequence of squiggles in the sand." "In crossing a heath, suppose I pitched my foot against a stone." As if the shared conceit were not enough, the two scenes also share a doubled structure, in which the question of intention comes to be felt not after the first discovery (the first stanza and the stone) but only after the second discovery (the second stanza and the watch). This new information forces questions of meaning and significance upon the subject. And that subject himself is a remarkably modern figure, thrown without warning or preparation into a world where anonymous but powerful voices demand an account: "suppose . . . it should be inquired how the watch happened to be in that place," writes Paley; "You will now . . . feel compelled to explain what you have just seen," write Knapp and Michaels. Who is doing this inquiring? Why should I feel compelled by it? Neither account tells us, yet both presume that there is no escape from the drama of interpretation.

The texts that must be interpreted, however, differ in one crucial respect. Paley turns a meaningless stone into a meaningful watch; Wordsworth's poem turns a human being into a stone, which by Paley's lights makes her an object without meaning because there is no way to read in her the intentions of a creator. The very fact that Wordsworth's poem does *not* strip meaning from Lucy as she joins the "rocks, and stones, and trees" but actually adds meaning through this transformation may be taken as example of the power of "literature" in relation to design that Wordsworth came to understand. Wordsworth does what Paley cannot do, for he is able to describe a world in which nature's supreme agency does not come at the expense of human meaning. There are still intentions in this poem, but they seem to have no source beyond the generalized meaning and significance with which literature imbues the entire natural world. Thus does literature both shape and embrace a differentiated world of intentionless meaning when it writes Lucy's human story into the larger story of rocks and stones and trees. In transforming design into a vision of the natural world full of intentionality without an intender, Wordsworth's poem invites theoretical reflection. Paley's design argument does not, since Paley remains committed to the idea that meaning only comes from specific intentions: that is why he can find nothing of interest to say about the very stones in which Wordsworth seems most interested.

At this juncture it does not seem like an urgent task to evaluate the philosophical worthiness of "Against Theory," just as it may seem irrelevant to debate the epistemological merits of intelligent design.[14] More interesting is the desire that both positions evidently share. In each case the critique is aimed at a certain differentiated way of doing business (theory, evolution), and the goal is to defeat differentiation by linking intention to meaning through the offices of an author. Insofar as differentiation is central to the experience of modernity, the desire to get beyond or behind or before theory is the desire to escape from modernity by restoring intentionality to the world. Yet because the desire to escape modernity is also one of the things that it means to *be* modern, "litera-ture" as we have come to understand it since the romantics names the impossible desire to escape ourselves. Knapp and Michaels want to es-cape from theory into a world of intention; proponents of intelligent de-sign want to escape evolution into a world of intention. The temptation to offer "literature" as an alternative to "theory," as if literature were something whose unified sensibility would counter differentiation by de-riving meaning from intention, is only a temptation because literature as we know it perpetually reminds us of our proximity to the kind of differ-entiated activity that goes by the name of theory. In Wordsworth's poem, "theory" is simply the proclivity to find meaning in stones. To read litera-ture without theory, then, is like reading the world as the Book of God; from the differentiated place where we now stand, perhaps the best we can do is try to imagine how such a reading might be possible.

Notes

Introduction

1. M. H. Abrams, *Natural Supernaturalism: Tradition and Revolution in Romantic Literature* (New York and London: W. W. Norton, 1971) 12, 13. More recent books that contest, with various levels of success, Abrams's coordination of romanticism with secularization include Stephen Prickett, *Origins of Narrative: The Romantic Appropriation of the Bible* (Cambridge: Cambridge University Press, 1996); Robert M. Ryan, *The Romantic Reformation: Religious Politics in English Literature, 1789–1824* (Cambridge: Cambridge University Press, 1997); David Jasper, *The Sacred and Secular Canon in Romanticism: Preserving the Sacred Truths* (Houndmills: Macmillan; New York: St. Martin's, 1999); Martin Priestman, *Romantic Atheism: Poetry and Freethought, 1780–1830* (Cambridge: Cambridge University Press, 1999); and Mark Canuel, *Religion, Toleration, and British Writing, 1790–1830* (Cambridge: Cambridge University Press, 2002). Of these, Canuel offers the most helpful redefinition of secularization: "secularization did not emerge as a change in individuals' beliefs, or a change in collective beliefs, but as a shift in the means through which distinct beliefs could be coordinated or organized under the auspices of more capacious and elaborate structures of government" (4). Canuel here coordinates secularization with tolerance; both secularization and tolerance, however, can be brought under the larger rubric of differentiation.

2. It is worth pointing out that the premise "design requires a designer" is axiomatic during this period. The idea of design without a designer—as posited by evolutionary theory, for instance—was apparently inconceivable at this historical juncture.

3. D. L. LeMahieu, *The Mind of William Paley: A Philosopher and His Age* (Lincoln: University of Nebraska Press, 1976) 32–40, gives a thorough account of the interrelation of teleology and induction in the British Enlightenment.

4. On the relations of science and theology during the early modern period, see Amos Funkenstein, *Theology and the Scientific Imagination: From the Middle Ages to the Seventeenth Century* (Princeton, N.J.: Princeton University Press, 1986) esp. chapter 5. For a good overview of the intellectual issues surrounding natural theology in the eighteenth and early nineteenth centuries, see John Hedley Brooke, *Science and Religion: Some Historical Perspectives* (Cambridge: Cambridge University Press, 1991) 192–225.

5. Charles Taylor, *Modern Social Imaginaries* (Durham, N.C.: Duke University Press, 2004) 13–14. For a good introduction to the differences between design and the Great Chain of Being, see Peter J. Bowler, *Evolution: The History of an Idea* (Berkeley: University of California Press, 1989) 50–89.

6. Taylor, *Modern Social Imaginaries*, 2.

7. Under the rubric of "intelligent design," the design argument is currently enjoying something of a renaissance, at least in the United States. The best introduction to the present debate from a philosophical perspective is Neil A. Manson, ed., *God and Design: The Teleological Argument and Modern Science*, (London: Routledge, 2003). For more on intelligent design, see my Afterword.

8. LeMahieu, *The Mind of William Paley*, 31. For an elegant description of the centrality of eighteenth-century natural theology, see Norman Sykes, *Church and State in England in the XVIIIth Century: The Birkbeck Lectures in Ecclesiastical History* (Cambridge: Cambridge University Press, 1934) 341–45.

9. "Sermon I: The Wisdom of Being Religious," *The Works of the Most Reverend Dr. John Tillotson, Late Lord Archbishop of Canterbury, Containing Fifty Four Sermons and Discourses, on Several Occasions. Together with The Rule of Faith. Being All that Were Published by His Grace Himself. And Now Collected into One Volume* (London: B. Aylmer and W. Rogers, 1696) 1–33, 15. Thanks to Charles Weiss for securing my entrance to the Fellows Library of Clare College, Cambridge, where I consulted this work.

10. To give some sense of the parameters: The trope runs from Bacon's *Novum Organum* in 1620 to Mill's *Three Essays on Religion* in 1870. See "The Argument from Marks of Design in Nature," in "Theism," *Three Essays on Religion*, 3rd ed. (London: Longmans, Green & Co., 1885) 167–75. On John Keble's use of the trope in *The Christian Year*, see Stephen Prickett, *Words and The Word: Language, Poetics, and Biblical Interpretation* (Cambridge: Cambridge University Press, 1986) 123–48.

11. Psalm 19:1–4. All biblical references are to the King James Version; italics are in the original.

12. August 23, 1712 (no. 465), *The Spectator*, ed. Donald F. Bond, vol. 4 (Oxford: Clarendon Press, 1965) 141–45.

13. Isaac Watts, *The Psalms of David Imitated in the Language of the New Testament* (London: Printed for J. Clark; R. Ford; and R. Cruttenden, 1719) 56–57, lines 1–4, 13–16, http://galenet.galegroup.com/servlet/ECCO.

14. John Milton, *Paradise Lost*, 1674 ed., in *John Milton: Complete Poems and Major Prose*, ed. Merritt Y. Hughes (Indianapolis, Ind.: Odyssey Press, Bobbs-Merrill, 1983), book 8, lines 70–75. All further references will be to this edition.

15. For this argument, see Stanley Fish, *How Milton Works* (Cambridge, Mass.: Harvard University Press, 2001) 43.

16. See Edward Stillingfleet, *Origines Sacrae, or a Rational Account of the Grounds of Christian Faith* (London: Printed by R. W. for Henry Mortlock, 1662); and Ralph Cudworth, *The True Intellectual System of the Universe* (London: Printed for Richard Royston, 1678). John Wilkins, *Of The Principles and Duties of Natural Religion: Two Books* (London: Printed for T. Basset, 1678).

17. See Isabel Rivers, "'Galen's Muscles': Wilkins, Hume, and the Educational Use of the Argument from Design," *Historical Journal* 36 (1993): 577–97, 585.

18. As I discuss in the second chapter, Clarke's cosmological argument is a modification of the design argument.

19. "Dedication: To the Honourable and Right Reverend Shute Barrington,

LL.D., Lord Bishop of Durham," *The Works of William Paley, D. D.*, 5 vols. (London: William Baynes and Son, 1825), 4: vii.

20. There is a large and growing literature on this topic. See, among others, Annette C. Baier, *A Progress of Sentiments: Reflections on Hume's Treatise* (Cambridge: Harvard University Press, 1991); G. J. Barker-Benfield, *The Culture of Sensibility: Sex and Society in Eighteenth-Century Britain* (Chicago: University of Chicago Press, 1992); Claudia L. Johnson, *Equivocal Beings: Politics, Gender, and Sentimentality in the 1790s* (Chicago: University of Chicago Press, 1995); Adela Pinch, *Strange Fits of Passion: Epistemologies of Emotion, Hume to Austen* (Stanford, Calif.: Stanford University Press, 1996); and Julie Ellison, *Cato's Tears and the Making of Anglo-American Emotion* (Chicago: University of Chicago Press, 1999).

21. Thomas Sprat, *History of the Royal Society* (London, 1667, facsimile ed.), ed. Jackson I. Cope and Harold Whitmore Jones (1958; St. Louis: Washington University Press; London: Routledge and Kegan Paul, 1966) 82. I first discovered this quotation in Funkenstein, *Theology and the Scientific Imagination*, 8–9.

22. Thus *The British Critic*, dispatching with the unfortunate author of a book entitled *The Sacred Scripture Theory of the Earth*, remarks acidly in 1799: "to instruct us in any particular system of philosophy, was by no means the design of the sacred writings; it is not astronomical, but divine and moral precepts that are there meant to be inculcated; and he who labours to deduce from them arguments in support of any particular branch of human science, or build upon them any fabric of philosophy, evidently mistakes their ultimate object and end, which are to improve the *heart* rather than the *head*." *The British Critic* 14 (August 1799): 113–15, 114–15.

23. Mill, *Three Essays on Religion*, 169.

24. *Analytical Review* 8 (1790): 325.

25. *The British Critic*, n.s., 3 (May 1815): 449–67, 452.

26. Samuel Taylor Coleridge, *Marginalia*, vol. 12, pt. 3, ed. H. J. Jackson and George Whalley, in *The Collected Works of Samuel Taylor Coleridge*, ed. Kathleen Coburn (Princeton, N.J.: Princeton University Press; London: Routledge, 1992) 763. On Coleridge and Paley, see Douglas Hedley, *Coleridge, Philosophy and Religion: Aids to Reflection and the Mirror of the Spirit* (Cambridge: Cambridge University Press, 2000) 45–49.

27. *Shelley's Poetry and Prose*, 2nd ed., ed. Donald H. Reiman and Neil Fraistat (New York: W. W. Norton, 2002) 209.

28. Wednesday, September 14, 1814, in *The Journals of Mary Shelley, 1814–1844*, ed. Paula R. Feldman and Diana Scott-Kilvert (Oxford: Clarendon Press, 1987) 1: 25.

29. See Earl R. Wasserman, "Nature Moralized: The Divine Analogy in the Eighteenth Century," *English Literary History* 20, no. 1 (1953): 39–76.

30. "Why do we admit design in any machine of human contrivance? Simply because innumerable instances of machines having been contrived by human art are present to our mind, because we are acquainted with persons who could construct such machines; but if, having no previous knowledge of any artificial contrivance, we had accidentally found a watch upon the ground, we should have been justified in concluding, that it was a thing of Nature, that it was a combination of matter with whose cause we were unacquainted, and that any attempt to account for the origin of its existence would be equally presumptuous and unsatisfactory." Percy Shelley, "A Refutation of Deism," in *The Complete Works of Shelley*, ed. Roger Ingpen and Walter E. Peck (New York: Gordian Press) 6: 46. See also "A Refutation of Deism: Fragment of a Draft," in *The Complete Works*, 7: 281–82.

31. William Wordsworth, *"The Prelude": 1799, 1805, 1850*, ed. Jonathan Wordsworth, M. H. Abrams, and Stephen Gill (New York and London: W. W. Norton, 1979). The Norton editors call this passage an "unequivocal restatement of the pantheist position of *Tintern Abbey*" (152). Given the "Dream of the Arab" passage that shortly follows, this seems to me an overstatement. Unless otherwise noted, quotations from *The Prelude* will be from the 1805 version in this edition.

32. See Andrzej Warminski, "Missed Crossing: Wordsworth's Apocalypses," *MLN* 99 (1984): 983–1006, esp. 998; and Warminski, "Facing Language: Wordsworth's First Poetic Spirits," *diacritics* 17, no. 4 (1987): 18–31, esp. 25–29. In Warminski's reading of the drowned man passage, the sudden appearance of the corpse interrupts the stable, and implicitly orthodox, analogy between nature and books, inaugurating a semiotic, anti-incarnational, and implicitly secular poetics.

33. See J. Hillis Miller, *The Linguistic Moment: From Wordsworth to Stevens* (Princeton, N.J.: Princeton University Press, 1985) 88–96.

34. For a winsomely self-conscious example of that normativity, see W. J. T. Mitchell, "Romanticism and the Life of Things: Fossils, Totems, and Images," *Critical Inquiry* 28, no. 1 (2001): 167–84, esp. 169, 170. For a discussion of the relationship of romanticism to modernity, see Orrin N. C. Wang, *Fantastic Modernity: Dialectical Readings in Romanticism and Theory* (Baltimore: Johns Hopkins University Press, 1996).

35. C. P. Snow, *The Two Cultures and the Scientific Revolution: The Rede Lecture* (Cambridge: Cambridge University Press, 1959).

36. See Philip Connell, *Romanticism, Economics, and the Question of "Culture"* (Oxford: Oxford University Press, 2001), for a more complex analysis of the relationship between romanticism and scientific culture.

37. For the first part of this story, see Connell, *Romanticism, Economics, and the Question of "Culture"*; for the second part of it, see John Guillory, *Cultural Capital: The Problem of Literary Canon Formation* (Chicago: University of Chicago Press, 1993) 134–75.

38. The canonical example is Max Horkheimer and Theodor W. Adorno, *Dialectic of Enlightenment,* trans. John Cumming (New York: Continuum, 1991); for more recent versions, see Michael Lowy and Robert Sayre, *Romanticism Against the Tide of Modernity,* trans. Catherine Porter (Durham, N.C.: Duke University Press, 2001), and Robert Kaufman's series of attempts to link the Frankfurt School to romanticism, most notably in "Legislators of the Post-Everything World: Shelley's *Defence* of Adorno," *English Literary History* 63, no. 3 (1996): 707–33.

39. This does not mean that the "two cultures" split is the first of its kind; its importance, however, comes in the way that it helps to make romanticism part of a cluster of ideas pitched decisively toward a secularized vision of modernity.

40. Geoffrey H. Hartman, "Romanticism and 'Anti-Self-Consciousness,'" in *Romanticism and Consciousness: Essays in Criticism,* ed. Harold Bloom (New York: W. W. Norton, 1970) 46–56, 48.

41. Hartman, "Romanticism and 'Anti-Self-Consciousness,'" 49. Hartman quotes from William Wallace, *The Logic of Hegel: Translated from the Encyclopedia of the Philosophical Sciences,* 2nd rev. ed. (1892; London: Oxford University Press, 1972) 54–57, 55.

42. Hartman, "Romanticism and 'Anti-Self-Consciousness,'" 52.

43. Warminski, "Facing Language," 20.

44. Warminski, "Facing Language," 29.

45. Bruce C. MacIntyre, *Haydn: "The Creation"* (New York: Schirmer Books, Simon and Schuster, Macmillan, 1998) 41.

46. For an interpretation of *The Creation* within the context of Pythagorean and Platonic thought, see Lawrence Kramer, "Music and Representation: The Instance of Haydn's *Creation*," in *Music and Text: Critical Inquiries*, ed. Steven Paul Scher (Cambridge: Cambridge University Press, 1992) 139–62. Kramer begins by supposing that science and religion contradict each other when it comes to understanding the world, and thus that Haydn ingeniously turns to the idea of the *harmonia mundi* to resolve this difficulty. My position, in contrast, is that for Haydn and the librettist there is no conflict between science and religion to begin with.

47. Nicholas Temperley, *Haydn: "The Creation"* (Cambridge: Cambridge University Press, 1991) 12. See also MacIntyre, *Haydn*, 41–44, on the possible Masonic connections.

48. See Temperley, *Hayden*, 39–46.

49. MacIntyre, *Hayden*, 266–67.

50. MacIntyre calls these early passages "a tour de force of proto-romantic tone painting" (80). For the libretto, see Temperley, *Haydn*, 52–64, 52. Temperely reprints the first editions of the German and English texts side by side. Other references will be to Temperley's edition.

51. Quotted in MacIntyre, *Haydn*, 81. MacIntyre is quoting C. G. Stellan Mörner, "Haydniana aus Schweden um 1800," *Haydn-Studien* 2, no. 1 (1969): 28, cited and translated in H. C. Robbins Landon, *Haydn: The Years of "The Creation," 1796–1800*, in *Haydn: Chronicle and Works*, vol. 4 (Bloomington, Ind.: Indiana University Press, 1977) 318.

52. See MacIntyre, *Haydn*, 120.

53. Mary Wollstonecraft Shelley, *The Last Man*, ed. Anne McWhir (Peterborough, Ontario: Broadview, 1996) 328–29.

54. The only other suggestion that creation's perfection will ever be marred comes in a dark hint from Uriel just before the final chorus:

O happy pair! and always happy yet
If not, mislead by false conceit,
ye strive at more, as granted is;
and more to know, as know ye should! (64)

55. See Rodney Stark, "Secularization, R. I. P.," *Sociology of Religion* 60, no. 3 (1999): 249–73, 252, 251. The causal connection between institutional decline and personal belief was criticized already by Alasdair MacIntyre in *Secularization and Moral Change* (London: Oxford University Press, 1967). One historical account of secularization that tries to avoid normative considerations is C. John Sommerville, *The Secularization of Early Modern England: From Religious Culture to Religious Faith* (New York: Oxford University Press, 1992).

56. Abrams's emphasis on ideas makes him typical of his age. In the introduction to *The Secularization of the European Mind in the Nineteenth Century* (Cambridge: Cambridge University Press, 1975), for example, Owen Chadwick meditates on the need to combine social and intellectual history—yet the balance of his book, too, tilts toward the intellectual. See 1–14.

57. The literature on this phenomenon is immense and growing quickly. See, for example, Peter Berger, ed., *The Desecularization of the World: Resurgent Religion*

and World Politics (Washington, D.C.: Ethics and Public Policy Center; Grand Rapids, Mich.: Wm. B. Eerdmans, 1999); and Philip Jenkins, *The Next Christendom: The Coming of Global Christianity* (Oxford: Oxford University Press, 2002).

58. See Callum G. Brown, "A Revisionist Approach to Religious Change," in *Religion and Modernization: Sociologists and Historians Debate the Secularization Thesis,* ed. Steve Bruce (Oxford: Clarendon Press, 1992) 31–58. One aspect of the debate pits those who advocate a marketplace model of religious change against those who remain committed to some version of modernization theory. For the former, see Rodney Stark, "Must All Religions Be Supernatural?" in *The Social Impact of New Religious Movements,* ed. Bryan Wilson (New York: Rose of Sharon Press, 1981) 159–77; Rodney Stark and Laurence R. Iannaccone, "A Supply-Side Reinterpretation of the 'Secularization' of Europe," *Journal for the Scientific Study of Religion* 33 (1994): 230–52; and Roger Finke and Rodney Stark, *The Churching of America, 1776–1990: Winners and Losers in Our Religious Economy* (New Brunswick, N.J.: Rutgers University Press, 1992); for the latter, see Steve Bruce, *Choice and Religion: A Critique of Rational Choice Theory* (Oxford: Oxford University Press, 1999), and *God Is Dead: Secularization in the West* (Oxford: Blackwell, 2002). For an overview that looks beyond Europe and North America, see Grace Davie, *Europe: The Exceptional Case: Parameters of Faith in the Modern World* (London: Darton, Longman and Todd, 2002).

59. See the figures in Brown, "A Revisionist Approach," 42–47. For the situation in the United States, see Andrew M. Greeley, *Religious Change in America* (Cambridge, Mass.: Harvard University Press, 1989). For the earlier situation in England, see Mark Smith, *Religion in Industrial Society: Oldham and Saddleworth, 1740–1865* (Oxford: Clarendon Press, 1994), which argues that religious participation in two communities remained constant during a 120-year period of rapid industrialization and modernization. For the English data between 1800 and 1900, see Robert Currie, Alan D. Gilbert, and Lee Horsley, *Churches and Churchgoers: Patterns of Church Growth in the British Isles Since 1700* (Oxford: Clarendon Press, 1977). Among historians, J. C. D. Clark, *English Society, 1660–1832,* 2nd rev. ed. (Cambridge: Cambridge University Press, 2000), critiques secularization, though he views religion largely through a political lens.

60. Indeed, sociologists of religion often explained away countervailing data as an "exception." The highly modernized and differentiated United States has been viewed as an "exception" to the thesis that modernization leads to secularization, for example. Grace Davie, "Europe: The Exception that Proves the Rule?" in *Desecularization of the World,* ed. Berger, suggests that it is time the analytic poles were reversed: "The secularization thesis developed within a European framework, and for certain stages in Europe's religious development there is a convincing fit between the argument and the data. . . . Bit by bit, however, the thesis rather than the data began to dominate the agenda. The 'fit' became axiomatic, theoretically necessary rather than empirically founded—so much so that Europe's religious life was considered a prototype of global religiosity: what Europe did today, everyone else would do tomorrow" (76). And see Jeffrey K. Hadden, "Toward Desacralizing Secularization Theory," *Social Forces* 65, no. 3 (1987): 587–611, for secularization's ideological status: "secularization theory has not been subjected to systematic scrutiny because it is a *doctrine* more than it is a theory. Its moorings are located in presuppositions that have gone unexamined because they represent a taken-for-granted *ideology* rather than a systematic set of interrelated propositions" (588).

61. S. N. Eisenstadt, "Multiple Modernities," *Daedalus* 129, no. 1 (2000): 1–29, 2.

See also the essays collected in *Alternative Modernities*, ed. Dilip Parameshwar Gaonkar (Durham, N.C.: Duke University Press, 2001).

62. Charles Taylor and Benjamin Lee, *Multiple Modernities Project*, "Modernity and Difference," working draft, http://www.sas.upenn.edu/transcult/promad .html (accessed December 17, 2005).

63. As noted previously, romanticism's investment in the "two cultures" divide means that it can be enlisted as one powerful method for transforming the negative Weberian interpretation of modernity into a positive, "spiritual" interpretation.

64. "[T]he majority of sociologists of religion . . . have abandoned the paradigm with the same uncritical haste with which they previously embraced it." José Casanova, *Public Religions in the Modern World* (Chicago: University of Chicago Press, 1994) 11.

65. Casanova, *Public Religions*, 14. One consequence of treating secularization as differentiation means that the personal opinions, beliefs, and practices of the writers under consideration are largely irrelevant. Thus, what Wordsworth believed about the relation of the natural and supernatural worlds is of less interest than the manner in which Wordsworth and his later interpreters conceive of "literature" as a differentiated sphere, one that takes over some of the functions formerly attributed to religion.

66. Casanova, *Public Religions*, 6, 15. Interestingly, Abrams's own argument sounds a functionalist note from time to time: "the ancient problems, terminology, and ways of thinking about human nature and history survived, as the implicit distinctions and categories through which even radically secular writers saw themselves and their world . . ." (*Natural Supernaturalism*, 13). Unfortunately, insights like these, which point toward a theory of secularization as differentiation, are generally buried by Abrams's focus on ideas and their transformation.

67. *Novum Organum*, in *The Works of Francis Bacon*, ed. and trans. James Spedding, Robert Leslie Ellis, and Douglas Denon Heath (Boston: Taggard and Thompson, 1863) vol. 8, Aphorism 9, 368–69. Bacon's strictures were very severe; under the influence primarily of Newton, eighteenth-century natural theologians were more comfortable reading nature teleologically. On Bacon, see Michael McKeon, *The Origins of the English Novel, 1600–1740* (Baltimore: Johns Hopkins University Press, 1987) 65–68.

68. *The Works of Joseph Butler, D. C. L.*, 2 vols., ed. W. E. Gladstone (Oxford: Clarendon Press, 1896) 1: 365. For a discussion of the difference between medieval and early modern conceptions of revelation, see John Montag, SJ, "Revelation: The False Legacy of Suarez," in *Radical Orthodoxy*, ed. John Milbank, Catherine Pickstock, and Graham Ward (London: Routledge, 1999) 38–63.

69. Casanova, *Public Religions*, 24. Thus in the *Novum Organum*, Bacon singles out teleology as the enemy of scientific inquiry: "the final cause," he writes, "rather corrupts than advances the sciences" (168). And yet his solution is not to abandon teleology but to put it in its proper place, namely that of "theology and tradition" (91).

70. Alvin Gouldner, *The Future of Intellectuals and the Rise of the New Class* (New York: Seabury Press, 1979) 1. For a more nuanced account of intellectuals as a new class, see Andrew Ross, "Defenders of the Faith and the New Class," in *Intellectuals: Aesthetics, Politics, Academics*, ed. Bruce Robbins (Minneapolis: University of Minnesota Press, 1990) 101–32.

71. Berger, "The Desecularization of the World: A Global Overview," in *Desecularization of the World*, ed. Berger, 10.

72. Christian Smith, "Introduction: Rethinking the Secularization of American Public Life," in *The Secular Revolution: Power, Interests, and Conflict in the Secularization of American Public Life*, ed. Christian Smith (Berkeley: University of California Press, 2003) 1–96, 33.

73. Smith, *Secular Revolution*, 38.

74. Pierre Bourdieu and Loïc J. D. Wacquant, *An Invitation to Reflexive Sociology* (Chicago: University of Chicago Press, 1992) 64.

75. For differing views on Europe's representativeness, see Bruce, *God Is Dead*; Davie, *Europe: The Exceptional Case*; and Davie, "Europe: The Exception that Proves the Rule?" in *Desecularization of the World*, ed. Berger, 65–83.

76. Jane Austen, *Mansfield Park*, ed. Kathryn Sutherland (New York: Penguin Books, 1996) 73.

77. On this transformation, see Steven M. Wasserstrom, *Religion After Religion: Gershom Scholem, Mircea Eliade, and Henry Corbin at Eranos* (Princeton, N.J.: Princeton University Press, 1999).

78. William H. Swatos, Jr., and Kevin J. Christiano, "Secularization Theory: The Course of a Concept," *Sociology of Religion* 60, no. 3 (1999): 209–28, 210. One helpful book on secularization that nevertheless participates in this general *Zeitgeist* is Vernon Pratt, *Religion and Secularisation* (London: Macmillan, 1970).

79. Abrams, *Natural Supernaturalism*, 13.

80. Gene W. Ruoff, "Romantic Lyric and the Problem of Belief," in *The Romantics and Us: Essays on Literature and Culture*, ed. Gene W. Ruoff (New Brunswick, N.J.: Rutgers University Press, 1990) 288–302, 289.

81. Cleanth Brooks, "The Language of Paradox," *The Well Wrought Urn: Studies in the Structure of Poetry* (1947; San Diego: Harvest Book, 1975) 3–21. See also Guillory, *Cultural Capital*, 134–75.

82. Why this development caught most analysts and intellectuals by surprise is the subject of Casanova's *Public Religions*.

83. Ruoff, "Romantic Lyric and the Problem of Belief," 289.

84. This is not to deny, of course, that events such as the Iranian Revolution were not also a response to global politics, the legacies of colonialism, and so on. It *is* to deny, though, that what was, and was understood to be, a religious event can be simply transcoded into these other domains.

85. Jerome J. McGann, "The Meaning of the Ancient Mariner," *Critical Inquiry* 8 (1981): 35–67, 65.

Chapter 1

1. Richard Blackmore, *Creation. A Philosophical Poem Demonstrating the Existence and Providence of a God*, 2nd ed. (London: Printed for S. Buckley and J. Tonson, 1712), book 1, 1–13, http://galenet.galegroup.com/servlet/ECCO (accessed December 15, 2005).

2. Char[les] Blount, Mr. Gildon, and others, *The Oracles of Reason* (London, 1693) 88. *Early English Books Online,* image 48367. The term "deism" itself had been in common currency in England since Stillingfleet's 1677 "Letter to a Deist." Lord Herbert of Cherbury is sometimes called the "first English Deist"; Blount helped to popularize Lord Herbert's arguments. Blount's own contributions to deism, meanwhile, are somewhat obscure. *The Oracles of Reason* itself is a collection of texts, many of them written by Blount in the 1680s. "A Summary Account of the Deists Religion" has no authorial attribution, but it is preceded

by a letter from Blount to "the most Ingenuous and Learned Dr. Sydnham," in which Blount claims to be passing on, at Sydnham's request, this text that "I had sometimes by me." In the letter, dated 1686, Blount avoids endorsing deism. "[H]uman Reason," he writes, "like a Pitcher with two Ears, may be taken on either side; However, undoubtedly in our Travails to the other World the common Road is the safest; and tho Deism is a good manuring of a man's Conscience, yet certainly if sowed with Christianity it will produce the most profitable Crop" (87).

3. A. W., "To Charles Blount, Esq., of Natural Religion, as Opposed to Divine Revelation," in *Oracles of Reason*, 196.

4. John Toland, "Preface," in *Christianity Not Mysterious: or, A Treatise Shewing, That There Is Nothing in the Gospel Contrary to Reason, Nor Above It: And That No Christian Doctrine Can Be Properly Call'd a Mystery*, 2nd enl. ed. (London: Printed for Sam. Buckley, 1696) iv. *Early English Books Online*, image 55936.

5. Quoted in David A. Pailin, "The Confused and Confusing Story of Natural Religion," *Religion* 24 (1994): 202. Pailin's source is Viscount Henry St. John Bolingbroke, *The Works of the Late Right Honorable Henry St. John, Lord Viscount Bolingbroke*, vol. 3 (London: David Mallett, 1754) 347.

6. Matthew Tindal, *An Essay Concerning the Power of the Magistrate, and the Rights of Mankind, in Matters of Religion. With Some Reasons in Particular for Dissenters Not Being Obliged to Take the Sacramental Test but in Their Own Churches; and for General Naturalization. Together with a Postscript in Answer to the Letter to a Convocation-Man* (London: Printed by J. D. for Andrew Bell, 1697) 47. *Early English Books Online*, image 51550.

7. Tindal, *An Essay*, 51.

8. On the relationship of deism to the enlightenment, see Frederick C. Beiser, *The Sovereignty of Reason: The Defense of Rationality in the Early English Enlightenment* (Princeton, N.J.: Princeton University Press, 1996).

9. Northrop Frye, *Fearful Symmetry: A Study of William Blake* (1947; Princeton, N.J.: Princeton University Press, 1990) 67.

10. William Blake, *There Is No Natural Religion*, in *The Complete Poetry and Prose of William Blake*, rev. ed., ed. David V. Erdman (1965; New York: Anchor Books, Doubleday, 1988) 2.

11. William Blake, *The Marriage of Heaven and Hell*, plate 22, in *Complete Poetry and Prose*, ed. Erdman, 43.

12. *Jerusalem: The Emanation of the Giant Albion*, plate 52, "To the Deists," in *Complete Poetry and Prose*, ed. Erdman, 201.

13. However, see Celeste Langan's comments on analogy in *Romantic Vagrancy: Wordsworth and the Simulation of Freedom* (Cambridge: Cambridge University Press, 1995) 1–12, 15. I disagree with Langan's argument that analogy always represents a relation of abstract equivalence. For helpful though quite different discussions of theological uses of analogy, see Humphrey Palmer, *Analogy: A Study of Qualification and Argument in Theology* (London: Macmillan, 1973); and Richard Swinburne, *Revelation: From Metaphor to Analogy* (Oxford: Clarendon Press, 1992). The so-called "Radical Orthodox" theologians have also made significant use of analogy, though they associate it with ontological uniformity, whereas for me analogy is rhetorical. See, among others, John Milbank, *Theology and Social Theory: Beyond Secular Reason* (1990; Oxford: Blackwell, 1997) 302–6; Graham Ward, *Cities of God* (London: Routledge, 2000) 79–202; and John Milbank and Catherine Pickstock, "Truth in Correspondence," in *Truth in Aquinas* (London: Routledge, 2001) 1–18.

14. Wallace Stevens, "Effects of Analogy," in *The Necessary Angel: Essays on Reality and the Imagination* (1942; New York: Vintage, 1951) 117–18. See also Michel Foucault's discussion of analogy in *The Order of Things: An Archeology of the Human Sciences* (London: Tavistock; New York: Routledge, 1970) 46–77. Though Foucault also sees analogy as a structure of similitude, he does recognize its figural nature; analogy, he writes, is "an attempt to transform reality into a sign" (47).

15. "Sunday Morning," in *The Collected Poems of Wallace Stevens*, vol. 1 (1954; New York: Knopf; New York: Vintage, 1990) 56–60.

16. In many ways this account is correct, though it perhaps overlooks the fact that metaphor and symbol are not new inventions but rather analogies whose logical structure has been buried or obscured. The relation between metaphor and analogy is discussed by Aristotle in the *Poetics*, 1457b. See *The Complete Works of Aristotle: The Revised Oxford Translation*, 2 vols., ed. Jonathan Barnes (Princeton, N.J.: Princeton University Press, 1984) 2: 2333. See chapter 1 of Robert Weisbuch, *Emily Dickinson's Poetry* (1972; Chicago: University of Chicago Press, 1975) esp. 13, for an application of this argument, as well as for a treatment of analogy and poetic language.

17. Earl R. Wasserman, *The Subtler Language: Critical Readings of Neoclassic and Romantic Poems* (1959; Baltimore: Johns Hopkins University Press, 1964) 183. I quote from an excerpt reprinted in Robert F. Gleckner and Gerald E. Enscoe, eds., *Romanticism: Points of View* (Englewood Cliffs, N.J.: Prentice Hall, 1962) 257.

18. M. H. Abrams, "Structure and Style in the Greater Romantic Lyric," in *From Sensibility to Romanticism: Essays Presented to Frederick A. Pottle*, ed. Frederick W. Hilles and Harold Bloom (New York: Oxford University Press, 1965) 527–60, 533. I quote from a collection of Abrams's essays, *The Correspondent Breeze: Essays on English Romanticism* (New York: W. W. Norton, 1984) 87.

19. Blake, *Visions of the Daughters of Albion*, plate 7, in *Complete Poetry and Prose*, ed. Erdman, 50.

20. Matthew Tindal, *Christianity as Old as the Creation; or, the Gospel, a Republication of the Religion of Nature*, 2nd ed. (London, 1731) 42. Quoted in Pailin, "Confused and Confusing Story of Natural Religion," 202.

21. William Godwin, *Things as They Are or The Adventures of Caleb Williams*, ed. Maurice Hindle (London: Penguin, 1988) 129.

22. Paul de Man, "The Rhetoric of Temporality," in *Blindness and Insight: Essays in the Rhetoric of Contemporary Criticism*, 2nd ed. (Minneapolis: University of Minnesota Press, 1983) 187–228, 207.

23. Paul de Man, "Preface" to *The Rhetoric of Romanticism* (New York: Columbia University Press, 1984) ix.

24. For a recent tacit acknowledgment of this from within humanistic studies, see "Forum: Responses to Bill Brown's 'The Dark Wood of Postmodernity (Space, Faith, Allegory),'" particularly the responses by Rey Chow and Simon During, *PMLA* 120, no. 3 (2005): 874–85.

Chapter 2

1. At the end of the last chapter, I cast this situation as an allegory of enlightened critical models in general, whose tendency to treat religion in terms of an argument keeps running up against the melancholy truth that critique does not, of itself, accomplish the kind of secularization for which it aims. Critical vigilance,

for which de Manian deconstruction can stand as an exemplary model, confesses itself consistently surprised and disappointed by this fact. Yet because its only recommendation is yet more vigilance, it arrives at a strangely symbiotic relationship with its object of critique: like the deist, the deconstructive reader perpetually identifies secrets in order to expose them.

2. David Hume, *Dialogues Concerning Natural Religion*, in *Principal Writings on Religion, Including Dialogues Concerning Natural Religion; and The Natural History of Religion*, ed. J. C. A. Gaskin, World's Clasics (Oxford: Oxford University Press, 1993) 43.

3. *Analogy of Religion, Natural and Revealed, to the Constitution and Course of Nature*, in *The Works of Joseph Butler*, ed. W. E. Gladstone (Oxford: Clarendon Press, 1896) 1: 8, 9.

4. Here Hume revisits the arguments of his *Enquiry* (1748), particularly of the chapter entitled "Of a Particular Providence and of a Future State." He had argued there that the effort to establish God's attributes inductively from the design of the world was circular. See Hume, *An Enquiry Concerning Human Understanding*, ed. Eric Steinberg (Indianapolis: Hackett, 1977) 90–102.

5. 116. Were Cleanthes a little sharper, he might have noticed the equivocation in Philo's apparently conciliatory remark. That evidence of contrivance and design will necessarily strike "the most careless, the most stupid thinker" can of course be taken to mean that only stupid and careless thinkers (like Cleanthes) will insist on seeing design in the world; and Philo's further claim that "no man can be so hardened in absurd systems, as at all times to reject" evidence of design may very well be a recapitulation of the skeptical pose of the *Enquiry*: no one can *at all times* reject the design argument, but some (like Philo) do indeed reject it some of the time.

6. Keith E. Yandell, *Hume's "Inexplicable Mystery": His Views on Religion* (Philadelphia: Temple University Press, 1990) 43.

7. On the "Cleanthes is Hume" side, the chief texts are Charles William Hendel, *Studies in the Philosophy of David Hume* (Princeton, N.J.: Princeton University Press, 1925); B. M. Laing, "Hume's *Dialogues Concerning Natural Religion*," *Philosophy* 12 (1937): 175–90; Nelson Pike's edition of the *Dialogues Concerning Natural Religion* (Indianapolis, Ind.: Bobbs-Merrill, 1970); J. Y. T. Greig, *David Hume* (New York: Garland, 1983); and Jeffrey Wieand, "Pamphilus in Hume's *Dialogues*," *Journal of Religion* 65 (1985): 35–45. The more popular "Philo is Hume" position can be found in Norman Kemp Smith's edition of *Hume's Dialogues Concerning Natural Religion* (New York: Social Science Publishers, 1948); J. C. A. Gaskin, *Hume's Philosophy of Religion*, 2nd ed. (Houndmills: Macmillan, 1988); Dorothy P. Coleman, "Interpreting Hume's *Dialogues*," *Religious Studies* 25 (1989): 179–90; and John Valdimer Price, *David Hume*, rev. ed. (Boston: Twayne, 1991). John Bricke, "On the Interpretation of Hume's *Dialogues*," *Religious Studies* 11 (1975): 1–18, and Yandell, *Hume's "Inexplicable Mystery"* both argue that no single character speaks for Hume.

8. These figures are quoted by Price, *David Hume*, 109. Price gets them from E. C. Mossner, "The Enigma of Hume," *Mind*, n.s., 45 (1936): 334–49, 348.

9. Further evidence: Hume's model in constructing the *Dialogues* was Cicero's *De Natura Deorum*. Cicero himself studied under Philo (160–80 B.C.), the philosopher credited with founding the Fourth Academy, which became synonymous with skepticism.

10. For a good description and interpretation of the historical situation surrounding the *Dialogues*, see Robert John Sheffler Manning, "David Hume's

Dialogues Concerning Natural Religion: Otherness in History and in Text," *Religious Studies* 26 (1990): 415–26, esp. 421–26.

11. These letters are quoted in Manning, "David Hume's *Dialogues,*" 421, 422. Manning quotes, respectively, Raymond Klibansky and Ernest C. Mossner, eds., *New Letters of David Hume* (1954; Oxford: Clarendon Press; New York: Garland, 1983) 72–73; and Mossner, *The Life of David Hume* (Edinburgh: Thomas Nelson and Sons; Austin: University of Texas Press, 1954) 354.

12. Quoted in Norman Kemp Smith's introduction to *Hume's Dialogues,* 90.

13. "Review of *Dialogues Concerning Natural Religion,*" *The Weekly Magazine, or Edinburgh Amusement* 46 (October and November 1779): 113–15, 136–38, 162–64; William Rose, "Review of Hume's *Dialogues,*" *Monthly Review* 61 (November 1779): 347.

14. Hume wrote that "almost all my life has been spent in literary pursuits and occupations." By "literary," of course, Hume means "letters," a broader category than what the nineteenth century understood as "literature." See David Hume, "My Own Life," in *Principal Writings on Religion, Including Dialogues Concerning Natural Religion,* ed. J. C. A. Gaskin, 3–10.

15. Michael B. Prince, "Hume and the End of Religious Dialogue," *Eighteenth-Century Studies* 25 (1992): 283–308.

16. George Berkeley, "Preface to *Three Dialogues Between Hylas and Philonus,*" in *Principles, Dialogues, and Correspondence,* ed. Colin Murray Turbayne (Indianapolis, Ind.: Bobbs-Merrill, 1965) 106–7.

17. Demea's argument here doesn't sit well with his earlier claim that God's nature is incomprehensible. A consistent application of this first claim is in fact impossible, since saying God is incomprehensible means that no concept applies to him. But this would have to include the concept "that no concept applies to God," which means that in its strong form the incomprehensibility thesis is incoherent. But with his cosmological proof, of course, Demea is claiming not only to possess certain concepts about God but also that these concepts correspond to certain properties (such as necessity) that God possesses. See Yandell, *Hume's "Inexplicable Mystery,"* 148, on this point.

18. Demea's language recalls especially Clarke's *A Demonstration of the Being and Attributes of God More Particularly in Answer to Mr. Hobbs, Spinoza, and Their Followers* (London: Printed by W. Botham for James Knapton, 1705), based on his first series of Boyle lectures. The following year he gave a second series of Boyle lectures, published as *A Discourse Concerning the Unchangeable Obligations of Natural Religion and the Truth and Certainty of the Christian Revelation* (London: Printed by W. Botham for James Knapton, 1706). Later the two texts were combined as *A Discourse Concerning the Being and Attributes of God, the Obligations of Natural Religion, and the Truth and Certainty of the Christian Revelation.* This composite text had gone through nine editions by 1738. For more on Clarke, see Edward J. Khamara, "Hume *versus* Clarke on the Cosmological Argument," *Philosophical Quarterly* 42 (1992): 34–55.

19. Hume's statement is quoted in Manfred Kuehn, "Kant's Critique of Hume's Theory of Faith," in *Hume and Hume's Connexions,* ed. M. A. Stewart and John P. Wright (Edinburgh: Edinburgh University Press, 1994) 241. Locke, like Cleanthes, attempted to demonstrate the existence of a contingent but eternal being. Clarke, like Demea, argued that God is a necessary being.

20. Prince, "Hume and the End of Religious Dialogue," 299.

21. According to the *Oxford English Dictionary,* "arbitrary" was undergoing a

gradual transition in the eighteenth century, from meaning simply individual discretion to a discretion derived from authority.

22. David Hume, *A Treatise of Human Nature*, ed. L. A. Selby-Bigge; 2nd rev. ed. P. H. Nidditch (Oxford: Clarendon Press, 1978) 263–64.

23. Susan Manning discusses how Hume's writing is pulled simultaneously toward fragmentation and sociality in *Fragments of Union: Making Connections in Scottish and American Writing* (Houndmills: Palgrave, St. Martin's Press, 2002) esp. 18, 32–64.

Chapter 3

1. David Hume, *Dialogues Concerning Natural Religion*, in *Principal Writings on Religion Concerning Natural Religion; and The Natural History of Religion*, ed. J. C. A. Gaskin, World's Classics (Oxford: Oxford University Press, 1993) 33–34.

2. David Burrell, *Analogy and Philosophical Language* (New Haven, Conn.: Yale University Press, 1973) 5.

3. This interpretation has been subject to substantial critique. But for a cautious refashioning of it, see James E. Bradley, *Religion, Revolution, and English Radicalism: Nonconformity in Eighteenth-Century Politics and Society* (Cambridge: Cambridge University Press, 1990) 18–30.

4. On the Anglican resurgence, see J. C. D. Clark, *English Society 1660–1832: Religion, Ideology, and Politics During the Ancien Regime,* rev. ed. (Cambridge: Cambridge University Press, 2000) 216–35.

5. On the varieties of dissent, see Daniel E. White, "'Properer for a Sermon': Particularities of Dissent and Coleridge's Conversational Mode," *Studies in Romanticisim* 40 (2001): 175–98.

6. All quotations from Barbauld's poetry are from *The Poems of Anna Letitia Barbauld*, ed. William McCarthy and Elizabeth Kraft (Athens: University of Georgia Press, 1994). McCarthy and Kraft's introduction points out that dating Barbauld's poems accurately is virtually impossible, since besides the thirty-three poems in the 1773 volume, and individual publication of a few others, such as the "Epistle to Wilberforce" and *Eighteen Hundred and Eleven*, most of her poetic output appeared posthumously, in her niece Lucy Aikin's *Works* of 1825. It is likely, too, that some of Barbauld's poetry has been lost permanently; Lucy Aikin acknowledged that she did not reprint all of the poems in her possession, and whatever manuscript materials might have remained were destroyed in the bombing of London in 1940.

7. David Hume, *Enquiries Concerning Human Understanding and Concerning the Principles of Morals*, 3rd ed., ed. L. A. Selby-Bigge and P. H. Nidditch (Oxford: Clarendon Press, 1975) 109.

8. J. F. Ross, *Portraying Analogy* (Cambridge: Cambridge University Press, 1981) 1.

9. Burrell, *Analogy and Philosophical Language*, 5.

10. The distinction made here between "theory" and "philosophical practice" may be more familiar to some readers as a debate about the centrality of figurative language within philosophical texts. From this perspective, the attempt to stabilize analogy so that it means only one thing looks like what Derrida identifies as the philosophical tradition's inability to account for the basic metaphoricity of its procedures. See, for instance, Jacques Derrida, "White

Mythology: Metaphor in the Text of Philosophy," in *Margins of Philosophy*, trans. Alan Bass (Chicago: University of Chicago Press, 1982) 207–71. In associating Barbauld with the tradition of philosophical practice, then, I am also linking her to a procedure quite amenable to the deconstructive idea that the presence of figurative language renders all philosophy a kind of literature.

11. For a technical version of this claim, see Donald Davidson, "On the Very Idea of a Conceptual Scheme," in *Inquiries into Truth and Interpretation* (Oxford: Clarendon Press, 1984) 183–98.

12. It is possible that Barbauld would have read the arguments against natural and revealed religion in Hume's *Enquiry*. Even if she did not experience Hume firsthand, the dissenting culture in which she spent her entire life would have alerted her to Hume's arguments and their possible ramifications. For instance, Philip Doddridge, tutor at the Northampton dissenting academy from 1729 to 1751, encouraged his students to read widely among deists and skeptics, especially Shaftesbury, Tindal, and Hume. His lecture notes, published posthumously in 1763, circulated extensively in dissenting circles.

13. Priestley arrived at Warrington Academy in 1761, when Barbauld (then Anna Aikin) was eighteen. Barbauld's father, John Aikin, was Warrington's theological tutor, and the two families had almost daily contact until 1767, when Priestley left for a career in the ministry.

14. Joseph Priestley, *Autobiography of Joseph Priestley: Memoirs Written by Himself, with An Account of Further Discoveries in Air*, ed. Jack Lindsay (Teaneck, N.J.: Fairleigh Dickinson University Press, 1970) 89.

15. According to Priestley's monism, the mind is a wholly material entity; fixed, objective laws discernible through observation determine all aspects of subjectivity. Beyond the esoteric details of the theory, its aim is to respond to skepticism by simply canceling the distinction between mind and world, showing them to be different versions of the same mechanical phenomena. See, in particular, *The Doctrine of Philosophical Necessity Illustrated* (1777) in *The Theological and Miscellaneous Works of Joseph Priestley*, 25 vols., ed. J. T. Rutt (Hackney: G. Smallfield, 1817–31) 3: 453. Priestley derived his notion of necessity largely from David Hartley. "Dr. Hartley," Priestley wrote, "has thrown more useful light upon the theory of the mind than Newton did upon the theory of the natural world." See *An Examination of Dr. Reid's Enquiry* (1774), vol. 3 of *The Theological and Miscellaneous Works of Joseph Priestley*.

16. Priestley, *The History and Present State of Electricity* (London, 1769) iv. Quoted in Isaac Kramnick, "Eighteenth-Century Science and Radical Social Theory: The Case of Joseph Priestley's Scientific Liberalism," *Journal of British Studies* 25, no. 1 (1986): 8.

17. Thomas Cooper, *Introductory Lecture of T. Cooper, Professor of Chemistry at Carlisle College* (Carlisle, 1812) 7. Quoted in Kramnick, "Eighteenth-Century Science," 9. Cooper went on to a successful career as a scientist in America.

18. See William Blake, *The Marriage of Heaven and Hell*, plates 5 and 6, *The Illuminated Books*, 5 vols., vol. 3: *The Early Illuminated Books*, ed. Morris Eaves, Robert N. Essick, and Joseph Viscomi (1993; Princeton, N.J.: Princeton University Press, 1998). The question of a "romantic" reading of Milton is a vexed one. For opposing views, see Lucy Newlyn, *Paradise Lost and the Romantic Reader* (Oxford: Oxford University Press, 1993); and Stanley Fish, *How Milton Works* (Cambridge, Mass.: Harvard University Press, 2001).

19. This distinction comes from the *Categories*, 1a1–1a5. See *The Complete Works of Aristotle: The Revised Oxford Translation*, 2 vols., ed. Jonathan Barnes

(Princeton, N.J.: Princeton University Press, 1984) 1: 3. See also versions of this distinction in *De Interpretatione*, the *Topics*, and the *Metaphysics*. Aristotle calls equivocal words "homonymous," but they are not homonyms in the English sense of the word. He calls univocal words "synonymous," but, again, they are not equivalent to English synonyms.

20. *Metaphysics*, 1003a33, in *The Complete Works of Aristotle*, vol. 2, ed. Barnes, 1584.

21. Coleridge's example suggests the prevalence of the watch analogy even before Paley took it up in 1802. See "Lecture 1," in *Lectures on Revealed Religion Its Corruptions and Political Views*, vol. 1, ed. Lewis Patton and Peter Mann, in *The Collected Works of Samuel Taylor Coleridge*, ed. Kathleen Coburn (Princeton, N.J.: Princeton University Press; London: Routledge, 1971) 98.

22. *Table Talk*, February 22, 1834, vol. 14, pt. 2, ed. Carl Woodring, in *The Collected Works of Samuel Taylor Coleridge*, ed. Coburn, 276. *Aids to Reflection* contains similar observations, some of them implicitly Humean. See, for instance, the section entitled "Aphorisms on that Which Is Indeed Spiritual Religion," particularly Aphorism II and Aphorism Xa in "Aphorisms on Spiritual Religion B," *Aids to Reflection*, vol. 9, ed. John Beer, in *The Collected Works of Samuel Taylor Coleridge*, ed. Coburn.

23. Samuel Taylor Coleridge, *Biographia Literaria; or, Biographical Sketches of My Literary Life and Opinions*, vol. 7, pt. 1, ed. James Engell and M. Jackson Bate, 1983, in *The Collected Works of Samuel Taylor Coleridge*, ed. Coburn, chapter 13, 295–306.

24. On the relationship of theory and practice in the *Biographia*, see Paul Hamilton, *Coleridge's Poetics* (Stanford, Calif.: Stanford University Press, 1983) esp. 7–12.

25. See Julie Ellison, " 'Nice Arts' and 'Potent Enginery': The Gendered Economy of Wordsworth's Fancy," *The Centennial Review* 33 (1989): 441–67, 442.

26. William Cowper, "The Winter Evening," in *The Task, and Other Selected Poems*, ed. James Sambrook (London: Longman, 1994) book 4, 118–19. Orig. pub. 1785.

27. See Lisa Vargo, "The Case of Anna Laetitia Barbauld's 'To Mr C[olerid]ge,' " *Charles Lamb Bulletin* 102 (April 1998): 55–63, for a discussion of the relationship of these two poets.

28. Julie Ellison, "The Politics of Fancy in the Age of Sensibility," in *Re-Visioning Romanticism: British Women Writers, 1776–1837*, ed. Carol Shiner Wilson and Joel Haefner (Philadelphia: University of Pennsylvania Press, 1994) 228–55, 250.

29. Judith Butler, *The Psychic Life of Power: Theories in Subjection* (Stanford, Calif.: Stanford University Press, 1997) 6. Also: "But if, following Foucault, we understand power as *forming* the subject as well, as providing the very condition of its existence and the trajectory of its desire, then power is not simply what we oppose but also, in a strong sense, what we depend on for our existence and what we harbor and preserve in the beings that we are" (2).

30. Gilles Deleuze, *Difference and Repetition*, trans. Paul Patton (New York: Columbia University Press, 1994) esp. 70 ff.

31. Judith Butler, *Gender Trouble: Feminism and the Subversion of Identity* (New York: Routledge, 1990) 145.

32. Judith Butler, "Variations on Sex and Gender: Beauvoir, Wittig, and Foucault," in *Feminism as Critique: On the Politics of Gender*, ed. Seyla Benhabib and Drucilla Cornell (Minneapolis: University of Minnesota Press, 1987) 131.

244 Notes to Pages 100–112

33. Saba Mahmood, *Politics of Piety: The Islamic Revival and the Feminist Subject* (Princeton, N.J.: Princeton University Press, 2005) 23.

34. Of particular relevance here is Mahmood's analysis of modesty, in which the feeling of modesty is *created* by bodily acts. See *Politics of Piety*, 153–60.

35. Abrams's "Structure and Style in the Greater Romantic Lyric" depends heavily upon the idea that the romantics secularized a meditative structure learned from metaphysical poets such as Vaughn. My position, in contrast, is that meditation does not necessarily need to be secularized in order for it to be modern.

Chapter 4

1. In the half century between Hume's essay on miracles and the publication of Paley's *Evidences of Christianity*, many divines targeted Hume's skepticism regarding the evidence of the senses. See, for instance, William Warburton's *Remarks on Mr. David Hume's Essay on the Natural History of Religion* (1757), in *A Selection from Unpublished Papers of the Right Reverend William Warburton*, ed. Francis Kilvert (London: J. Bowyer Nichols and Son, 1841) 311–15; and his short essay "Of Miracles," reprinted in *Early Responses to Hume's Writings on Religion*, vol. 1, ed. James Fieser (Bristol: Thoemmes Press, 2001) 301–48, 9–12.

2. For more on this environment, see D. L. LeMahieu, *The Mind of William Paley: A Philosopher and His Age* (Lincoln: University of Nebraska Press, 1976); Mark Francis, "Naturalism and William Paley," *History of European Ideas* 10 (1989): 203–20; and the chapter on Watson in Norman Sykes, *Church and State in England in the XVIIIth Century: The Birkbeck Lectures in Ecclesiastical History* (Cambridge: Cambridge University Press, 1934) 332–78.

3. Quoted in LeMahieu, *Mind of William Paley*, 156. From Richard Whately, ed., *Paley's Moral Philosophy*, with Annotations (London, 1859) iii.

4. *Shelley's Poetry and Prose*, 2nd ed., ed. Donald H. Reiman and Neil Fraistat (New York: W. W. Norton, 2002) 209.

5. William Paley, *Natural Theology; or, Evidences of the Existence and Attributes of the Deity*, in *The Works of William Paley, D.D.*, vol. 4 (London: William Baynes and Son, 1825) 1–2. By the time Paley composed *Natural Theology*, the intricacy and workmanship of a watch was the standard trope of the design argument. Its first appearance may be in Cicero's *De natura Deorum*, in which the narrator Balbus compares the world to a sundial. The source for Paley's watch is generally thought to be the Dutch theologian Bernard Nieuwentyt, whose *The Religious Philosopher; or, The Right Use of Contemplating the Works of the Creator* appeared in translation in 1718. See LeMahieu, *Mind of William Paley*, 59–60.

6. "Review of *Natural Theology*," in *Edinburgh Review* 1, no. 2 (January 1803): 287–305, 295.

7. Isabel Rivers, "'Galen's Muscles': Wilkins, Hume, and the Educational Use of Argument from Design," *Historical Journal* 36 (1993): 594.

8. Hume, *Dialogues* 49. Paley's strategy is not unprecedented. Earlier theologians had indeed relied upon the specific characteristics of objects to prove the existence of a designer. Rivers, "'Galen's Muscles,'" traces the use of a particular motif, that of Galen's work on the muscles, in works of eighteenth-century natural theology. Paley's contribution to natural theology is thus not so much a new argument as it is a strategic assertion of one resource within natural theology against the threat embodied by Hume's *Dialogues*. LeMahieu, *Mind of William*

Paley, makes a similar point when he notes that Paley's response to Hume hinges as much on *feeling* as on reason.

9. Earl R. Wasserman, "Nature Moralized: The Divine Analogy in the Eighteenth Century," *English Literary History* 20, no. 1 (1953): 67.

10. Indeed, the intelligent design movement has effectively exploited this tendency. See, esp., William Dembski, *The Design Inference* (Cambridge: Cambridge University Press, 1998); and Michael Behe, *Darwin's Black Box: The Biochemical Challenge to Evolution* (New York: Free Press, 1996). See also the essays collected in Neil A. Manson, ed., *God and Design: The Teleological Argument and Modern Science* (London: Routledge, 2003).

11. Immanuel Kant, *Critique of Judgment*, trans. Werner S. Pluhar (Indianapolis, Ind.: Hackett, 1987) §61, emphasis in original. References are to section numbers.

12. For a reading of Kant along these lines, see Jerome McGann, *Social Values and Poetic Acts: The Historical Judgment of Literary Work* (Cambridge, Mass.: Harvard University Press, 1988), 39–43; and Terry Eagleton, *The Ideology of the Aesthetic* (Oxford: Blackwell, 1990).

13. On this point, see Simon Malpas, "In What Sense 'Communis'? Kantian Aesthetics and Romantic Ideology," *Romanticism on the Net* 17, no. 1 (February 2000), http://www.erudit.org/revue/ron17/2000/v/n17; and Tobin Siebers, "Kant and the Politics of Beauty," *Philosophy and Literature* 22, no. 1 (1998): 31–50.

14. Michel Foucault makes a similar point with regard to similitude, which he says haunts the enlightenment effort of discrimination and separation. See Foucault, *The Order of Things: An Archeology of the Human Sciences* (London: Tavistock; New York: Routledge, 1970) esp. 67–68.

15. Foucault, *The Order of Things*, 239.

16. See Peter J. Bowler, *Evolution: The History of an Idea* (Berkeley: University of California Press, 1983) 55–56.

17. *Reasons for Contentment; Addressed to the Labouring Part of the British Public*," in *The Works of William Paley, D. D.*, 4: 391–403, 396. The pamphlet was initially published in Carlisle in 1792 and reprinted in London in 1793. On Paley's rhetorical strategies, as the well the historical context of his pamphlet, see Kevin Gilmartin, "In the Theater of Counterrevolution: Loyalist Association and Conservative Opinion in the 1790s," *Journal of British Studies* 41, no. 3 (2002): 291–328.

18. Jerome Christensen, *Romanticism at the End of History* (Baltimore: Johns Hopkins University Press, 2000) 6.

19. The book in question is *Sketch of the Professional Life and Character of John Clarke, M.D.* (Newcastle: S. Hodgson, 1806). Clarke was Paley's doctor.

20. See Alexander Pope, *An Essay on Man*, 3: 7–8, 21–26 (originally published 1733–34), in *Poetry and Prose of Alexander Pope*, ed. Aubrey Williams (Boston: Houghton Mifflin, 1969).

21. See Arthur O. Lovejoy, *The Great Chain of Being: A Study of the History of an Idea* (1936; Cambridge, Mass.: Harvard University Press, 1964) 186, 187–88.

22. John Donne, *An Anatomie of the World* (1611; London: Printed by W. Stansby for Tho. Dewe, 1625) 21, line 213. *Early English Books Online*, image 10345.

23. Charles Taylor, *Modern Social Imaginaries* (Durham, N.C.: Duke University Press, 2004) 12.

24. For one important example, see Kant's essay "What Is Enlightenment," which distinguishes between the role of a clergyman as the guardian of a religion

and the role of a clergyman as a public intellectual. Kant does not think that religion is *prima facie* incompatible with enlightenment, and he has no trouble imagining a clergyman who is also an enlightened intellectual; he simply thinks of himself as setting the conditions under which religion may join enlightenment. Those conditions are that religion surrender its claim to a distinctive public voice and content itself with speaking directly to the heart. See Immanuel Kant, "What Is Enlightenment?" in Immanuel Kant, *Philosophical Writings*, ed. Ernst Behler, trans. Lewis White Beck (New York: Continuum, 1986) 263–69, esp. 266.

Chapter 5

1. George Douglass Campbell, 8th duke of Argyll, "What Is Science?" in *Good Words* (April 1885): 236–45, 244. Argyll's own theistic agenda doubtless accounts for some of the pathos of this account. Quoted in Del Ratzsch, "Perceiving Design," in *God and Design*, ed. Manson 124–44, 124. Ratzsch links the notion of design perception to Thomas Reid's response to Hume.

2. John Henry Newman, "Letter to Mrs. John Mozley, 10 January 1837," in *Letters and Correspondence of John Henry Newman During His Life in the English Church*, vol. 2, ed. Anne Mozley (London: Longman, Green and Co., 1891). Quoted in B. C. Southam, ed., *Jane Austen: The Critical Heritage* (London: Routledge and Kegan Paul; New York: Barnes and Noble, 1968) 117.

3. This seeming disjunction between Austen the realist and Austen the Christian novelist has led a few critics to the resolutely modern conclusion that whatever her personal beliefs, Austen's art is secular. See, for instance, Laurence Lerner, *The Truthtellers: Jane Austen, George Eliot, D. H. Lawrence* (New York: Schocken, 1967); and Gilbert Ryle, "Jane Austen and the Moralists," in *Critical Essays on Jane Austen*, ed. B. C. Southam (London: Routledge and Kegan Paul, 1968) 106–22.

4. Richard Whately [unsigned], "Review of *Northanger Abbey* and *Persuasion*," *Quarterly Review* (January 1821): xxiv, 352–76, in *Jane Austen: The Critical Heritage*, ed. Southam, 92, 95.

5. The notion of a hermetically sealed Austen has more or less been laid to rest. Along with Butler's groundbreaking work, see esp. Claudia L. Johnson, *Jane Austen: Women, Politics, and the Novel* (Chicago: University of Chicago Press, 1988); Margaret Kirkham, *Jane Austen, Feminism and Fiction* (Sussex: Harvester Press, 1983); the essays in Devoney Looser, ed., *Jane Austen and Discourses of Feminism* (New York: St. Martin's Press, 1995); and William H. Galperin, *The Historical Austen* (Philadelphia: University of Pennsylvania Press, 2003).

6. Marilyn Butler, *Jane Austen and the War of Ideas* (Oxford: Clarendon Press, 1975) 3.

7. Important recent treatments of history in relation to Austen include Edward Said, "Jane Austen and Empire," in *Culture and Imperialism* (New York: Vintage, 1994) 80–96; Brean S. Hammond, "The Political Unconscious in *Mansfield Park*," in *Mansfield Park*, ed. Nigel Wood (Buckingham: Open University Press, 1993); and Galperin, *The Historical Austen*.

8. *Mansfield Park*, ed. Kathryn Sutherland (New York: Penguin, 1996) 72.

9. See Rudolf Otto, *The Idea of the Holy: An Inquiry into the Non-rational Factor in the Idea of the Divine and Its Relation to the Rational*, trans. John W. Harvey (New York: Oxford University Press, 1958) 19, 36.

10. On the critical possibilities of romance, see Theodor Adorno, "Reconciliation Under Duress," *Aesthetics and Politics*, ed. Ernst Bloch et al. (London: NLB, 1977); and Fredric Jameson, *The Political Unconscious: Narrative as a Socially Symbolic Act* (Ithaca, N.Y.: Cornell University Press, 1981) 206–80.

11. The appearance of James II here also suggests a complex relation between Austen's representation of Sotherton and her own family politics. Jane Austen's maternal family, the Leighs, were strongly royalist. Adlestrop, a property acquired by the Leighs in the reign of Elizabeth, had served as a sometime safe house for royalists; Theophilus, Jane Austen's great-grandfather, had gone so far as to gather the men of Adlestrop together and march to oppose the landing of William. Stoneleigh, the other Leigh property from another branch of the family, was during Jane Austen's lifetime united with Adlestrop under the proprietorship of Reverend Thomas Leigh. Stoneleigh was also historically Stuart. Charles I had sheltered at Stoneleigh while on the run from Cromwell; one hundred years later, in 1745, the Leighs prepared to receive the Young Pretender there. As Jacobites the Leighs kept to themselves, and they kept the style of the house consistent with pre-Hanoverian style. They even worshipped at the chapel at Stoneleigh so that they would not have to pray for the House of Hanover at the parish church.

12. The trials that succeeded Monmouth's rebellion give a good measure of this changed tone. As the historian David Ogg mildly puts it, "[c]lemency was not a Stuart virtue" (149). The most notorious examples are the so-called Bloody Assizes, where those found guilty of supporting the rebellion were sentenced to be whipped through all the market towns of a county. Besides the whippings, Lord Chief Justice Jeffreys's commission executed 300 people and transported another 800 to the West Indies. See David Ogg, *England in the Reigns of James II and William III* (Oxford: Clarendon Press, 1955).

13. Vacancies among judges and heads of colleges were invariably filled with Catholics, as were military positions. By 1688, 24 percent of the justices of the peace were Catholic; 13 of the 43 privy counselors were Catholic; and 16 of 43 lord lieutenants—figures vastly out of proportion to the 2 to 4 percent of English citizens who were Catholic. See John Miller, *Popery and Politics in England, 1660–1688* (Cambridge: Cambridge University Press, 1973) 218–20.

14. See J. G. A. Pocock, "The Significance of 1688: Some Reflections on Whig History," in *The Revolutions of 1688: The Andrew Browning Lectures, 1988*, ed. Robert Beddard (Oxford: Clarendon Press, 1991) 271–92.

15. Defying standard protocol, William promoted Tillotson from a deanship to Archbishop of Canterbury in April 1691. Tillotson remained close to both William and Mary until his death in 1694. Gilbert Burnet, also a longtime friend of William and Mary's, was made bishop of Salisbury and became chaplain to Mary; under his influence one of William's first acts was to pass a Toleration Bill, which extended limited liberties to all religious dissenters except Catholics. Within three years William had consecrated fifteen new bishops, all of them latitudinarian. Locke, too, was a latitudinarian Anglican whose fortunes fluctuated with those of William. Though there is no evidence that he was directly involved in the Rye House plot, his close association with Shaftesbury made it prudent for him to leave England for Holland in 1683. There he finished *An Essay Concerning Human Understanding* and the *Epistola de Tolerantia*. He may also have contributed 400 pounds to Monmouth's cause. See Richard L. Greaves, *Secrets of the Kingdom: British Radicals from the Popish Plot to the Revolution of 1688–1689* (Stanford, Calif.: Stanford University Press, 1992) 285. Locke returned from Holland

in 1689, on the same boat that bore the new Queen Mary to England. An English version of the *Letter Concerning Toleration*, translated by William Popple, was published anonymously in October of that same year.

16. John Locke, *The Reasonableness of Christianity, with A Discourse of Miracles and part of A Third Letter Concerning Toleration*, ed. I. T. Ramsey (Stanford, Calif.: Stanford University Press, 1958) 90.

17. *A Letter Concerning Toleration*, trans. William Popple (London, 1689), ed. James H. Tully (Indianapolis, Ind.: Hackett, 1983) 67, para. 28.

18. *Reasonableness of Christianity*, #244. Locke is speaking here of Judaism before the coming of Christ. The association of Catholicism and Judaism runs strong in liberal Protestantism, exploiting anti-Semitism in order to score points against Catholicism.

19. Burnet's opinion is quoted in Norman Sykes, *Church and State in England in the XVIIIth Century: The Birkbeck Lectures in Ecclesiastical History* (Cambridge: Cambridge University Press, 1934) 423; Locke's dictum is quoted in Christopher Hill, *The Century of Revolution, 1603–1714* (Edinburgh: Thomas Nelson, 1961) 303.

20. Quoted in Irene Collins, *Jane Austen and the Clergy* (London: Hambledon Press, 1994) 43.

21. The curriculum at this time was still largely the same as the one defended by Thomas Secker, bishop of Oxford (1737–58) and later Archbishop of Canterbury (1758–68), who declared in his charges to the clergy in 1738 that the prerequisites for embarking on a study of the Christian faith were "a due knowledge of the rules of right reasoning, and of the moral and religious truths which nature teaches; of the state of the world in its earlier ages, and in that when Christianity first appeared." Only then should come, he continues, a "diligent search into Holy Scripture." See *The Works of Thomas Secker, LL.D.*, 4 vols., ed. T. Hardy (London, 1805) 4: 67.

22. See R. Greaves, "Religion in the University, 1715–1800," in *The History of the University of Oxford*, ed. T. H. Ashton, vol. 5, *The Eighteenth Century*, ed. L. S. Sutherland and L. G. Mitchell (Oxford: Clarendon Press, 1986) 401–24, 405.

23. Edmund Burke, *Reflections on the Revolution in France*, ed. L. G. Mitchell (Oxford: Oxford University Press, 1993) 31, 32.

24. From one perspective, certainly, it looked very much like a revolution: an armed uprising against a sovereign, that sovereign's subsequent hasty flight, and the possibility of a violent reversal of these events focused on the many long years of the Stuart court in exile. Throughout December there were rumors of bands of Irish mercenaries roaming the countryside. On December 12, the day after the king left, London caught the alarm and people stayed up all night, banging kettles and firing muskets. A band of renegade Papists was supposed to be plundering the country around Northampton. There were rumors that 8,000 Irish and Scots had massacred the people of Birmingham. Similar rumors were heard in Wendover, Wigan, Norfolk, and Berwick in the middle days of December. For more detail on these rumors see Miller, *Popery and Politics*, 260.

25. See Johnson, *Jane Austen: Women, Politics, and the Novel*, 13–14.

26. Burke, *Reflections*, 80.

27. See Claudia L. Johnson, *Equivocal Beings: Politics, Gender, and Sentimentality in the 1790s* (Chicago: University of Chicago Press, 1995) 2, 6; and Michael McKeon, "Tacit Knowledge: Tradition and Its Aftermath," *Storiographia* 2 (1998): 233–52, 247.

28. "Reformed" refers specifically to the 39 Articles, drawn up in the reign of Elizabeth. In making William a defender of the reformed religion, the coronation

oath thus reasserted the perceived glories of Elizabeth's reign and implicitly elevated Tudor over Stuart. See Ogg, *England in the Reign of James II and William III*, 235–37, for more detail on the coronation oath.

29. Most of the established churchmen strongly opposed the wording of William's oath, with its historical references and implications; some 400 ecclesiastics resigned their offices in protest around the time of William's ascension.

30. Jane Austen, *The History of England, from the Reign of Henry the Fourth to the Death of Charles the First, by a Partial, Prejudiced, and Ignorant Historian* (facsimile ed.), ed. Deirdre Le Faye (Chapel Hill, N.C.: Algonquin Books, 1993) 33.

31. On possibility and probability in Austen, see Galperin, *The Historical Austen*, 42–43.

32. "The order commanding the reading," writes the historian Michael Mullett, "seemed to require the Anglican clergy to act as accomplices in the assassination of their own Church." Some clergy did comply; many more, noting that the proviso didn't require anybody to stay and listen to the declaration, encouraged their congregants to depart before it was read. And many refused the order altogether. See Michael Mullett, *James II and English Politics, 1678–1688* (London: Routledge, 1994) 68.

33. Oliver Goldsmith, *The History of England, from the Earliest Times to the Death of George II, by Dr. Goldsmith*, 8th ed. (London: G. G. & J. Robinson, 1800) 3: 123–24. Hume's generally more critical *History of England* (1778) paints a similar scene, though more self-consciously:

The whole shore was covered with crowds of prostrate spectators, who at once implored the blessing of those holy pastors, and addressed their petition towards Heaven for protection during this extreme danger, to which their country and their religion stood exposed. Even the soldiers, seized with the contagion of the same spirit, flung themselves on their knees before the distressed prelates, and craved the benediction of those criminals, whom they were appointed to guard.

See David Hume, *The History of England from the Invasion of Julius Caesar to the Revolution in 1688*, 6 vols. (Indianapolis, Ind.: Liberty Classics, 1983) 491.

34. See Mark Goldie, "The Political Thought of the Anglican Revolution," in *The Revolutions of 1688*, ed. Robert Beddard, esp. 107–12.

35. See chapter 5 of Jameson, *The Political Unconscious*, esp. 206–28.

36. Walter Scott, *The Lay of the Last Minstrel*, 11th ed. (London: Printed for Longman, Hurst, Rees, and Orme, 1810) 2.11.

37. Scott's theory of history, writes Avrom Fleishman, "is both an entry into the past—often achieving an interior sense of past life—and a coherent interpretation of that past from a particular standpoint in the present." Fleishman, *The English Historical Novel: Walter Scott to Virginia Woolf* (Baltimore and London: Johns Hopkins University Press, 1971) 24.

38. I am not suggesting an allegorical reading, in which Edmund stands for a capitulating clergyman and Crawford, Yates, et al. stand for the tyrannical James. Rather, Edmund has available to him, as a clergyman-to-be, a historical model of sturdy independence in the face of coercion, a model specifically built around a refusal to read out a prepared script that violates religious principles—and he fails to draw upon this history. This is a failure of historical imagination that attends the process of differentiation.

39. See William Galperin, "The Theatre at Mansfield Park: From Classic to Romantic Once More," *Eighteenth-Century Life* 16, no. 3 (1992): 247–71; Joseph Litvak, *Caught in the Act: Theatricality in the Nineteenth-Century English Novel*

(Berkeley: University of California Press, 1992); and David Marshall, "True Acting and the Language of Real Feeling: *Mansfield Park*," *Yale Journal of Criticism* 3, no. 1 (1989): 87–106.

40. *Mansfield Park*, ed. Sutherland, 341. One reason for hesitating before accepting Fanny's piece of moral philosophy as the ethical zenith of the novel is that its genealogy is uncertain. The most likely source for Fanny's claim, after all, is the moral sense school descended from Shaftesbury through Hutcheson and Smith. It is unlikely that Austen's narrator would have much sympathy for such an ethical scheme; indeed, the genealogy behind it is satirized in *Sense and Sensibility*.

41. Austen experienced landscape improvements firsthand, for Repton himself transformed Stoneleigh Abbey. Repton was hired in 1808, and Jane Austen doubtless saw his Red Book, presented to the family in 1809, on one of her visits to Stoneleigh. Mavis Batey, *Jane Austen and the English Landscape* (London: Barn Elms, 1996), has excellent reproductions of Repton's Red Book for Stoneleigh Abbey. See esp. 79–93.

42. On *Mansfield Park* and slavery, see Moira Ferguson, "Mansfield Park: Slavery, Colonialism, and Gender," *Oxford Literary Review* 13 (1991): 118–39; Said, "Jane Austen and Empire," 80–97; Judith Terry, "Sir Thomas Bertram's 'Business in Antigua,'" *Persuasions* 17 (1995): 97–105; and Susan Fraiman, "Jane Austen and Edward Said: Gender, Culture, and Imperialism," *Critical Inquiry* 21 (1995): 805–21.

43. On the relationship between text and context, see Alan Liu's discussion in the second chapter of *Wordsworth: The Sense of History* (Stanford, Calif.: Stanford University Press, 1989) esp. 46–51.

44. *Natural Theology*, in *The Works of William Paley, D. D.* (London: William Baynes and Son, 1825) 4: 1.

45. On watches, see C. John Sommerville, *The Secularization of Early Modern England: From Religious Culture to Religious Faith* (New York: Oxford University Press) 41–42.

46. "Review of *Natural Theology*," *Edinburgh Review* 1, no. 2 (January 1803): 289.

47. Marcel Gauchet, *The Disenchantment of the World: A Political History of Religion*, trans. Oscar Burge (Princeton, N.J.: Princeton University Press, 1997) 12.

Chapter 6

1. On the question of Wordsworth and religion, see also J. R. Watson, *Wordsworth's Vital Soul: The Sacred and Profane in Wordsworth's Poetry* (Atlantic Highlands, N.J.: Humanities Press, 1982); and Nancy Easterlin, *Wordsworth and the Question of "Romantic Religion"* (Lewisburg, Pa.: Bucknell University Press; London: Associated University Presses, 1996). Watson is influenced by anthropological studies of religion, Easterlin by religious psychology. Both agree, however, that the poetry tries to stand in for "religious experience."

2. Deeanne Westbrook, *Wordsworth's Biblical Ghosts* (New York: St. Martin's Press, Palgrave, 2001) 2.

3. From the third of *Essays Upon Epitaphs*, in *The Prose Works of William Wordsworth*, vol. 2, ed. W. J. B. Owen and Jane Worthington Smyser (Oxford: Oxford University Press, 1974) 85. Quoted in Westbrook, *Wordsworth's Biblical Ghosts*, 15.

4. For an example of such a deconstructive interpretation, see Frances Ferguson, *Wordsworth: Language as Counter-Spirit* (New Haven, Conn.: Yale University Press, 1977). For a different reading of Wordsworth's incarnation metaphor, see David P. Haney, *William Wordsworth and the Hermeneutics of Incarnation* (University Park: Pennsylvania State University Press, 1993).

5. William A. Ulmer, *The Christian Wordsworth, 1798–1805* (Albany: State University of New York Press, 2001) 7.

6. An example of such opportunism: Stephen Prickett, in *Words and* The Word, identifies Platonism and typology in the famous Snowdon passage of *The Prelude*; in the same passage I find Aristotelianism and analogy. I suspect we are both right. See Prickett, *Words and* The Word: *Language, Poetics and Biblical Interpretation* (Cambridge: Cambridge University Press, 1996) 129–30.

7. Mark Schoenfield, *The Professional Wordsworth: Law, Labor, and the Poet's Contract* (Athens: University of Georgia Press, 1996) 2. For an evocative account of how "literature" changes in the aftermath of natural theology, see Donald G. Marshall, "Religion and Literature After Enlightenment: Schleiermacher and Wordsworth," *Christianity and Literature* 50 (2000): 53–68.

8. Of interest here is the relation between religion and the New Critical love of a paradox. On paradox, see particularly Cleanth Brooks, "The Language of Paradox," in *The Well Wrought Urn: Studies in the Structure of Poetry* (1947; San Diego: Harcourt Brace and World, Harvest Book, 1975) 3–21. For a related discussion, see Guillory's chapter on the New Criticism in *Cultural Capital: The Problem of Literary Canon Formation* (Chicago: University of Chicago Press, 1993) 134–75.

9. Wordsworth to Charles James Fox, January 14, 1801, in *The Letters of William and Dorothy Wordsworth*, 2nd ed., rev. Chester L. Shaver, vol. 1, *The Early Years 1787–1805*, ed. Ernest De Selincourt (Oxford: Clarendon Press, 1967) 313, 314.

10. I will use the text of the first edition of the poem (1819), except where it differs substantially from Wordsworth's drafts of 1798 and 1799. When I use these latter texts, I will mark them as "MS." Reference throughout is to the Cornell Wordsworth edition of *Peter Bell*, ed. John E. Jordan (Ithaca, N.Y.: Cornell University Press, 1985). This edition prints the MS and the 1819 texts side-by-side, and Jordan's introduction gives a thorough overview of *Peter Bell's* complicated textual history.

11. Fredric Jameson, *The Political Unconscious: Narrative as a Socially Symbolic Act* (Ithaca, N.Y.: Cornell University Press, 1981) 28–32.

12. *"The Prelude,"* 11.342. Unless noted, all references are to 1805 edition found in *"The Prelude": 1799, 1805, 1850*, ed. Jonathan Wordsworth, M. H. Abrams, and Stephen Gill (New York: W. W. Norton, 1979).

13. This is essentially Alan Liu's argument in *Wordsworth: The Sense of History* (Stanford, Calif.: Stanford University Press, 1989) esp. 280–310. For a similar argument about the relationship between primal violence and the poetic self of *The Prelude*, see Alan Bewell, "Wordsworth's Primal Scene: Retrospective Tales of Idiots, Wild Children, and Savages," *English Literary History* 50, no. 2 (1983): 321–46.

14. Michel Foucault, *Discipline and Punish: The Birth of the Prison*, trans. Alan Sheridan (New York: Vintage, 1979) 46.

15. See Liu's use of Foucault in *Wordsworth: The Sense of History*, 297–99. On *Peter Bell*, in particular, see Alan Bewell, *Wordsworth and the Enlightenment: Nature, Man, and Society in the Experimental Poetry* (New Haven, Conn.: Yale University Press, 1989).

16. As the body of the criminal gradually withdraws behind prison walls, the trial and the sentence, not the punishment itself, become the public markers of justice. Punishment "leaves the domain of more or less everyday perception and enters that of abstract consciousness; . . . it is the certainty of being punished and not the horrifying spectacle of public punishment that must discourage crime." Foucault, *Discipline and Punish*, 9.

17. See James K. Chandler, *Wordsworth's Second Nature: A Study of the Poetry and Politics* (Chicago: University of Chicago Press, 1984) 190.

18. *"The Ruined Cottage" and "The Pedlar,"* ed. James Butler (Ithaca, N.Y.: Cornell University Press, 1979) lines 508–25.

19. Wordsworth never refers to the Poet by that name; within the poem he is simply "I." Dorothy, however, refers to the poem's narrator as the "Poet," in *Letters of William and Dorothy Wordsworth*, 1: 200.

20. *The Fenwick Notes of William Wordsworth*, ed. Jared Curtis (London: Bristol Classical Press, 1993) 79.

21. Wordsworth's process of revision here can be dated with some accuracy. He originally composed the passage in February and March of 1798; by December of 1801 he had added it, as a first-person description, to the two-book *Prelude*, which he was now thinking of as a five-book poem. See the Norton critical edition, 516.

22. Emile Durkheim, *The Elementary Forms of Religious Life*, trans. Karen E. Fields (1912; New York: Free Press, 1995). See esp. chapters 1 and 2.

23. Marcel Gauchet, *The Disenchantment of the World: A Political History of Religion*, trans. Oscar Burge (Princeton, N.J.: Princeton University Press, 1997) esp. 23–32. The bulk of Gauchet's book traces out the consequences of his thesis by distinguishing between the "end of religion," which he thinks has already happened, and the disappearance of religion as a cultural phenomenon, which has not. Religion no longer saturates a now-differentiated social space, so humans must face questions of meaning on an individual level. Religion remains, however, perhaps the single most potent force in such individual self-organization. Like C. John Sommerville's much more empirical account in *The Secularization of Early Modern England: From Religious Culture to Religious Faith* (New York: Oxford University Press, 1992), Gauchet finds this process of creative restructuring to be typical of enlightenment and postenlightenment culture.

24. Geoffrey H. Hartman, *Wordsworth's Poetry, 1787–1814* (New Haven, Conn., and London: Yale University Press, 1964) 49.

25. Hartman calls the Snowdon episode "Wordsworth's most astonishing avoidance of apocalypse" (*Wordsworth's Poetry*, 61). For Wordsworth as an antinature poet, see also Harold Bloom, "The Internalization of Quest-Romance," in *Romanticism and Consciousness: Essays in Criticism*, ed. Harold Bloom (New York: W. W. Norton, 1970) 3–24, esp. 8–11; and Paul de Man, "Wordsworth and Holderlin," trans. Timothy Bahti, in *The Rhetoric of Romanticism* (New York: Columbia University Press, 1984) 47–65. Of particular interest is de Man's reference to "the analogical echo, the overcoming of which is a major theme of Wordsworth's work" (59).

26. Hancy, *Wordsworth and the Hermeneutics of Incarnation*, 125. For a reading of the Snowdon passage in terms of platonic typology, see Prickett, *Words and The Word*, 129.

27. *The Five-Book Prelude*, ed. Duncan Wu (Oxford: Blackwell, 1997) 197–204, lines 27–28, 24–25. The Norton critical edition of *The Prelude* provides an earlier and slightly shorter draft of the Analogy Passage. See 496–500.

28. Here I follow Jonathan Wordsworth's dating in "The Five-Book *Prelude* of

Early Spring 1804," *Journal of English and Germanic Philology* 76, no. 1 (1977): 1–25, 24.

29. Among other evidence, Kishel cites two letters from this period. In early February 1804, Wordsworth wrote to Francis Wrangham: "You do not know what a task it is to me, to write a Letter; I absolutely loath the sight of a Pen when I am to use it. . . . I have great things in meditation but as yet I have only been doing little ones" (436). On March 6, in a letter to De Quincey, he sounded a similar theme: "I have a kind of derangement in my stomach and digestive organs which makes writing painful to me" (453). See Joseph F. Kishel, "The 'Analogy Passage' from Wordsworth's Five-Book *Prelude*," in *The Five-Book Prelude*, ed. Wu, 155–56. For the letters, see *The Letters of William and Dorothy Wordsworth*, 1: 436, 453.

30. Kishel, "The 'Analogy Passage,'" esp. 155. Letters again help to make Kishel's point. Dorothy wrote to Catherine Clarkson on March 25: "A great addition to the poem on my Brother's life he has made since C[oleridge] left us, 1500 Lines" (*Early Years*, 459). And on April 29, William wrote to Richard Sharp: "I have been very busy these past 10 weeks, [having?] written between two and three thousand lines, accurately near three thousand, in that time, namely 4 books, and a third of another. . . . I am at present in the 7th book of this work, which will turn out far longer than I ever dreamt of" (*Early Years*, 470). For a different reading of Coleridge's presence in the Snowdon passage, see William Galperin, *Revision and Authority in Wordsworth: The Interpretation of a Career* (Philadelphia: University of Pennsylvania Press, 1989) 189.

31. See Jerry E. Sobel, "Arguing, Accepting, and Preserving Design in Heidegger, Hume, and Kant," in *Essays in Kant's Aesthetics*, ed. Ted Cohen and Paul Guyer (Chicago: University of Chicago Press, 1982) 271–305. Of particular interest is Sobel's claim that, when it comes to design, "the logic or grammar of religion remains alive for us in the grammar of art" (297).

32. W. K. Wimsatt, Jr., and Monroe C. Beardsley, "The Intentional Fallacy," in W. K. Wimsatt, Jr., *The Verbal Icon: Studies in the Meaning of Poetry* (Lexington: University of Kentucky Press, 1954) 3–18. Wimsatt and Beardsley use the word "design" several times as a cognate for "intention."

33. Brian Goldberg, "'Ministry More Palpable': William Wordsworth and the Making of Romantic Professionalism," *Studies in Romanticism* 36, no. 3 (1997): 327–47, 334.

34. Characteristically, Wordsworth goes on to say that he is able to understand revolutionary France with the help of imagination, literature, and a measured distance from the events: "But that night/When on my bed I lay, I was most moved/And felt most deeply in what world I was" (10.54–56).

35. Chandler, *Wordsworth's Second Nature*, 57. Wordsworth composed the "Genius of Burke" passage that appears in the 1850 *Prelude* sometime during the 1820s. However, Chandler demonstrates that Burke shapes even the 1805 version of events. See also the argument in chapter 3, 31–61.

Chapter 7

1. Susan Neiman, "What's the Problem of Evil?" in *Rethinking Evil: Contemporary Perspectives*, ed. María Pía Lara (Berkeley: University of California Press, 2001) 27–45, esp. 32.

2. See Richard J. Bernstein, "Radical Evil: Kant at War with Himself," in *Rethinking Evil*, ed. Lara, 55–85.

3. See Odo Marquard, "Unburdenings: Theodicy Motives in Modern Philosophy," in *In Defense of the Accidental: Philosophical Studies*, trans. Robert M. Wallace (New York: Oxford University Press, 1991) 8–28. See also Mark Lilla, "The Big E," a review of Susan Neiman's *Evil in Modern Thought*, in *The New York Review of Books*, June 12, 2003, 46.

4. See, among others, Reeve Parker, " 'Finer Distance': The Narrative Art of Wordsworth's 'The Wanderer,' " *English Literary History* 39, no. 1 (1972): 87–111; Alan Liu, *Wordsworth: The Sense of History* (Stanford, Calif.: Stanford University Press) 320; and William A. Ulmer, *The Christian Wordsworth, 1798–1805* (Albany, N.Y.: State University of New York Press, 2001) 55–66.

5. Cleanth Brooks, "Wordsworth and Human Suffering: Notes on Two Early Poems," in *From Sensibility to Romanticism: Essays Presented to Frederick A. Pottle*, ed. Frederick W. Hilles and Harold Bloom (New York: Oxford University Press, 1965) 373–87, 385–86.

6. Augustine, *Confessions*, trans. R. S. Pine-Coffin (New York: Penguin, 1961) book 7, sec. 13, 149.

7. Remarking upon the role of religion in the transition from sensibility to romanticism, Colin Campbell writes that "a theodicy of creativity finally displaced the existing theodicy of benevolence," a comment that nicely accords with the dispute between the sentimental Poet and the creative Pedlar. See Colin Campbell, *The Romantic Ethic and the Spirit of Modern Consumerism* (Oxford: Blackwell, 1987) 205.

8. "It is in fact possible for totally heterogeneous contents to take on identical functions in specific positions in the system of man's interpretation of the world and of himself." See Hans Blumenberg, *The Legitimacy of the Modern Age*, trans. Robert M. Wallace (Cambridge, Mass.: MIT Press, 1983) 64–65.

9. Liu, *Worthsworth: The Sense of History*, 320.

10. William L. Rowe, "The Problem of Evil and Some Varieties of Atheism," in *The Problem of Evil*, ed. Marilyn McCord Adams and Robert Merrihew Adams (Oxford: Oxford University Press, 1990) 126–37, 129–30. Originally published in *American Philosophical Quarterly*, 16 (1979): 335–41.

11. See Stephen J. Wykstra's response to Rowe, "The Humean Obstacle to Evidential Arguments from Suffering: On Avoiding the Evils of 'Appearance,' " *The Problem of Evil*, ed. Adams and Adams, 138–60. Originally published in *International Journal for Philosophy of Religion* 16 (1984): 73–93.

12. William Ulmer argues that Wordsworth was already unhappy with the Pedlar's consolatory conclusion to *The Ruined Cottage* by late 1798. See *The Christian Wordsworth*, 66.

13. *The Excursion*, book 1, 932–41, in *William Wordsworth: The Poems*, vol. 2, ed. John O. Hayden (New Haven, Conn., and London: Yale University Press, 1977).

14. Diogenes Allen, "Natural Evil and the Love of God," in *The Problem of Evil*, ed. Adams and Adams, 189–208, 192–93.

15. Slavoj Žižek, *The Puppet and the Dwarf: The Perverse Core of Christianity* (Cambridge, Mass., and London: MIT Press, 2003) 41–42.

16. See Galperin, *Revision and Authority in Wordsworth*, which argues that such acts of poetic revision determine the very notion of a poetic career.

Chapter 8

1. This is a very complex transformation, of course. But its two most prominent moments are the Protestant Reformation and its aftermath, whereby the

emphasis on religion as a kind of "saving knowledge" tended to define it in terms of correct belief; and the later eighteenth century and early nineteenth centuries, when religion came to be understood as a universal essence associated with feeling and intuition—a change that made such disciplines as anthropology and religious studies conceptually possible. On the former, see Peter Harrison, *"Religion" and the Religions in the English Enlightenment* (Cambridge University Press, 1990); and C. John Sommerville, *The Secularization of Early Modern England: From Religious Culture to Religious Faith* (New York: Oxford University Press, 1992). On the latter, see Talal Asad, *Genealogies of Religion: Discipline and Reasons of Power in Christianity and Islam* (Baltimore: Johns Hopkins University Press, 1993); and, most influentially for the history of theology, Friedrich Schleiermacher, *On Religion: Speeches to Its Cultured Despisers,* trans. Richard Crouter (Cambridge: Cambridge University Press, 1996).

2. See the subtitle of Sommerville's book: *The Secularization of Early Modern England: From Religious Culture to Religious Faith.*

3. John D. Caputo, *On Religion* (London: Routledge, 2001) 39.

4. Marcel Gauchet, *The Disenchantment of the World: A Political History of Religion,* trans. Oscar Burge (Princeton, N.J.: Princeton University Press, 1997) 164.

5. Elaine Pagels, *Beyond Belief: The Secret Gospel of Thomas* (New York: Random House, 2003).

6. Harrison, *"Religion" and the Religions,* 1–2.

7. Rabbi Marc Gellman and Monsignor Thomas Hartman, *Religion for Dummies* (New York: Wiley, 2002) 10.

8. John Montag, "Revelation: The False Legacy of Suárez," in *Radical Orthodoxy: A New Theology,* ed. John Milbank, Catherine Pickstock, and Graham Ward (London: Routledge, 1999) 43.

9. See Harrison, *"Religion" and the Religions,* esp. 25.

10. Michel de Certeau, *The Mystic Fable: The Sixteenth and Seventeenth Centuries,* trans. Michael B. Smith (Chicago: University of Chicago Press, 1992) 123. Quoted in Montag, "Revelation," 50–51.

11. Alfred Jules Ayer, *Language, Truth, and Logic* (1936; London: Victor Gollancz, 1967) 115.

12. Steve Bruce, "Introduction," in *Religion and Modernization: Sociologists and Historians Debate the Secularization Thesis,* ed. Steve Bruce (Oxford: Clarendon Press, 1992) 6.

13. Roy Wallis and Steve Bruce, "Secularization: The Orthodox Model," in *Religion and Modernization,* ed. Bruce, 8–30, 10.

14. The association of religion with belief has influenced romantic scholarship, particularly the empirically oriented historicist criticism of the 1990s. By highlighting the fact that many of the most important national political debates during the romantic age had their origin in religious issues, from the question of how to accommodate dissenters in the 1780s and 1790s to Catholic enfranchisement in the 1820s, this work complicated prevailing ideas about the cultural work that religion might do. See, for example, Iain McCalman, *Radical Underworld: Prophets, Revolutionaries and Pornographers in London, 1795–1840* (Cambridge: Cambridge University Press, 1988); Robert M. Ryan, *The Romantic Reformation: Religious Politics in English Literature, 1789–1824* (Cambridge: Cambridge University Press, 1997); and Martin Priestman, *Romantic Atheism: Poetry and Freethought, 1780–1830* (Cambridge: Cambridge University Press, 1999) . Yet such empirical studies do not offer a theory of how religion relates to aesthetic production. Poems, as well as a more broadly conceived "culture," are mined

for content, and occasionally for theme, but critical interest resides in the world of the poet rather than the world of the poem. The result is a broad but also rather thin conception of religion as "belief." In this sense, a modern understanding of religion is built into this methodology, even though the express purpose of its historicization is to trouble the link between romanticism and modernity.

15. Asad, *Genealogies of Religion*, 46.

16. Xan Brooks, *Choose Life: Ewan McGregor and the British Film Revival* (London: Chameleon Books, 1998) 7.

17. Karl Marx and Frederick Engels, *The German Ideology*, ed. C. J. Arthur (1970; New York: International Publishers, 1995) 47.

18. Jerome Christensen even suggests that this consciousness is ideology itself. See *Romanticism at the End of History* (Baltimore: Johns Hopkins University Press, 2000) 16. Christensen cites, in turn, Louis Althusser's "Preface to *Capital*," reprinted in *Lenin and Philosophy and Other Essays*, trans. Ben Brewster (New York: Monthly Review Press, 1971) 71–106; and Paul Ricoeur, *Lectures on Ideology and Utopia*, ed. George H. Taylor (New York: Columbia University Press, 1986).

19. W. J. T. Mitchell, *Iconology: Image, Text, Ideology* (Chicago: University of Chicago Press, 1986) 175.

20. Sommerville, *The Secularization of Early Modern England*, 134–35.

21. Karl Marx, *Capital*, vol. 1, trans. Ben Fowkes (New York: Vintage, 1977) 163.

22. Asad, *Genealogies of Religion*, 207.

23. *Poems in Two Volumes and Other Poems, 1800–1807*, ed. Jared Curtis (Ithaca, N.Y.: Cornell University Press, 1983) 133.

24. Herbert Tucker offers a related argument when he writes that "[t]hey who choose to write and read sonnets not only exercise but contemplate the grounds and limits of their freedom. For better or worse, the sonnet as Wordsworth presents it is liberal space par excellence." See Herbert F. Tucker, "Of Monuments and Moments: Spacetime in Nineteenth-Century Poetry," *MLQ* 58, no. 3 (1997): 269–97, 280–81.

25. The nonspecialist reader may wish to know that Petrarchan sonnets generally begin with eight lines rhymed abba, abba, known as the *octave*; following the turn, or *volta*, which usually coincides with a change in image or argument, the sonnet finishes with six lines of more varying rhyme (often abc, abc, or cde, cde), called the *sestet*.

26. Saba Mahmood, "Feminist Theory, Embodiment, and the Docile Agent: Some Reflections on the Egyptian Islamic Revival," *Cultural Anthropology* 16, no. 2 (2001): 202–36.

Afterword

1. See Karen Armstrong, *The Battle for God: A History of Fundamentalism* (New York: Ballantine, 2001) 175–83, 214–18.

2. Claudia Wallis, "The Evolution Wars," *Time*, August 15, 2005, 27–35. Visually, *Time* sends yet another signal. The cover shows an image of God from Michelangelo's *The Creation of Adam*, but in *Time*'s version God's finger points not to Adam but to a monkey. The cover thus seems to endorse the traditional compromise position often called "theistic evolution."

3. Dennis Overbye, "Philosophers Notwithstanding, Kansas School Board Redefines Science," *New York Times*, November 15, 2005. In fact, the minimalist definition of intelligent design favored by many of its proponents—that some aspects of the natural world are best explained by a cause other than natural selection—is specifically designed *not* to bring religion into the discussion, but only to leave the door open for religious explanations.

4. Laurie Goodstein, "Closing Arguments Made in Trial on Intelligent Design," *New York Times*, November 5, 2005, A14. Around 1870 John Stuart Mill offered an interesting intertext for this dispute in his essay "Theism." Remarking that Paley's watch "puts the case much too strongly," Mill writes that "the evidence of design in creation can never reach the height of direct induction; it amounts only to the inferior kind of inductive evidence known as analogy." See John Stuart Mill, "Theism," in *Three Essays on Religion*, 3rd ed. (London: Longmans, Green & Co., 1885) 168.

5. Daniel C. Dennett, "Show Me the Science," *New York Times*, August 28, 2005, 11.

6. Saba Mahmood, *Politics of Piety: The Islamic Revival and the Feminist Subject* (Princeton, N.J.: Princeton University Press, 2005) 5.

7. "'Both sides ought to be properly taught,' said the president, who appeared to choose his words with care, 'so people can understand what the debate is about. . . . I think that part of education is to expose people to different schools of thought.' " See Wallis, "The Evolution Wars," 28.

8. This is one possible reading of Bruno Latour's work, for instance, though Latour himself has backed away from such radical implications. See Latour, *We Have Never Been Modern* (Cambridge, Mass.: Harvard University Press, 1993). The epistemological issues surrounding science studies came to a head during the so-called "Sokal hoax" and its aftermath. See Alan Sokal, "Transgressing the Boundaries: Toward a Transformative Hermeneutics of Quantum Gravity," *Social Text* 46–47 (1996): 217–52; and Sokal, "A Physicist Experiments with Cultural Studies," *Lingua Franca* 6 (May 1996): 62–64. For an erudite reading of the larger significance of the Sokal affair, see John Guillory, "The Sokal Affair and the History of Criticism," *Critical Inquiry* 28, no. 2 (2002): 470–508.

9. The bacterial flagellum, for example, is a constant reference point for intelligent design proponents. It figured prominently in the Dover trial. See Margaret Talbot, "Darwin in the Dock," *The New Yorker*, December 5, 2005, 66–77, 68.

10. A recent Pew Poll puts those who believe in evolution at between 40 and 50 percent—numbers that suggest the distance between the American populace and the scientific community on this issue. See "Reading the Polls on Evolution and Creationism," released September 28, 2005, http://people-press.org/commentary/display.php3?AnalysisID=118 (accessed November 11, 2005).

11. Steven Knapp and Walter Benn Michaels, "Against Theory," *Critical Inquiry* 8, no. 4 (1982): 723–42, 723.

12. Knapp and Michaels, "Against Theory," 724; emphasis in original.

13. William Paley, *Natural Theology; or, Evidences of the Existence and Attributs of the Deity*, in *The Works of William Paley, D.D.*, vol. 4 (London: William Baynes and Son, 1825) 1. The uncanny similarity between Paley's opening pages and Knapp and Michael's "Against Theory" continues when Paley entertains the possibility that the watch has the ability to reproduce itself, and Knapp and Michaels offer the equally mechanical possibility that a group of scientists in a submarine just off the shore have invented a technology for getting waves to write poetry. See "Against Theory," 729. As Orrin Wang points out in his discussion of "Against

Theory," there are numerous other possible predecessors to Knapp and Michaels's primal scene, including Robinson Crusoe. See Wang, "Mute Bodies, Fanatical Seeing: Against Romanticism Beside Theory" (unpublished manuscript).

14. See the responses collected in *Against Theory: Literary Studies and the New Pragmatism* ed. W.J.T. Mitchell (Chicago: University of Chicago Press, 1989). See also Peggy Kamuf, "Floating Authorship," *diacritics* 16, no. 4 (Winter 1986): 3–13.

Selected Bibliography

This bibliography assembles primary and secondary material most germane to the book's argument. Readers may consult the notes for additional texts.

Abrams, M. H. *Natural Supernaturalism: Tradition and Revolution in Romantic Literature.* New York: W. W. Norton, 1971.
———. "Structure and Style in the Greater Romantic Lyric." In *The Correspondent Breeze: Essays on English Romanticism.* New York: W. W. Norton, 1984. 76–108.
Adams, Marilyn McCord, and Robert Merrihew Adams, eds. *The Problem of Evil.* Oxford: Oxford University Press, 1990.
Addison, Joseph. *The Spectator,* no. 465 (August 23, 1712). Edited by Donald F. Bond. Vol. 4. Oxford: Clarendon Press, 1965. 141–45.
Analytical Review or History of Literature, Domestic and Foreign (London) 8 (September–December 1790).
Aristotle. *Metaphysics, Poetics, Rhetoric,* and *Topics.* In *The Complete Works of Aristotle: The Revised Oxford Translation.* Edited by Jonathan Barnes. 2 vols. Princeton, N.J.: Princeton University Press, 1984.
Asad, Talal. *Genealogies of Religion: Discipline and Reasons of Power in Christianity and Islam.* Baltimore: Johns Hopkins University Press, 1993.
Augustine, Saint. *Confessions.* Translated by R. S. Pine-Coffin. New York: Penguin, 1961.
Austen, Jane. *Mansfield Park.* Edited with introduction and notes by Kathryn Sutherland. New ed. New York: Penguin Books, 1996.
Bacon, Francis. *Novum Organum and Preparative Towards a Natural and Experimental History.* In vol. 8 of *The Works of Francis Bacon.* Edited and translated by James Spedding, Robert Leslie Ellis, and Douglas Denon Heath. Boston: Taggard and Thompson, 1863. 57–371.
Barbauld, Anna Letitia. *The Poems of Anna Letitia Barbauld.* Edited by William McCarthy and Elizabeth Kraft. Athens: University of Georgia Press, 1994.
Berger, Peter L., ed. *The Desecularization of the World: Resurgent Religion and World Politics.* Washington, D.C.: Ethics and Public Policy Center; Grand Rapids, Mich.: Wm. B. Eerdmans, 1999.
Bewell, Alan. *Wordsworth and the Enlightenment.* New Haven, Conn.: Yale University Press, 1989.
———. "Wordsworth's Primal Scene: Retrospective Tales of Idiots, Wild Children, and Savages." *English Literary History* 50, no. 2 (1983): 312–46.

Blackmore, Richard. *Creation. A Philosophical Poem Demonstrating the Existence and Providence of a God.* 2nd ed. London: Printed for S. Buckley and J. Tonson, 1712. http://galenet.galegroup.com/servlet/ECCO

Blake, William. *The Complete Poetry and Prose of William Blake.* Edited by David V. Erdman. Rev. ed. 1965; New York: Doubleday, Anchor, 1988.

Blount, Char[les], [Charles] Gildon, et al. *The Oracles of Reason.* London, 1693. *Early English Books Online,* image 48367.

Blumenberg, Hans. *The Legitimacy of the Modern Age.* Translated by Robert M. Wallace. Cambridge, Mass.: MIT Press, 1983.

Bourdieu, Pierre, and Loïc J. D. Wacquant. *An Invitation to Reflexive Sociology.* Chicago: University of Chicago Press, 1992.

Brooks, Cleanth. "The Language of Paradox" and "The Heresy of Paraphrase." In *The Well Wrought Urn: Studies in the Structure of Poetry.* 1947; San Diego: Harcourt Brace and World, Harvest Book, 1975. 3–21, 192–214.

———. "Wordsworth and Human Suffering: Notes on Two Early Poems." In *From Sensibility to Romanticism: Essays Presented to Frederick A. Pottle.* Edited by Frederick W. Hilles and Harold Bloom. New York: Oxford University Press, 1965. 373–87.

Bruce, Steve, ed. *Religion and Modernization: Sociologists and Historians Debate the Secularization Thesis.* Oxford: Clarendon Press, 1992.

Burke, Edmund. *Reflections on the Revolution in France.* Edited by L. G. Mitchell. World's Classics. Oxford: Oxford University Press, 1993.

Burrell, David. *Analogy and Philosophical Language.* New Haven, Conn.: Yale University Press, 1973.

Butler, Judith. *Gender Trouble: Feminism and the Subversion of Identity.* New York: Routledge, 1990.

Butler, Marilyn. *Jane Austen and the War of Ideas.* Oxford: Clarendon Press, 1975.

Casanova, José. *Public Religions in the Modern World.* Chicago: University of Chicago Press, 1994.

Chandler, James K. *Wordsworth's Second Nature: A Study of the Poetry and Politics.* Chicago: University of Chicago Press, 1984.

Christensen, Jerome. *Romanticism at the End of History.* Baltimore: Johns Hopkins University Press, 2000.

Coleridge, Samuel Taylor. *The Collected Works of Samuel Taylor Coleridge.* Edited by Kathleen Coburn. Princeton, N.J.: Princeton University Press; London: Routledge; 1970.

de Man, Paul. "The Rhetoric of Temporality." In *Blindness and Insight: Essays in the Rhetoric of Contemporary Criticism.* 2nd ed. 1971; Minneapolis: University of Minnesota Press, 1983. 187–228.

———. "Wordsworth and Hölderlin." Translated by Timothy Bahti and preface by de Man. In *The Rhetoric of Romanticism.* New York: Columbia University Press, 1984. 47–65, vii–ix. Essay originally published as "Wordsworth and Hölderlin," in *Schweizer Monatshefte* 45, no. 5 (March 1966): 1141–55.

Durkheim, Emile. *The Elementary Forms of Religious Life.* Translated by Karen E. Fields. New York: Free Press, 1995. Originally published as *Les Formes élémentaires de la vie religieuse: Le Systèm de totémique en Australie* (Paris: F. Alcan, 1912).

Eisenstadt, S. N. "Multiple Modernities." *Daedalus* 129, no. 1 (2000): 1–29.

Foucault, Michel. *Discipline and Punish: The Birth of the Prison.* Translated by Alan Sheridan. New York: Vintage, 1979.

———. *The Order of Things: An Archeology of the Human Sciences.* London: Tavistock; New York: Routledge, 1970.

Frye, Northrop. *Fearful Symmetry: A Study of William Blake.* 1947; Princeton, N.J.: Princeton University Press, 1990.

Gauchet, Marcel. *The Disenchantment of the World: A Political History of Religion.* Translated by Oscar Burge. Princeton, N.J.: Princeton University Press, 1997.

Godwin, William. *Things as They Are or The Adventures of Caleb Williams.* Edited by Maurice Hindle. 1794; London: Penguin Books, 1988.

Goldie, Mark. "The Political Thought of the Anglican Revolution." In *The Revolutions of 1688, The Andrew Browning Lectures, 1988.* Edited by Robert Beddard. Oxford: Clarendon Press, 1991.

Goldsmith, Oliver. *The History of England, from the Earliest Times to the Death of George II, by Dr. Goldsmith.* 8th ed. London: G. G. & J. Robinson, 1800.

Greaves, Richard L. *Secrets of the Kingdom: British Radicals from the Popish Plot to the Revolution of 1688–1689.* Stanford, Calif.: Stanford University Press, 1992.

Haney, David P. *William Wordsworth and the Hermeneutics of Incarnation.* University Park: Pennsylvania State University Press, 1993.

Harrison, Peter. *"Religion" and the Religions in the English Enlightenment.* Cambridge: Cambridge University Press, 1990.

Hartman, Geoffrey H. "Romanticism and 'Anti-Self-Consciousness.'" In *Romanticism and Consciousness: Essays in Criticism.* Edited by Harold Bloom. New York: W. W. Norton, 1970. 46–56.

———. *Wordsworth's Poetry, 1787–1814.* New Haven, Conn.: Yale University Press, 1964.

Hume, David. *Dialogues Concerning Natural Religion.* In *Principal Writings on Religion, Including Dialogues Concerning Natural Religion; and, The Natural History of Religion.* Edited by J. C. A. Gaskin. World's Classics. Oxford: Oxford University Press, 1993. 29–133.

———. *A Treatise of Human Nature.* Edited by L. A. Selby-Bigge. 2nd rev. ed. Edited by P. H. Nidditch. 1888; Oxford: Clarendon Press, 1978.

Jameson, Fredric. *The Political Unconscious: Narrative as a Socially Symbolic Act.* Ithaca, N.Y.: Cornell University Press, 1981.

Kant, Immanuel. *Critique of Judgment.* Translated with introduction by Werner S. Pluhar. 1790; Indianapolis, Ind.: Hackett, 1987.

Kishel, Joseph F. "The 'Analogy Passage' from Wordsworth's Five-Book *Prelude.*" In *The Five-Book Prelude.* Edited by Duncan Wu. Oxford: Blackwell, 1977. 153–65.

Kramnick, Isaac. "Eighteenth-Century Science and Radical Social Theory: The Case of Joseph Priestley's Scientific Liberalism." *Journal of British Studies* 25 (1986): 1–30.

LeMahieu, D. L. *The Mind of William Paley: A Philosopher and His Age.* Lincoln: University of Nebraska Press, 1976.

Liu, Alan. *Wordsworth: The Sense of History.* Stanford, Calif.: Stanford University Press, 1989.

Locke, John. *Letter Concerning Toleration* [Epistola de Tolerantia]. Translated by William Popple. London: Printed for Awnsham Churchill, 1689. Edited and introduced by James H. Tully. Indianapolis, Ind.: Hackett, 1983.

———. *The Reasonableness of Christianity, with A Discourse of Miracles and Part of A Third Letter Concerning Toleration.* Edited by I. T. Ramsey. Stanford, Calif.: Stanford University Press, 1958.

Lovejoy, Arthur O. *The Great Chain of Being: A Study of the History of an Idea.* 1936; Cambridge, Mass.: Harvard University Press, 1964.

MacIntyre, Bruce C. *Haydn: "The Creation."* New York: Schirmer Books, Simon & Schuster Macmillan, 1998.

Mahmood, Saba. "Feminist Theory, Embodiment, and the Docile Agent: Some Reflections on the Egyptian Islamic Revival." *Cultural Anthropology* 16 (2001): 202–36.

———. *Politics of Piety: The Islamic Revival and the Feminist Subject.* Princeton, N.J.: Princeton University Press, 2005.

Manson, Neil A., ed. *God and Design: The Teleological Argument and Modern Science.* London: Routledge, 2003.

Marquard, Odo. "Unburdenings: Theodicy Motives in Modern Philosophy." In *Defense of the Accidental: Philosophical Studies.* Translated by Robert M. Wallace. New York: Oxford University Press, 1991.

McGann, Jerome J. *The Romantic Ideology: A Critical Investigation.* Chicago: University of Chicago Press, 1983.

Milton, John. *Paradise Lost.* 1674 ed. In *John Milton: Complete Poems and Major Prose.* Edited by Merritt Y. Hughes. 1957; Indianapolis, Ind.: Odyssey Press, Bobbs-Merrill, 1983.

Mitchell, W. J. T. *Iconology: Image, Text, Ideology.* Chicago: University of Chicago Press, 1986.

Montag, John, SJ. "Revelation: The False Legacy of Suarez." In *Radical Orthodoxy: A New Theology.* Edited by John Milbank, Catherine Pickstock, and Graham Ward. London: Routledge, 1999. 38–63.

Otto, Rudolph. *The Idea of the Holy: An Inquiry into the Non-rational Factor in the Idea of the Divine and Its Relation to the Rational.* Translated by John W. Harvey. New York: Oxford University Press, 1958.

Paley, William. *The Works of William Paley, D. D. with Extracts from His Correspondence: and a Life of the Author.* By the Rev. Robert Lynam. 5 vols. London: William Baynes and Son, 1825.

Pocock, J. G. A. "The Significance of 1688: Some Reflections on Whig Historiography." In *The Revolutions of 1688: The Andrew Browning Lectures, 1988.* Edited by Robert Beddard. Oxford: Clarendon Press, 1991.

Priestley, Joseph. *Autobiography of Joseph Priestley: Memoirs Written by Himself, with An Account of Further Discoveries in Air.* Edited by Jack Lindsay. Teaneck, N.J.: Fairleigh Dickinson University Press, 1970.

———. *The Theological and Miscellaneous Works of Joseph Priestley.* Edited by J. T. Rutt. Hackney: G. Smallfield, 1817–31.

Prince, Michael B. "Hume and the End of Religious Dialogue." *Eighteenth-Century Studies* 25 (1992): 283–308.

Rowe, William L. "The Problem of Evil and Varieties of Atheism." In *The Problem of Evil.* Edited by Marilyn McCord Adams and Robert Merrihew Adams. Oxford: Oxford University Press, 1990. 126–37. Originally published in *American Philosophical Quarterly* 16 (1979): 335–41.

Ruoff, Gene W. "Romantic Lyric and the Problem of Belief." In *The Romantics and Us: Essays on Literature and Culture.* Edited by Gene W. Ruoff. New Brunswick, N.J.: Rutgers University Press, 1990. 288–302.

Shelley, Percy Bysshe. *The Complete Works of Percy Bysshe Shelley.* Edited by Roger Ingpen and Walter E. Peck. New York: Gordian Press, 1965.

Smith, Christian, ed. *The Secular Revolution: Power, Interests, and Conflict in the Secularization of American Public Life.* Berkeley: University of California Press, 2003.

Snow, C. P. *The Two Cultures and the Scientific Revolution: The Rede Lecture.* Cambridge: Cambridge University Press, 1959.

Sommerville, C. John. *The Secularization of Early Modern England: From Religious Culture to Religious Faith.* New York: Oxford University Press, 1992.

Sprat, Thomas. *History of the Royal Society.* Facsimile of 1667 ed. Edited by Jackson I. Cope and Harold Whitmore Jones. 1958; St. Louis: Washington University Press; London: Routledge and Kegan Paul, 1966.

Swatos, William H., Jr., and Kevin J. Christiano. "Secularization Theory: The Course of a Concept." *Sociology of Religion* 60, no. 3 (1999): 209–28.

Taylor, Charles. *Modern Social Imaginaries.* Durham, N.C.: Duke University Press, 2004.

Taylor, Charles, and Benjamin Lee. *Multiple Modernities Project.* "Modernity and Difference." Working Draft. http://www.sas.upenn.edu/transcult/promad .html (accessed December 17, 2005).

Tillotson, John. "Sermon I: The Wisdom of Being Religious." In *The Works of the Most Reverend Dr. John Tillotson, Late Lord Archbishop of Canterbury, Containing Fifty Four Sermons and Discourses, on Several Occasions. Together with The Rule of Faith. Being All That Were Published by His Grace Himself. And Now Collected into One Volume.* London: B. Aylmer and W. Rogers, 1696. 1–33.

Tindal, Matthew. *Christianity as Old as the Creation; or, the Gospel, a Republication of the Religion of Nature.* London 1731. http://galenet.galegroup.com/servlet/ECCO

Toland, John. Preface to *Christianity Not Mysterious: or, A Treatise Shewing, That There Is Nothing in the Gospel Contrary to Reason, Nor Above It: And that No Christian Doctrine Can Be Properly Call'd a Mystery.* 2nd ed. London: Printed for Sam. Buckley, 1696. *Early English Books Online,* image 55936.

Ulmer, William A. *The Christian Wordsworth, 1798–1805.* Albany, N.Y.: State University of New York Press, 2001.

Wallis, Roy, and Steve Bruce. "Secularization: The Orthodox Model." In *Religion and Modernization.* Oxford: Clarendon Press. 8–30.

Warminski, Andrzej. "Facing Language: Wordsworth's First Poetic Spirits." *diacritics* 17, no. 4 (1987): 18–31.

———. "Missed Crossing: Wordsworth's Apocalypses." *MLN* 99 (1984): 983–1006.

Wasserman, Earl R. "Metaphors for Poetry." In *The Subtler Language: Critical Readings of Neoclassic and Romantic Poems.* 1959; Baltimore: Johns Hopkins University Press, 1964. 169–88. Reprinted in *Romanticism: Points of View.* Edited by Robert F. Gleckner and Gerald E. Enscoe. Englewood Cliffs: Prentice Hall, 1962. 247–59. All references to reprinted edition.

———. "Nature Moralized: The Divine Analogy in the Eighteenth Century." *English Literary History* 20, no. 1 (1953): 39–76.

Westbrook, Deeanne. *Wordsworth's Biblical Ghosts.* New York: St. Martin's Press, Palgrave, 2001.

Wimsatt, W. K., Jr., and Monroe C. Beardsley. "The Intentional Fallacy." In *The Verbal Icon: Studies in the Meaning of Poetry.* By W. K. Wimsatt, Jr. Lexington: University of Kentucky Press, 1954. 3–18.

Wordsworth, William. *Peter Bell.* Edited by John E. Jordan. Ithaca, N.Y.: Cornell University Press, 1985.

———. *"The Prelude": 1799, 1805, 1850.* Edited by Jonathan Wordsworth, M. H. Abrams, and Stephen Gill. New York: W. W. Norton, 1979.

———. *The Prose Works of William Wordsworth.* Edited by W. J. B. Owen and Jane Worthington Smyser. Oxford: Clarendon Press, 1974. 49–96.

———. *"The Ruined Cottage" and "The Pedlar."* Edited by James Butler. Ithaca, N.Y.: Cornell University Press, 1979.

Index

Abrams, M. H., 1, 18, 19, 25, 26, 49, 158; and personalistic approach to religion, 29; on poetry, 50; on "progressive secularization," 34

Addison, Joseph, 6–8, 23

"Address to the Diety, An" (Barbauld), 85

Adorno, Theodor, 19

"Against Theory" (Knapp and Michaels), 222–27, 257–58 n.13

agency, 99–101

Aids to Reflection (Coleridge), 15

Allen, Diogenes, 198

analogy, 237 n.13, 238 n.14; arguments by in the form *a:b::c:d*, 81–82, 113; and Blake, 46–51; as "elaboration," 48; as "imagination," 48; as a linguistic practice, 83; persistence of, 113–21; as a rhetorical activity, 119–21; as a source of possibility, 120; and the unknown God, 88–93. See also *Prelude* (Wordsworth), "Analogy Passage" of; *Prelude* (Wordsworth), and the design analogy; *Prelude* (Wordsworth), and the pathway of analogy; secularization, and analogy; "Summer Evening's Meditation, A" (Barbauld), analogy in

Analogy of Religion, The (Butler), 30

Analytical Review, 13–14

"Anatomie of the World, An" (Donne), 122

Ancient Mariner (Coleridge), 35

Anglican Revolution, and the seven bishops, 138–42

Anglicans/Anglicanism, 130, 131, 132, 249 n.32; Anglican theology, 133;

liberal, 134; Tory, 139. *See also* Anglican Revolution

animism, 172, 173

Anselm, 201–2

anti-Jacobins, 135

apologetics, 194–97

Aquinas, Thomas, 30, 82

Arendt, Hannah, 189

"argument against design," 56–57, 59. *See also* analogy; deism

Aristotle, 82, 191; distinction of between two types of words, 91, 242–43 n.19; on metaphor, 91–92

Arnold, Matthew, 18

Asad, Talal, 206–7, 210–11

atheism, 135

Austen, Cassandra, 138

Austen, Jane, 11, 38, 138, 246 n.3, 250 n.41; Christianity of, 126; historical skepticism of, 138; maternal family of (the Leighs), 247 n.11; religion in the novels of, 125–27, 158

Ayer, A. J., 205

Bacon, Francis, 30–31, 235 n.67; on teleology, 235 n.69

bacterial flagellum, 257 n.9

Barbauld, Anna, 38, 74–75; dating of her poems, 241 n.6; and differentiation, 75–76; possible influence of Hume on, 84, 242 n.12; relationship with Priestley, 85, 242 n.13

Barnes, Robert, 208

Beardsley, Monroe, 160, 182–83, 184

Bentley, Richard, 10

Berger, Peter, 31, 32
Berkeley, George, 70
Biographia Literaria (Coleridge), 95, 97; modernization narrative in, 98
Blackmore, Richard, 41–42, 46
Blair, Hugh, 13, 65
Blake, William, 37, 58; and analogy, 46–51; and "Deism," 46–48; description of theology, 47; on Milton, 89
Bloom, Harold, 18, 158
Blount, Charles, 43, 44, 236–37 n.2
Blumenberg, Hans, 192–93, 217–18, 254 n.8
Boswell, James, 67
Bourdieu, Pierre, 32
Boyle, Robert, 10, 15, 67
British Critic, 15, 16, 17
Brooks, Cleanth, 34, 161, 190–91, 193–94
Bruce, Steve, 206
Burke, Edmund, 11, 14, 130, 134–35, 185
Burnet, Gilbert, 130, 140
Burrell, David, 75, 82–83, 86
Bush, George W., 216, 220, 257 n.7
Butler, Joseph, 30–31
Butler, Judith, 99–100; on power, 243 n.19
Butler, Marilyn, 126–27

Caleb Williams (Godwin), 52–56
camera obscura, 207, 209
Campbell, Colin, 254 n.7
Campbell, George Douglas (8th Duke of Argyll), 125, 130, 246 n.1
Canuel, Mark, 229 n.1
Capital (Marx), 209
Caputo, John D., 201–2
Casanova, José, 28–29, 36, 38; on cultural acceptance of modernity, 39
Categories (Aristotle), 91
Catholics/Catholicism, 129–30, 134, 247 n.13, 247–48 n.15; and the Catholic Counter-Reformation, 202
Chadwick, Owen, 233 n.56
Chandler, James, 185
"Character of Joseph Priestley, A" (Barbauld), 87
Charles I (king of England), 247 n.11
Chesterton, G. K., 198
Christensen, Jerome, 118
Christianity, 13, 131, 201, 216; "displaced," 159; eschatology of, 193, 195–96; and the Eucharist, 209; and intellectuals,

86–87. *See also* Priestley, Joseph, defense of Christianity by; Protestants
Christianity Not Mysterious (Toland), 44–45
Christian Wordsworth, The (Ulmer), 159
Cicero, 239 n.9, 244 n.5
Clarke, Samuel, 10, 67
Coleridge, Samuel Taylor, 15–16, 35, 74, 75, 179; departure of to Malta, 180; on design, 93–94; on imagination, 94–95, 97–98
Confessions (Augustine), 191
cosmology, 122–23
Council of Nicea, 202
Cowper, William, 97
Creation (Blackmore), 41
Creation, The (Haydn), 21–25, 233 nn. 46, 50; dark tones in, 24, 233 n.54; ecumenism of, 21, 23; influence of *Paradise Lost* on, 21, 24–25; premiers of, 22; Mary Shelley's depiction of, 23–25
"Creation of the World considered, as displaying in the Great Creator, Supreme Power, Wisdom, and Goodness" (Blair), 13
Critique of Judgment (Kant), 103, 114–17
Critique of Pure Reason (Kant), 114
Cudworth, Ralph, 9
culture, 19, 255–56 n.14; diversity in, 3; elite, 31–32; "two cultures" distinction, 232 n.39, 235 n.63

Darwin, Charles, 10, 125, 246 n.1
Dawkins, Richard, 216–17, 218
de Certeau, Michel, 204
deconstruction, 25, 159, 238–39 n.1; methodologies of, 26
deism, 37, 43–46, 236–37 n.2; controversy over, 102–3; deism/orthodox design distinction, 45–46; and the design argument, 46; and secrets/secrecy, 52–53
Deleuze, Gilles, 99
de Man, Paul, 18, 19, 238–39 n.1; on secularization as melancholy and necessary, 54–56
De Quincey, Thomas, 179
Dennett, Daniel, 219
Descartes, René, 17
desecularization, 35
Desecularization of the World, The (Berger), 31

design, argument(s) from, 1–14 passim, 29–30, 146–48, 196–97, 229 n.2; analogical arguments concerning, 2, 12–13, 62–63; and the argument from perception, 11–13, 110–13, 182, 219; bivalent nature of, 8; classic example of (the word as machine argument), 60–62; critiques of, 10–12; design arguments as part of larger context of argument, 9–10; discourse of, 150; throughout history, 5–6; and inductive reasoning, 2–3; and poetry, 15; teleological arguments concerning, 2, 3, 60, 115, 116, 221. *See also* analogy

Dialogues Concerning Natural Religion (Hume), 11, 37, 58–59, 73, 83–84, 96, 102, 124–25, 187, 205, 239 n.5, 244 n.5; and the "arbitrary act of mind" argument, 69–72; and the argument from design, 59–64; and Cicero, 239 n.9; and dogmatism, 68–69; and God's nature, 240 n.17; and Hume's true opinion of religion, 64–65; publication history of, 63; reviews of, 110; as a threat to prevailing orthodoxy of the time, 65–66; vulnerability of skepticism in, 110–12

Difference and Repetition (Deleuze), 99

differentiation, 75–76; and intentionality, 183–87, 224; and secularization, 28–30, 32–33, 38–39, 198

Discipline and Punishment (Foucault), 168

Disenchantment of the World, The (Gauchet), 174, 252 n.23

dissent/dissenters, 75–76, 242 n.12, 247–48 n.15

Donne, John, 122–23

Durkheim, Emile, 172

Edinburgh Review, 107, 108; on natural theology, 109–10, 152

Eichmann in Jerusalem (Arendt), 189

Elementary Forms of Religious Life, The (Durkheim), 172

Eliade, Mircea, 34

Eliot, T. S., 18, 182

Ellison, Julie, 98

empiricism, 30

Engels, Friedrich, 207

Enquiry Concerning Human Understanding (Hume), 65, 239 n.4

Essay Concerning Human Understanding, An (Locke), 67

Essay on Man, An (Pope), 121

Essays Upon Epigraphs (Wordsworth), 159

Evidences of Christianity (Paley), 10, 104, 105

evil, problem of, 188–90, 198–99; Augustinian perspective on, 194; as an empirical problem, 194–95; as a hermeneutical problem, 196–97

evolution, 217–18, 219–20; believers in, 257 n.10; as "just a theory," 220–24

Excursion, The (Wordsworth), 15–16, 25, 188; and the attainment of belief, 197–200

Falwell, Jerry, 34

fancy, 78, 80; and agency, 99; as an "allegory of women's literary ambition," 98; and imagination, 93–99

fetishism, 173; fetishization of science, 220

Flatow, Ira, 216

Fleishman, Avrom, 249 n.37

Foucault, Michel, 53, 117, 168, 243 n.29; on analogy, 238 n.14; on similitude, 245 n.14

Fox, James, 162

"Fragment of an Epic Poem, Occasioned by the Loss of a Game of Chess to Dr. Priestley, in Consequence of an Unseasonable Drowsiness" (Barbauld), 85–86

Frankfurt School, 19

French Revolution, 126, 127, 134, 135, 177, 185

Frye, Northrop, 46

Gauchet, Marcel, 174, 175, 202, 252 n.23

gender, 74; sex/gender distinction, 99–100

Gender Trouble (Judith Butler), 100

Genealogies of Religion (Asad), 206–7, 210–11

George III (king of England), 104

German Ideology, The (Engels and Marx), 207

God, 13, 81, 87–88, 189; belief in, 96; creative word of, 97; nature of, 59–60, 240 n.17; wisdom of, 107–8. *See also* evil, problem of; God, existence of

God, existence of, 2–3, 30, 196–97, 205, 240 n.19; ontological argument for, 201–2. *See also* design, argument(s) from

Godwin, William, 37, 52, 53, 58, 177

Goldberg, Brian, 183

Goldie, Mark, 139
Goldsmith, Oliver, 138, 139, 249 n.33
Gouldner, Alvin W., 31
Great Chain of Being, 3, 117, 122

Hall, Joseph, 15
Harrison, Peter, 203, 206
Hartman, Geoffrey, 19–21, 25, 26, 158;
    emphasis of on self-consciousness,
    20–21; on the imagination, 176–77
Hastings, Warren, 11
Haydn, Josef, 21–24
Hazlitt, William, 15
"Heavens Declare Thy Glory, Lord, The"
    (Watts), 8
Hegel, G. W. F., 20
Henry VIII (king of England), 137
hermeneutics, 194–97. See also Peter Bell
    (Wordsworth), and biblical hermeneu-
    tic of Old and New Testament linkage
Herschel, William, 14
History of England (Goldsmith), 138, 139
History of England (Hume), 249 n.33
History of England, A (Trevelyan), 75
History of England, The: From the Reign of
    Henry the Fourth to the Death of Charles the
    First (C. Austen and J. Austen), 138
History of the Royal Society (Sprat), 12, 29–30
Hume, David, 10–11, 37–38, 48, 114, 125,
    151, 219; on design as a lived practice,
    57; "literary" career of, 239 n.14; on
    nature, 79–80; on religion, 102–3;
    skepticism of, 96–97, 244 n.1
Hyson Club, 103–4

Iconology (Mitchell), 208
Idea of the Holy, The (Otto), 128
imagination, 176–77, 180, 184; and fancy,
    93–99; and temporality, 20
industrialization, 29, 234 n.59
intellectuals, 31–32, 235 n.70. See also
    Christianity, and intellectuals
intelligent design, 37, 217–18, 220, 221,
    226, 230 n.7, 257 n.4; minimalist defini-
    tion of, 257 n.3. See also design, argu-
    ment(s) from
"Intentional Fallacy, The" (Wimsatt and
    Beardsley), 160, 182
intentionality, 222–24; and differentiation,
    183–87, 224; and "intentionless
    meaning," 223; and literary effect,

181–83. See also Wordsworth, William,
    intentionality in
intertextuality, 158–59
Iranian Revolution, 34, 236 n.84

James II (king of England), 129–30, 131,
    136–37, 247 n.11; extension of religious
    tolerance to Protestants by, 138–39;
    violent uprising during his reign, 135,
    248 n.24
Jameson, Frederic, 164
Jebb, John, 104
Jerusalem (Blake), 47
Job, 189
John, Gospel of, 202
Judaism, 248 n.18

Kant, Immanuel, 48, 58, 103; on aesthetic
    judgment, 115–16; and analogy, 116–17;
    analysis of evil by, 189; on the distinc-
    tion between the sublime and the beau-
    tiful, 114–15; and the persistence of
    analogy, 113–17; on pure and practical
    reason, 95
Kishel, Joseph F., 179–80, 253 nn. 29, 30
Knapp, Steven, 222–27
Kramer, Lawrence, 233 n.46

Langan, Celeste, 237 n.13
Language, Truth, and Logic (Ayer), 205
Last Man, The (M. Shelley), 23–24
latitudinarians/latitudinarianism, 127,
    131–32, 134, 136; appointment of latitu-
    dinarian bishops by William of Orange,
    139–40; tolerance of, 137
Latour, Bruno, 257 n.8
Law, John, 104
Lay of the Last Minstrel, The (Scott), 128–29,
    141, 142
Leavis, F. R., 18
Lectures on Revealed Religion (Coleridge), 93
Lee, Benjamin, 27–28
Legitimacy of the Modern Age, The (Blumen-
    berg), 192–93
Leibniz, Gottfried, 194
Letter Concerning Toleration (Locke), 131,
    247–48 n.15
liberalism, 136
literary culture, 18–19
literature, 240 n.14, 251 n.7; as an alterna-
    tive to theory, 225; and doctrine, 34

Liu, Alan, 193, 251 n.13
Locke, John, 67, 104, 130, 247–48 n.15; on religion, 131, 154
Lovejoy, Arthur, 122
Lover's Vows, 141
"Love Song of Alfred J. Prufrock, The" (Eliot), 182
Lynam, Robert, 119

Mahmood, Saba, 99–100; on modesty, 244 n.34; on the women's mosque movement, 214
Malthus, Thomas, 16, 162
Mansfield Park (J. Austen), 11, 38, 39, 124–25, 127; ambiguities in, 127–28; authentic voice of Fanny Price in, 142–43; and the book of nature, 152–57; chapel (Sotherton chapel) motif in, 129–30, 131, 133, 135–36, 138, 140–41, 154; desire in, 151, 156–57; Edmund Bertram character in, 132–34, 135–36, 140–42, 248 n.21, 249 n.38; and the end of natural theology, 145–52; failed dialogues of, 151–52; Fanny Price character in, 128–29, 140, 250 n.40; and "fraternal love," 155–56; Mary Crawford character in, 33, 36, 155–57; and naturalization, 143–45; piety/knowledge debate in, 203; religious dialogue of, 153; Sir Thomas character in, 144–45, 155, 156; theatricality in, 142, 143–44
Marquard, Odo, 189–90
Marriage of Heaven and Hell, The (Blake), 46–47, 89
Marx, Karl, 19, 207; fetish example of, 209–10
McGann, Jerome J., 35–36
McGregor, Ewan, 207, 208, 209
Memoirs (Priestley), 85, 86
metaphor, 49, 238 n.16. *See also* Aristotle, on metaphor
Metaphysics (Aristotle), 91, 92
"Michael" (Wordsworth), 161, 162
Michaels, Walter Benn, 222–27
Mill, John Stuart, 12–13, 257 n.4
Milton, John, 9, 15, 74
Minnich, Scott A., 218
Mitchell, W. J. T., 208, 210
modernity, 1, 16, 25, 26, 28, 39, 175, 190, 193, 226; convergence theories of, 27–28; "multiple" ("alternative")

modernities, 26, 29, 39–40, 188; and poetic growth, 166–69; and "reoccupation theory," 193, 217–18, 254 n.8; and romanticism, 18
modernization, 16, 26, 189, 234 n.59; as a myth, 28; narrative of, 175; and secularization, 27, 73, 174, 234 nn. 58, 60; Western, 27, 234 n.60
Montag, John, 204–5
Moral Majority, 34–35
Mullett, Michael, 249 n.32

natural supernaturalism, 77, 78, 181
Natural Supernaturalism (Abrams), 1, 26
natural theology (natural religion), 3–4, 14, 21, 25, 97; critiques of, 37, 109–10; and naturalization, 146; orthodox, 102; paradox of, 42–43; and social bonds, 59; "truth" of, 71. *See also* deism; *Dialogues Concerning Natural Religion*; *Mansfield Park* (J. Austen), and the end of natural theology
Natural Theology (Paley), 10, 103, 105, 148–49, 152, 154, 210; and the argument from perception, 111–13; and the Augustinian argument, 191, 195–96; excessive description and detail in, 108–9; and the persistence of analogy, 117–21; rhetorical concept of, 119–20
nature, 170, 180; as another "Book of God" alongside the Scriptures, 6, 17, 20, 21, 30–31, 41, 178, 221; as distinct from theology, 13–14; diversity in, 3; as a reflection of its Creator's glory, 2–3
Neely, Samuel, 13
Newman, John Henry, 153
Newton, Isaac, 10
Northanger Abbey (J. Austen), 126
Novum Organum (Bacon), 30
"Nuns fret not at their Convent's narrow room" (Wordsworth), 211–15

"Ocean, The; Displays of the Divine Perfections in it; and the Moral Instructions to be derived from it" (Neely), 13
"Of Miracles" (Hume), 79, 205
Of the Principles and Duties of Natural Religion (Wilkins), 9–10
Ogg, David, 247 n.12
"Old Man Travelling" (Wordsworth), 161
"On the Abuse of Reason" (Twining), 13

Oracles of Reason (Blount), 43–44, 236–37 n.2
Order of Things, The (Foucault), 117
Otto, Rudolf, 128; on the conception of the holy, 153–54

Pagels, Elaine, 202
Paley, William, 10, 15, 38, 39, 102, 103, 124, 125, 219; career of, 103–4; comparison of the universe to a watch, 48, 106–10, 148–49, 225–26, 243 n.21, 244–45 n.8, 257–58 n.13; education of, 103; influence of, 103, 105–6; opinion of astronomy, 108, 148; use of mechanical language, 107, 149; and the persistence of analogy, 117–21; physical pain experienced by, 119; and secularization, 121–23; struggles with classification, 117–18
Paradise Lost (Milton), 9, 21, 41–42, 187; and God's language, 85; and justifying the ways of God to men, 88–89
Paul, Saint, 6; in Athens, 90–91, 92
Persuasion (J. Austen), 126
Peter Bell (Wordsworth), 161–66; allegory in, 163–64, 166, 169; and biblical hermeneutic of Old and New Testament linkage, 164–65; character of Peter in, 162–63; corporal punishment theme in, 167–69, 252 n.16; psychology of Peter in, 166; as a sacred story, 165–66
philosophy, 231 n.22; of science, 220; two types of, 81–84. *See also* theory, and philosophical practice
Platonism, 251 n.6; neo-Platonism, 3, 17; Platonic tradition, 122–23
Pocock, J. G. A., 130, 134
poetry/poetics, 170; and accuracy in representing the world, 177; and analogy, 101; fancy as a device of, 78, 101; Greek, 92; metaphysical, 49; nonintentional, 181; and the "poetic faculty," 47; sonnets, 256 nn. 24, 25. *See also* romanticism, and the revival of poetic language
Political Unconscious, The (Jameson), 164
politics. *See* religion, and politics
Pope, Alexander, 121–22
Popple, William, 247–48 n.15
Prelude (Wordsworth), 15, 17, 19–21, 25, 168, 171–72, 175, 221–22, 232 n.31; "Analogy Passage" of, 179–81; and the

design analogy, 161; as an example of literature as an entity set apart, 160–61; imagination in, 176–77; and the pathway of analogy, 176–81; Simplon Pass episode in, 176–78, 184; textual history of, 172, 179–80, 252 n.21. *See also* intentionality
Priestley, Joseph, 74, 84, 85; defense of Christianity by, 86–87; monism of, 87, 242 n.15
primitivism, 174–76
Prince, Michael, 66, 68
Principles of Moral and Political Philosophy (Paley), 10, 104, 105
Principles of Population (Malthus), 162
Prometheus Unbound (P. Shelley), 16, 106
Protestant Reformed Religion, 137, 248–49 n.28
Protestant Reformation, 254–55 n.1
Protestants, 130, 138, 201, 248 n.18
Psalm 19, 6–7, 8, 23
Psychic Life of Power, The (Judith Butler), 243 n.29
Public Religions in the Modern World (Casanova), 28

Quarterly Review, 126

Ray, John, 10, 117
Reasonableness of Christianity, The (Locke), 131
reason/revelation distinction, 204
"Reasons for Contentment" (Paley), 105, 118–19, 245 n.17
Reflections on the Revolution in France (Burke), 14
"Refutation of Deism, A" (P. Shelley), 17, 231 n.30
religion, 74, 200, 245–46 n.24, 252 n.23; abstract conception of, 46–47; as belief, 202–6, 255–56 n.14; as discipline, 210–15; as false consciousness, 206–7; hypocrisy of, 209; as ideology, 206–10; as an inner phenomenon, 201, 254–55 n.1; institutional decline of, 26–27; and politics, 216–17; public role of, 35; scientific study of, 205–6; as a set of beliefs that can be lost, 26. *See also* science, divisions between science and religion; science, and religion
Religion for Dummies, 203–4

Religion Within the Limits of Reason Alone (Kant), 189
religious dialogue: and arbitrariness, 70; binary structure of, 66
religious dissent, 75
repetition, 99
"Resolution and Independence" (Wordsworth), 161
revelation. *See* reason/revelation distinction
Rhetoric (Aristotle), 91–92
"Rhetoric of Temporality, The" (de Man), 54
Rights of Man, The (Paine), 105
Rivers, Isabel, 109
"romantic exceptionalism," 18, 73
Romantic Ideology (McGann), 35
romanticism, 1–2, 14–26 passim, 32–34, 39, 73; attempts to pluralize, 74; and the "death of the author" guise, 25–26; entanglement of in the narrative of secularization, 19–26, 35, 50, 97; relation of to modernity, 26; and the revival of poetic language, 49–50; romantic historicism, 35; two types of, 17, 33. *See also* analogy
"Romanticism and 'Anti-Self-Consciousness' " (Hartman), 19
Rose, William, 65–66
Rowe, William, 195, 196
Ruined Cottage (Wordsworth), 37, 161, 188, 199–200, 210; animism in, 172, 173; growth of the poet theme in (personal growth narratives), 169–75; and literary interpretation, 169–70; publication of, 198; revisions of, 201; and suffering, 190–94, 195, 198
Ruoff, Gene W., 34, 35
Ruskin, John, 18

Salomon, Johann Peter, 22
Satan, 87–88, 98
Schoenfield, Mark, 160
science, 18, 220, 257 n.8; differentiated model of, 224; divisions between science and religion, 4, 12, 30; fetishization of, 220; and religion, 218–20
Scott, Walter, 128, 140–41; theory of history of, 249 n.37
secularization, 1–2, 17, 26–36 passim, 39, 121–23, 206, 215; and analogy, 31; definition of, 29, 229 n.1; as differentiation,

28–30, 32–33, 38–39, 198, 235 nn. 65, 66; and global elites, 31–32; masculine versus feminine, 74; and primitivism, 174–76; "progressive," 34, 74; "reoccupation" theory of, 192–93, 217–18; and "romantic exceptionalism," 18; secret of, 51–57; as a theory of religious decline, 28, 32, 35. *See also* modernization, and secularization; romanticism, entanglement of in the narrative of secularization
Sermons (Blair), 13
Shaftesbury, Earl of, 135, 250 n.40
Shelley, Mary, 16, 23–24
Shelley, Percy, 15, 16–17; on design, 231 n.30; hostility toward Paley, 16, 18; on religion, 16–17
"Simon Lee," 161, 162
skepticism, 72, 74, 96–97; allegorizing of, 70
slavery/slave trade, 144–45
Smith, Adam, 65
Smith, Christian, 32, 36
Snow, C. P., 18
Socrates, 82
Sommerville, C. John, 208
"Spacious Firmament on High, The" (Addison), 8, 23
Spectator, The, 6, 8
Spinozism, 17
Stevens, Wallace, 48
Stillingfleet, Edward, 9
"Structure and Style in the Greater Romantic Lyric" (Abrams), 50, 244 n.35
Subtler Language, The (Wasserman), 49
suffering, 190–94, 195, 198
"Summary Account of the Deists Religion" (Blount), 43
"Summer Evening's Meditation, A" (Barbauld), 76–81, 84, 97–98; analogy in, 88–93; and cognitive failure, 78–79; decomposition of the divine in, 76–77; and fancy, 78, 99; influence of *Paradise Lost* on, 84–85; influence of Priestley on, 85–88; and natural supernaturalism, 77, 78; and the natural world, 100; and repetition, 99; and Satanic desire, 85; and wisdom, 77–78
"Sunday Morning" (Stevens), 48–49

Task, The (Cowper), 97
Taylor, Charles, 4, 27–28

Temperley, Nicholas, 21
Test Acts, 138, 202
"Theism" (Mill), 257 n.4
theodicy, 192, 254 n.7 *See also* evil,
    problem of
theology, 81, 109, 114; and the aesthetic,
    116; as "conservative," 4; and the design
    argument, 46; rational, 153; of redemp-
    tion, 30; and science, 4. *See also* natural
    theology
theory, 93; cost of, 96; "devilish enginery"
    of, 84–88, 89; literature as an alternative
    to, 225; and philosophical practice,
    82–83, 241–42 n.10; "theory construc-
    tion," 75. *See also* evolution, as "just a
    theory"
There Is No Natural Religion (Blake), 47
Time, 218, 256 n.2
"Thorn, The" (Wordsworth), 161
Three Dialogues Between Hylas and Philonous
    (Berkeley), 66
Tillotson, John, 4–5, 130, 132,
    140, 225
Tindal, Matthew, 44, 52
"To an Unknown God" (Barbauld),
    89–90
Toland, John, 44–45, 46; on the definition
    of reason, 45
Topics (Aristotle), 91
tradition, and resistance to modernization,
    27–28
Treatise on Human Nature, A (Hume), 65,
    79–80, 83
Treaty of Amiens, 118
Twining, Thomas, 13
"two cultures" hypothesis, 18–19
Tucker, Herbert, 256 n.24

Ulmer, William A., 159, 160, 254 n.12
United States, religious vibrancy of, 27

Vatican II (1962–65), 34
vision/seeing, 207–8, 210. *See also* camera
    obscura
Visions of the Daughters of Albion, The
    (Blake), 51–52
von Swieten, Gottfried, 22

Wang, Orrin, 257–58 n.13
Warminski, Andrzej, 20–21, 25, 26, 232 n.32
Wasserman, Earl, 34, 49–50, 113
Watson, Richard, 104, 134
Watts, Isaac, 8
Weber, Max, 18, 19
Westbrook, 158–59
"What Is Enlightenment?" (Kant),
    245–46 n.24
Whatley, Richard, 105, 125–26, 133, 154
Whigs, 130, 131, 135, 136, 137, 139
Wilkins, John, 9–10
William of Orange, 131, 139–40, 247–48
    n.15, 248–49 n.28, 249 n.29
Wimsatt, W. K., 160, 182–83, 184
"Wisdom of Being Religious, The" (Tillot-
    son), 4–5, 225
*Wisdom of God Manifested in the Works of Cre-
    ation, The* (Ray), 10, 117
Wittgenstein, Ludwig, 80, 82
Woolston, Thomas, 102
Wordsworth, William, 15–16, 38, 50; and
    Christianity, 158–59; on the effect of in-
    dustrialization on the rural poor,
    162–63; "Great Decade" (1797–1807) of,
    158; intentionality in, 159–60, 181–87;
    on revolutionary France, 184, 253 n. 34
Wordsworth's Biblical Ghosts (Westbrook),
    158–59
World Council of Churches, 33–34
Wrangham, Francis, 253 n.29

Žižek, Slavoj, 198–99

Acknowledgments

Parts of this book have appeared in print previously. Chapter 4 originally appeared as "Natural Designs: Romanticism, Secularization, Theory," *European Romantic Review*, 12, no. 1 (2001): 53–91; used by permission of Taylor and Francis, http://www.tandf.co.uk. Chapter 5 originally appeared as "*Mansfield Park* and the End of Natural Theology," *Modern Language Quarterly*, 63, no. 1, pp. 31–63, Copyright 2002, University of Washington, all rights reserved; used by permission of the publisher.

* * *

Friends and colleagues at a number of institutions have aided this book materially and conceptually. I thank the president and fellows of Clare Hall, University of Cambridge, for an outstanding sabbatical year. For romantic conversation at Cambridge, I thank Phil Connell, Mary Jacobus, Simon Jarvis, Nigel Leask, and Reeve Parker. At the University of Michigan, Lincoln Faller, Jessica Lieberman, James Porter, Amit Ray, Marlon Ross, Tobin Siebers, Sondra Smith, and Jeremy Wells offered advice and encouragement. I thank Adela Pinch for interventions too numerous to record, including returning to Michigan at just the right time. Marjorie Levinson's combination of intellectual rigor and supportive encouragement remains a model for me.

Jonathan Van Antwerpen has been a friend and intellectual interlocutor for many years now. In bringing this book to fruition, the University of Pennsylvania Press has been a pleasure to work with. I thank Eric Halpern especially. Orrin Wang was an exemplary reader. The Plangere Writing Center at Rutgers offered financial support at a crucial moment, for which I thank Richard Miller in particular. Sharon McGrady has my sincere gratitude for heroic work that saved me from a variety of errors. Any that remain are of course my own.

At Rutgers University, where I am fortunate to teach in the English Department, numerous friends and colleagues have offered advice and encouragement. I thank Chris Chism, Brad Evans, Stacy Klein, Daphne Lamothe, George Levine, Mary Sheridan-Rabideau, and Shuang Shen for reading bits and pieces. Jonathan Kramnick and Michael McKeon read the whole thing and made it a better book; even more crucially, conversations with Michael Warner altered the book's scope and ambition. William Galperin has been a terrific senior colleague; I hope my own subsequent career will adequately honor his many virtues.

I come now to those obligations that perhaps can never be adequately honored. My parents, Ronald and Grace Jager, have always been for me models of unconditional love and support. They have also listened kind-heartedly to this project's various permutations over the years. My patient father has read countless drafts and made each one better. I am thankful for my parents every day.

Olivia Grace Jager was born while I was in the midst of this book; Eliot John Jager arrived near its completion. I cannot now imagine life without them, and I thank them for sharing their father with this strange stepchild.

Finally, my wife, Wendy, has borne with this project magnificently and is doubtless even more pleased than I am to bid it farewell. Along the way, she has made our life together rich with meaning, helping me understand what Donne meant when he wrote that when it comes to love there is only the present: *Running it never runs from us away.*

GAYLORD No. 2333

PRINTED IN U.S.A.

DATE DUE

GAYLORD No. 2333   PRINTED IN U.S.A.